Robert Solow and the Development
of Growth Economics

Robert Solow and the Development of Growth Economics

Annual Supplement to Volume 41
History of Political Economy

Edited by Mauro Boianovsky and Kevin D. Hoover

Duke University Press
Durham and London 2009

Contents

The Neoclassical Growth Model and Twentieth-Century Economics

Mauro Boianovsky and Kevin D. Hoover

While growth has been a central element of economic thought at least since the physiocrats and Adam Smith, the modern analysis of growth using formal models began only in the middle of the twentieth century. Thanks largely to Robert Solow's two articles, "A Contribution to the Theory of Economic Growth" (1956) and "Technical Change and the Aggregate Production Function" (1957), growth economics developed into a major area of research in macroeconomics and economic theory, attracting the attention of a significant part of the economics profession.

The current volume collects most of the papers from the twentieth annual *HOPE* conference, held 25–27 April 2008 at Duke University. The conference addressed the history of modern growth economics, taking Solow's key papers from the 1950s as its anchor. The conference was not about Solow's work per se, but addressed the intellectual currents that formed the background to that work and the history of the growth economics that it subsequently informed. The conference considered the rise of growth economics as an active field of research in the 1950s, its extension to several branches of the discipline in the 1960s, its decline in the 1970s, and its return to the center stage of macroeconomics over the last twenty years. In addition to sixteen essays presented at the conference, we are fortunate to be able to include transcripts of two less formal talks. The first is Professor Solow's keynote lecture to the conference on the future of growth economics. This lecture was delivered as part of a celebration

History of Political Economy 41 (annual suppl.) DOI 10.1215/00182702-2009-013

of Professor Solow's commitment of his papers to the Economists' Papers Project of Duke University's Rare Book, Manuscript, and Special Collections Library. The second is Edwin Burmeister's recollections of his time as Solow's student in the graduate program in economics at the Massachusetts Institute of Technology (MIT)—an after-dinner talk on the first night of the conference.

Although it was a relatively minor field in the early days of macroeconomics, growth economics exploded in the decade and a half after Solow's 1956 paper (see table 1). Through the 1960s the basic neoclassical growth model was extended in several directions, by Hirofumi Uzawa (two-sector model), Kenneth Arrow (learning by doing), James Tobin (money and growth), Peter Diamond (fiscal policy and overlapping generations), and many others. Edward Denison, Zvi Griliches, and Dale Jorgenson, among others, elaborated Solow's (1957) approach to growth accounting. Solow himself modified the simple model to introduce the notion of vintage capital with embodied technological change and worked out a new version without direct substitution between factors of production. During that same period, Edmund Phelps and others used Solow's model—now frequently known simply as the *neoclassical growth model*—to establish the golden rule of growth, while David Cass and others combined it with Frank Ramsey's much older model of capital accumulation to study optimal growth. At the same time, the growth models of Roy Harrod, Evsey Domar, and John von Neumann continued to attract some (declining) attention, while alternative approaches to growth theory (especially those of Nicholas Kaldor and other Cambridge economists) were still very much on the agenda. F. H. Hahn and R. C. O. Matthews's famous survey of growth economics, published in the *Economic Journal* in 1964, summed up the main results and stabilized the discussion for some time.

Under the influence of Solow and Paul Samuelson, MIT quickly became the main center of research in growth theory, with several PhD students rising to prominence as growth theorists, including Diamond, Eytan Sheshinski, William Nordhaus, Burmeister, Joseph Stiglitz, A. Rodney Dobell, and Avinash Dixit (see the Festschrift edited by Diamond in celebration of Solow's sixty-fifth birthday). In 1965–66 Karl Shell organized an influential seminar on optimal economic growth at MIT, which resulted in a conference volume published the next year. By 1970 economists started to take stock, and growth theory began to be consolidated in textbooks, including those of Burmeister and Dobell (1970) and Henry

Table 1   Attention Paid to Growth by Economists

Period	Articles with "growth" in title (as percentage of all articles)	Change from previous period (percent)
1936–55	0.95	
1956–70	4.64	388
1971–85	2.71	−42
1986–2006	2.67	−2

Data derived from JSTOR journal archive (30 October 2006) based on the *American Economic Review*, the *Journal of Political Economy*, the *Review of Economic Studies*, the *Review of Economics and Statistics*, the *Economic Journal*, and *Econometrica*.

Wan (1971), also an MIT PhD. Solow's 1969 Radcliffe Lectures (published in 1970 as the first edition of his *Growth Theory: An Exposition*) became a standard reference, along with two collections of readings in growth economics—one edited by Amartya Sen (1970), the other by Stiglitz and Uzawa (1969).

Interest in the theory of economic growth subsided in the 1970s and early 1980s, when only a few new results were produced, such as the application of the neoclassical growth model to the economics of exhaustible resources by Solow and others in the wake of the surge in the price of oil following the Yom Kippur War of 1973. Although the main focus of macroeconomic research shifted in this period back toward short-term fluctuations, table 1 shows that interest in growth did not fall back to its pre-1956 level. The middle 1980s seemed to provide a new beginning for the economics of growth. Even though interest in growth measured by the crude statistics of table 1 was merely steady, Paul Romer and Robert Lucas opened up a new research agenda, one that has persisted for the last two decades (see also Kim, Morse, and Zingales 2006).

The *new growth theory* extended the neoclassical model by treating the steady-state rate of growth as itself endogenous, in the sense that it is affected by taste parameters (such as the savings rate) and/or is determined within the model. At first, an endogenous growth rate was secured by replacing Solow's assumption of diminishing returns to capital by constant returns to capital broadly defined. A second phase focused on monopolistically competitive models in which the rate of technological progress was endogenous (see David Warsh's 2006 fascinating historical account, focused on Romer's contributions).

Solow engaged in the debate, and he reacted critically to the theoretical and empirical aspects of new growth economics in his 1992 Siena Lectures (revised and incorporated into the second edition of his *Growth Theory*, published in 2000), in his contributions to the *Handbook of Macroeconomics* in 1999 and to the *Handbook of Economic Growth* in 2005, and elsewhere. By the mid-1990s textbooks started to discuss endogenous growth models extensively (Barro and Sala-i-Martin 1995; Jones 1998; Aghion and Howitt 1998), yet they continued to take the basic neoclassical growth model as their common starting point.

I

Solow (1956) set out an aggregate, competitive general equilibrium perfect-foresight growth model built around three equations: a constant-returns-to-scale production function with smooth substitution and diminishing returns to capital and labor; an equation describing capital accumulation on the assumption of a constant rate of savings (investment) as a fraction of output; and a labor-supply function in which labor (population) grows at an exogenously given rate.[1] The system generated a first-order differential equation that showed how the current level of the capital-labor ratio and two parameters (the savings rate and the rate of population growth) determine the rate of change of the capital-labor ratio. Solow provided quantitative solutions for specific constant-returns production functions (such as the Cobb-Douglas and CES functions). Solow first analyzed the dynamic stability of equilibrium qualitatively using a diagram—known as the "Solow diagram"—depicting the equilibrium value of the capital-labor ratio in the steady state. The diagram showed how the economy would converge to a steady-state growth path along which output and the capital stock both grew at the exogenous rate of population growth. To account for increasing income per capita, Solow briefly introduced technical change and worked out the solution for the Cobb-Douglas case, with the result that, along the balanced growth path, output per worker and capital per worker both grow at the same rate of exogenous technologi-

---

1. What Solow and others characterize as the savings function would more naturally be thought of as the investment function. The identification works only because Solow assumes continuous full employment and the equality of *ex ante* and *ex post* savings and investment rates, which guarantee that both planned and realized investment and savings are equal.

cal progress.[2] Technological improvement, therefore, offsets diminishing returns to capital accumulation, permitting steadily rising labor productivity and output per worker.

While Karl Marx, Knut Wicksell, and Alfred Marshall may have known the notion of steady-state growth in an incipient form already in the nineteenth century, it was Gustav Cassel in the early twentieth century who elaborated the idea and introduced it into the literature under the guise of "the uniformly progressing state." Mauro Boianovsky's essay in this volume documents the influence of Cassel's growth model on other Swedish economists, especially Erik Lundberg, who shared with Harrod's and Domar's later formulations not just the growth equations but also (differently from Cassel) their implications for economic instability. Cassel's and Lundberg's contributions were not themselves enough to set off growth economics as a main field of research worldwide. Things started to change in the late 1940s, not just because of the publication of Harrod's book (*Towards a Dynamic Economics* [1948]) and Domar's articles ("Capital Expansion, Rate of Growth, and Employment" [1946] and "Expansion and Employment" [1947]) but also because of the general concern with economic development and growth after the Second World War.[3]

At the outset of his 1956 paper, Solow claims that he was reacting to what he described as the "knife-edge" property of the "Harrod-Domar model." Solow sees this knife-edge property as the result of an inconsistency between Harrod's *warranted rate* of growth, determined as the ratio of the savings rate and the capital-output ratio, and his *natural rate* of growth, determined by the rates of technical progress and population growth. Solow argues that Harrod's and Domar's models assume that the capital-output ratio is rigidly determined by a fixed-coefficients production function and, therefore, that no mechanism exists to bring the warranted and natural rates into line. He proposes that a flexible production function with substitutability between capital and labor will provide a mechanism for establishing the equality between the two rates and so

2. Technical progress in the form Solow employs later became known as *output-augmenting* or *Hicks-neutral* technical progress. A few years later, Hirofumi Uzawa (1961) established that only *labor-augmenting* or *Harrod-neutral* technical progress is compatible with steady-state growth (see also Solow [1970] 2000, 30–35). However, the Cobb-Douglas production function is a special case in which Hicks-neutral and Harrod-neutral technical progress are equivalent.

3. Harrod's 1939 essay went relatively unnoticed until the late 1940s.

will eliminate the knife-edge. In his essay in this volume, Harald Hagemann shows that Solow's framework was quite distinct from Domar's and Harrod's. In particular, Solow excluded from his model the possibility of divergence between Harrod's warranted (or equilibrium) and actual rates of growth. Harrod relied on such divergences and the resulting instability of the warranted rate, itself caused by discrepancies between savings and planned investment in his complex interpretation of cyclical fluctuations. As Hahn and Matthews (1964) and Sen (1970, introduction) point out, Solow considered only one aspect of Harrod's instability problem (the balance between warranted and natural growth). He neglected the balance between warranted and actual growth, which Harrod related to entrepreneurial expectations.

Solow wrote to Sen (14 January 1970) that he agreed with the introduction to Sen's anthology. He acknowledged that "it is clear to me that my general discussion in the 1956 article was ambiguous, for the simple reason that it wasn't clear to me at the time exactly what I was doing."[4] In another letter, Solow acknowledged that the object of the 1956 model was to trace full-employment (not actual) paths toward the steady state (quoted in Sen 1970, 24 n. 15; see also Solow [1970] 2000, 21). Solow returned to the topic in his 1987 Nobel lecture, in which he referred to his "youthful confusion" between Harrod's two instability problems (Solow [1970] 2000, xiv).

By the mid-1960s, Solow (1966) had resolved the confusion in his own mind:

It is clear to me that I oversimplified matters in 1956. The model was new and I didn't understand all its implications. Some of what Harrod called instability is, of course, a matter of the behavior of effective demand, off equilibrium paths. Harrod never specified very clearly what he had in mind, and indeed there is very little in the literature even now that marries the theory of growth and effective demand. What I was getting at in 1956 was this: the special character of Harrod's model rests in the fact that the natural and warranted rates of growth are independent numbers. . . . That characteristic of the model rests on fixed

4. In describing the balance between warranted and natural growth in Harrod's model as a fluke, Solow was in good company: Joan Robinson (1956, 404–6) and other Cambridge economists held similar views, although their solution in terms of the adjustment of saving propensity caused by changes in income distribution along the growth path was quite distinct from Solow's (see Kregel 1980).

proportions. (It is immaterial whether Harrod believed that factor proportions are technically fixed or simply never change.) In turn, at least some aspects of "instability" arise because the economy is always being pulled away from the warranted path because it differs from the natural path.

Solow (1956, 91), therefore, maintained his earlier position that aggregate disequilibrium should not be ascribed to any deviation from a narrow balance between warranted and natural growth, though it might arise from the "difficulties and rigidities" highlighted by Keynesian short-run analysis.[5] After Kaldor (1961) put forward his famous "stylized facts" of long-run growth, Solow reaffirmed the ability of the neoclassical growth model to account for the main empirical features of steady growth as opposed to the sharp instability results of the Harrod-Domar model, especially if another "stylized fact" is added to the list—the fluctuation of the unemployment rate within fairly narrow limits in modern industrial economies (Solow [1970] 2000, chap. 1, esp. 28).

Domar reacted positively to Solow's aggregative neoclassical growth model (Hagemann, this volume; Easterly 2001, 28). Domar (1957, 7–8) later noted that before the Solow 1956 paper, he had treated capital as the only explicit production factor because he thought including labor as well would require a complex, highly disaggregated production function along the lines of Wassily Leontief's dynamic input-output system. Indeed, Domar (1947, 45) had already referred to Tinbergen's (1942) neoclassical treatment, which he did not follow on the grounds that he wanted to "express the idea of growth in the simplest possible manner."

In contrast, Harrod (1960) denied Solow's interpretation. He claimed that he had not omitted the influence of the rate of interest on the capital-output ratio, but he also acknowledged that he had not paid enough attention to that effect in the long run. To "remedy this defect" he developed—under the partial influence of Ramsey—the notion of a "natural rate of interest" and of an "optimum rate of saving" corresponding to the natural rate of growth, which was the object of correspondence with Solow and led to a further restatement by Harrod (1963, 404–10).

---

5. Solow fails to acknowledge Harrod's focus is directed exactly to the Keynesian short run. Harrod's dynamic problem is not Solow's long-term growth problem. For a more detailed contrast between Solow's and Harrod's approaches, see Hoover 2008, which also investigates the empirical performance of Harrod's model in accounting for growth fluctuations in the American economy in the twentieth century.

Whereas some commentators have identified the neglect of the business cycle and the ensuing lack of integration between short-run and long-run macroeconomics as the main shortcoming of neoclassical growth theory, Lionello Punzo argues in his essay in this volume that Solow's model was born precisely from the failure of the research program of "classical macrodynamics" to find a unified explanation for cycles and growth. That is, by separating growth and fluctuations, Solow succeeded where other macroeconomists—including not only Harrod and Domar but also Ragnar Frisch, John Hicks, and Richard Goodwin, among others—had failed before him. That "success," however, was achieved by changing the question. While Harrod considered disequilibrium dynamics, neoclassical growth theory considered only equilibrium dynamics. Punzo maintains that the origins and relative success of neoclassical growth theory should be sought less in the influence of the general equilibrium theory and Samuelsonian stability analysis than in its ability to forge a new concept of a dynamics driven by exogenous forces rather than endogenous fluctuations.

As Solow points out in his keynote address to the *HOPE* conference, the development of new theories and approaches in economics is more the result of the collective effort of research communities than of single individuals. Although Solow's contributions have been particularly influential, several aspects of the neoclassical growth model were advanced somewhat earlier or simultaneously with Solow 1956 by Jan Tinbergen ([1942] 1959), James Tobin (1955), and especially the Australian economist Trevor Swan (1956).

In their essay in this volume, Robert Dimand and Barbara Spencer discuss the similarities and differences between Swan's and Solow's presentations of the same basic growth model and assess why, despite the fact that it is often rightly called the "Solow-Swan model," it was Solow's version that caught the eyes of the profession.[6] Both Solow and Swan established mathematically and diagrammatically how the economy finds the steady-state growth path in a one-commodity world. Instead of a general constant-returns production function, Swan worked out the mathematics of growth under the assumption of a Cobb-Douglas function. What is more, it is the capital-output ratio rather than Solow's capital-labor ratio that takes pride of place in Swan's diagram.[7]

6. Barbara Swan Spencer is Trevor Swan's daughter.
7. See also Harcourt's (2006, 110–13) detailed discussion of Swan's diagram. According to Harcourt, "Generations of Australians have been brought up on this and other famous Swan diagrams."

Whereas Solow reacted to what he perceived as the "knife-edge" property of the Harrod-Domar model, Swan sought to contrast the role of capital accumulation in the classical (Ricardian) and neoclassical frameworks, and to criticize Joan Robinson's (1956) views about growth and capital. With that target in mind, Swan used his model to clarify the role of land in classical growth theory (an issue set aside by Solow 1956) and, more important, to show for the first time that in the neoclassical approach with diminishing returns to capital and exogenous population growth a higher savings propensity brings about only a temporary, not a steady-state, increase of the rate of output growth (an implication of Solow's model, but not one stressed in his original paper). Swan saw a contrast between the neoclassical growth model, in which the steady-state growth rate is independent of the savings rate (a property that he notes generally vanishes, even in the neoclassical model, if the rate of population growth is endogenously determined by income per capita), and both the classical growth economics and the Harrod-Domar model as it was typically applied to planning for economic development (Easterly 2001). Harrod and Domar themselves were much more careful about the implications of higher savings for economic growth than were the development economists. And, of course, *classical* growth models typically assume endogenous labor-force growth in the form of Malthus's population mechanism. Swan confirms a well-known classical proposition: the combination of diminishing returns to land and Malthusian population dynamics in the absence of technical progress results in an equilibrium with declining output per head that converges to a stationary state in which population does not grow and capital does not accumulate. Swan's independence proposition soon became recognized as one of the main implications of diminishing returns to capital in the neoclassical growth model (see Meade 1961, 42–46; Solow [1970] 2000, 22–24).

As Steven Durlauf observed at the *HOPE* conference, despite the striking similarities of their theoretical models, Solow's research program was empirical in a sense that Swan's was not. Indeed, Solow followed up his 1956 paper with the equally influential empirical study of the sources of U.S. economic growth between 1909 and 1949 (Solow 1957). The 1957 paper does not refer directly to the 1956 paper, yet the connection between the two is clear enough. Both model the economy in which a neoclassical aggregate production function governs output and in which each factor price equals its marginal productivity. These assumptions allowed Solow (1957) to parameterize the production function.

Solow decomposed the growth of output into the sum of the capital and labor inputs, each weighted by their shares in national income, plus a term that captured Hicks-neutral shifts of the production function. Although he dubbed such shifts "technical change," he acknowledged that they comprised not just technological progress in the narrow sense but also any other changes that affected the productivity of inputs, such as increasing skills among workers. Domar (1961) soon described the contribution of technical change broadly defined to the growth of output per head as the "residual," since it was obtained after calculating the contribution of capital. (The residual is also often called "total factor productivity" [TFP], a term introduced by John Kendrick [1956].) Solow concluded from his 1957 study that about seven-eighths of the increase in output per head in the American economy was traceable to technical change.[8] That was a surprising result, since, although the irrelevance of the investment rate for steady-state growth was clear enough from the 1956 model, its measured small effect even in the transition to the steady state was unexpected.

The massive importance of "technical change" in explaining growth, the exogenous and disembodied manner in which it enters the production function, and the ambiguity of its interpretation (what are its sources? how does it work?) encouraged Solow to investigate further. Solow (1960) offers a model of the accumulation of vintage capital with embodied technical progress. In this model, investment is the vehicle that transmits new ideas. Solow's new approach was the culmination of a line of research that Ingvar Svennilson had begun in Sweden in the mid-1940s (see Boianovsky, this volume).

Domar (1961), among others, noted the clear methodological difference between Solow's aggregative approach to technical change and the disaggregated dynamic input-output approach of Leontief et al. (1953). Marcel Boumans (this volume) argues that Solow's representation of technical change evolved from his work in the early 1950s (frequently with Samuelson) on the stability of dynamic linear systems. Tinbergen advanced a similar representation of technical change in an article originally published in German in 1942 (translated into English in 1959).[9] Indeed, Tinbergen's approach to growth accounting was also based on the notion of

8. According to Warsh (2006, chap. 11), Solow's theoretical and empirical conclusions about the pivotal role of technological progress in the growth process were significant at the time in the context of the Cold War.

9. Although, as he informed the *HOPE* conference, he could read German, Solow did not know of Tinbergen's article at the time he formulated his own growth model.

the residual ("efficiency"), measured with the aid of a neoclassical (Cobb-Douglas) production function.[10] Tinbergen's model was based on the explicit separation between trend and fluctuations. He referred to Cassel, but not to Harrod. The model comprises three equations: a Cobb-Douglas function, which shifts over time; an equation governing equilibrium in the labor market; and an equation governing capital accumulation through proportional savings. Tinbergen assumed numerical values for the parameters of the production function (based on Paul Douglas's previous studies) and solved for the rate of growth of capital. His main concern was to estimate the factors determining long-run growth, without a close theoretical investigation of the steady-state path.

II

In the final pages of his 1956 article, Solow mentions various "cobwebs," including uncertainty and price rigidity, as potentially practically important but foreign to the central message of his model. During the process of spread and consolidation, later neoclassical growth economists have typically followed Solow's lead and neglected to clear the cobwebs—or even to investigate them closely. William Darity (this volume) claims that once (Keynesian) uncertainty is incorporated, the structure of the model itself is affected by the expectations of economic agents, in a manner reminiscent of Harrod's growth dynamics. Darity, a former student of Solow's, adds another cobweb to Solow's list: increasing returns to scale, which would render orthodox marginalist distribution theory useless. Piero Sraffa's (1926) discussion of returns to scale more than eighty years ago set off a debate that led to monopolistic competition models, which have been applied to growth economics by Romer and others since the 1980s.[11]

In contrast, Darity develops another path from Sraffa's criticism of neoclassical theory to a reformed model of growth: the classical surplus

10. Before Tinbergen, Cassel (1935, chap. 6) had considered the empirical extension of the Cobb-Douglas function to the aggregate growing economy. He rejected the idea on the grounds that it would imply a constant capital-labor ratio in a growing economy, which data would not support. That is, Cassel did not take into account the possibility of introducing steady technological progress into the aggregate production function, as Tinbergen and Solow would do later.

11. Solow (1956, 79 n. 7) considered replacing perfect competition with monopolist competition in his model. He gave it up because of the analytic problems involved in its introduction into aggregative models. The first general equilibrium models of monopolist competition were advanced in the 1970s by Avinash Dixit and Joseph Stiglitz (1977) and others.

approach to distribution and growth, which was intertwined with the famous "two Cambridges" controversy in capital theory of the 1950s and 1960s. In his talk (reproduced in this volume), Ed Burmeister, who participated actively in those debates, offers a vivid recollection of that intense discussion from the MIT (Cambridge, Massachusetts) point of view.[12]

Another important development in the 1960s was the shift in focus of growth economics from production to consumption and saving. David Cass and Tjalling Koopmans combined Frank Ramsey's 1928 model of optimal saving with the golden rule of capital accumulation, originally proposed by Edmund Phelps and others in the context of a Solow-Swan model, to create a theory of optimal growth.[13] Although it was initially interpreted as a study of the normative implications of neoclassical growth models, in the hands of Miguel Sidrauski (1967) and especially William Brock (1974) and others in the 1970s (see McCallum 1996, 49) optimal growth gradually came to be seen as offering a positive theory of the actual accumulation path of the market economy as described by the behavior of a representative economic agent with perfect foresight—a transformation that Solow ([1970] 2000, 109) criticized. In comparison with the original Solow-Swan model, the optimal version of the neoclassical growth model yields the same steady-state growth rate, but typically a different steady-state rate of output per worker, as well as different paths away from the steady state.

Had Ramsey's model of optimal savings been ignored before the arrival of the optimal growth literature? In his essay in this volume, Pedro Garcia Duarte argues that Ramsey's 1928 article was read and appreciated by a significant number of economists even before the 1950s, but that it was only after the neoclassical synthesis that dynamic welfare economics and, therefore, Ramsey's approach (as rediscovered and transformed by Cass and Koopmans) were fully integrated into economic theory.

The Solow-Swan growth model abstracted from monetary problems. In their contribution to this volume, Robert Dimand and Steven Durlauf trace the introduction of money into neoclassical growth economics mainly to two articles by James Tobin (1955, 1965). Tobin's 1955 article anticipated Solow and Swan by introducing factor substitution into Harrod-Domar type models and went farther by introducing monetary effects.

12. Stiglitz (1990), also a student of Solow, provides another account of growth economics at MIT in the 1960s.

13. Ramsey's insights were anticipated by Wicksell (see Boianovsky, this volume).

Despite incorporating a neoclassical production function, Tobin's main purpose, unlike Solow's or Swan's, was not to analyze steady-state growth but to investigate the interplay between money, nominal prices, growth, and fluctuations.

Tobin showed Solow a draft of his paper in November 1954. Solow replied in February 1955 and sent Tobin a first version of his own growth model:

> Way back in November I was absolutely fascinated when I read your paper on the train to Boston. When you look at the paper I am now sending you, you will see why. We had both been thinking almost exactly the same thoughts. . . . Strangely, there is practically no overlap between us, since you were interested mainly in the monetary and I in the real aspects. My paper at that time existed only in notes, and I decided it would hardly make any sense to send yours back until I could enclose a completed version. . . . Thank god I can *prove* I'm not a plagiarist— I gave a talk embodying essentially all of this paper at Chicago two weeks before I saw you at New Haven!

Solow's letter implies that he had set out the basic ideas of his growth paper around the end of October/beginning of November 1954 and wrote it in the first quarter of the next year. Tobin's first article on money and growth had only limited influence, probably, as Dimand and Durlauf observe, because it contained too much information. His 1965 paper received much more notice. With it, Tobin effectively initiated a new research program into the effects of monetary growth and inflation on the steady-state values of capital and output per worker. As an attempt to extend Keynesian economics into the long run, it was natural for Tobin to cite Harrod, Robinson, and Kaldor. While Tobin's model supports the neutrality of money, it also shows that a growing money supply can affect the real economy—that is, money is not *superneutral*. Sidrauski (1967) soon challenged Tobin's conclusion using an optimal monetary growth model.

Economic historians have studied the process of economic growth at least since the classic contributions of Alexander Gerschenkron, Simon Kuznets, and Walt Rostow in the 1950s. In his essay in this volume, Nicholas Crafts discusses the instrumental role of growth accounting methods— as developed and refined by Solow, Denison, and others—in the interpretation of key historical episodes (such as the Industrial Revolution) by modern quantitative economic historians. Economic historians have

generally supported Solow's (1957) result that the growth of TFP is particularly important in explaining the development of old industrial economies, with the proviso that major technological changes affect the growth
of output per worker only after an extended time lag. Things appear different for the relatively new industrialized countries, such as the so-called
Asian tigers.

The growth accounting studies of Alwyn Young (1995) and others have
provided evidence that factor accumulation—that is, increases in investment in capital and education, increases in labor force participation,
and shift from agriculture to manufacturing—accounts for a large part of
their growth. The evidence on newly industrialized economies, as Crafts
observes, is consistent with Gerschenkron's hypothesis, which posits that
the growth of relatively backward countries (as compared with the pioneers) depends mainly on capital accumulation, particularly when technology is able to flow relatively freely among countries. The heightened
importance of factor accumulation relative to the "Solow residual" might
be consistent with the neoclassical growth model as well, provided that
historical experience can be interpreted as a dynamic transition path from
one steady state to another with a higher rate of investment.[14]

Young's study in conjunction with versions of the neoclassical growth
model that include human capital as a separate factor of production contributed to a "neoclassical revival" in growth theory in the 1990s. After
Gregory Mankiw, David Romer, and David Weil's (1992) influential
econometric study of the differences in growth rates among countries,
cross-country econometric studies have often deployed an expanded neoclassical growth model to counter the claims of the so-called *new* growth
theorists that only a model of endogenous technical progress could account
for the historical record of national growth rates and income levels (Durlauf, this volume; see also Warsh 2006, 272–74, 319–21).

Gerschenkron (1952) first advanced the notion of "convergence" of
incomes per capita among countries in elaborating his concept of
"advantage of backwardness"—the hypothesis that relatively backward
economies tend to grow at a faster rate than the first industrial countries
because they borrow modern techniques of production and search for

---

14. The emphasis on transition dynamics became prominent in the early 1990s. While
they were not stressed in the original formulations of the Solow and Swan models, some of
the elements can be found already in Solow's 1969 Radcliffe Lectures.

"substitutes for prerequisites" for the productive factors, internal demand, or institutions that they lack. The neoclassical growth model also makes a prediction about convergence, albeit based on a different framework (diminishing returns to capital). Among countries that have the same steady state, those with current lower-income per capita should grow faster than rich countries and eventually catch up.

Convergence (or the lack of it) was not on Solow's or Swan's original agenda. Both restricted their investigation to the growth path within a single economy, without much concern about international comparisons. Indeed, while discussing Kaldor's stylized facts, Solow ([1970] 2000, 3) remarked that facts relating to differences between economies—such as the variety of growth rates across countries—were largely alien to his model. In their contributions to this volume, John Toye and Brian Snowdon note that the questions posed by pure growth theory in the 1950s and 1960s were generally distinct from the ones posed in development economics, which emerged as a field around the same time (e.g., Lewis 1954).

The neoclassical growth model was originally designed for a closed economy—under the double assumption of constant returns to scale and exogenous technological progress. Trade was not modeled as an important factor for economic growth. However, once increasing returns are introduced, the scale effects of international trade become crucial in explaining growth. Solow notes in his keynote address that, despite a few important contributions (especially Helpman and Krugman 1985, and Grossman and Helpman 1991), open economy growth theory has not attracted wide attention. Convergence of levels of income per head is explained with the standard neoclassical model by common technology, savings rate, and population growth. When a technological laggard gets access to more-advanced technology, a fast rate of growth is possible until the steady state is achieved and both countries share the same per capita income level and growth rate. Trade theory provides a second mechanism for convergence—factor price equalization as predicted by Eli Heckscher and Bertil Ohlin. Toye argues that trade theory and policy has thus significantly influenced (old and new) development economics.

More recently, (modified versions of) the neoclassical growth model have been used to study convergence and poverty traps, helping diminish the gap between growth and development economics. Solow (1956, 90) showed that, when there is some absolute minimum to consumption per capita and endogenous population growth, multiple equilibria are possible.

The idea of such multiple equilibria has played an important role in modern debates about poverty traps and foreign aid.[15] Snowdon also notes studies of the role of institutions in the growth process as another connection between growth theory and economic development (see also Solow 2005, 6).

The scarcity of natural resources is an important aspect of the growth process that affects developed and underdeveloped countries alike. Scarce natural resources, of course, were a crucial element of the classical Malthusian approach to growth in the early nineteenth century. Although Swan (1956) and, particularly, Meade (1961) had previously studied the analytic consequences of a finite supply of land for the neoclassical growth model, it was only in the 1970s that nonrenewable natural resources were integrated into growth economics (the topic is not mentioned in Hahn and Matthews's 1964 survey), even though the literature on the economics of exhaustible resources had existed at least since Harold Hotelling's (1931) contribution in the early 1930s. Guido Erreygers shows in his essay that it was the debate over the "limits to growth," together with the publication of John Rawls's *Theory of Justice*, that prompted Solow and others to develop the first growth models addressed to optimal capital accumulation with nonrenewable resources. In the early 1970s Solow criticized the Club of Rome report *Limits to Growth* for building models that, because they ignored substitution in the face of rising relative prices for scarce natural resources, could not help but bounce off the ceiling. In his keynote address to the *HOPE* conference, Solow suggests that the situation may be different nowadays because of large demands on natural resources associated with intensive growth in India, China, and other densely populated countries.

III

One of the main conclusions of the Solow-Swan model was that, under the assumption of diminishing returns to capital, the steady-state rate of growth of income per capita is governed by the rate of technological

---

15. Another source of multiple equilibria in Solow's 1956 model was the convexity of the production function provoked by increasing returns to capital at low levels of the capital stock. This would lead to a positive relation between the capital-output ratio (and so the rate of increase of capital) and the capital stock, similarly to the insights of early development economists.

progress.[16] Solow (see, e.g., [1970] 2000, 98) acknowledges that the theory left an obvious gap, since technological progress is an exogenous variable not explained within the model. What is more, if technology were regarded as an input in an economy that otherwise displays constant returns to scale in labor and capital, the economy would exhibit increasing returns in respect to all factors. As Kaldor (1961) first pointed out, in the face of such nonconvexities, not all factors can be paid their marginal products as is typically assumed in the analysis of perfect competition. In his classic paper on "learning by doing," Arrow (1962) suggested that the growth of technical knowledge was an unintended consequence of the experience of producing new capital goods and, therefore, external to the firms. Kaldor's (1957) "technical progress function" was an earlier attempt to capture a similar insight.[17] The alternative would be to deploy imperfectly competitive models, but that option was not open to growth economists at the time (Stiglitz 1990). Things started to change when Romer (1990) argued that ideas are nonrival, partially excludable goods, which implies the presence of increasing returns and the existence of monopolistically competitive rents used to pay for the resources used in the generation of innovations.[18]

Historically, the notion that economic growth is largely the result of increasing returns was first forcefully advanced in Allyn Young's 1928 address, which was a reelaboration of Adam Smith's theme about the

16. There may be another way to offset the diminishing returns to capital accumulation in the neoclassical growth model. If the aggregative elasticity of substitution between capital and labor is large enough (higher than one), the capital-labor ratio will increase indefinitely, accompanied by sustained growth in income per head (Solow 1956, 77; 2005, 8–9).

17. See Hahn and Matthews 1964, sec. 2.4, for a contemporary overview of the attempts of learning models to deal with growth and technical progress in a competitive framework. Solow, in his Arrow Lectures delivered at Stanford in 1993 and published in 1997, would later examine learning by doing in detail. In both Arrow's and Kaldor's models the steady-state rate of growth was, as in the Solow-Swan model, independent of savings behavior. They were not, therefore, "endogenous" in that sense. Erik Lundberg and some other economists trained in the Harrod-Domar tradition were dismayed by that result. In a contribution that went largely unnoticed until recently, Marvin Frankel (1962) advanced the first model of "endogenous" growth of the AK variety with constant returns to capital because of externalities at the firm level (Aghion and Howitt 1998, 26–27; Cannon 2000; see also Pomini and Tondini 2006).

18. The insight that nonrival knowledge is a main source of increasing returns may be found already in J. Maurice Clark's (1923, 119–23) treatment of overhead costs: "In a sense, knowledge is the only instrument of production that is not subject to diminishing returns. . . . The same research department can serve a large plant as well as a small one. Indeed, in technical matters where a law, once learned, is universal, one laboratory could serve the entire business of the country. . . . The costs of intellectual equipment, then, are one of the big sources of economy in large-scale production."

dynamic role of the division of labor. Young's approach to the growth process influenced the first generation of development economists in the 1940s and 1950s, but—with a few exceptions such as Svennilson and Kaldor—not growth theorists. Hahn and Matthews (1964, sec. 2.2) clarified the conditions under which increasing returns can be readily incorporated into a steady-state growth model. Output and capital will grow at the same rate, which is a multiple of the rate of growth of population. Even in the absence of technical progress, the economies of scale will bring about a permanent increase in income per capita so long as the rate of population growth is positive.[19]

Young's central message, on the other hand, was that progress is determined by the increased specialization of labor across a growing variety of goods—the extent to which capital is used in relation to labor is mainly governed by the scale of operations, that is, the capital-labor ratio depends on a larger extent on the size of the market rather than on factor prices. Young's notion of increasing returns through continuing specialization in production would have a marked influence on Kaldor's interpretation of growth as a disequilibrium process after the 1960s (Wulwick 1993) and on Romer's (1990) modeling of technological progress as creating new varieties of capital goods. However, as Roger Sandilands (this volume) argues, Romer's formalization leaves out of the picture important features of Young's notion of macroeconomic increasing returns and the role of the growth of demand in deciding the scope for application of knowledge to the productive process.[20]

Whereas Young stressed increasing returns, Joseph Schumpeter—another crucial intellectual source of non-steady-state growth economics—argued that growth results from technological progress through "creative destruction." Schumpeter taught Solow at Harvard in the 1940s, but made no lasting impression on him. In particular, although Solow's (1956) model may look like a vindication of Schumpeter's insight about the pivotal role of technical change in the growth process, there is no real connection between their analyses.

---

19. Such "scale effects" are a controversial feature of several growth models, e.g., Arrow 1962 and Romer 1990. Solow ([1970] 2000, 113) points out that just allowing for increasing returns is not enough to generate a fully "endogenous" growth model—in the sense that the rate of growth is explained within the model—since the long-run rate of growth is still exogenous.

20. While commenting at the *HOPE* conference on Young's notion that growth generates growth in cumulative fashion, Solow pondered whether there is no analogue to diminishing returns in specialization.

Schumpeter's approach, as William Baumol (this volume) reminds us, was especially relevant for the microeconomics of technological progress, based on the study of competition between firms through innovation. Although Schumpeter's approach influenced important aspects of new growth theory (see especially Aghion and Howitt 1998), a full formal investigation of entrepreneurship is still missing. From a methodological standpoint, one should distinguish between macroeconomic growth theory—the study of the long-run performance of the economy conditioned on the evolution of technology—and the microeconomic investigation of the process of technological change (Solow [1970] 2000, 101).

Solow's main criticism of endogenous new growth theory—partly supported by Baumol—is the special character of the assumption that the production function for ideas is a linear differential equation. The "linearity critique" (Jones 1998, chaps. 5, 8) has played an important role because, among other reasons, linearity ensures that, in contrast to the conclusions of the Solow-Swan model, changes in economic policy that affect, say, the savings rate can permanently increase the growth rate of output.

Twenty years after their first appearance, none of the new growth theory models or any synthesis model has definitively supplanted the old neoclassical growth model. Durlauf (this volume) ascribes the failure to the "open-endedness" of growth models—that is, to the mutual compatibility of different growth theories.[21] Another factor is undoubtedly the difficulties in adequately testing the models against data. Although the recent literature on economic growth is more empirically orientated than the older literature—as witnessed especially by the boom in cross-country growth regressions after the early 1990s—the methodological role of growth econometrics is still an open issue. Durlauf suggests that the relationship between new growth theory and growth empirics will tend to mirror that between neoclassical growth theory and data, with growth regressions taking over the role of growth accounting as a supplier of stylized facts that models need to capture.

The interpretation of one particular piece of empirical evidence—the Solow residual—has played an important role in the controversy about the interconnection between short- and long-run macroeconomics. Beginning in the 1980s, real business cycle theorists have argued that, at business

21. Solow (2005, 4) has claimed that "there is not really any competing model" to the basic neoclassical growth model, since, in a broad sense, the new growth theories are completely neoclassical. See Helpman 2005 for a different opinion.

cycle frequencies, total factor productivity is strongly correlated with output and hours worked. Procyclical labor supply and investment propagate shocks to total factor productivity (TFP), generating fluctuations in output and labor productivity in economy well described by an optimal growth model. New Keynesian macroeconomists have challenged this interpretation of the residual. They argue that short-run fluctuations of TFP reflect departures from perfect competition and from constant returns to scale.

In the final essay in this volume, Tiago Mata and Francisco Louçã recount the debate. They argue that, as often happens in economics, the concept of the residual has been used in ways quite distinct from the original context in which it was formulated. While Solow himself has not been deeply engaged in this controversy, he did recall in his reaction to the contributions to a Festschrift in his honor that in his 1957 article he was interested in the trend, not in year-to-year oscillations, of TFP, but, if asked about the meaning of such yearly fluctuations, he would largely side with the new Keynesians in emphasizing increasing returns in the short run, when output is below capacity (Solow 1990, 224–26).

References

Aghion, Philippe, and Peter Howitt. 1998. *Endogenous Growth Theory*. Cambridge: MIT Press.

Arrow, Kenneth J. 1962. The Economic Implications of Learning by Doing. *Review of Economic Studies* 29:155–73.

Barro, Robert, and Xavier Sala-i-Martin. 1995. *Economic Growth*. New York: McGraw-Hill.

Brock, William. 1974. Comments. In vol. 2 of *Frontiers of Quantitative Economics*. Amsterdam: North-Holland.

Burmeister, Edwin, and A. Rodney Dobell. 1970. *Mathematical Theories of Economic Growth*. New York: Macmillan.

Cannon, Edwin. 2000. Economies of Scale and Constant Returns to Capital: A Neglected Early Contribution to the Theory of Economic Growth. *American Economic Review* 90.1:292–95.

Cassel, Gustav. 1935. *On Quantitative Thinking in Economics*. Oxford: Clarendon.

Clark, John M. 1923. *Studies in the Economics of Overhead Costs*. Chicago: University of Chicago Press.

Diamond, Peter. 1990. *Growth/Productivity/Unemployment: Essays to Celebrate Bob Solow's Birthday*. Cambridge: MIT Press.

Dixit, Avinash K., and Joseph E. Stiglitz. 1977. Monopolistic Competition and Optimum Product Diversity. *American Economic Review* 67:297–308.

Domar, Evsey. 1946. Capital Expansion, Rate of Growth, and Employment. *Econometrica* 14:137–47.

——. 1947. Expansion and Employment. *American Economic Review* 37:34–55.

——. 1957. *Essays in the Theory of Economic Growth*. New York: Oxford University Press.

——. 1961. On the Measurement of Technological Change. *Economic Journal* 71:709–29.

Easterly, William. 2001. *The Elusive Quest for Growth: Economists' Adventures and Misadventures in the Tropics*. Cambridge: MIT Press.

Frankel, Marvin. 1962. The Production Function in Allocation and Growth: A Synthesis. *American Economic Review* 52:995–1022.

Gerschenkron, Alexander. 1952. Economic Backwardness in Historical Perspective. In Hoselitz 1952.

Grossman, Gene, and Elhanan Helpman. 1991. *Innovation and Growth in the Global Economy*. Cambridge: MIT Press.

Hahn, Frank, and R. C. O. Matthews. 1964. The Theory of Economic Growth: A Survey. *Economic Journal* 74:779–902.

Harcourt, Geoffrey C. 2006. *The Structure of Post-Keynesian Economics: The Core Contributions of the Pioneers*. Cambridge: Cambridge University Press.

Harrod, Roy F. 1939. An Essay in Dynamic Theory. *Economic Journal* 49:14–33.

——. 1948. *Towards a Dynamic Economics*. London: Macmillan.

——. 1960. Second Essay in Dynamic Theory. *Economic Journal* 70:277–93.

——. 1963. Themes in Dynamic Theory. *Economic Journal* 73:401–21.

Helpman, Elhanan. 2005. *The Mystery of Economic Growth*. Cambridge: Harvard University Press.

Helpman, Elhanan, and Paul Krugman. 1985. *Trade Policy and Market Structure*. Cambridge: MIT Press.

Hoover, Kevin D. 2008. Was Harrod Right? Unpublished typescript, 25 May, Department of Economics, Duke University. www.econ.duke.edu/~kdh9/.

Hoselitz, Bert F., ed. 1952. *The Progress of Underdeveloped Areas*. Chicago: University of Chicago Press.

Hotelling, Harold. 1931. The Economics of Exhaustible Resources. *Journal of Political Economy* 39:137–75.

Jones, Charles. 1998. *Introduction to Economic Growth*. New York: Norton.

Kaldor, Nicholas. 1957. A Model of Economic Growth. *Economic Journal* 67:591–624.

——. 1961. Capital Accumulation and Economic Growth. In Lutz and Hague 1961.

Kendrick, John W. 1956. Productivity Trends: Capital and Labor. *Review of Economics and Statistics* 38:248–57.

Kim, E. Han, Adair Morse, and Luigi Zingales. 2006. What Has Mattered to Economics since 1970. NBER Working Paper No. 12526.

Kregel, Jan. 1980. Economic Dynamics and the Theory of Steady Growth: An Historical Essay on Harrod's "Knife-Edge." *HOPE* 12.1:97–123.

Leontief, Wassily, et al. 1953. *Studies in the Structure of the American Economy*. New York: Oxford University Press.

Lewis, W. Arthur. 1954. Economic Development with Unlimited Supplies of Labor. *Manchester School* 22:139–91.

Lutz, F. A., and D. C. Hague, eds. 1961. *The Theory of Capital*. London: Macmillan.

Mankiw, N. Gregory, David Romer, and David Weil. 1992. A Contribution to the Empirics of Economic Growth. *Quarterly Journal of Economics* 107:407–38.

McCallum, Bennett T. 1996. Neoclassical vs. Endogenous Growth Analysis: An Overview. *Federal Reserve Bank of Richmond Economic Quarterly* 82.4:41–71.

Meade, James. 1961. *A Neo-classical Theory of Economic Growth*. London: Unwin.

Pomini, Mario, and Giovanni Tondini. 2006. The Idea of Increasing Returns in Neoclassical Growth Models. *European Journal of the History of Economic Thought* 13.3:365–86.

Ramsey, Frank P. 1928. A Mathematical Theory of Saving. *Economic Journal* 38:543–59.

Robinson, Joan V. 1956. *The Accumulation of Capital*. London: Macmillan.

Romer, Paul. 1990. Endogenous Technological Change. *Journal of Political Economy* 98:S71–S102.

Sen, Amartya, ed. 1970. *Growth Economics*. Middlesex, U.K.: Penguin.

Sidrauski, Miguel. 1967. Rational Choices and Patterns of Growth in a Monetary Economy. *American Economic Review* 57.2:534–44.

Solow, Robert M. 1955. Letter to James Tobin, 16 February. Duke University Rare Book, Manuscript, and Special Collections Library, Durham, N.C.

——. 1956. A Contribution to the Theory of Economic Growth. *Quarterly Journal of Economics* 70:65–94.

——. 1957. Technical Change and the Aggregate Production Function. *Review of Economics and Statistics* 39:748–62.

——. 1960. Investment and Technical Progress. In *Mathematical Methods in the Social Sciences, 1959*, edited by K. Arrow, S. Karlin, and P. Suppes. Stanford, Calif.: Stanford University Press.

——. 1966. Letter to Ernst Helmstädter, 11 February. Duke University Rare Book, Manuscript, and Special Collections Library, Durham, N.C.

——. 1970. Letter to Amartya Sen, 14 January. Duke University Rare Book, Manuscript, and Special Collections Library, Durham, N.C.

——. 1990. Reactions to Conference Papers. In Diamond 1990.

——. 1994. Perspectives on Growth Theory. *Journal of Economic Perspectives* 8.1:45–54.

——. 1997. *Learning from "Learning from Doing": Lessons for Economic Growth*. Stanford, Calif.: Stanford University Press.

——. 1999. Neoclassical Growth Theory. In vol. 1 of *Handbook of Macroeconomics*, edited by J. B. Taylor and M. Woodford. Amsterdam: Elsevier.

——. [1970] 2000. *Growth Theory: An Exposition*. 2nd ed. New York: Oxford University Press.

——. 2005. Reflections on Growth Theory. In *Handbook of Economic Growth*, edited by P. Aghion and S. Durlauf. Amsterdam: Elsevier.

Sraffa, Piero. 1926. The Laws of Returns under Competitive Conditions. *Economic Journal* 36.144:535–50.

Stiglitz, Joseph E. 1990. Comments: Some Retrospective Views on Growth Theory. In Diamond 1990.

Stiglitz, Joseph E., and Hirofumi Uzawa, eds. 1969. *Readings in the Modern Theory of Economic Growth*. Cambridge: MIT Press.

Swan, Trevor. 1956. Economic Growth and Capital Accumulation. *Economic Record* 32:334–61.

Tinbergen, Jan. [1942] 1959. On the Theory of Trend Movements. In *Selected Papers*, edited by L. Klaassen, L. Koyck, and H. Witteveen. Amsterdam: North-Holland.

Tobin, James. 1955. A Dynamic Aggregative Model. *Journal of Political Economy* 63:103–15.

———. 1965. Money and Economic Growth. *Econometrica* 33:671–84.

Uzawa, Hirofumi. 1961. Neutral Inventions and the Stability of Growth Equilibrium. *Review of Economic Studies* 28:117–24.

Wan, Henry Y. 1971. *Economic Growth*. New York: Harcourt Brace Jovanovich.

Warsh, David. 2006. *Knowledge and the Wealth of Nations: A Story of Economic Discovery*. New York: Norton.

Wulwick, Nancy. 1993. What Remains of the Growth Controversy. *Review of Political Economy* 5.3:321–43.

Young, Allyn A. 1928. Increasing Returns and Economic Progress. *Economic Journal* 38:527–42.

Young, Alwyn. 1995. The Tyranny of Numbers: Confronting the Statistical Realities of East Asian Growth Experience. *Quarterly Journal of Economics* 110:641–80.

Part 1
Growth Economics in the First Person

Does Growth Have a Future?
Does Growth Theory Have a Future?
Are These Questions Related?

Robert M. Solow

I do intend to provide answers, at least my answers, to the questions that make up the title of this talk. Before that, however, I would like to make a few brief comments on the conference that forms the basis of this occasion and this issue. It consisted of two days devoted to scholarly and historical discussion of a couple of papers that I wrote in 1956 and 1957, thus fifty or fifty-one years ago. Participating in that conference has been an unusual experience, maybe a bit too much like Tom Sawyer attending his own funeral. The phrase "dead white male" keeps hovering in my mind. Two out of three ain't bad, especially if you get the luckier two of the three.

There is a piece of background wisdom that historians of economic thought must all know in their bones, but that they may tend to forget in the momentum of later discussion. When I did the research and wrote those papers more than fifty years ago, I had no inkling that they would be important or influential papers. As far as I was concerned, I was just doing what a junior academic was supposed to do. I had an idea; I worked it out; and I wrote a paper. I had no premonition that these two pieces of work would become the foundation for a minor, and in some ways much more than a minor, intellectual industry. The point for historians of thought is that works that look like monuments and function like monuments fifty years later were not necessarily looking like monuments or thought of that way when they were new.

History of Political Economy 41 (annual suppl.) DOI 10.1215/00182702-2009-014

It is interesting, especially to me, that in the course of the conference, Olivier de La Grandville of the University of Geneva, with whom I have worked before, produced what was to me a new and surprising consequence of a paper that I had written fifty-two years ago. What I had used as the ordinary everyday market-clearing condition that the marginal product of capital should be equal to the cost of capital is also, within the model, an optimization condition for an intertemporal problem that I had not really been considering at all. So here I am, an old gentleman fifty-two years after having written a paper, learning something about it that had not occurred to me at the time, or later. (Maybe it is not so surprising: my children, also in their fifties, occasionally tell me something about their early years that I had not known and was probably better off not knowing.)

Here is one more historical note before I turn to my stated business. I was very glad that this conference has also taken notice of other people who were more or less simultaneously contributing to the kind of theory of economic growth that I was then working on. I tend to believe that real progress in economics—and, I presume although I don't know this, in other disciplines—is made by small research communities more than by individuals, in ways that the individuals themselves may not realize. The fact that Trevor Swan and James Tobin, two of my favorite macroeconomists of all time (and, in the case of Tobin, one of my closest friends), got their due in this conference has been a good thing. It speaks well for this research community that it saw this and did that.

Of the three questions I have posed, the easiest to answer is the third: and the answer is yes. One can foresee some likely changes in the character of future economic growth even in the developed world. Some of those changes are already partially visible, and others seem at least probable. In my view, growth theory is not an abstract discipline; it is not a project you would pursue for its own intrinsic beauty. Instead it is a discipline you pursue in the belief that it will tell you something useful about the longer-run evolution—past and future—of our own economic system. I would hope that the research community of growth economists will turn its energy toward modeling these already visible or apparently likely changes in the character of growth in advanced economies, and toward trying to see how to fit them into the theoretical story, the analytical story that we tell. No doubt there will need to be changes in the standard models—like those of 1956 and 1957—in order to accommodate such new factual developments.

In this connection, the one thing I have found lacking in the program of the conference so far is some serious attention to the stylized facts of economic growth, that is to say, the facts of economic growth as seen from a distance. A central part of the history of the subdiscipline is how those basic facts have influenced what economists interested in economic growth write down, how they decide to model the process of economic growth, how indeed they think about it. Steve Durlauf seems to share my regret. His paper suggests a reason for the gap: the recent empirical literature on economic growth has shied away from a direct concern with the gross facts and the theoretical hints that they may contain. He and I both think that cross-country regressions are not a satisfactory substitute.

My answer to the first two questions of my title will come in the course of describing two or three of these shifts in the pattern of economic growth that seem likely to be with us. They certainly provide some kind of "future" for economic growth. If economists younger than I are worth their salt, they will correspondingly provide a future for growth theory that is related precisely to those changes. Since I have thought of only a few such changes, it will not take me long to discuss them. Do not be surprised if they sound commonplace; if they were not commonplace, they would not be worth talking about in this way.

The first structural change that calls for attention is the shift from a goods-producing to a service-producing economy. This is most pronounced in the United States, though other advanced economies are following with varying degrees of reluctance. In this country, as most of us are aware, only about one in six of every person employed is employed in producing goods, that is, something with mass and weight; the other five are engaged in the production of immaterial services. It is odd: I have spent a certain amount of time as an economist trying to explain to lay people that there is not much difference between goods and services as objects of production, the main one being that you can't hold an inventory of a service, as you can of a material good. The principles of economics hold for both. That is an important lesson for lay people. In terms of the standard categories of growth theory, however, there may be important *quantitative* differences between a service-dominated economy and one in which manufacturing, construction, and agriculture are the main income-originating activities.

The growth theorist of the future may find it most useful to think of a two-sector model whose two sectors are goods production and service production, instead of the more traditional division between consumer goods and capital goods, or between industry and subsistence agriculture. (One might even need three sectors to distinguish high-productivity services—like finance—from personal services like child care and elder care; health care is obviously a complicated case.) It might even be necessary to subdivide labor input into skilled and unskilled to allow for persistent differences in factor intensity among these sectors. Why go to this trouble?

We anticipate, or have anticipated in the past, that an important, usually the most important, element in the growth of a modern economy is the sustained increase of total factor productivity. We do not have any very clear and empirically defensible idea about how fast and how far total factor productivity is likely to increase in the service sectors, whether it is bounded or whether one could imagine total factor productivity increasing for a long time beyond any bounds that we can now imagine. Nor do we know what the likely incidence of total factor productivity improvement in a service economy would be: labor augmenting, skilled-labor augmenting, or what?

Here is a second relevant way in which a service economy might differ systematically from a goods economy. I have no idea to what extent the law of diminishing returns applies to the service sector. I assume that it does apply, because I am much too old to start assuming it does not. But there could easily be a different pace with which diminishing returns asserts itself. Remarkably enough, there does not seem to be any reliable generalization about the capital intensity of service production. My dentist's office looks capital intensive; that little room where I sit in a mechanized chair seems to contain as much sophisticated capital equipment as any place else that I go. On the other hand, a nursery school is not very capital intensive. Naturally, then, we are pretty much in the dark about the rate of return on service-sector capital. That is all information that will be needed by the theorist of the future as he or she grapples with the growth patterns of a service economy. It appears to the casual eye that many intrinsically low-productivity consumer services have high income-elasticity of demand, so they will bulk larger in the economy as income per person increases. I am thinking of leisure activities, resort hotels and the like. If that generalization is really so, it will affect many aspects of the market system; it will also affect the resource-allocation and growth patterns of the whole economy.

The nature of returns to scale may also be systematically altered by a continuing shift to the production of services. Casual observation suggests that it might not go all one way: communications-based services may become more efficient at larger scales, but personal services (including many business services) may not. This is yet another case where systematic empirical research is needed.

Before I leave this issue of the service economy, I should raise one more question. Is a service economy easier on the environment than a goods economy? Much environmental damage is done through the mining and processing of bulky materials. It is a reasonable hypothesis that the production of services requires less of that sort of thing, but a serious analysis depends on the capital intensity of the service sector, as well as its energy intensity. There are some surprisingly capital-intensive personal services—I mentioned dentistry a moment ago—but even they may use little energy.

This brings me directly to the second way in which I suspect that changes in the economy will affect both real economic growth and the way growth theory tries to understand it. I mean the related issues of natural resource scarcity and environmental preservation. Whenever it was that the Club of Rome burst onto the scene—two or three decades ago?—I thought that its message was mostly hot air. I have not changed my mind about then. Thirty years later, the situation may have changed. It is possible that real demands on natural resources, and therefore on the natural environment, will be dramatically different in a world in which India and China, and other countries, too, grow at 8 or 10 percent a year, and need to pass through the material-goods-intensive phase of growth before they arrive at the service economy. The necessary process of (very material-intensive) urbanization is an outstanding example of what I mean. So it will probably be more important in the future to deal intellectually, quantitatively, as well as practically, with the mutual interdependence of economic growth, natural-resource availability, and environmental constraints.

The research community does respond. Economists are intelligent, clever people, and they do think about these things in their own way. There is already the beginning of growth theory with nonrenewable resources, with renewable resources, and there has even been some attention to the more difficult problem of the transition from one to the other. Once again, however, we need some basic stylized facts that I have not seen properly discussed. For example, I have read—I am in no position to make critical judgments—that the current (2008) spike in food prices is not a fundamental; it may be mainly a short-run phenomenon. Even if food prices may tend to rise relative to goods in general, the future will not look like the past six months or so. Even so, it is possible that one will have to pay more attention to the role of agriculture in economic growth, something that we have not had to do for a long time. You will notice that I am not going to touch on the issue of climate change, though it so obviously looms; there is too much controversy about the stylized facts. Nevertheless, it is hard to avoid the thought that there is here a whole set of questions posed for real economic growth and for growth theory that will have to be answered.

A third set of issues about the world and its representation in growth theory arises from the enormous expansion of international trade. I have been surprised at how little interest the community has shown in open-economy growth theory, the modeling of growth in a group of differently situated trading economies. There was one excellent book published on that subject by Gene Grossman and Elhanan Helpman, rather a long time ago. It was not really followed up. The community seemed to focus on a side issue—the way they modeled new goods as quality ladders—and left aside what they had to say about trade between growing economies. That needs to be discussed.

All these open or partially open questions are interrelated. For instance, the character of world economic growth will surely change as India and especially China evolve from export-orientation to internal demand, and from goods-intensive to service-intensive growth. In some ways the most burning issue of all, one that needs some reasoned hypotheses about stylized facts to come, is this: given what we know currently about rates of growth and technological change, and about income elasticities of demand, how long is it likely to take before the real-wage level in China gets closer to the real-wage level in the Western world? Are we talking about a century or about less? Remember, I am leaving aside the possibility that the normal economic tendency for real wages to rise might be suppressed politically and for political reasons: that would create problems that are well beyond the capacity of the theory of economic growth even to discuss.

Finally, I would like to mention a wholly different kind of question for the growth theory of the future: the question of growth with equity. I will be thinking mainly about advanced economies, but many of the same issues arise in middle-income countries like Turkey and Chile. The first defining question to ask is, How is income inequality likely to change endogenously as growth continues? That has something to do with the functional distribution of income among labor, capital, and natural resources, but much of the inequality and inequity arises *within* functional categories, especially labor (where human-capital issues play a role).

Here I want to state a presumption that goes rather against the economist's instincts, but that is made plausible by some recent research. There is considerable evidence that, within the group of advanced capitalist economies, the fundamentals of technology and market competition impose only fairly loose constraints on the size distribution of wage incomes. Societies as similar as the United States and Western Europe seem to have a lot of room for maneuver: the size distribution of wage incomes can be strongly influenced by both formal legislation and the informal social norms that govern relations between employers and employees. In particular, the dispersion of wage incomes below the median—which is where equity issues bite—can differ substantially among economies exposed to the same technology and to the same international market.

If that is so, there is good cause for the research community to investigate what it is in our countries that governs the size distribution at the bottom end of each factor share, as well as the distribution between broad factors of production. An answer to that question would lead directly to the growth-with-equity issue: what our societies can do so that, as income rises, the left-hand tail of the income distribution does not just get longer and longer, straying farther behind the median. Something like that seems to be happening in the United States and in some, though not all, European economies as well.

Suppose, to take an extreme but not unthinkable case, the nature of changing technology and demand, even as we shift to service production, were such that the market wants to impute more and more income to capital, to property in general. Then, if we are concerned with preserving equity as the economy grows, we would have to think of ways to—so to speak—democratize the ownership of capital. There was a similar scare, in the early 1960s, that the process of the automation of production could lead to a situation in which labor was essentially dispensable in production. That fear, the fear that all the jobs are going to go away, is still common outside the world of economists. Suppose that this time the nightmare came true, or nearly true. How would one find a way of distributing income if annual wage rates became negligible relative to incomes from capital? We would have to find some way to widen the ownership of capital, whether through an analog of pension funds or in some other way. We would have to make a reality of Henry Luce's "people's capitalism," not an empty slogan.

I don't intend to make a proposal. My goal is to point out that this is the kind of shift that the process of economic growth might eventually entail. If elasticities of substitution are very large, and if the stock of capital grows much more rapidly than the supply of labor, then one might have to face that kind of story, and it will be the job of growth theory to tell the story analytically.

These are some of the issues that your students and your students' students may have to deal with if the process of economic growth in the future differs in some systematic ways from past patterns. The ones I picked out are the shift from goods to services, the constraints arising from the provision of natural resource products and energy from nonrenewable or renewable resources, and the resulting strains on the environment, and the possible need to worry more explicitly about the distribution of income in order not to run into our own version of a poverty trap. And my limited imagination may have missed what turns out to be the Big Deal in economic growth a few decades from now.

So I feel pretty safe in thinking that anyone who gets a PhD in economics from Duke thirty or forty years from now will probably be taking a course on the theory of economic growth; some of them will be writing PhD theses in the field and finding no need to pay attention to the papers that I wrote fifty years ago, and that got me here in this rather awkward position.

Reflections

Edwin Burmeister

In thinking about giving this talk, I asked myself if I possessed some special knowledge about any aspect of growth theory that no one else in the room would know about, or at least not know much about. Well, one other person in this room knows about the growth theory course that I took in 1962–1963—but probably no one else does.

So I will start with some fond reflections about Bob Solow's course entitled 14.123. Usually we left the decimal point out and simply said, "fourteen one twenty-three." Yes, that really is how things were done at M.I.T. We were in Building E52, Economics was Course 14, and Advanced Economic Theory was 14.123. At the time I remember wondering if there was some kind of inside joke meant to imply that advanced economic theory was easy—you know, like Lotus 123. Well, later it became quite clear that this was not the case, and I decided that 1, 2, and 3 were merely random numbers that had drifted over from the physics department.

Imagine that we found one of those wormholes and could go back in time to Monday, September 17, 1962, the first day of Fall semester classes at M.I.T. Those were the days of sensible schedules; the Fall semester did not end until Wednesday, January 23, 1963. We would find that John F. Kennedy is President, and everyone is excited about his proposed tax cut.

Editors' note: Transcript of Edwin Burmeister's after-dinner talk at the *HOPE* conference, "Robert Solow and the Development of Growth Economics," delivered on 25 April 2008, with Robert Solow as the guest of honor.

History of Political Economy 41 (annual suppl.) DOI 10.1215/00182702-2009-015

14.123 is a Wednesday-Friday class, so its first meeting is on September 19, 1962. I arrive at M.I.T. with an M.A. degree from Cornell, and this somehow qualifies me to enroll in Advanced Economic Theory without having had its normal prerequisites.

Well, being naïve sometimes has its advantages. I had no idea that I should have been impressed by the intellectual power of the other people who showed up on that first day. These included:

1. Edmund S. Phelps, who was a visiting assistant professor at M.I.T. (from Yale) and who was a co-instructor with Bob Solow.
2. Prof. Dr. Carl Christian von Weizsäcker, who hedged his bets by having a post-doc fellowship at both M.I.T. and the University of Cambridge.
3. Christopher Bliss, who writes me now that he was ". . . a junior short-term visitor to M.I.T."
4. A. Rodney Dobell, who subsequently co-authored a book with me.
5. David Levhari, who became famous for the wrong reason; more about that later.
6. And perhaps five or six other M.I.T. Ph.D. students.

Suffice it to say that this was not the kind of class that I was used to from Cornell.

My notes from 14.123 have survived all these years, and so I actually have documentation for events that occurred some forty-six years ago. Bob's 14.123 course began in earnest on Friday, September 21, 1962. Here is his very first sentence:

> We will first study a model of a one-product economy in which production takes the form of using labor in one point of time and then harvesting product (with no further use of scarce resources) at a later point in time.

And so we were off and running. Analysis of the model resulted in two equations in three unknowns, the real wage rate w/p, the rate of interest r, and the optimal time to harvest T. The conclusion was that a determinate model required either fixing r, as in Joan Robinson, or introducing a savings function or a rate of time preference. This conclusion turned out to be amazingly robust across the models that we were to study for the remainder of the semester.

From this pure Austrian tree model, the focus moved on to a Lange circulating capital model and then on to Wicksell's fixed capital model where the durability of machines is a choice variable.

Beginning on Wednesday, October 17th, the emphasis changed to notions of productivity growth and technological change. Many of these models invented the wheels for other people to later reinvent. But to say more here would be to digress.

Even outside of Economics 14.123, these were exciting times: on Sunday, October 14th reconnaissance photos taken by an American U-2 spy plane revealed missile bases being built in Cuba. The first public statement by President Kennedy was made on Monday, October 22nd when he said:

> It shall be the policy of this nation to regard any nuclear missile launched from Cuba against any nation in the Western Hemisphere as an attack on the United States, requiring a full retaliatory response upon the Soviet Union.

This may have been the closest we have ever been to destroying the world—and back then I had seen so little of it. At Harvard Law School Henry Kissinger was teaching a course entitled "Strategic Decision Making"—or something like that—and the entire three-hour lecture for that week was about what Kissinger would do if *he* were in Washington. (I was taking this course and remember it well because Kissinger did not like and/or understand my concept of equal-probability-of-destruction curves, with quantities of offensive and defensive missiles on the axes; he gave my brilliant effort an A minus.)

But in 14.123 the subject on Friday, October 26th was the growth of productivity and technical change. Nowhere in my notes can I find any mention of the Cuban Missile Crisis, nor do I remember any reference to it in class. In 14.123 we did *economics*, and that was the sole focus of our attention. It was beautiful, and I loved it.

However, on Friday, November 2nd my notes read: "Phelps (Solow in Washington)." Now Ned implied that Bob was in Washington to consult with the Council of Economic Advisors: Walter W. Heller, Kermit Gordon, and Gardner Ackley. But could it have been that he also consulted with McGeorge Bundy, Dean Rusk, and Robert F. Kennedy? Well, the timing for this wild notion is not quite right; the Cuban Missile Crisis was officially over the preceding Sunday, October 28, 1962. Nevertheless, no doubt Bobby Kennedy and his colleagues would have benefited from Solow's advice, even if it were not about economic growth.

For me the highlight of 14.123 came in a pair of Solow lectures on Wednesday, November 14 and Wednesday, November 21. (I have no idea what happened on the intervening Friday.) The first lecture started with these words:

> This will be a funny lecture because I have not solved the problem of
> the rate of return to saving under technical change.

And then we were given a very clear picture of exactly what problem
was unsolved.

The very next lecture begins with just three words from Bob: "Problem now solved." And then we were walked through the details of the
solution.

As you know, Bob's abilities as a lecturer are legendary, and here I can
confirm that the legend is true. But as this example so wonderfully illustrates, Bob teaches much more than facts. He also teaches how to do genuine research. Those of us who were lucky enough to benefit from his
most extraordinary skill are greatly indebted to him. Thanks!

In retrospect 14.123 was not just on the frontier of economic research;
often it was beyond the ordinary frontier at the best universities. Here
is another example. On Wednesday, December 12, 1962 the subject was
Optimality Problems in Capital Theory. We were shown how to use the
Minimum Principle of Pontryagin to solve the famous Ramsey problem
of optimal saving over time. In this lecture we covered essentially everything that is contained in the famous David Cass paper that was not published until the July 1965 issue of the *Review of Economic Studies*! M.I.T.
students were indeed well prepared.

By way of completeness I mention here that we studied several other
capital theory topics in 14.123. In particular, Arrow's learning-by-doing
paper was examined in detail, and, of course, Phelps gave us a comprehensive treatment of the Golden Rule. But he only dared do so on Friday,
December 14 when Bob was absent. And only then did I learn that in his
1961–1962 German Ph.D. thesis, Christian von Weizsäcker had discovered the Golden Rule independently of Ned Phelps. Thoughts of, "What
am I doing here?" went through my mind.

If 14.123 were to be taught today, what might be the most important
subject that would be added that was not known about in 1962–1963?
Well, of course there are rational expectations, endogenous growth theory,
and all of that. But something that at least in some ways is even more
fundamental is what later became known as the Capital Theory Controversies. Since I was very much a player in these controversies, I will
try to convey to you how they unfolded for me as a student and later as a
brand new assistant professor.

Essentially the "controversies" illustrate that in general a well-behaved aggregate index of capital does not exist. Now, in 14.123 Solow and Phelps were very careful to talk about "schmoos" or "leets" ("steel" spelled backwards) as the magical thing that was output, output that could either be consumed or used along with labor as a factor of production. But we never discussed exactly how one measured the number of schmoos.

What was the prevailing view about capital, saving, and the rate of interest among U.S. economists in 1962 or 1963? Well, I do not need to consult any of you economic historians to find the answer to this one. On pages 595–597 of Samuelson's elementary text we find a very clear answer. This is in the 1964 Sixth Edition, so it probably was written sometime in 1963. Here is the story:

1. An economy starting from some steady-state equilibrium cuts back on consumption for a period of time.
2. This lowering of consumption enables the economy to accumulate more capital.
3. The economy then can move into a new steady-state with a permanently higher level of consumption. This new steady-state will have a larger capital stock and a lower rate of interest than the first.
4. Now repeat an identical cut-back in consumption.
5. One can then move to another higher permanent consumption level with an even lower rate of interest, but the consumption gain will be less than the first time because of diminishing returns.

This story is exactly true for a one-sector Solow growth model. The fact that it appears in Samuelson's elementary text is ample evidence that the story was thought to be generally true. A few technical details needed to be filled in, but the basic truth was thought known.

So what happened to change this M.I.T. view of the world?

In the Spring semester of 1963 Paul Samuelson taught a seminar—I do not remember its exact title—and most of us from 14.123 were enrolled. One day Paul was talking about what Joan Robinson called the Ruth Cohen curiosum, namely it is possible that the same linear technique (for producing a single good) is cost minimizing at both high and low interest rates, but not in-between. As I recall Paul conjectured something like, "You know, I bet that cannot happen for the whole economy if it is indecomposable." Not long thereafter David Levhari produced a "proof" of this conjecture. David's results were published as the second part of his paper in the February 1965 issue of the *Quarterly Journal of Economics*. Only a few months later—in September 1965—the First World Congress of the Econometric Society was held in Rome. There Luigi Pasinetti presented a paper containing a counterexample to both Levhari's "proof" and Samuelson's conjecture.

I had been at Penn as a new Assistant Professor for only a couple of weeks when I heard the news. I was astonished. To me it was as if someone had established that the earth was indeed flat. How could it be that everyone at M.I.T. had overlooked the mistake? I am included in this "everyone." I well remember attending the thesis-writing seminar where David presented his "proof." We all thought it was elegant.

Perhaps there is a role for behavioral economists here. It seems to me that if you believe strongly enough that something is true, then it can be very difficult to correctly evaluate facts that stand in contradiction. And similarly, it is very easy to believe assertions that are consistent with your prior beliefs. But I want to quickly abandon this line of inquiry . . .

The entire November 1966 issue of the *Quarterly Journal of Economics* was devoted to David's false theorem and the related questions it inspired. It includes a note by Levhari and Samuelson in which they candidly admit the mistake. It also includes my very first publication, coauthored with Michael Bruno and Eytan Shesinski. And thus it came to be that certain economists in Cambridge, England, claimed their victory over those of us in Cambridge, USA.

What does victory mean? It means that the story of consumption, capital accumulation, and the rate of interest told in Samuelson's Sixth Edition is not generally true. And since the story is not generally true, it follows that a well-behaved index of aggregate capital generally does not exist, even if joint production is ruled out. Furthermore, if joint production is admitted, then the Samuelson Sixth Edition story is not true even when there is only a single type of capital good (and hence no capital aggregation issue)!

Most of these facts are no longer disputed, but heated discussions about how important all this is still occur. As one example, Avi Cohen and Geoff Harcourt present their Cambridge, England views in a paper "What Ever Happened to the Cambridge Theory Controversies?" published in the Winter 2003 issue of the *Journal of Economic Perspectives*. This inspired replies by no less than five economists in the Fall 2003 issue, including for example Luigi Pasinetti (remember he and Levhari started all this) and Frank Fisher.

But the reply by Robert Greenfield is what caught my special attention. He wrote:

For me, [the controversies] ended when Leland Yeager wrote "Toward Understanding Some Paradoxes in Capital Theory," showing that the paradoxes traced to measuring capital in purely physical terms and thus were not paradoxical at all. The article took *Economic Inquiry* article-of-the-year honors for 1976. . . .

Well, in 1976 I moved from the University of Pennsylvania to the University of Virginia, and I was given an office across the hall from Leland. In preparation for meeting him, I did some homework and read his prize-winning paper. To my horror, I discovered that it was wrong and immediately produced a counterexample. So our first meeting went something like this:

Hi, Leland. I'm Ed Burmeister. By the way, that paper of yours that just won you a prize is completely wrong.

Probably it would have been better to wait until our second meeting.

Anyway, after talking with me Leland became convinced that his index of roundaboutness of production methods was—shall we say—"ill conceived." In January 1978 we published a jointly authored correction to his paper. But I think that they let him keep his prize. . . .

At least three lessons are to be learned here:

1. False ideas about capital theory have been pervasive in our profession and even Austrian economics is not exempt.
2. Some bad ideas are hard to stamp out.
3. Referees occasionally do awful jobs.

To bring this matter really up-to-date, I mention that the upcoming 2009 AEA meeting in San Francisco includes a Union of Radical Political Economics (URPE) session entitled "The Capital Theory Controversy Revisited." I was asked to participate along with Avi Cohen, Christopher Bliss, and, yes, Luigi Pasinetti. In an e-mail Christopher gave me the excuse that, "The truth is that England in January is fairly awful." Well, Durham is really quite nice in January, and I turned down the invitation. Then they asked me for the name of a younger person who might be able to participate. So I suggested Bob. . . .

A few years ago Frank Fisher told me that the large portion of my career that I had devoted to studying issues related to the Capital Theory Controversies was wasted. Those of you who know Frank will recognize that this statement is almost a compliment; had he not liked my work at all, he would have said, "Stupidly wasted."

But I want to share with you what I have concluded after all these years, or perhaps stupidly concluded:

1. First, it is true that the existence of a well-behaved index of capital and an aggregate production function do not exist in general. In this conclusion I am in apparent agreement with Frank Fisher, though my work follows a different line of attack than his in that I restrict myself to steady-state comparisons and he does not. My conclusion is that, except for freak cases, rigorous aggregation is possible if and only if there is Equal Organic Composition of Capital (which is equivalent to all prices being an equal markup over labor cost, implying that relative prices are constant for all interest rates).

2. Second, it is not of much practical significance that aggregate production functions and indices of aggregate capital do not have any rigorous theoretical foundation. In particular, this fact does nothing to undermine the neoclassical theory of income distribution, a theory that in no way depends upon the aggregation of anything. Moreover, Solow-type aggregate models provide tools necessary for analyzing many important economic problems—and they still are the only game in town.

3. Third, I completely agree with the view about growth models that is expressed in the one-page Conclusions section of Solow's 1969 Radcliffe Lectures book. But for a completely independent reinforcement, here I turn to another teacher of mine, Mark Kac, a mathematician known for his work in physics. Mark wrote:

> Models are, for the most part, caricatures of reality, but if they are good, then, like good caricatures, they portray, though perhaps in distorted manner, some of the features of the real world. The main role of models is not so much to explain and predict— though ultimately these are the main functions of science—as to polarize thinking and to pose sharp questions. Above all, they are fun to invent and to play with, and they have a peculiar life of their own. The "survival of the fittest" applies to models even more than it does to living creatures. [*Science*, November 1969]

Solow-type growth models meet all of these criteria admirably. They are certainly fun, and they have enabled economists to pose literally thousands of sharp questions. The fact that we are all here today attests to their survival. While I recognize that philosophers and others may have much more to say about this issue, for me what I have said already is enough.

And speaking of "enough," I want to quit before it becomes too obvious that the third stage of diminishing returns has kicked in. I have just one more short tale to relate.

For Bob the course 14.123 did not end with the last day of classes on Wednesday, January 23, 1963. I have in my hand an envelope that required 9 cents of U.S. postage. In it are some old notes of mine and a letter from Bob Solow dated June 25, 1963. He writes:

> Dear Ed:
> I never got around to giving this note back to you during the term, but it just floated to the top of the pile, so here it is.

His letter goes on to provide both encouragement and incredibly useful comments about my little model of technological change.

And this is yet another example why it is such an honor to have had Bob Solow as a teacher. Bob, thank you.

Part 2
Origins of Growth Economics

Some Swedish Stepping-Stones to Growth Economics

Mauro Boianovsky

Ever since Abba Lerner's 1940 review essay, Swedish economics has become well known in the history of thought for devising dynamic methods to study fluctuations of macroeconomic variables as part of expectation formation mechanisms. After the breakthroughs made by Roy Harrod (1939, 1948), Evsey Domar (1946), Robert Solow (1956, 1957, 1960), Trevor Swan (1956), and—although less influential—Jan Tinbergen ([1942] 1959), dynamics became associated with growth economics as it started to investigate what growth economics had already been investigating, rates of change of economic variables along a growth path. The purpose of the present article is to show that, besides their contributions to monetary macroeconomics, Swedish economists—namely, the founding fathers of Swedish economics, Knut Wicksell and Gustav Cassel, and two members of the young Stockholm school of economics, Erik Lundberg and Ingvar Svennilson—put forward new insights to interpret the process of economic growth.

Some of the concepts advanced by those authors have been discussed in a larger degree in the literature, others less so. Cassel's ([1918] 1932)

I would like to thank William Baumol, Rodolphe dos Santos Ferreira, Geoff Harcourt, Kevin Hoover, Hans-Michael Trautwein, Warren Young, and (other) participants at the 2008 *HOPE* and ESHET conferences for helpful comments. Financial support from CNPq (Brazilian Research Council) is gratefully acknowledged.

History of Political Economy 41 (annual suppl.) DOI 10.1215/00182702-2009-016

"uniformly progressing state" is probably the best-known Swedish stepping-stone to growth economics (Tinbergen [1942] 1959, 187; Robinson 1952; Schumpeter 1954, 966; Brems 1989). We shall see that Cassel's concept of uniform growth was adumbrated by Wicksell's ([1893] 1954) discussion of "dynamic equilibrium."

Apart from the notion of steady state in economies with a growing population, the contributions examined below include (1) Cassel's and Lundberg's earlier formulations of the Harrod-Domar condition; (2) Wicksell's application of the aggregate production function approach to growth with land scarcity; (3) Wicksell's study of the optimal capital accumulation path; (4) Cassel's proposition that the rate of growth is equal to the interest rate under certain circumstances; (5) Cassel's result that the steady-state growth rate of output is the sum of population growth and the rate of neutral technological progress; (6) Svennilson's hypothesis that high production growth leads to high productivity growth; (7) Lundberg's work on the variability of the accelerator coefficient and the propensity to save as stabilizing factors; (8) Svennilson's view that technical progress takes place through replacing old capital goods by more efficient new ones; and (9) Lundberg's distinct notion that pure productivity growth results from adopting more efficient methods of production at suboptimal disequilibrium positions, called the "Horndal effect."

Wicksell on "Dynamic Equilibrium"

Following the presentation of the theory of a stationary economy, Wicksell ([1893] 1954, 164–65) briefly turned to the "dynamics of economic phenomena," in the sense of the disturbance of equilibrium caused by changes in the value of economic variables. Wicksell's definition pointed the way to Harrod's (1939, 17) notion of "dynamic as referring to propositions in which a rate of growth appears as an unknown variable."

> If in all these relationships a certain *rate* of progression may be assumed to be given, then it is clear that equations of production and exchange can be laid down. We have then, so to speak, a problem of dynamic equilibrium instead of static equilibrium with which to deal. (Wicksell [1893] 1954, 165; see also [1896] 1997, 93)

After that promising start Wicksell ([1893] 1954, 165) refrained from developing a growth model, on the grounds that "it would be quite a different matter to try to lay down laws for determining the rate of progression itself. I personally make no attempt in this direction." Wicksell's first exploration into the determinants of saving may be found in his *Lectures*. From the perspective of an average individual or of society as a whole ("regarded as an individual who never ages or dies"), capital accumulation should continue, at a diminishing rate, until maximum permanent consumption is reached at zero rate of interest (Wicksell [1901] 1934, 209). Wicksell's view about saving by a single immortal representative individual that optimizes its consumption plans over infinite time is akin to Frank Ramsey's (1928) optimizing tradition (Solow 1999, 646–50). Maximum permanent consumption is reached only if there is no subjective undervaluation of future needs, that is, Böhm-Bawerk's second reason is not operative.

Wicksell again tackled the problem of capital accumulation in his 1914 obituary piece about Böhm-Bawerk and in his posthumous 1928 article. In the obituary Wicksell worked out the precise relation between Böhm-Bawerk's three reasons for the existence of a positive rate of interest. Under dynamic equilibrium there is a permanent difference between the interest rate determined by the return on productive capital (the third reason) and the rate of discount of the future. The gap between the two is filled by means of the first reason (the expectation of an objectively more abundant satisfaction of future needs). "Capital accumulation and saving are constantly pushed to the limit where the *under*weight of present supply, and hence the *over*weight of present marginal utility, exactly corresponds to this difference" (Wicksell [1914] 1997, 36). The argument was illustrated by a numerical example. If the expected rate of return on capital is 5 percent and the subjective underestimation of the future is 3 percent, "then saving does not stop until the level at which present marginal utility is 2% higher than the future level. The dynamic equilibrium will be expressed by the equality 5 = 3 + 2" (36). The momentary rate of decline of the marginal utility of consumption is 2 percent. During this process of capital deepening, diminishing returns imply that the marginal productivity of capital falls asymptotically to the value of the rate of net time preference, and the pace of net saving declines accordingly.[1]

Wicksell ([1928] 1997) clarified the role of the introduction of successive longer investment periods: once the superior technique is extended to the whole economy and capital has reached saturation point, the rate

---

1. Wicksell all but wrote Ramsey's (1928, 554) equation $[du(x)/dt]/u(x) = -[(df/dc) - \varrho]$, where $u(x)$ is the utility function, f is the production function, c is capital, and ϱ is the rate of time preference (Boianovsky 1998, 145–48).

of interest becomes zero (if net time preference is assumed away), a point Joseph Schumpeter had tried to establish unsuccessfully (Boianovsky 1998, 153–54). The main reason why capital accumulation is not in fact accompanied by a falling rate of interest is population growth (Wicksell ([1901] 1934, 213–14). The introduction of population growth into Ramsey's savings model would be performed by Tjalling Koopmans (1965), who replaced the Wicksell-Ramsey capital saturation requirement by the corresponding golden rule condition. The steady population growth that had taken place in the nineteenth century was regarded by Wicksell ([1901] 1934, 214) as an exception to the oscillating pattern of previous ages and to the (approximately) stationary population he foresaw for the future (Boianovsky 2001).

Interestingly enough, there is no mention of land scarcity in Wicksell's ([1893] 1954, [1896] 1997) discussion of dynamic equilibrium. This would change in his later articles ([1907] 1953, 65; 1918, 70; [1919] 1934, 226–27 n. 1), where Wicksell argued that uniform growth is inconceivable in a progressive economy, unless (what we now call) land-augmenting technical change proceeds steadily. Wicksell's discussion of dynamic equilibrium–cum–land scarcity was probably prompted by his pioneer treatment of linear homogeneous production functions in general and of the so-called Cobb-Douglas production function in particular (Wicksell [1900] 1958, 98; [1901] 1934, 128).[2] As explained by Wicksell ([1916] 1958, 133), if one assumes a production function of the form $a^\alpha b^\beta c^\gamma = p$ (where α, β, and γ are three fractions whose sum is unity, p is output, and a, b, and c stand for labor, land, and capital), an increase of 10 percent in capital would increase p by 10γ percent, the two increases of capital and labor together giving $10 (\alpha + \gamma)$ percent.

Wicksell was the first to apply the theory of marginal productivity to the interpretation of technical change and its effect on output and distribution (Boianovsky and Hagemann 2005). Land-saving technical progress was defined as an increase of the marginal product of labor at the expense of land caused by some invention such that "the existing supply of natural resources is, as it were, increased" (Wicksell [1901] 1934, 135–36). As pointed out by Wicksell (1910), "during the last half century 'land' has been increasing much faster than men." He did not develop that insight

---

2. Wicksell (1918, 70) would reject Marx's scheme of "expanded reproduction" (the first outline of a model of balanced growth) because it "fails in the fundamental respect that its assumptions, that not only labor and capital but also natural resources uniformly increase, are of course against reality."

into a growth model with land scarcity and steady technological progress (Swan 1956, 340–42).[3] Instead, he used it as a building block of his influential "rocking horse" approach to economic fluctuations as provoked by the impact of technological shocks on a stable economic structure (Wicksell 1918, 70–71; Boianovsky 1995, 378–83).

Cassel's "Uniformly Progressing State"

The full elaboration of the notion of steady growth was provided by Cassel ([1918] 1932, sec. 6). He had probably been exposed to Wicksell's 1893 dynamic equilibrium and to Marshall's remark about an economy in "steady motion."[4] Cassel (1925, 27) defined the "uniformly progressive economy" as the stage in economic investigation when we can introduce "such dynamic conditions as we are able to treat in a static form." Under the (provisional) assumption of absence of technical change, economic progress is equal to the rate of population growth in steady state: "If the annual percentage increase of the population is given, then we know the rate at which the economic system as a whole is progressing" (Cassel [1918] 1932, 34).

Another feature of uniform growth is that capital and income increase at the same pace, which means that the capital-output ratio and the proportion of income saved are both constant in equilibrium (34). Cassel's description of the steady state is consistent with Nicholas Kaldor's (1961, 178–79) later "stylized facts." To bring this out it is necessary to introduce technical progress into the picture. Economic data indicate that both capital and income grow at an average rate of 3 percent a year, whereas population grows by 1 percent (Cassel 1935, 127–28). Economic growth has displayed comparatively small deviations from the curve of uniform progress (127–28), accompanied by continuous increase of the average productivity of labor and of the capital-labor ratio. "In our typical progressive economy the product per unit of labor shows an annual growth of 2%,

3. Steady growth with land scarcity is possible if there is land-augmenting technical change, or if the elasticity of substitution between land and capital is higher than one (Jones 2002, chap. 9). Wicksell discussed the first possibility, but not the second (which was adumbrated by Walras [1874] 1954, lesson 36), probably because he assumed a Cobb-Douglas function, which features unitary elasticity of substitution between factors.

4. "Nearly all the distinctive portions of the stationary state may be exhibited in a place where population and wealth are both growing, provided they are growing at about the same rate, and there is no scarcity of land" (Marshall 1898, 41). Marshall got the idea of "steady motion" from a letter of Albert Flux, who in 1894 had reviewed Wicksell 1893.

whereas the product per unit of capital remains constant" (138). The rate of interest is constant in the steady state, as Cassel observed against the view that it tends to fall.[5] With steady values of the capital-output ratio and interest rate, the share of interest in income is also constant, which completes the stylized facts. Moreover, technical progress must be of such a neutral form in the aggregate that the capital-output ratio remains constant. Cassel assumed that a higher rate of increase of capital in some sectors is compensated by a lower one in others (143; cf. Harrod 1948, 83).

Cassel ([1918] 1932, 61–63; 1935, 134–35) put forward a simple model expressing the relation between the rate of growth of both income and capital of p (equal to the increase of the effective labor force), the stock of capital C, the level of income I, and the degree of saving I/s. In equilibrium, the proportion of income saved and used to purchase capital is equal to the production of capital goods: $I/s = pC$. Using familiar notation, we may replace Cassel's p with n, I/s with s, I with Y, and C with K, and define v as K/Y. His equation then reads $sY = nK$. It was used by Cassel to find the income level for an initial capital stock and to find v for given n and s. It may also be used to establish Cassel's (1900, secs. 41, 43; 1903, 178–79; [1904] 2005, 29) proposition that the rate of interest is equal to the rate of growth if interest is all saved and wages all consumed, as in a "socialist" economy (Boianovsky 1999, 52–53). If there is no saving out of wages, the equation may be written as $s_p P = nK$, where P and s_p stand for interest (or "profits") and the proportion of profits saved, respectively. Hence $P/K = n / s_p$, which implies that the rate of interest is equal to the rate of growth if s_p is unity.[6]

Cassel's equations are a description of the steady state, with no indication of how and whether it is reached. Their main purpose is to show that capital accumulation may go on forever without turning into stagnation (Cassel [1918] 1932, 62; [1904] 2005, 23–30; Robinson 1952, 42; Niehans 1990, 452). Cassel's ([1918] 1932, 62) remark that "only during transition periods will there be a material difference between the rate of increase of capital and of income" suggests that there must be an economic

5. The rate of interest will change if the parameters that determine the steady state (n and s) change.

6. An outcome of John von Neumann's ([1937] 1945) model was the equality between the rates of growth and interest. Von Neumann's argument was that Cassel's ([1918] 1932, 152–54) microeconomic growth model can be in balanced growth at different growth rates, but only one of these rates is efficient—the maximal growth rate, equal to the minimal interest rate (see Niehans 1990, 400–404).

mechanism leading the economy back to its steady growth path once it departs from equilibrium, but that is not spelled out in that section. This has led commentators to interpret Cassel's equations as a fixed-coefficient model of an unstable economy (Lundberg 1967; Brems 1989) or to criticize him for not explaining convergence to the full-employment path (Tinbergen and Polack 1950, 125; Svennilson 1954, 5). However, if one reads elsewhere (Cassel [1918] 1932, secs. 23, 25; 1903, chaps. 2, 3) it is clear that equilibrium is reached through the effects of interest-rate changes on the average capital-output ratio. Cassel acknowledged the possibility of substituting capital for other factors in the production of each commodity, but stressed instead that the capital-output ratio varies among different sectors. The emphasis was not on substitution between capital and labor on the production side but on substitution of goods on the consumption side according to their relative price, which is consistent with his general equilibrium system.

Cassel (1903, 121) discussed how changes in the rate of interest would bring the economy back to equilibrium if there was a "large and continuous growth of capital" in excess of demand determined by population growth. The ratio v is below the level required to make $nv = s$: there is excess supply of savings and the rate of interest falls accordingly. The ensuing rise of v continues until it has increased the amount of widening investment to a point where savings are fully absorbed, which interrupts the interest rate fall: "Every fall of this rate [of interest] will widen the field for the use of durable instruments and thus call out forces counteracting the fall." The outcome is similar to Solow's (1956, 68–70) convergence toward a steady-state path, although the argument is not quite the same and not as fully elaborated.

One result of the Solow-Swan growth model is that a higher s increases the income level, without any permanent effect on growth (Swan 1956, 337–38; Solow [1970] 2000, 22–24). That is also implied by the logic of Cassel's growth model, but he was ambiguous about it. Cassel (1934, 88) carried out an exercise in the Swedish edition about the consequences of a reduction of the degree of saving from 20 percent to 10 percent. The economy is initially growing at a steady rate of 3 percent, and the output-capital ratio is accordingly 15 percent. Cassel's model indicates that the long-run effect should be an increase of the output-capital rate to 30 percent accompanied by higher output level. In the Domar model the new steady-state growth rate would fall to 1.5 percent. Curiously enough, Cassel gave an answer that is in between the two results. In his exercise, the reduction of the savings coefficient will raise the value of the output-capital ratio to 20 percent and reduce growth to 2 percent. One way to make sense of Cassel's inference is to assume that the growth of the labor force is affected by capital accumulation in classical fashion (cf. Swan 1956, 338–39; Solow 1956, 90–91). This is consistent with Cassel's ([1918] 1932, 564) notion that the migration of rural workers accounts for the increasing labor supply in periods of intense growth (Spengler 1969).

As observed by Warren Young (1989, 150–52), Harrod read *Social Economy* and kept an annotated copy of the book, but it is not clear whether the 1918 growth model had any direct influence on the 1939 one. It is likely that Cassel influenced Harrod indirectly via John Maynard Keynes's ([1937] 1973) essay about growth and population, which deployed Cassel's framework.[7] Keynes assumed a (steady) capital-output ratio of 4 percent and a proportion of saving from full-employment income between 8 and 15 percent. Hence the rate of growth of capital (and income) lay between 2 and 4 percent (129). A decline of population growth would bring about a reduction of the natural growth rate below its warranted level, unless the proportion of income saved came down and/or the rate of interest was reduced to the extent necessary to induce a higher capital-output ratio (130–31). The latter is Cassel's equilibrating mechanism, about which Keynes was skeptical.

One feature of Cassel's approach, shared by Harrod (1939), John von Neumann ([1937] 1945), and Solow (1956), is that natural resources scarcity does not constrain growth. This set Cassel apart from Léon Walras, Alfred Marshall, and Wicksell, and is probably the reason why the model did not catch the latter's attention (Wicksell [1919] 1934, 241). Cassel ([1918] 1932, 35, 95, 152–53) assumed that the quantities of *all* production factors are subject to uniform increase in the steady state. He did not expect steady growth in the provision of raw materials to continue in the future (159–60). Cassel, however, did not incorporate that into his model of a uniformly progressive economy, which reflected the growth process in the nineteenth and early twentieth centuries.

Lundberg on the (In)stability of Growth

Cassel's steady growth attracted Lundberg's attention, and Lundberg made it the starting point of the model sequences of chapter 9 of his *Studies in*

---

7. Keynes did not refer to Cassel in that connection, but he read Cassel carefully (Leijon-hufvud 1968, 250).

the Theory of Economic Expansion. That chapter provided a theoretical interpretation of the cyclical instability of the economy based on an original combination of the multiplier and accelerator principles. The subject matter of the 1937 book was "an economic system during a period of expansion" (Lundberg [1937] 1955, 283). Cassel's assumption of a uniformly progressive economy was therefore "viewed as a problem to be investigated" (283).

According to Lundberg ([1987] 1995, 497), his contribution was "to analyze the *dual role of investments.*" On the one hand, investment decides the level of effective demand; on the other, it determines the growth of capital stock. The interaction between the multiplier and the accelerator generates a growth process that may or may not be a dynamic equilibrium.

> The demand for consumption goods has to increase in a certain tempo, in order to give rise to a volume of new investment which has to be so large that in turn an increase of income is generated which gives the necessary impulse to the demand for consumption goods. The possibility of reaching such a dynamic equilibrium depends upon the size of certain constants. (Lundberg [1937] 1955, 253–54)

Dynamic equilibrium was formally expressed by an equation, almost hidden in a footnote, which gives the rate of growth that equilibrates the market for goods. Using E, S, I, and K for income, saving, investment, and capital, respectively, Lundberg ([1937] 1955, 185 n. 1) writes the saving function $S = \Lambda E\,(t)$, the accelerator relation $K = \mu E,$ and the definition $Kt = K0 + \int_0^t I(t)dt$. Assuming equilibrium in the goods market ($I = S$), this can be written as $\mu E(t) = K0 + \Lambda \int^t E(t)dt$. After derivation, the equilibrium condition for the goods market reads $\mu E'(t) = \Lambda E(t)$. The solution for the time path of income is $E(t) = c \cdot e^{(\Lambda/\mu)\cdot t}$ and the (warranted) growth rate is accordingly Λ/μ in Lundberg's notation.

This is the same as the expression given by Harrod's (1939) "fundamental equation." Apparently Domar (1952, 480–81) was the first to acknowledge Lundberg's anticipation, followed by Schumpeter (1954, 966 n. 8), R. G. D. Allen ([1956] 1959, 64–65), and Dale Jorgenson (1960, 420). It was after the publication of Harrod 1948 that Lundberg claimed priority:

> In contemplating his formulae . . . Harrod [1948, 85] declares, with that typical tendency of British economists to be, as Myrdal [(1939) 1965, 8] says, "unnecessarily original": "I ask you to join me in thinking it extraordinarily impressive." With all due modesty I must point out that

the model sequences in my doctor's thesis are based on various manip-
ulations of Harrod's particular relations. Indeed, the note on p. 185 contains a derivation of Harrod's fundamental relation. (Lundberg [1950]
1995, 108 n. 14)

Harrod (1937) reviewed Lundberg's book—hence, Jürg Niehans's (1990,
453) statement that Harrod was unaware of Lundberg when he wrote down
his growth model is incorrect. He did not refer to Lundberg's growth equation though—nor did other reviewers of the book, for that matter. Instead,
Harrod criticized the dynamic method adopted in Lundberg's "model
sequences," based on the introduction of time lags that prevent the *ex ante*
equality between saving and investment in successive periods (Baumol
1991; Berg 1991). As suggested by Young (1989, 163), Lundberg 1937 provided Harrod less the growth equation than the inherent systematic instability notion.

Lundberg's focus in the 1950s was growth, not fluctuations as in the
1930s. As Lundberg ([1950] 1995, 90) put it, in a remark that could well
be applied to his own work, "It is striking how little analysis has been
made of the determinants of the rate of progress . . . in relation to the
enormous amount of work which has been devoted to throwing light on
the 'small dips' in the trend of expansion." The double assumption of constant values for the propensity to save and the accelerator coefficient—
found, for example, in Hicks 1950—had led to underestimating the stability of expansion. The procyclical behavior of the savings ratio, because
of changes in income distribution, worked as a stabilizing factor of aggregate demand. The variability of the capital-output ratio reflected changes
in the composition of investment between short- and long-term investment.[8] Moreover, according to Lundberg ([1950] 1995, 105), Harrod and
Hicks had assumed that technical progress continues "on a sufficiently
large scale and more or less automatically." This was in contrast with the
Schumpeterian approach, which had just been applied by Erik Dahmén
([1950] 1970) to Swedish industry.

Lundberg's (1959, 1961) agenda in the 1950s set out to investigate productivity increase and the investment process through interview studies
in Swedish industry (Ohlin 1962). Disequilibrium positions were again at
the center stage of Lundberg's dynamics, but this time as part of his insight
about the microfoundations of growth.

8. The variability of the accelerator coefficient is conspicuous in Lundberg [1937] 1955,
216, 230, 254. He was followed by Harrod 1939, 27, 32.

The investment process can be understood only when the reference basis is an economy perpetually out of static equilibrium . . . that is, with a below-optimum allocation of resources. . . . [This] will mean a stream of efficiency gains at the various points in the economy, which may be assumed to sum up to a yearly increase in productivity for the economy as a whole. (Lundberg 1959, 662–63)[9]

Confirmation of Lundberg's hypothesis came from his study of a steel plant at Horndal. The plant was left to operate without any new investment in fixed capital for fifteen years, yet labor productivity rose on average 2 percent per year. This was called the "Horndal effect" by Lundberg (1961, 129–33; see also 1959, 663–64; Arrow 1962, 156; Hahn and Matthews [1964] 1965, 68).

It follows that there is a lack of relation between *ex post* profitability of investment and its private (and social) marginal efficiency, which is an *ex ante* concept. Data indicated that the *ex ante* expectations of profitability were higher than their measured values. That was relevant for investigating the effects of savings on growth (Lundberg 1959, 656). Whereas in neoclassical theory the contribution of capital is quite small—profit rate times the net rate of investment (Meade 1961, 17)—this is not so under the fixed capital-output ratio assumption (Lundberg 1959, 656; 1961, 170–73; the latter was the only approach discussed by Lundberg 1955). The answer should be sought by investigating the effect of savings on the speed at which innovations are applied—that is, the slope of Kaldor's (1957) technical progress function. Lundberg (1959) proposed that the empirical study of profitability and expectations of returns could provide such information. The 1937 accelerator model was gone, replaced by expectations of profits from technical change as best suited to explaining growth.

Svennilson on Technical Progress and the Capital Structure

Svennilson was one of the two people (the other was Dag Hammarskjöld) who read drafts of Lundberg's thesis ([1937] 1955, vi). They were colleagues at the University of Stockholm, where in 1938 Svennilson defended his thesis on intertemporal decisions under risk (Siven 1991, 147–50). He

---

9. The production function concept, on the other hand, assumes that it is not possible to increase output "by a more suitable arrangement of the labor and capital already available," that is, entrepreneurs have reached "*a certain average level of . . . skill and experience*" (Wicksell ([1916] 1958, 132).

came back to the treatment of investment in his contribution to the Heckscher Festschrift, when he investigated the connection between technical progress, the scale of production, and the introduction of new machines. Svennilson (1944, 239) argued that capital accumulation is the transmission mechanism for new ideas.

> The most modern production technique is normally applied in an *expansion* of the productive capacity. (240)

> The volume of investment, whether it constitutes a net addition to the stock of capital or not, can . . . be said to measure the rate at which capital is being modernized. (Svennilson 1954, 208)

> Technical progress will mean that old capital goods are eliminated and new ones substituted. (Svennilson 1956, 325)

This corresponds to what Edmund Phelps called the "new view of investment." It was first formalized in Solow's (1960) vintage model, although the notion could be traced back to the *Economic Survey of Europe in 1958*, prepared by the UN Economic Commission for Europe (Phelps 1962, 458–51). It is likely that Svennilson influenced that survey, for he had been a member of the commission. The first author to take notice of Svennilson's new approach was Leif Johansen (1956, 1959), whose article on substitution versus fixed coefficients Solow (1983, 445) read in manuscript form.[10]

According to Svennilson, it is only with a "lag" that capital goods that represent new techniques are integrated into an existing structure made up of durable means of production of several ages. This "inertia"—a phenomenon noticed but regarded as irrational "friction" by Cassel (1903, 119–21)—is explained by the fact that "old machinery can, while it lasts, continue to compete on a basis of prices which do not cover replacement costs" (Svennilson 1954, 10; cf. 1944, 240). Old machines have to cover only their variable costs, whereas new machines have to expect to cover their total costs. This is the same answer given by W. E. G. Salter (1960, chap. 4) in his discussion of why old machines operate side by side with new and more efficient ones. The speed with which technical innovations make their breakthrough is affected also by the rate of increase of production, since new capacity will be built in accordance with the most modern technology.

---

10. The notion that greater durability of new machines is generally combined with greater efficiency may be found in Wicksell [1923] 1934, 299.

The slower production is growing and the more durable its capital equipment, the bigger the lag in relation to the newest technique. (Svennilson 1944, 240)

The proportion of modern equipment in an industry will increase in proportion to the rapidity of the industry's growth. This leads to the conclusion that, *ceteris paribus*, the efficiency of an industry increases accordingly to the rapidity of expansion. (Svennilson 1954, 10)

Svennilson (1944, 242–43) compared his "dynamic" explanation of the relation between the *growth rates* of productivity and production with what he called the "static" connection—advanced by Young (1928)—between the *levels* of productivity and production through economies of scale and increasing returns. He claimed that the statistical evidence for the British and American economies pointed to a positive relation between relative *changes* of production and productivity. Svennilson (1944, 243–52) carried out correlation analysis for the Swedish industry for the periods 1915–29 and 1929–39, which corroborated his insight. Svennilson's positive relation between the rates of growth of productivity and production was very close to "Verdoorn's Law," established by P. J. Verdoorn in 1949 (Lundberg 1972, 315–16). However, Verdoorn's economic interpretation of the positive correlation, based on increasing returns to scale, was distinct from Svennilson's and not fully consistent with Verdoorn's own model (Rowthorn 1979). The two economists worked together at the UN Economic Commission for Europe in the late 1940s, which opens up the possibility of Svennilson's influence on Verdoorn (Erixon 2005, 191). Inertia in the renewal of equipment was one of the main factors determining poor growth performance in interwar Europe (Svennilson 1954). The association between productivity and output tends to make the growth process cumulative (in Wicksell's sense), especially if technical progress is induced by changes in demand and prices (Svennilson 1954, 6 n. 1, 7 n. 1, 9; 1956, 320, 331–32).

Svennilson (1956, 1964) made two attempts to model economic growth as the result of competition between old and new capital.[11] In his contribution to the Lindahl Festschrift, Svennilson tackled the analytic problems

---

11. Svennilson's interpretation of growth "as a result of a dialectic conflict between the new and the old" was shared by Johan Åkerman and Dahmén (Lebraty 1968, 446). Dan Johansson and Nils Karlson (2002) have applied the term "Swedish growth school" to the trio formed by Svennilson, Åkerman, and Dahmén. However, only the former attempted to build formal growth models.

involved in the existence of a capital structure formed by different kinds of machines embodying the technology corresponding to their construction dates. The variety of capital goods makes it necessary to elaborate an index to measure the age composition of "national real capital" (NRC; cf. Solow 1960, 91–93).

Assuming that a constant fraction u of every age group of capital is eliminated each year and that the rate of growth of gross investment is indicated by v, Svennilson (1956, 329) writes the formula

$$NRC = \sum_{n=0}^{\infty} I \cdot \frac{(1-u)^n}{(1+v)^n}.$$

The change in NRC between years 1 and 0 is then given by $\Delta NRC = I_0 \cdot v(1+v)/(v+u)$. The other two equations follow the Lundberg-Harrod-Domar model: $I = s \cdot O$ and $\Delta O = \alpha \cdot \Delta NRC$, or $O \cdot v = \alpha \cdot \Delta NRC$, where α is the marginal productivity of capital and O is output. By combining the equations, Svennilson gets the expression $1 + v = (1 - u)/(1 - \alpha s)$. The parameters s, u, and α determine the rate of growth of output, the rate of capital accumulation, and the age-structure of the capital stock. The assumption that α is the same for all age groups of capital contradicts the notion of increasing efficiency of capital (Johansen 1956, a comment on a preliminary version of Svennilson 1956), a criticism accepted by Svennilson (1956, 331). If the parameters are causally interrelated (along the lines of his 1944 paper), the economy will experience a "cumulative" instead of steady process of growth (Svennilson 1956, 332–33).

Nevertheless, the idea of steady-state growth is conspicuous in Svennilson 1964, which is an elaboration of the 1956 piece modified by the impact of the vintage literature plus Lundberg's Horndal effect. Svennilson now adopted a neoclassical perspective. Full employment was assumed, with a "Wicksell-Cobb-Douglas" (Svennilson 1964, 110) production function featuring the possibility of capital-labor substitution *ex ante* investment. He distinguished between two types of technical progress: the "F-type" (for "fixed"), which takes place from period $t - 1$ to t in the efficiency with which inherited equipment is used, and the "N-type" (for "new"), which takes place at the new equipment created in period t. The rate of replacement depends on trends in productivity with new and old equipment. Svennilson's model aimed to show how labor is allocated between new and inherited equipment in each period, which is similar to the problem tackled by Solow (1960). Indeed, in a letter of 12 July 1965, Solow wrote to Svennilson that his paper was "exactly in the right direction." Like other vintage models at the time, Svennilson's did not explain what factors govern the growth of productivity (Kaldor 1964, 142). From that point of view, the promises of the insights advanced in 1944 remained partly unfulfilled.

Conclusion

Several elements of the Swedish contributions to economic dynamics directly or indirectly influenced the formation of the field of growth economics. As Solow ([1970] 2000, xiii) recalled, he had inherited his "instincts" as an economist from Wicksell and Paul Samuelson. Wicksell's production function concept and marginal productivity theory are an obvious influence. Wicksell was also carefully read by Swan, who regarded the *Lectures* as the best source to learn economics (personal communication by Barbara Spencer). The Solow-Swan result that the long-run rate of growth does not change with changes in the savings ratio is the dynamic counterpart of Wicksell's process of capital accumulation toward the stationary state. Solow (1961) was the first author to apply Wicksell's ([1923] 1934) model of fixed capital to growth. Indeed, it was in the discussion that followed the 1958 presentation of his paper that Solow advanced his ideas about a vintage model (Lutz and Hague 1961, 384). On the other hand, some insights suggested by the Swedes—for example, Wicksell's Ramsey-like equation—have remained relatively unknown.

Wicksell and Cassel developed their notions of "dynamic equilibrium" and "uniformly progressive economy" around the analytic consequences of an increasing population, the same perspective adopted by neoclassical growth economics. Solow's ([1970] 2000, 4, 97–98) description of the steady state and of the determinants of the growth rate is reminiscent of Cassel's. Domar (1944, 809 n. 26) mentioned Cassel's argument that the capital-output ratio is constant in the steady state, a principle Domar would apply to his 1946 model (cf. Young 1989, 176). Moreover, Domar's (1946) emphasis on the "dual" character of investment was quite close to Lundberg's approach. Like Domar, Harrod was probably influenced, directly or indirectly, by Cassel's or Lundberg's theoretical frameworks. As Lundberg in the 1950s shifted from the study of fluctuations to long-run growth, he, like Solow and others, came to focus on the relation between investment and productivity. That was also the main topic of Svennilson's research agenda, which culminated with the introduction of the "new view" of investment into growth economics. His notion of "inertia," together with

Lundberg's emphasis on disequilibrium, shows how Wicksell's and Cassel's earlier views about economic dynamics were further developed to lay down some stepping-stones to growth economics.

References

Allen, R. G. D. [1956] 1959. *Mathematical Economics*. 2nd ed. London: Macmillan.

Arrow, K. J. 1962. The Economic Implications of Learning by Doing. *Review of Economic Studies* 29:155–73.

Baumol, W. 1991. On Formal Dynamics: From Lundberg to Chaos Analysis. In Jonung 1991.

Berg, C. 1991. Lundberg, Keynes, and the Riddles of a General Theory. In Jonung 1991.

Boianovsky, M. 1995. Wicksell's Business Cycle. *European Journal of the History of Economic Thought* 2.2:375–411.

———. 1998. Wicksell, Ramsey, and the Theory of Interest. *European Journal of the History of Economic Thought* 5.1:140–68.

———. 1999. Cassel on Cyclical Growth. In *Keynes, Post-Keynesianism, and Political Economy: Essays in Honour of Geoff Harcourt*, edited by C. Sardoni and P. Kriesler. London: Routledge.

———. 2001. Economists as Demographers: Wicksell and Pareto on Population. In *Economics and Interdisciplinary Exchange*, edited by G. Erreygers. London: Routledge.

Boianovsky, M., and H. Hagemann. 2005. Wicksell on Technical Change, Real Wages, and Employment. In *Evolution of the Market Process: Austrian and Swedish Economics*, edited by M. Bellet, S. Gloria-Palermo, and A. Zouache. London: Routledge.

Brems, H. 1989. Gustav Cassel Revisited. *HOPE* 21.2:165–78.

Cassel, G. 1900. *Das Recht auf den vollen Arbeiterstrag*. Göttingen: Vandenhoech & Ruprecht.

———. 1903. *The Nature and Necessity of Interest*. London: Macmillan.

———. 1925. *Fundamental Thoughts in Economics*. London: Unwin.

———. [1918] 1932. *The Theory of Social Economy*. New York: Harcourt, Brace.

———. 1934. *Teoretisk socialekonomi*. Stockholm: Forbundets.

———. 1935. *On Quantitative Thinking in Economics*. Oxford: Clarendon.

———. [1904] 2005. Of Crisis and Bad Times. In vol. 6 of *Business Cycle Theory: Selected Texts, 1860–1939*, edited by M. Boianovsky. London: Pickering and Chatto.

Dahmén, E. [1950] 1970. *Entrepreneurial Activity and the Development of Swedish Industry, 1919–1939*. Translated by Axel Leijonhufvud. Georgetown, Ont.: Irwin-Dorsey.

Domar, E. 1944. The "Burden of Debt" and the National Income. *American Economic Review* 34:798–827.

——. 1946. Capital Expansion, Rate of Growth, and Employment. *Econometrica* 14.2:137–47.

——. 1952. Economic Growth: An Econometric Approach. *American Economic Review* 42:479–95.

Erixon, L. 2005. Combining Keynes and Schumpeter: Ingvar Svennilson's Contributions to the Swedish Growth School and Modern Economics. *Journal of Evolutionary Economics* 15:187–210.

Flux, A. W. 1894. Review of Wicksell 1893. *Economic Journal* 14:305–13.

Hahn, F., and R. Matthews. [1964] 1965. The Theory of Economic Growth: A Survey. In vol. 2 of *Surveys of Economic Theory*. London: Macmillan.

Harrod, R. 1937. Review of Lundberg [1937] 1955. *Zeitschrift für Nationalökonomie* 8:494–48.

——. 1939. An Essay in Dynamic Theory. *Economic Journal* 49.193:14–33.

——. 1948. *Towards a Dynamic Economics*. London: Macmillan.

Hicks, J. 1950. *A Contribution to the Theory of Trade Cycle*. Oxford: Clarendon.

Johansen, L. 1956. A Model of Economic Growth with Increasing Efficiency of Capital. *Ekonomisk tidskrift* 58:237–40.

——. 1959. Substitution vs. Fixed Production Coefficients in the Theory of Economic Growth: A Synthesis. *Econometrica* 27:157–76.

Johansson, D., and N. Karlson, eds. 2002. *Den svenska tillväxtskolan*. Stockholm: Ratio Institute.

Jones, C. 2002. *Introduction to Economic Growth*. 2nd ed. New York: Norton.

Jonung, L., ed. 1991. *The Stockholm School of Economics Revisited*. Cambridge: Cambridge University Press.

Jorgenson, D. W. 1960. Growth and Fluctuations: A Causal Interpretation. *Quarterly Journal of Economics* 74:416–36.

Kaldor, N. 1957. A Model of Economic Growth. *Economic Journal* 67:591–624.

——. 1961. Capital Accumulation and Economic Growth. In Lutz and Hague 1961.

——. 1964. Comments on Svennilson. In *The Residual Factor and Economic Growth*. Paris: OECD.

Keynes, J. M. [1937] 1973. The Economic Consequences of a Declining Population. In vol. 14 of *The Collected Writings of John Maynard Keynes*, edited by D. Moggridge. Cambridge: Cambridge University Press.

Koopmans, T. [1965] 1970. On the Concept of Optimal Economic Growth. In *Scientific Papers of Tjalling C. Koopmans*. Berlin: Springer.

Lebraty, J. 1968. Analyse critique de la fonction a generation de capital de R. M. Solow. *Revue économique* 19:411–61.

Leijonhufvud, A. 1968. *On Keynesian Economics and the Economics of Keynes*. New York: Oxford University Press.

Lerner, A. 1940. Some Swedish Stepping Stones in Economic Theory. *Canadian Journal of Economics and Political Sciences* 6:574–91.

Lindahl, E., ed. 1958. *Knut Wicksell: Selected Papers on Economic Theory*. London: Allen and Unwin.

Lundberg, E. [1937] 1955. *Studies in the Theory of Economic Expansion*. New York: Kelley.

———. 1955. Capital Formation and Economic Progress. *Skandinaviska Banken Quarterly Review* 36:103–9.

———. 1959. The Profitability of Investment. *Economic Journal* 69:653–77.

———. 1961. *Produktivitet och räntabilitet*. Stockholm: Norstedt.

———. 1967. The Influence of Gustav Cassel on Economic Doctrine and Policy. *Skandinaviska Banken Quarterly Review* 48:1–6.

———. 1972. Ingvar Svennilson: A Note on His Scientific Achievements and a Bibliography of His Contributions to Economics. *Scandinavian Journal of Economics* 74:313–28.

———. [1950] 1995. The Stability of Economic Growth: A Critique of Statistical and Theoretical Investigations. Translated in *International Economic Papers*, no. 8. Reprinted in Lundberg 1995.

———. [1987] 1995. Memories of the Stockholm School. In Lundberg 1995.

———. 1995. *Instability and Economic Change*, edited by R. Henriksson. Stockholm: SNS.

Lutz, F. A., and D. C. Hague, eds. 1961. *The Theory of Capital*. London: Macmillan.

Marshall, A. 1898. Distribution and Exchange. *Economic Journal* 8:37–59.

Meade, J. 1961. *A Neo-Classical Theory of Economic Growth*. London: Allen and Unwin.

Myrdal, G. [1939] 1965. *Monetary Equilibrium*. New York: Kelley.

Niehans, J. 1990. *A History of Economic Theory*. Baltimore, Md.: Johns Hopkins University Press.

Ohlin, G. 1962. Review of Lundberg 1961. *American Economic Review* 52:827–29.

Phelps, E. 1962. The New View of Investment: A Neoclassical Analysis. *Quarterly Journal of Economics* 76:548–67.

Ramsey, F. 1928. A Mathematical Theory of Saving. *Economic Journal* 38:543–59.

Robinson, J. 1952. The Model of an Expanding Economy. *Economic Journal* 62:42–53.

Rowthorn, R. E. 1979. A Note on Verdoorn's Law. *Economic Journal* 89:131–33.

Salter, W. E. G. 1960. *Productivity and Technical Change*. Cambridge: Cambridge University Press.

Sandelin, B., ed. 1997–99. *Knut Wicksell: Selected Essays in Economics*. Vols. 1 and 2. London: Routledge.

Schumpeter, J. A. 1954. *History of Economic Analysis*. New York: Oxford University Press.

Siven, C.-H. 1991. Expectations and Plan: The Microeconomics of the Stockholm School. In Jonung 1991.

Solow, R. M. 1956. A Contribution to the Theory of Economic Growth. *Quarterly Journal of Economics* 70.1:65–94.

———. 1957. Technical Change and the Aggregate Production Function. *Review of Economics and Statistics* 39:312–20.

———. 1960. Investment and Technical Progress. In *Mathematical Methods in the Social Sciences, 1959*, edited by K. Arrow, S. Karlin, and P. Suppes. Stanford, Calif.: Stanford University Press.

———. 1961. Notes towards a Wicksellian Model of Distributive Shares. In Lutz and Hague 1961.

———. 1965. Letter to Ingvar Svennilson, 12 July. Duke University Rare Book, Manuscript, and Special Collections Library.

———. 1983. Leif Johansen (1930–1982): A Memorial. *Scandinavian Journal of Economics* 85:445–56.

———. 1999. Neoclassical Growth Theory. In vol. 1A of the *Handbook of Macroeconomics*, edited by J. B. Taylor and M. Woodford. Amsterdam: Elsevier.

———. [1970] 2000. *Growth Theory: An Exposition.* 2nd ed. New York: Oxford University Press.

Spengler, J. 1969. Cassel on Population. *HOPE* 1.1:151–72.

Svennilson, I. 1938. *Ekonomisk planering.* Uppsala: Akademisk avhandling.

———. 1944. Industriarbets växande avkastning i belysning av svenska erfarehenter (The Increasing Returns of Labor in Sweden). In *Studier i ekonomi och historia, tillägnade Eli F. Heckscher.* Uppsala: Almqvist & Wiksell.

———. 1954. *Growth and Stagnation in the European Economy.* Geneva: United Nations Economic Commission for Europe.

———. 1956. Capital Accumulation and National Wealth in an Expanding Economy. In *25 Essays in English, German, and Scandinavian Languages in Honour of Erik Lindahl.* Stockholm: Ekonomisk Tidskrift.

———. 1964. Economic Growth and Technical Progress: An Essay in Sequence Analysis. In *The Residual Factor and Economic Growth.* Paris: OECD.

Swan, T. 1956. Economic Growth and Capital Accumulation. *Economic Record* 32.63:334–61.

Tinbergen, J. [1942] 1959. On the Theory of Trend Movements. In *Jan Tinbergen: Selected Papers*, edited by L. Klaassen, L. Koyck, and H. Witteveen. Amsterdam: North-Holland.

Tinbergen, J., and J. Polack. 1950. *The Dynamics of Business Cycles.* London: Routledge and Kegan Paul.

Verdoorn, P. J. 1949. Fattori che regolano lo sviluppo della productivitá del lavoro. *L'industria* 1:45–53.

Von Neumann, J. [1937] 1945. A Model of General Economic Equilibrium. *Review of Economic Studies* 13:1–9.

Walras, L. [1874] 1954. *Elements of Pure Economics.* Homewood, Ill.: Irwin.

Wicksell, K. 1910. The Laws of Increasing and Diminishing Returns. Unpublished manuscript. Lund University Archives.

———. 1918. Ett bidrag till krisernas teori. *Ekonomisk tidskrift* 20:66–75.

———. [1901] 1934. *Lectures on Political Economy.* Vol. 1. London: Routledge and Kegan Paul.

———. [1919] 1934. Professor Cassel's System of Economics. In Wicksell [1901] 1934.

———. [1923] 1934. Real Capital and Interest. In Wicksell [1901] 1934.

———. [1907] 1953. The Enigma of Business Cycles. *International Economic Papers*, no. 3:58–74.

———. [1893] 1954. *Value, Capital, and Rent.* London: Allen and Unwin.

———. [1900] 1958. Marginal Productivity as the Basis of Distribution in Economics. In Lindahl 1958.

———. [1916] 1958. The "Critical Point" in the Law of Decreasing Agricultural Productivity. In Lindahl 1958.

———. [1896] 1997. On the Theory of Tax Incidence. In Sandelin 1997–99.

———. [1914] 1997. Lexis and Böhm-Bawerk. In Sandelin 1997–99.

———. [1928] 1997. On the Theory of Interest. In Sandelin 1997–99.

Young, A. A. 1928. Increasing Returns and Economic Progress. *Economic Journal* 38:527–42.

Young, W. 1989. *Harrod and His Trade Cycle Group.* London: Macmillan.

Solow's 1956 Contribution in the Context of the Harrod-Domar Model

Harald Hagemann

Starting with Adam Smith's *Wealth of Nations*, the classical economists were concerned with the long-run development of an economy. This holds in particular for Karl Marx, who in chapter 21 of volume 2 of his *Capital* elaborated a two-sector steady-state growth model, comprising a capital goods and a consumption goods sector, which functioned as a reference path that irritated friends and foes alike. Thereafter, apart from very few exceptions, growth theory stopped being a major issue for most economists until the end of World War II, when modern growth theory was born with the works of Roy Harrod (1939, 1948) and Evsey Domar (1946, 1947). Growth became almost everybody's concern, first because of fear of stagnation and soon afterward because of reflections on the remarkable growth process in the Western world since the early 1950s.

The first wave of interest in growth theory associated with the contributions of Harrod and Domar came into existence as a by-product of John Maynard Keynes's *General Theory*, as best seen in Harrod's early correspondence with Keynes and in his seminal 1939 paper, "An Essay on Dynamic Theory," published in the *Economic Journal*. Harrod as well as Domar aimed to extend Keynes's analysis into the long run by considering under what conditions a growing economy could realize full-capacity utilization and full employment. Whereas Harrod (1939, 21) regarded the

I thank Robert M. Solow, Mauro Boianovsky, and two anonymous referees for valuable suggestions.

History of Political Economy 41 (annual suppl.) DOI 10.1215/00182702-2009-017

"dynamic equilibrium" "as a necessary propaedeutic to trade-cycle study," Domar was less ambitious. The complex stability problems of a growing capitalist economy were not a central feature of his analysis. Instead he concentrated his attention on the requirements for equilibrium of supply and demand along a steady growth path. However, despite some important differences in their analyses and because of a formal identity in their results for growth equilibrium, the Harrod-Domar model of economic growth emerged as a standard textbook model.

The second wave of interest in growth theory was launched by the development of the neoclassical model by Robert Solow (1956, 1957) and Trevor Swan (1956), with such precursors as Jan Tinbergen ([1942] 1959) and James Tobin (1955).[1] In his 1942 article "Zur Theorie der langfristigen Wirtschaftsentwicklung" ("On the Theory of Trend Movements"), Tinbergen had investigated the long-run development of the economy under the influence of population growth, technical progress, and capital formation and used a linear-homogenous Cobb-Douglas function with a geometric trend factor for technological development, probably the most advanced precursor of the Solow model.

Solow's neoclassical model came into existence as a reaction to the Harrod-Domar model and some deficiencies associated with it, in particular the enormous instability problems. "An economy evolving according to Harrod-Domar rules would be expected to alternate long periods of intensifying labor shortage and long periods of unemployment" (Solow 1999, 641). The empirical observation that real economies were not as wildly unstable as the Harrod-Domar model suggested propelled Solow to develop the basic neoclassical model. He made this clear from the very beginning. "The characteristic and powerful conclusion of the Harrod-Domar line of thought is that even for the long run the economic system is at best balanced on a knife-edge of equilibrium growth" (Solow 1956, 65). Solow (1994, 45 n. 1) attributed this suspicious result to dubious assumptions, in particular the assumption of fixed-production coefficients for the economy as a whole, which implied that any deviation from growth equilibrium would cause cumulative processes to move farther away from equilibrium, and to the fact that "Harrod's exposition tended to rest on incompletely specified behavioural and expectational hypotheses." Abandoning the fixed-coefficients technology and replacing it by a technology

---

1. For a more detailed discussion of the contributions by Tinbergen and Tobin, see the articles by Marcel Boumans and Robert Dimand and Steven Durlauf in this volume.

that allows substitution between the two factors of production capital and labor would make the capital-labor ratio and the capital-output ratio flexible, would guarantee convergence to a balanced growth path, and would establish stability of growth equilibrium.

In the following I first present the Harrod-Domar model, which was the main initial challenge and drove Solow to develop neoclassical growth theory. Section 2 puts forward the basic neoclassical model and discusses its key characteristics. In section 3 I focus on some early reactions by Harrod and Domar as well as on the distinction between two different instability problems, namely, the divergence between the warranted and the natural rates of growth, which marked, on the one hand, the starting point for the neoclassical reaction and, on the other, the divergence between the warranted and the actual rates of growth creating a business cycle problem. The article concludes with some reflections on the problem of combining long-run and short-run issues in macroeconomics in Solow's final section ("Qualifications") in his 1956 paper and in some of his more recent comments on the cycle-trend problem.

1. The Harrod-Domar Model of Economic Growth

The approaches by Harrod and Domar both start from a fundamentally Keynesian framework and extend it to the long run, analyzing the requirements for maintaining full employment over time. According to the Harrod-Domar model, to maintain full employment, the economy must invest the amount of saving related to full-employment income every year; but that alone is not sufficient. Production capacities have to be fully utilized as well, and capital accumulation has to be synchronized with the growth of the labor force. At first, "Keynes's peculiar treatment of investment" (Domar 1957, 6) had to be overcome and the *dual character of the investment process* had to be recognized. This implies that investment not only generates income as in the Keynesian multiplier analysis but also increases the economy's productive capacity. Whereas the first effect appears on the demand side and is of a short-run nature, the latter effect appears on the supply side and is a long-run effect (over the lifetime of the capital goods). Furthermore, whereas every positive net investment I has a capacity-enhancing effect, only an increment of investment $\dot{I}$ leads to an increase in income $\dot{Y}$. Assuming that the economy initially is in a position of full-employment equilibrium, we can formulate a Domar-type model

Table 1 Domar

	Flows	Stocks
Income effect	$\dot{Y}_D = \dfrac{1}{s}\, \dot{I}$	$\dot{K} \equiv I = S = sY_D$
Supply-side capacity effect	$\dot{Y}_{cap} = \dfrac{1}{v_{cap}}\, I$	$Y_{cap} = \dfrac{1}{v_{cap}}\, K$
Equilibrium condition	$\dot{Y}_D \overset{!}{=} \dot{Y}_{cap}$	$Y_D \overset{!}{=} Y_{cap}$
Solution	$\dfrac{\dot{I}}{I} = \hat{I} = \dfrac{s}{v_{cap}} = g$	$\dfrac{\dot{K}}{K} = \hat{K} = \dfrac{s}{v_{cap}} = g$

with production coefficients either for the flow variable I or for the stock variable K and get the solution for capital accumulation, $\hat{I} = \hat{K} = s\,/\,v_{cap}$. Table 1 contains Domar's equations.

Here s denotes the constant average and marginal propensity to save, with a proportional savings function $S = sY$; v_{cap} is the capital-output ratio in growth equilibrium, that is, with full-capacity utilization and full employment. Y_{cap} is full-capacity output, Y_D denotes aggregate demand, and the operator $\hat{x}$ is the growth rate of a variable x.

Although Domar's solution for equilibrium growth resembles Harrod's "fundamental equation," it has to be emphasized that Domar's (1946, 140) σ, "the potential social average investment productivity," is not the reciprocal of v. Since "its magnitude depends to a very great extent on technological progress" (140), Domar's σ measures more than the increase in potential output caused by investment; it embodies the effects of the labor force and technical progress on the productive potential and thus embodies Harrod's natural rate of growth. The maintenance of full employment over time requires investment, or the capital stock, to grow at a certain constant rate. However, Domar's approach, which focuses on the consistency conditions between supply and demand in dynamic equilibrium, does not include an investment function.

Probably the greatest difference between the approaches of Harrod and Domar is the incorporation of an investment function of the accelerator type

$$I_t = v_w(D_t - Y_{t-1}), \tag{1}$$

Table 2   Harrod

	Flows	Stocks
I-S-Condition (= capital accumulation)	$I \overset{!}{=} S = sY$	$I \equiv \dot{K} = sY$
Investment function/ warranted capital stock	$\dot{K} = I_w = v_w \dot{Y}$	$K_w = v_w Y$
Solution	$\dfrac{\dot{Y}}{Y} = \hat{Y} = \dfrac{s}{v_w} = g$	$\dfrac{\dot{K}}{K} = \hat{K} = \dfrac{s}{v_w} = g$
	$\hat{I} = \hat{Y} = \hat{K} = \dfrac{s}{v} = g$	

where the level of investment I_t in period t equals the difference between the expected demand for overall output D_t and the actual output in the last period Y_{t-1} times the desired capital-output ratio v_w (acceleration coefficient).[2] Harrod's (1939, 14) growth model is based on the "marriage of the 'acceleration principle' and the 'multiplier' theory," where the actual output Y_t in year t will equal the investment level I_t times the multiplier $1/s$, that is,

$$Y_t = \frac{1}{s} I_t. \tag{2}$$

We can easily derive Harrod's "fundamental equation" for the equilibrium or "warranted rate of growth" in a similar way as for Domar's production coefficient version based either on flows or on stocks. Harrod's equations are in table 2.

According to Harrod (1939, 16), "The warranted rate of growth is taken to be that rate of growth which, if it occurs, will leave all parties satisfied that they have produced neither more nor less than the right amount." So far the equilibrium growth rate for investment, output (income), or the capital stock $g = s/v$ describes a capital accumulation equilibrium in which investors would be satisfied because there is no underutilization of production capacities (*full-capacity growth*). It does not necessarily

---

2. Harrod (1959, 452) "stressed that subject to two relatively minor reservations . . . Domar's equation is identical with mine," and identified one in the difference of Domar's σ and v_w, or what he denoted C (Harrod 1939) and C_r, respectively (Harrod 1948).

please the workers, however, because the labor market is not yet integrated. There is no reason for the warranted rate to be associated with full employment.

Growth equilibrium therefore requires that not only the full-capacity condition but also the full-employment condition be fulfilled. Assume that labor supply in an initial period $t = 0$ equals L_0 and grows with a constant rate n over time; then labor supply in period t equals

$$L_t^s = L_0 e^{nt}. \tag{3}$$

Labor demand in period t equals overall output Y_t times the labor-output coefficient u_t, that is,

$$L_t^D = u_t Y_t. \tag{4}$$

Full employment therefore requires

$$u_t Y_t = L_0 e^{nt}. \tag{5}$$

The "natural" rate of growth g_n, which marks a maximum rate of growth or ceiling for the economy in the long run, equals

$$g_n = n + m, \tag{6}$$

where m denotes the rate of labor-augmenting technical progress. Growth equilibrium, that is, the simultaneous accomplishment of full-capacity growth and full-employment growth, therefore requires the conformity of the warranted with the natural rate of growth. However, according to Harrod (1939, 30), "there is no inherent tendency for these two rates to coincide."

This creates a secular instability problem, which is thoroughly Keynesian in spirit and a kind of extension of the unemployment problem to the long run. If all four parameters s, v, n, and m are exogenously given, then an equilibrium growth path can come about only as a lucky coincidence. It is highly probable that the rate of growth s/v, warranted by saving and investment behavior, will differ from the natural rate $n + m$, which would ensure full employment. However, the two disequilibrium cases are thoroughly asymmetrical. Whereas in the case $g_n > g_w$ there is a chronic tendency toward growing unemployment, in the opposite case $g_w > g_n$ the shortage of labor that arises as soon as the full-employment barrier is encountered would have a negative impact on investment and prevent the economy from growing at the warranted rate, which probably will also affect employment negatively. In the absence of any adjustment mecha-

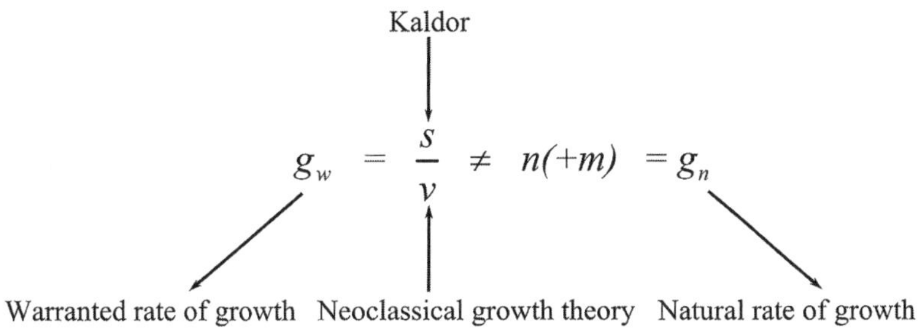

Kaldor

$$g_w \;=\; \frac{s}{v} \;\neq\; n(+m) \;=\; g_n$$

Warranted rate of growth   Neoclassical growth theory   Natural rate of growth

Figure 1 Potential solutions for the secular instability problem

nism to bring the warranted and the natural rates of growth closer together, economies would face most of their time either prolonged periods of rising or falling unemployment and/or periods of a decline or increase in the degree of capacity utilization. No wonder that the subsequent development of growth theory explored all four possible avenues to endogenize the parameters that allow the equalization of the warranted and the natural rates of growth. The four possibilities are indicated in figure 1. Two of these routes, which link up with the warranted rate, have become more popular. In retrospect, Solow (1994, 47 n. 2) argues that "in principle there is no reason to exclude the endogeneity of m and n. But induced changes in population growth, although an important matter in economic development, seemed not to figure essentially in the rich countries for which these models were devised. The idea of endogenous technological progress was never far below the surface." It may be recalled that migration very often depends on economic factors. Thus several Western European countries in the 1960s, after facing the full-employment ceiling, tried to overcome the shortage of labor in a period that may be interpreted as an $s/v > g_n$ constellation by hiring "guest workers" from southern Europe.[3]

As is well known, the favorite post-Keynesian solution for overcoming the secular Harrod problem was elaborated by Nicholas Kaldor (1956), who distinguishes between savings out of profits s_p and savings out of wages s_w, with $1 \geq s_p \geq s_w \geq 0$, which allows the endogenization of the overall savings propensity s. As in Keynes, the theory of income distribution has not been addressed in the basic Harrod-Domar model. In

---

3. According to the Federal Statistical Office, in Germany, for example, the number of guest workers increased from less than 300,000 in 1960 to nearly 2.5 million in 1973.

"Jean Baptiste" (as Samuelson teasingly called Kaldor) Kaldor's (1956, 94) second use of the multiplier principle, the level of output and employment is taken as given, and the multiplier analysis serves to develop a theory of the distribution of income between the two factors of production:

$$\frac{P}{Y} = \frac{I/Y - s_w}{s_p - s_w},$$ (7)

where the share of profits in income P/Y depends on the ratio of investment to output I/Y and the two saving propensities. Despite the full-employment assumption made by Kaldor, the critical hypothesis that investment decisions are independent from saving decisions has a strong Keynesian flavor and contrasts heavily with neoclassical growth theory.

In a longer passage it becomes clear that it has been one of Kaldor's major aims in formulating a Keynesian theory of income distribution to overcome the secular Harrod problem by endogenization of the overall savings ratio, which now amounts to

$$s = \frac{I}{Y} = \left(s_p - s_w\right)\frac{P}{Y} + s_w.$$ (8)

"Hence the 'warranted' and the 'natural' rates of growth are not independent of one another; if profit margins are flexible, the former will adjust itself to the latter through a consequential change in P/Y" (Kaldor 1956, 97).

Whereas James Meade (1961) was open to the use of a Kaldorian saving function with different saving rates out of wages and profits and the associated adjustment mechanism within a neoclassical theory of economic growth, Solow (1994, 57) always had been skeptical and pointed out "that this way of resolving the problem did not catch on, partly for empirical reasons and partly because the mechanism seemed to require that factor prices be completely divorced from productivity considerations."

2. Solow's Neoclassical Model
of Economic Growth

The very first pages of his 1956 classic elucidate how much Solow had been challenged by the secular instability problem of an incompatibility of the natural and warranted rates of growth, and the main route he took to overcome this problem, improving on the Harrod-Domar model.

But this fundamental opposition of warranted and natural rates turns out in the end to flow from the crucial assumption that production takes place under conditions of *fixed proportions*. There is no possibility of substituting labour for capital in production. If this assumption is abandoned, the knife-edge notion of unstable balance seems to go with it. . . . The bulk of this paper is devoted to a model of long-run growth which accepts all the Harrod-Domar assumptions except that of fixed proportions. Instead I suppose that the single composite commodity is produced by labor and capital under the standard neoclassical conditions. . . . The price-wage-interest reactions play an important role in this neoclassical adjustment process, so they are analyzed too. (Solow 1956, 65–66)

Thus the neoclassical adjustment mechanism rests on *two* decisive assumptions: *substitution* between the two factors of production, capital and labor, and *flexibility* of factor prices. In contrast to Kaldor's approach, where the burden of adjustment falls on the overall propensity to save s, in the neoclassical model the burden of adjustment falls on the capital-output ratio v.

Solow had already discussed Harrod's model before. As a former research assistant of Wassily Leontief, he was well trained in input-output systems or linear models (Solow 1952). In particular, his "Note on the Price Level and Interest Rate in a Growth Model" (Solow 1953–54), where he interprets the Harrod model as a special one-commodity case of the Leontief dynamic system, shows that Solow came to Harrod via his earlier work on linear systems.[4] There he noted that neither the more complex Leontief model nor the Harrod model "has anything to say about the actual time-path that will be followed by any economic system starting from arbitrary initial conditions" (Solow 1953–54, 75). Instead, "both models define equilibrium . . . by the perpetual appropriateness of the existing capital stock to the current level of output" (75). Solow had been critical not only of the missing disequilibrium dynamics in Harrod's system but also in particular of the fact that the equilibrium conditions for output and price are separated, that is, "that Harrod's discovery of an equilibrium growth of output required no formal consideration of prices, and the development of a price-interest equilibrium" (79).

4. This is also clearly reflected in Solow's 1956 paper when he discusses the fixed-proportions example or the Harrod-Domar case as the first of three examples of production functions to solve the differential equation (13). See Solow 1956, 73–76.

In Solow's 1956 model, technological possibilities are represented by the macroeconomic production function where output Y is produced with the help of the two input factors capital K and labor L.

$$Y = F(K, L). \tag{9}$$

With constant returns to scale the quantity of output per worker $y = Y/L$ becomes a function only of capital per worker $k = K/L$. Thus we get the per capita function

$$y = f(k).^5 \tag{10}$$

It is a one-commodity model, as are Swan's meccano sets, Meade's tons of steel (where the malleability character is more difficult to imagine than with "jelly" but comes in the backward reading of Joan Robinson's "leets"), or the Ricardian corn, which removes aggregation and capital measurement problems. The production function is "well behaved" (the later Inada conditions) and is homogeneous of the first degree, that is, it shows constant returns to scale that implies that the more general Euler theorem allows a logically consistent marginal productivity remuneration that overall income is exactly exhausted by payment to the two factors of production

$$Y = rK + wL, \tag{11}$$

with r as the rate of profit and w as the (real) wage rate. Investment is determined by the proportional saving function.

As Solow (2007, 13) has stated recently, "The Cobb-Douglas production function is a wonderful vehicle for generating instructive examples. But it has special Santa Claus properties, and we must not be misled about the generality of those examples." Among the "Santa Claus properties" are not only the evaporation of the distinction between labor-augmenting (Harrod-neutral), capital-augmenting (Solow-neutral), and

---

5. In Solow's original model, technical progress is widely absent. For growth equilibrium, it is necessary to assume that technical progress is of a labor-augmenting nature, that is, "neutral" in the sense of Harrod. The extension of a neutral technological change that Solow (1956, 85) discusses is a modification of (9) with increasing scale factor, that is, $Y = A(t)F(K, L)$, which is the Hicksian case of technical progress with a symmetrical productivity effect on both factors of production. However, Solow assumes a Cobb-Douglas production function, which is exactly the special case where "Hicks-neutral" technical progress (or "Solow-neutral" technical progress of the vintage capital model) coincides with the "Harrod-neutral" case. It should be pointed out, however, that, although Solow assumes a Cobb-Douglas function in his treatment of technical change, his theoretical model does only depend on a linear homogeneous function.

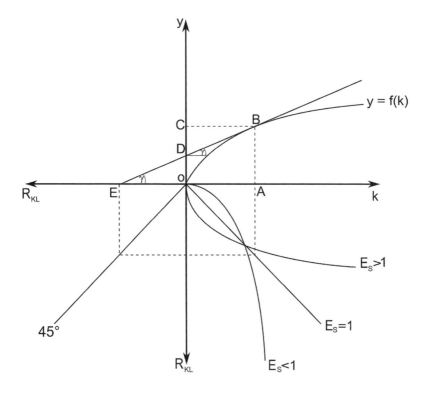

Figure 2 The central role of the elasticity of substitution

output-augmenting (Hicks-neutral) technical progress but also the constancy of the income shares of the factors of production.

The elasticity of substitution

$$E_s = \frac{dk/k}{dR_{KL}/R_{KL}} = \frac{dk/k}{d\left(\frac{w}{r}\right)/\frac{w}{r}} = \frac{d\left(\frac{0A}{0E}\right)}{\frac{0A}{0E}} \tag{12}$$

gives a measure for the easiness or difficulty of substitution between capital and labor. It addresses the central causal mechanism of neoclassical theory according to which a relative change in the (real) wage–rate of profit relation (or "factor-price" ratio) w/r leads to a relative change in the capital-labor ratio k. As figure 2 shows, only in the special case of a Cobb-Douglas production function with $E_s = 1$ will the shares of profit and wages in national income not be affected by substitution processes.

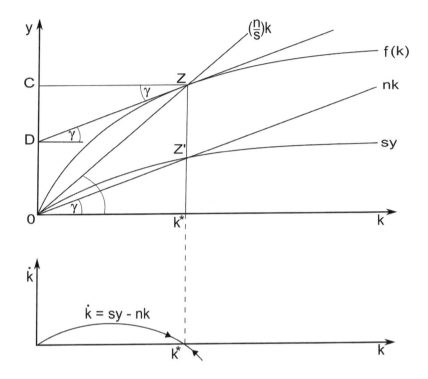

Figure 3 The fundamental equation of neoclassical economic growth

(In the figure, R_{KL} is the marginal rate of substitution between the two factors of production, tan γ indicates the rate of profit, and $0D$ represents the wage rate.) Similarly to Harrod's model of economic growth, which revolves around the warranted rate of growth derived from the marriage of the accelerator with the multiplier principle, there is also a "fundamental equation" (Solow 1956, 69) in Solow's neoclassical model of economic growth that outlines the change of the capital-labor ratio $\dot{k}$ over time. Figure 3 exhibits this "fundamental equation of neoclassical economic growth" (Jones 1975, 75–84).

Equation (10) gives output per worker y as a function of capital per worker or the capital-labor ratio k, sy denotes savings per capita, and nk denotes the investment necessary to supply the growing labor force with the same amount of capital ("capital widening"). If the initial capital stock is below the equilibrium level, that is, $sy > nk$, the investment volume increases with a declining r. Capital and output grow faster than the labor force, that is, a process of "capital deepening" takes place, until the equilibrium capital-labor ratio k^* is reached. The fundamental equation of neoclassical economic growth[6] is given by

$$\dot{k} = sy - nk. \tag{13}$$

"Whatever the initial value of the capital-labor ratio, the system will develop *toward* a state of balanced growth at the natural rate" (Solow 1956, 70).

In the Solovian model, the long-run equilibrium growth rate is independent of savings and investment decisions. As Solow (1988, 308) stated in his Nobel Prize lecture, "A developing economy that succeeds in permanently increasing its saving (investment) rate will have a higher level of output than if it had not done so, and must therefore grow faster for a while. But it will not achieve a permanently higher rate of growth of output." The impact of a permanent increase of the saving rate from a lower level s_1 toward a higher level s_2 is made plain in figure 4. An increase in s leads to an upward shift of the function sy. Because of the interest rate mechanism, these higher savings are invested. During the adjustment process, capital (which now grows with the rate s_2/v) grows faster than labor (output growth is always intermediate between the growth rates of capital and labor), that is, $\hat{K} > \hat{Y} > n$, so that the capital-labor ratio is increased until a new equilibrium value is reached in k_2^*. We have a partial factor variation, where finally the diminishing returns to capital take their toll. During the adjustment process the economy experiences

- a growing capital-labor ratio k,
- a growing output per capita y,
- a growing capital-output ratio v, and
- a growing wage-profit ratio $R_{KL} = w / r$.

Although the increase in saving (investment) leads to a higher *level* of output per unit of labor input in long-run equilibrium, the steady-state *rate* of growth is independent of capital formation. This irrelevance of savings for the long-run growth rate is one of the main results of Solow's 1956 contribution. The Solovian growth model has to rely on exogenous technical progress to increase the rate of growth of output per capita in long-run equilibrium.

6. See equation (6) in Solow 1956, 69.

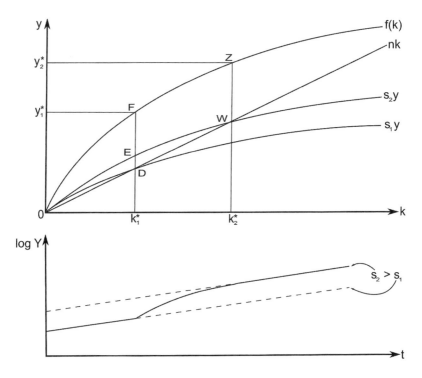

Figure 4 Effect of an increase in the saving rate

3. Early Reactions and Controversies

At the end of his presentation of the core of his neoclassical model of economic growth, Solow (1956, 73) sums up his major finding:

> The basic conclusion of this analysis is that, when production takes place under the usual neoclassical conditions of variable proportions and constant returns to scale, no simple opposition between natural and warranted rates of growth is possible. There may not be—in fact in the case of the Cobb-Douglas function there never can be—any knife-edge. The system can adjust to any given rate of growth of the labor force, and eventually approach a state of steady proportional expansion.

Solow seems to have convinced at least one of the founding fathers of the "Harrod-Domar model." Thus Domar (1957, 7–8) in the foreword to his *Essays in the Theory of Economic Growth*, published in 1957 when he was still at Johns Hopkins before moving to MIT and becoming Solow's colleague in the subsequent year, conceded that his "model employed an inadequate production function" and that "a recent article by Robert M. Solow, which appeared in print just as I was writing these lines, has shown how a growth model can be enriched by the use of a not very complex but less rigid production function."

Domar had entered this route away from the fixed-coefficient assumption toward a greater flexibility between the factors of production already in the debate on full-capacity versus full-employment growth that took place in the same *Quarterly Journal of Economics* where Solow's famous paper was published three years later. There Domar (1953, 560) expressed some skepticism concerning two convictions in the post-Keynesian literature: that a too-high saving ratio will lead to overaccumulation of capital and prolonged unemployment, a "belief which forms the basis of Harrod's distinction between the natural and the warranted rates of growth,"[7] and for which he diagnosed a lack of empirical evidence; and that "as an analytical device, a constant input coefficient is God-sent, but it is quite a simplification and it should be used with care, particularly over longer periods of time when it is known to be subject to change" (561). Since the production universe comprises elements of flexibility, Domar (1953, 562) credited Harold Pilvin (1953) for performing "a very useful service by stating explicitly the production function implied in the existing growth models as an extreme case of the more 'normal' one—the former does not allow for substitution between factors (capital and labour), the latter does."[8]

However, Harrod, the Cambridge Keynesians, and some American Keynesians such as Robert Eisner (1958), who set out to defend "what Harrod, Domar and Hicks really said" against the neoclassical "attacks" by Tobin (1955) and Solow, remained less convinced. One target of attack was the "pre-Keynesian" character of Solow's analysis, which lacks an investment function, and consequentially has no role for motivational and behavioral patterns of entrepreneurs, including investors' expectations. Instead *ex ante* savings determine investment. On the other hand, the independence of investment decisions, sometimes guided by "animal

---

7. The problem of chronic depression is emphasized by Harrod (1948, vi) in his foreword to *Towards a Dynamic Economics*.

8. Leland Yeager (1954) criticized the essentially *nonmonetary* nature of the analysis of Harrod and Domar, which does not allow the drawing of far-reaching instability conclusions for real economies.

spirits" but in any case independent from savings (which have only an adaptive role to play), is the core of the Keynesian revolution. This view is also shared by the author of the first textbook of neoclassical growth theory: "Keynes's intellectual revolution was to shift economists from thinking normally in terms of a model of reality in which a dog called *savings* wagged his tail labelled *investment* to thinking in terms of a model in which a dog called *investment* wagged his tail labelled *savings*" (Meade 1975, 82). This point comes out most clearly in the critique raised by Amartya Sen (1970, 22) in the introduction to his widespread collection of selected readings in *Growth Economics*, in which he emphasizes

> The oddity of the neo-classical assumptions. . . . for in the process of adjustment a rise in the real interest rate seems to induce a higher rate of growth. One would have expected a rise in the real interest rate to cut down the rate of expansion through the investment function, but in the neo-classical model there is no investment function and investment is assumed simply to be determined by savings behaviour.

Instead of explicitly working with fixed coefficients or a Leontief technology, Harrod has never been very clear about the production-theoretic basis of his growth model. The (post-)Keynesian inflexibility of the capital-output ratio v has been substantiated less with production arguments than with the supposed inflexibility of the rate of profit (as one element of Kaldor's "stylized facts"). Thus it is equally important that the adjustment mechanism of neoclassical growth theory rests not only on substitution of the factors of production but also on the flexibility of factor prices. This decisive contrast to the post-Keynesian approach is not only pointed out by Eisner (1958) but comes out most sharply in Harrod's comment on a 1953 article by Pilvin, who made an early contribution to endogenize the capital-labor and the capital-output ratios but did not yet investigate the time path of capital intensity outside the steady state as Solow 1956 did. Here we find Harrod pointing out the centrifugal forces surrounding the warranted rate of growth, but in particular arguing in great detail against Pilvin's supposition that the rate of interest will do the appropriate job to generate an increase in the capital-labor ratio. Harrod not only refers to the problem of a liquidity trap but also states that "the postulate of a continually falling rate of interest seems rather an awkward one in a mature economy where the rate of interest is already low" (Harrod 1953, 556), and he concludes with his important doubts whether in mature economies the rate of interest has a major impact on the choice of production methods when the producers are facing high degrees of uncertainty. These arguments elucidate that Harrod shares Keynes's fundamental skepticism concerning the required variations in the interest rate. Interestingly, Burmeister and Dobell (1970, 41), who follow Eisner (1958) in studying Harrod's position, conclude that to narrow Harrod's argument exclusively to a fixed-coefficient production function "misses the essential feature of Harrod's analysis," and on the basis of a Solovian neoclassical production function Burmeister and Dobell "have isolated the hypothesis about freely falling interest rates as the crucial consideration."

The intrinsic instability of equilibrium growth in the Harrod model has two dimensions: the divergence between the warranted and the natural rate, and the short-run instability problems that arise when the investors base their decisions on expectations of a higher or lower rate of growth than the warranted rate. The consequence is a much greater difference between the actual and the warranted rate of growth. Harrod's analysis of this instability problem leads to dramatic results because the market gives perverse signals to the investors. However, the results rely sensitively on the assumptions. This requires a thorough analysis of disequilibrium investment behavior, which is not properly elaborated by Harrod. Since Harrod originally came from trade cycle analysis, it is this cyclical stability problem that is normally more at the center of the "Harrod literature."[9]

The publication of "Second Essay in Dynamic Theory" by Harrod (1960), who sent an offprint to Solow, launched a correspondence between the two growth economists (see Young 1989, 183–85) that did not lead to greater agreement. Solow remained convinced that Harrod's "new" or "second" equation developed in that essay also presupposes a constant capital coefficient.

Solow (1988, 310) has always been well aware of the two dimensions of Harrod's instability problems, although he concedes in his Nobel Prize lecture that "I may not have been as clear then [1956] as I am now about the distinction between the two notions of instability." This becomes evident by the final section, "Qualifications," of his 1956 article, where he discusses "Keynesian" problems such as rigid wages and liquidity preference.[10] Thus he has been aware from the beginning that his neoclassical model of economic growth only "took the sting out of the first sort of

9. See, for example, Besomi 1999 and Young 1989.
10. See also Solow's reply to Eisner where Solow (1959) refers to that section and emphasizes that his main purpose had been to challenge the "tight-rope" view of economic growth.

instability," namely, the divergence between the warranted and the natural rates of growth.

I turn now to the "knife-edge" metaphor, which was used on the very first page of Solow's 1956 classic, was perpetuated in Edward Prescott's (1988, 8) remarks on Solow's contributions deserving the Nobel Prize, and is still commonly used today. What made Harrod furious, who fought a lifelong hopeless battle against "Harrod's knife-edge" (see, e.g., Harrod 1973, chap. 3), which he would have preferred to exorcize permanently from the economic literature and to replace by a corridor concept instead, was the fact that even Cambridge Keynesians such as Joan Robinson (1965)—in her "Chinese period" (Solow 2007, 4)—were using this term. In his response, Harrod (1970, 741) expressed his "hope that we shall hear no more of the 'Harrod knife-edge.'"

4. Separation or Integration of Cycle and Trend Analysis?

Things are more complicated than just separating the two stability problems into a cyclical one and a secular one. Harrod (1939, 22) himself always regarded the warranted rate of growth as intrinsically unstable, representing a "moving equilibrium," which raises the problem of interaction between the trend and the cycle to which he finally could not give a satisfying answer.

In contrast to Harrod, Solow has addressed a different conceptual problem, namely, the issue of long-run economic growth. Neoclassical growth theory of the Solow-Swan-Meade type clearly separates the cycle from the trend and focuses on the steady state. Solow (2005, 9) recently recognized this in his "Reflections on Growth Theory" in the Aghion-Durlauf *Handbook*. The point was made more explicitly than in Solow's original article in Meade's famous 1961 textbook; there, the exposition of a neoclassical growth theory was "based on the assumption of an ideally successful Keynesian policy which at every point of time manages to keep the value of investment at the desired level" (ix), which sounds a little bit strange for a neoclassical theory but serves the function of getting rid of the business cycle problem.[11]

---

11. In the same spirit we can read in Swan's ([1963] 1970, 205) reflections on "golden ages" that his "illustrations will be Keynesian, in the sense of the future as Keynes did, and assume either that the authorities have read the *General Theory* or that they are socialists who don't need to; in other words I assume that whatever is saved is invested."

Hahn and Matthews (1964, 805–9) may have been the first authors who, after Eisner's earlier attempt, not only clearly distinguished between two different notions of the knife-edge problem, namely, the inequality between the warranted and the natural rate of growth and the instability of the warranted rate itself, but also observed that Solow, in focusing exclusively on the first, had missed Harrod's emphasis on the second. Harrod, however, had not elaborated a convincing out-of-equilibrium dynamics in his model. As Sen's numerical example has shown, the slightest deviation from the warranted rate leads to extreme instability, which "rule[s] out the possibility of stabilizing price and interest rate movements" (Baumol [1951] 1970, 55) on the theoretical side but also is at odds with an important empirical observation: the growth process in advanced economies after the Second World War was not as wildly unstable as the Harrod-Domar model implied. As mentioned at the outset of this essay, that observation inspired Solow to develop his own neoclassical model, and one of the main reasons his model has been a success is that it projects an economy whose stability is closer to that of the real world.

Solow always has been a short-run Keynesian, as can be seen in the concluding "Qualifications" section of his 1956 contribution. However, "all the difficulties and rigidities which go into modern Keynesian income analysis have been shunted aside. It is not my contention that these problems don't exist, nor that they are of no significance in the long run" (Solow 1956, 91). However, the shunting aside opened up the opportunity for real-business-cycle theorists such as Finn Kydland and Prescott to use Solow's steady-state model, in which the economy in contrast to the Harrod model never deviates from the warranted rate, for their explanation of short-run fluctuations.

In his Nobel Prize lecture, Solow (1987, 311–12) pointed out that

> it is impossible to believe that the equilibrium growth path itself is unaffected by the short- to medium-run experience. In particular the amount and direction of capital formation is bound to be affected by the business cycle. . . . So a simultaneous analysis of trend and fluctuations really does involve an integration of long run and short run of equilibrium and disequilibrium.

Similar statements that breathe a kind of "Harrodian spirit" have been made by Solow since then, time and again. However, despite the development of such concepts as path dependency, and a great advancement in technical methods compared with the days of Harrod, this decisive problem of combining short-, medium-, and long-run macroeconomics two decades later still has not yet been solved, and probably will not be solved in the near future.

References

Baumol, W. J. [1951] 1970. *Economic Dynamics: An Introduction*. 3rd ed. London: Macmillan.

Besomi, D. 1999. *The Making of Harrod's Dynamics*. Houndmills, U.K.: Macmillan.

Burmeister, E., and R. Dobell. 1970. *Mathematical Theories of Economic Growth*. London: Macmillan.

Domar, E. D. 1946. Capital Expansion, Rate of Growth, and Employment. *Econometrica* 14 (April): 137–47.

———. 1947. Expansion and Employment. *American Economic Review* 37 (March): 34–55.

———. 1953. Full Capacity vs. Full Employment Growth: Further Comment. *Quarterly Journal of Economics* 67.4:559–63.

———. 1957. *Essays in the Theory of Economic Growth*. New York: Oxford University Press.

Eisner, R. 1958. On Growth Models and the Neo-classical Resurgence. *Economic Journal* 68 (December): 707–21.

Hahn, F. H., and R. C. O. Matthews. 1964. The Theory of Economic Growth: A Survey. *Economic Journal* 68 (December): 779–902.

Harrod, R. F. 1939. An Essay on Dynamic Theory. *Economic Journal* 49 (March): 14–33.

———. 1948. *Towards a Dynamic Economics*. London: Macmillan.

———. 1953. Comment [on Pilvin]. *Quarterly Journal of Economics* 67.4:553–59.

———. 1959. Domar and Dynamic Economics. *Economic Journal* 69 (September): 451–64.

———. 1960. Second Essay in Dynamic Theory. *Economic Journal* 70 (June): 277–93.

———. 1970. Harrod after Twenty-One Years: A Comment. *Economic Journal* 80 (September): 737–41.

———. 1973. *Economic Dynamics*. London: Macmillan.

Jones, H. 1975. *An Introduction to Modern Theories of Economic Growth*. Sunbury-on-Thames, U.K.: Nelson.

Kaldor, N. 1956. Alternative Theories of Distribution. *Review of Economic Studies* 23.2:83–100.

Meade, J. 1961. *A Neo-Classical Theory of Economic Growth*. London: Allen and Unwin.

———. 1975. The Keynesian Revolution. In *Essays on John Maynard Keynes*, edited by M. Keynes. Cambridge: Cambridge University Press.

Pilvin, H. 1953. Full Capacity vs. Full Employment Growth. *Quarterly Journal of Economics* 67.4:545–52.

Prescott, E. C. 1988. Robert M. Solow's Neoclassical Growth Model: An Influential Contribution to Economics. *Scandinavian Journal of Economics* 90.1:7–12.

Robinson, J. 1965. Harrod's Knife-Edge. In vol. 3 of *Collected Economic Papers*, by J. Robinson. Oxford: Blackwell.

Sen, A., ed. 1970. *Growth Economics: Selected Readings*. Harmondsworth, U.K.: Penguin Books.

Solow, R. M. 1952. On the Structure of Linear Models. *Econometrica* 20 (January): 29–46.

———. 1953–54. A Note on the Price Level and Interest Rate in a Growth Model. *Review of Economic Studies* 21.1:74–79.

———. 1956. A Contribution to the Theory of Economic Growth. *Quarterly Journal of Economics* 70 (February): 65–94.

———. 1957. Technical Change and the Aggregate Production Function. *Review of Economics and Statistics* 39 (August): 312–20.

———. 1959. Is Factor Substitution a Crime, and If So, How Bad? Reply to Professor Eisner. *Economic Journal* 69 (September): 597–99.

———. 1960. Investment and Technical Progress. In *Mathematical Methods in the Social Sciences, 1959*, edited by K. Arrow, S. Karlin, and P. Suppes. Stanford, Calif.: Stanford University Press.

———. 1988. Growth Theory and After. *American Economic Review* 78.3:307–17.

———. 1994. Perspectives on Growth Theory. *Journal of Economic Perspectives* 8.1:45–54.

———. 1999. Neoclassical Growth Theory. In vol. 1A of *Handbook of Macroeconomics*, edited by J. B. Taylor and M. Woodford. Amsterdam: Elsevier.

———. 2005. Reflections on Growth Theory. In vol. 1A of *Handbook of Economic Growth*, edited by P. Aghion and S. N. Durlauf. Amsterdam: Elsevier.

———. 2007. The Last 50 Years in Growth Theory and the Next 10. *Oxford Review of Economic Policy* 23.1:3–14.

Swan, T. W. 1956. Economic Growth and Capital Accumulation. *Economic Record* 32.63:334–61.

———. [1963] 1970. Golden Ages and Production Functions. In Sen 1970.

Tinbergen, J. [1942] 1959. Zur Theorie der langfristigen Wirtschaftsentwicklung. *Weltwirtschaftliches Archiv* 55:511–49. Translated as On the Theory of Trend Movements, in *Jan Tinbergen: Selected Papers,* edited by L. H. Klaassen, L. M. Koyck, and H. J. Witteveen. Amsterdam: North-Holland.

Tobin, J. 1955. A Dynamic Aggregative Model. *Journal of Political Economy* 63.2:103–15.

Yeager, L. B. 1954. Some Questions about Growth Economics. *American Economic Review* 44.1:53–63.

Young, W. 1989. *Harrod and His Trade Cycle Group: The Origins and Development of the Growth Research Programme*. Houndmills, U.K.: Macmillan.

A Nonlinear History
of Growth and Cycle Theories

Lionello F. Punzo

This article offers a reconstruction of the history of the formal theories of economic fluctuations vis-à-vis the history of the macroeconomic theories of growth.[1] It proposes an account of the birth of the neoclassical growth theory at the hands of Robert Solow and Trevor Swan, and of the ensuing evolution of aggregate growth theory. My main thesis is that modern macromodeling of growth phenomena grew out of the general equilibrium approach as much as from the attempt of what I call *classical macrodynamics* to construct a general theory explaining cycles and growth on the basis of a unique set of principles. To accomplish such an ambitious project, the marriage of macrodynamics with Keynesian aggregative analysis was temporarily thought to be useful. It is this peculiar blend that sets the resulting brand of dynamics apart from multisectoral growth theories, whose genealogy can instead be traced in, for example, the works of John von Neumann and Wassily Leontief.

Even restricting our focus to aggregate theories, history is not as straightforward as often implicitly suggested: the "same perennial issues seem to come back." Together with the peaks of three waves of interest in growth counted by Solow (1994, 45), we have witnessed the emergence and often reemergence of a variety of theories of economic fluctuations.

Financial support from UNISI as a 2007 PAR project and the hospitality of the INCTPPED at UFRJ, Rio de Janeiro, are gratefully acknowledged.

1. For more details, see Punzo 2006, in particular for the intellectual route of Richard M. Goodwin against the backdrop of the development of macrodynamics.

History of Political Economy 41 (annual suppl.) DOI 10.1215/00182702-2009-018

The history of the alternating interest in these two topics seems quite akin to that of a pair of coupled but out-of-phase oscillators. Such a peculiar association calls for an explanation. To find it, we look for their common path leading back to the origins of formal dynamics. At one point, this path led to the neoclassical growth theory. In a "nonlinear view of history," however, certain interpretive models from time to time reappear as long as certain theoretical issues remain unsolved, though each time they may result in some answers. I address one such unsolved issue.

In the 1960s, in an article reviewing the field, F. H. Hahn and R. C. O. Matthews concluded that growth theorizing had probably reached the end of its fruitful years. They may have been wrong. We might be again in the middle of another swing, waiting for the next peak.

The First Growth Wave

We teach Harrod-Domar as a single model of steady growth. And, in fact, Hahn and Matthews begin their review article with Roy Harrod's 1939 book and Evsey Domar's 1946 article (Solow 1956 refers to Harrod 1948, though). Although it is often mentioned that there are important differences between Harrod's and Domar's models, the consensus among economists is that the two form basically a single model, marking the beginning of the formal theory of growth. In the Harrod-Domar model we already find all the essential ingredients that ensuing models have tried to incorporate. There can be found the *method of growth theory*, which also "uses as central concept that of the equilibrium of an expanding economy" (Hicks 1965, vi).

From time to time, it is recalled that Harrod's 1939 *Essay* was preceded by his 1936 *Essay on the Trade Cycle*. This book is generally considered an unsuccessful and a really short-lived dash by Harrod into the theory of fluctuations. Its analysis is found to be full of ungranted, unclear assumptions and undefined concepts (see, e.g., Hansen 1937, Solow 1988). Domar would be clearer in focusing on the conditions characterizing an equilibrium growth path. The use of the method of growth should really be attributed to Domar, then.

The Harrod-Domar model, on the other hand, is the genealogical ancestor from which neoclassical growth theory claims to descend, for the latter's focus on proving the existence of a full-employment equilibrium path.

Naturally, together with the issue of such an equilibrium path, two additional related issues were to arise: uniqueness and stability. To be practically relevant as a *predictor*, an equilibrium has to be (at least, locally) unique, and the economy must be shown to be stable toward it. Solow's proof solves all three issues at once, while neither Domar nor Harrod (though trying hard) had succeeded. Thus neoclassical growth theory would be the successful end of their quest. On the other hand, if the accepted principal task of a formal theory is to generate predictions as testable hypotheses, growth theory was really born with the neoclassical model.

As the neoclassical response to the "Harrod-Domar impulse" (Solow 1994), neoclassical growth theory is, however, better split into a response to Domar as far as the analysis of the equilibrium properties, and to Harrod for the analysis of stability and uniqueness. And, in fact, rereading in the words of Solow the episode of the conception of neoclassical growth theory from the viewpoint of Harrod, rather than or even in opposition to that of Domar, affords us a new perspective. The conventional reconstruction inserts the birth of neoclassical growth theory into the process that produced the modern general equilibrium program, in particular linking it with the then ongoing research on stability with Paul Samuelson's dynamical approach on the front line (documented in, e.g., Weintraub 1991). The new perspective shows that episode as a temporary station of a longer intellectual process; it puts it in a distinct context and points to a new genealogical thread. It is to follow such a thread—thus entering a perhaps unexpected theoretical scenario—that we need to go back to Harrod of the *Trade Cycle.*

Such a book can be taken to represent the conceptual crossroads of a broad ongoing reflection on how to theorize about economic dynamics.[2] It is for this objectively ambiguous position at the junction of different strands of thought (the Keynesian being one of them), still largely in the making, that Harrod could so swiftly switch from his ambitious treatment of general dynamics in 1936 to the theory of growth of the 1939 *Essay.*

The *Trade Cycle* claimed to offer a "new theory" with a "precise and definite diagnosis" of the dynamics of a system out of its equilibrium path. There, we find probably the earliest conscious attempt to analyze both growth and the business cycle within a Keynesian framework, along with some intuitive ideas as to how they were to interact. The difficulty inherent in the search for an altogether new approach and a definitely poor com-

---

2. Young 1989 and Besomi 1999 give a detailed account of the evolution of Harrod's ideas leading to the *Trade Cycle*, as well as of the intellectual atmosphere and network of relations in which it took place. See in particular Young 1989, chaps. 4 and 5.

mand of the required mathematics thwarted the ambitious attempt. Harrod's own aim there was to deal with something much more complex than the mere (knife-edge) stability issue that was going to be read in it later. Once the concept of the warranted rate of growth is introduced, the thrust of the argument is to establish three propositions (Punzo 1988):

1. the warranted rate and the associated path are not unique (indeterminacy);
2. any equilibrium growth path (hence, also a warranted and the full employment paths) is empirically irrelevant: no economy would ever be seen on one such path (observability);
3. the economy is not stable toward any warranted path; it tends to exhibit explosive deviations from it starting from practically any initial condition (stability).

These propositions can be seen as exactly dual to those of neoclassical growth theory.[3] With the hindsight of the modern theory of dynamic complexity (that we have been taught by the chaos literature of the 1990s), in the *Trade Cycle*, the issue is not the instability of an equilibrium path.[4] The capitalist system is simply not *capable* of being stable.

The *Trade Cycle* is a good illustration of the fact that "successful (like, often, also unsuccessful) ideas are a group product" (Solow 1988; Young 1987). The intuitive notion that the capitalist system is basically unstable belonged to the perception of reality of a broad intellectual milieu, spread between Oxford, Cambridge, and probably the London School of Economics, and dominant in most Middle European circles. It was waiting to be made precise, which is precisely what Harrod was trying to do.

In such an international intellectual milieu, some thought that the classics (up until Knut Wicksell and Gustav Cassel) had provided an acceptable explanation of the economic long run, and this was what the established equilibrium analysis was really about. Cassel had shown an extension into dynamics (Boianovsky, this volume). What was missing was an explanation of the "shorter than long run" behavior of the economies. On the basis of current and recent experience, this behavior did not look at all like an equilibrium.

3. A similar thesis is expressed by Besomi 2001.
4. The latter amounts to saying more than simply that an economy "once it strays from equilibrium growth" never returns (e.g., Solow 1988, 310). Solow acknowledges that the issue of Harrod's (in)stability has two aspects and that this latter aspect was not dealt with by neoclassical growth theory.

All researchers in such varied milieu were looking for explanations of the more complex dynamics exhibited by "reality." They perceived that either this would lead to structural change (Leontief 1934, quoted in Goodwin 1947) or else it had to have some self-limiting behavior. They surmised that the economy would run into the former, as a result of deeply rooted destabilizing forces, when the latter failed to set in.

The program of (classical) macrodynamics, launched by Ragnar Frisch, was well aware of such an alternative (before Solow saw it in his 1956 paper). It set out to deal with the self-limiting kind of unstable dynamics. In doing so (or in order to single this out), it swept under the theoretical carpet the issue of structural change.

Frisch's Macrodynamics Manifesto

The suggested link of neoclassical growth theory to Harrod leads us farther back to classical macrodynamics. I believe that some key issues of modern dynamics have their roots in such a connection.

Generally, macrodynamics can be defined (after Frisch 1933) as the theory of the manifold dynamics exhibited by model economies when they are represented at certain levels of (dis-)aggregation. Born as a theory of real variables, it was later expanded to chart a much broader territory. Thus we may use the term to indicate a whole class of models, the evolution of which occurred in three phases: the 1930s and 1940s, which saw the origins of the models; the 1950s and 1960s, which represent a phase of transition; and the 1970s up to the present, which is marked by a varied landscape of modern and postmodern models. Thus one begins with Frisch (together with the other founders of the Econometric Society) and with Harrod, to end with real business cycles and endogenous models of various types producing growth or fluctuations, and often both at the same time. In parallel, we move from classical to neoclassical macrodynamics.[5] In my reconstruction, the birth of neoclassical theory is located at the junction between origins and transition. Really, it does not belong to either, as it shows traces of both phases and contributed to initializing transition.

Programmatically, the research territory of classical macrodynamics extends over growth as well as fluctuations at various frequencies,

---

5. Justification for calling it "classical" lies, in my view, in the fact that it does not have the ingredients of the so-called choice-theoretic framework, required in the neoclassical version of macrodynamics.

therefore including business cycles as special cases. Typical is its view (imported from physics) that fluctuations are intimately related with growth identified as an exponential motion and that the latter is but a specimen of the former: a fluctuation with a singular frequency. As a consequence, they ought to receive a unified mathematical treatment. Moreover, classical macrodynamics claimed to focus on, and it has to be at least credited for trying to deal with, non- or out-of-equilibrium dynamics. It proved, at the end, unfortunate that this latter came to be identified with any path different from the static equilibrium of the established Walrasian theory.

The formalism had two basic and simple conceptual ingredients: the notion of a given empirical structure, formalized as a collection of functional relations with given (i.e., observed) parameters, and the dual notion that dynamics was generated by exogenous impulse(s) activating a propagation mechanism, that is, the system structure. A dynamic *tableau économique* was offered to illustrate how a system of n interdependent equations could exhibit both growth and fluctuations (Frisch 1933, 173–75).

That explanatory scheme placed greater weight on the impulse, the real engine of dynamics, and relatively less on propagation, which was basically seen as a damping mechanism to be repeatedly reinitialized. Any motion (including exponential growth) has both its cause and the cause of its persistence in some specifically assumed, often ad hoc, impulse profile.

Such a scheme could be easily reversed, exchanging relative weights: the propagation mechanism being the dynamic engine and the impulse a mere disturbance. This, I believe, is the key to really understanding Harrod's 1936 book, marking its distance from the view of classical macrodynamics. On the other hand, the latter's approach based on the notion of a given system (macro-) structure made a marriage with Keynesian analysis of real variables relatively easy. The latter only needed the simplest structure, with the lowest dimension of one-state variable.

For the present history, the project of classical macrodynamics should be read against the backdrop of Keynes's attack on the classical stability postulate. Such a postulate was said to imply the view that an economy is a naturally stable system that, unless disturbed from outside, always lingers around a (possibly, locally unique) equilibrium state. The classical stability postulate was implicit in Frisch's view of a damping propagation mechanism: his analysis of dynamics had oscillations on the forefront, but a stable, though possibly moving, equilibrium lay at its core.

Therefore the simultaneous presence of growth and fluctuations places Harrod's effort within the paradigm and research program of macrodynamics. On the other hand, his rejection of global stability is the basic motivation behind the view of the trade cycle as an explosive but recurrent path systematically away from equilibrium, the warranted growth path. If intellectual history can at times be told as a spy story, Roy Harrod was the person who really tried to resolve the ambiguity in the classical macrodynamics program and to attack that stability postulate head-on.

The result of such an attack was the earliest programmatic attempt at founding an endogenous theory of economic dynamics, but also its temporary failure. Armed with the intuition that an economy should be conceived as an *autonomous system* (Punzo 2006) and that, therefore, the propagation mechanism embedded in its own structure would be capable, alone, of sustaining fluctuations, Harrod launched a wave of business cycle analysis. This was a crossbreed between a version of a Keynesian income determination model with a macrodynamic methodology drawn to its extreme consequences by unambiguously placing *structure* (instead of *impulse*) at its center. Voicing a latent demand, with perhaps a bad book and the poor mathematics he commanded, he set at least part of a generation to work.

A Project for Business Cycle Analysis

Thus Harrod tried to formulate his view of system instability but could not handle the mathematical complications. Apparently, as a result of realizing this inadequacy but also of other events, he gave up the attempt. According to this story, it was disappointment that produced the *Essay* and later work.[6] How to solve his problem, that is, how to get growth *and* fluctua-

6. Tinbergen's (1937) review of the *Trade Cycle* pointed out that its mathematical formulation was insufficient to yield fluctuations and could in fact only produce exponential growth. According to, for example, Goodwin 1982, vii–viii, and Goodwin 1985, this led Harrod to abandon the business cycle and to elaborate the growth interpretation that appears in the *Essay*, published shortly afterward. This anecdotal episode (argued to be true by Jolink 1995) shows the existence of an actual link between Harrod and the Middle European milieu associated with the macrodynamics program. Moreover, Warren Young (1989) produces convincing evidence of the atmosphere in which *Trade Cycle* was conceived, in particular of Harrod's great expectations that his book would be the center of debate at the forthcoming meeting of the Econometric Society in Oxford, just four months after its publication. Probably, the disillusion with that meeting contributed to Harrod's change of mind as much as the realization of the mathematical difficulties he could not cope with.

tions together, became the core issue in the thinking of a generation. To try to fix the mathematical problem inadequately dealt with in *Trade Cycle* (together with Harrod's strong argument against the ad hoc use of lags) seems to have been the fundamental motivation for certain people working on the business cycle at the time to move on to a nonlinear formulation.

In other words, while Harrod was evolving toward the theory of growth that we attribute to him, his earlier analysis contributed substantially to shaping the research agenda of the nonlinear endogenous approach to business cycle and other oscillations, the program whose fully blown version we may call classical business cycle analysis. In fact, well after the publication (1950) of John Hicks's *Contribution to the Theory of the Trade Cycle*, for instance, it was Harrod's *Trade Cycle* that was still cited as the key reference for dynamics.

Classical business cycle analysis generated a family of models trying to address and to provide analytic answers to what a generation interpreted as Keynes's (and Harrod's) search for a theory of non-self-adjusting economic system. It took the rejection of the stability postulate to its extreme logical consequences: self-sustained fluctuations were to be shown to be the *generic* motions whose explanation would be buried deep in the structure of the economy. Nonlinear mathematics was the adequate tool to represent such persistent "disequilibrium."

The twenty-year interval between *Trade Cycle* and the birth of neoclassical growth theory saw the development of such a research program. Practically all such models were aggregate, the offspring of a marriage of convenience between classical macrodynamics and Keynesian analysis. A whole group of researchers collaborated to arrange for such a marriage, by showing, for example, that the coupling of an income multiplier with a destabilizing mechanism (the accelerator) could in principle account for both growth and fluctuation. What at the time appeared to be reciprocal convenience was the fact that the one-dimensional Keynesian model was a mathematically simpler version of the *n*-dimensional *tableau économique* envisaged in Frisch's article. Unfortunately, the two frameworks eventually came to be identified with one another.[7]

Classical business cycle analysis was basically about a thought experiment: trying to construct a wholly endogenous explanation of dynamics

---

7. Goodwin's lifelong work in linear economics, in parallel with his nonlinear cycle modeling, shows the uneasiness generated by such marriage and an unresolved contradiction (Punzo 2006).

as if an economy could be observed in vitro, insulated from all sorts of exogenous, even stochastic, impulses. There was no clear predictive content in its models. This lack was felt to be one of its weakest points in an intellectual atmosphere where growing familiarity with modeling raised increasing expectations and demand for testable hypotheses.

Its models, on the other hand, were all deterministic, built around a common set of properties that could be represented only in nonlinear formulations more adequate than Harrod's own. Equilibrium growth (e.g., steady-state) paths were considered empirically irrelevant, rarely or never actually observed, and had to be understood as some of the modes in the complicated modal interlocking typical of large systems. They could be intellectual constructs or be caused by long-run forces exogenous to the natural mechanics of the economy. The task of explaining them, therefore, would be beyond the realm of theory and have no intrinsic interest (Goodwin 1951a). At times, reference was eclectically made to Harrod's full-employment path, sometimes to Joseph Schumpeter's view of innovation swarms (as, e.g., in Kaldor 1954) or else to autonomous investment expenditure, perhaps linked to technological progress (Hicks 1950). Observed fluctuations, instead, were interpreted as the visible manifestation of an inherent tendency to disequilibrium, their causes being ingrained in the internal wiring of an economic system. In other words, this approach to business cycle coordinated an endogenous explanation of fluctuations with an exogenous explanation of growth. However, the relationship between growth as a trend and fluctuation was still unclear. In fact, even in the most mature formulations, they were linearly superimposed on one another.

Thus that approach failed to reach the objective it had set for itself, a unified theory of dynamics. Nonlinearity per se was not adequate to the task, for a single state–variable model simply cannot yield, at the same time, fluctuations and exponential growth. Thus it cannot solve the problem that haunted the key argument in *Trade Cycle*. Sticking to nonlinearity only for mathematical convenience eventually led to focusing on fluctuations and abandoning all attempts to explain equilibrium growth paths, which were considered to be empirically irrelevant.

This left a hole in the theory of economic dynamics, and somebody was to look into it. The failure in addressing satisfactorily Harrod's issue is, therefore, the first key to understanding subsequent developments, among them the birth of growth theory as a dedicated, separate dynamic theory. Such separation was one cost of the initially promising marriage of convenience.

On the other hand, mathematically more robust formulations eventually elaborated by, for example, Richard Goodwin, produced only regular oscillations, which in fact still represent some sort of equilibrium. Thus, although the search was for a disequilibrium theory, fluctuations were obtained that were far *too* regular and did not look like real ones. The explanation of their irregularity was missing, at times receiving ad hoc and unconvincing treatment.

Finally, the difficulties associated with nonlinear formulations led to the introduction of qualitative analysis (in the style of Poincaré, Andronov, et al.). Important as it was in the history of economic analysis, such a passage was perceived as the abandonment of a quantitative approach, the divorce of theory and econometrics.

Thus the project of a theory of a self-sustained, endogenously generated or structural dynamics appeared to be impossible to realize. At the same time, the aim of constructing a *quantitative* theory also proved to be unreachable with the mathematics then familiar to most economists.[8] These two facts jointly declared the (temporary) end of classical business cycle analysis and thus liberated growth from the embrace with fluctuations. Failure exposed the hole.

The awareness of that failure contributed to the intellectual atmosphere that was to generate a theory of growth as an exogenously driven phenomenon.

The Right Place for Equilibrium Growth

Recalling the relevance of the full-employment equilibrium path as a predictor, one can appreciate how far neoclassical growth went from classical business cycle theory. The latter did not deny the possibility of an equilibrium, but it assigned to it the very limited role of a reference or benchmark behavior. In fact, there was no obstacle to make it fit into its framework, for example, keeping self-sustained fluctuations coupled with exogenously driven growth (i.e., using the model of a nonlinear *forced* instead of a *free* oscillator). This would simply require assuming an unstable equilibrium, which could be Harrod's own path (Kaldor 1940; Goodwin 1953, 1955), a response to some other exogenously given forcing function (e.g., Hicks's autonomous demand trend), or else having the

8. This is not to say that the mathematics of Frisch, Tinbergen, Hicks, and Goodwin was not adequate to the task.

full-employment path acting as a ceiling (Hicks 1950; Goodwin 1951b). Not everybody, at the time, found this solution satisfactory (e.g., Goodwin 1950), but apparently there was no other. There was, in fact, a mathematical problem in endogenizing growth.[9] Still, the conceptual question remains: why was the explanation of growth placed outside dynamic theory?

This is linked, I surmise, with the attitude of business cycle theorists of the time toward "relevant" exogenous impulses. These and generally any force exerting effects on equilibrium were deemed to also have other major effects. Even with greater determination than in macrodynamics, classical business cycle theory was looking for structural explanations referring to basic mechanisms supposedly regulating system functioning. Thus, consistently, it was thought that, behind any long-run tendency, there would be processes slowly shaping and most likely also changing the very economic structure. Demographic movements, structural change (of the resource reallocation type, and sectoral capital accumulation), technological progress and innovation were conceptualizations of such forces, which would interact with one another in a complicated way (a notion very close to Schumpeter's view; see Kaldor 1954). Though with different formulations, various models put forward the view that all those were discontinuous processes, possibly of a stochastic nature. At any rate, their interaction would produce complicated outcomes: for example, deforming an otherwise regular fluctuation, shifting equilibrium in unpredictable directions (Goodwin 1946), bringing about abrupt or catastrophic changes, and the like. All such nonsystematic forces at work were most unlikely to produce anything similar to an equilibrium or a smooth trend. Structural and technological change was the only explanation for irregularity left to classical business cycle analysis. On the other hand, *realism* seemed to be a justification for leaving them outside a theory of systematic dynamics.

Thus, shortly before the appearance of neoclassical theory, for theorists and theories in the business cycle program the issue was not to explain growth but to find a way to combine accepted unexplained growth with seemingly better-understood endogenous oscillations. One way to go about it was to make growth *look* endogenous, that is, by identifying it with a trend as a statistical average over actual oscillations. Alternatively to this

---

9. A problem that the multisectoral theories of growth did not encounter, precisely because of their higher dimension, a fact that partially explains their blossoming in the 1960s–70s (after Hicks's 1965 book), at a time of relative quiescence of aggregate growth theory.

practical answer, it could be argued, à la Schumpeter, that it was the oscillation that generated growth (Kaldor 1954). Neither of these solutions was really available for formal analysis, the former being premature, the latter implying formidable mathematical complications.[10]

A third conceivable solution was to have an economy switch frequency, from fluctuation to growth, and thus simply get rid of fluctuations from then on. This was impossible when structural change was not contemplated or even methodologically conceivable, as was the case in classical macrodynamics, but it was the only remaining alternative. It implied a mechanism by which an explosive motion (e.g., an oscillation) would be converted into smooth growth (e.g., growth along the full-employment path)—an explosive growth path limited by Hicks's and Goodwin's ceiling. Designing and embedding a *new* mechanism of structural adjustment was required.

Seen from the point of view of the classical business cycle program, this was the true innovation of neoclassical growth theory. It proved a relatively simple solution, which had far-reaching consequences.

The Neoclassical Revolution:
Continuous Technological Progress

To accomplish this feat, the interpretation of the formal model had to be altered. With the introduction of a production function, the structure on which a macrodynamic model was constructed was no longer an observed set of relations and realized values for variables and structural parameters. It became founded on realizable values of an *ex ante* functional approach. A silent paradigm shift took place launching the creation of modern macrodynamics endowed with what later, after a process of further enrichment, was to be called the "choice-theoretical framework."

Seen against the agenda of classical business cycle analysis and its relatively poor scores up to that time, the equilibrium path had suddenly become worth a closer look. This produced the well-known analysis of the dynamical properties around that equilibrium. The long-run path implied now-continuing full employment. It also proved that, under the assumed conditions and in a time horizon sufficiently long to be called *long run*, certain key variables of Harrod and the then contemporary business cycle research would cease to play a role and be replaced by other "determinants"

10. Although hinted at in various writings, the notion of a purely statistical trend came into the open only much later.

of growth. In particular, the self-feeding process of capital accumulation was superseded by exogenous technical progress as the explanation of growth performance. Moreover, their divorce was a surprising logical consequence.

As said, that technical progress could be a driving force of long-run equilibrium was not foreign to people in business cycle research. However, they were inclined to think that it induced an irregularly fluctuating path, hard to distinguish from endogenously driven oscillations (as in Schumpeter's theory, formalized in Goodwin 1946 and Kaldor 1954). However, only a steady and continuous process (at a positive rate) of productivity enhancement is compatible with smooth growth. It is this assumption that generates the steady-state path associated with neoclassical predictions and growth accounting. The basic difference of neoclassical growth theory from classical business cycle analysis, therefore, is in its treatment of technical progress as a continuous process. Such a hypothesis might appear hardly consistent with its assumed exogeneity, but it is also necessary to support the other, hardly intuitive but logical implication of the neoclassical model: that the pace of capital accumulation contributes to shaping long-run growth. With this move, a whole tradition of thought, which had Schumpeter as perhaps its most prominent representative, was buried.

However, something was felt to be wrong: either in the very conception of technical progress and, hence, of its relation to investment and the role of the latter, or else in the concept of a time horizon long enough to make capital disappear from the growth scenario. The often hot debate following the birth of neoclassical theory shows the varied reactions to those implications, with the appearance of theories of vintage capital goods, the discussion about embodied versus disembodied technical progress, Kaldor's attempt at formalizing a new technical progress (investment) function, and finally Arrow's learning by doing.[11]

At the time, the challenge was seen as how to keep capital accumulation (that neoclassical theory had expelled so as to secure global stability) *and* make it compatible with equilibrium growth. This debate never really abated. The third and most recent of the waves of interest in growth theory sprung up as a redefinition and reinterpretation of the role of capital accumulation in growth performance.

11. "Where recent discoveries have made a decisive contribution is in the recognition that investing and technical progress may be Siamese twins" (Hahn and Matthews 1964, 888–89).

An Intellectual Cycle?

Harrod's thesis, that growth would arise from the same endogenous sources of fluctuations, was left unproved, notwithstanding the vast number of publications up until shortly before the birth of neoclassical theory that marked the second wave of interest in growth. This can be seen as a reaction to the failure of the classical approach to business cycle.

Neoclassical growth theory did not address that thesis or share it. Simply, theoretical attention shifted from fluctuations without growth to growth without fluctuations. Correspondingly, the out-of-equilibrium interpretation of observed dynamics was abandoned in favor of one of equilibrium, and correspondingly the view spread that economic dynamics, rather than being essentially endogenously driven, was the response to external forces. This was a new phase of an intellectual cycle that had already had an early phase with endogeneity (i.e., an endogenous explanation) as the dominating paradigm, followed by the unsatisfactory mix produced by classical business cycle analysis.

In fact, the articulation, at about the same time, of the linear econometric methodology associated with the Cowles Commission (Morgan 1990) and its wide acceptance were the other logical consequences of the same fact. Like in neoclassical growth theory, a similarly exogenous theory of fluctuations was proposed, refreshing a view that had been at the origins of macrodynamics. Oscillations would again be transient deviations from a (globally) stable equilibrium, kept alive by an unexplained tendency to be hit by stochastic impulse(s), a view that had been contemplated but soon dismissed.

The conceptual match with neoclassical theory was practically perfect. The econometric model of the 1960s got along very well with a dynamic theory that focused only on stable equilibria and therefore guaranteed predictability in econometric models so that they complemented each other. The 1970s and the very early part of the 1980s happily lived in a new, finally unified paradigm of exogeneity. It was a sort of middle season in the nonlinear history of dynamics I am sketching out.

A winter of discontent arrived with the third growth wave, when the so-called endogenous theories became ripe. Perhaps, it was regretted that, in the effort to get rid of fluctuations, neoclassical growth theory had also got rid of capital accumulation. It was also thought that there was no longer such necessity. A search for a novel role for capital accumulation and technological progress in explaining growth performance, also in conjunction with the release of a massive new data bank to tap, ignited the wildfire of the so-called endogenous theory of growth. A set of older ideas made a comeback as growth determinants: in particular, the centrality of investment (though qualified to suit modern times, with education and R&D entering into it), innovation processes, international trade, and many others. What widely different models shared was their success in bending manifold phenomena, even the vision of the innovation process as essentially discontinuous (as was Schumpeter's), to fit steady-state analysis. They were the product of a discontent with certain, also empirical, implications of the neoclassical theory, more than of the search for a new theoretical framework.

Associations between varieties of dynamics and location of their sources changed dramatically. Once again, the unifying principle that had prevailed in the earlier season got lost, and we returned to a mix or spurious paradigm, dual though to the one unwillingly produced by what I have termed the classical analysis of business cycle. At the peak of that relatively short season, in fact, *endogenous* growth was coupled with the *exogenously* driven fluctuations of the still-surviving standard or linear econometric model and the new monetarist theory.

Each of these "seasons" represented a temporary equilibrium station as they had their own built-in destabilizer: the initial one was the search for a unified theory of growth and cycle; the second, the season of the classical analysis of business cycle ended in the failure of dealing with such issues. This last season sprang from the discontent with the limited relevance given to various forms of investment and to innovation, but it left the same open issue as the second. Giving opposite explanations for the modes of actual dynamics, it did not respond to the apparent demand for a unique dynamic paradigm.

A step further, into a fourth season, and a *new* brand of macrodynamics was produced. This fully adheres to the classical self-regulating principle: according to the real business cycle approach, all sorts of dynamics are taken to be optimal equilibrium responses to exogenous shocks and explained by the use of the choice-theoretic framework. The possibility of disequilibrium is not denied but is seen to be just a transient phenomenon (Mankiw 1989; Hartley et al. 1998).

In this last but one phase, there are many ideas that already belonged to classical macrodynamics, the first being that the distinction between growth and fluctuations is not really relevant: both are types of fluctuations with different frequencies. Moreover, just like in the older approach, real business cycle theory promotes a linear view of dynamics, and in

its extreme blown version (where growth as well as fluctuations are sto-
chastically induced), the unifying explanatory principle is exogeneity,
once again.[12]

Final Remarks: Newtonian Apples

The previous pages argue that the neoclassical theory of growth was an
answer to the failure of a research program to attain its self-assigned task,
to construct an all-encompassing theory of economic dynamics modeled after physics. Such failure was, eventually, the unexpected result of
its having been trapped in the marriage of convenience with the one-
dimensional Keynesian model, where there was no room for long-run
dynamics, hence for such phenomena as technological change and innovation, that is, the Schumpeterian tradition. By the mid-1950s that failure
was evident,[13] and this explains why two independent researchers could
provide basically the same solution, the Solow-Swan model: two Newtonian apples falling on two heads, at the same time.

To move on implied a divorce. This explains why, ever since, "when we
talk of growth we do not talk of fluctuations," to paraphrase Solow's words
in his 1992 Siena Lectures.[14]

Real business cycle theory is perhaps the most recent, and still ongoing,
phase of what seems to be a four-season intellectual cycle in our understanding of economic dynamics. As one of its original impulses, it had
the ideas of classical macrodynamic analysis, but it seems to have later
looked for new mechanisms of self-sustained oscillations.

In such new macrodynamics, structural problems of coordination disappear, and economies are enlarged replicas of a single clever economic

---

12. The fundamental debt of real business cycle theory to Eugen Slutzky is clearly acknowledged and well studied (Louçã 2004). I argued (Punzo 2006) that once the engine of dynamics
had been placed (by Frisch) into the *impulse*, a coherent approach could regard the propagation
mechanism as of minor interest. In this light (in which it was perceived, e.g., by Goodwin
1951a), Slutzky's contribution can be considered as an extreme version of Frisch's oscillatory
system, designed to explain persistence rather than existence of observed fluctuations. The latter, more general, category of dynamics includes regular cycles (and growth) as special cases.
I am grateful to an anonymous referee for pointing out the necessity of this clarification.

13. Hagemann, this volume, documents the collective effort being spent to cope with it
at that time.

14. "Growth theory was invented to provide a systematic way to talk about and to compare
paths. In the task it succeeded reasonably well. In doing so, however, it failed to come to grips
adequately with an equally important and interesting problem: the right way to deal with
deviations from equilibrium growth" (Solow 1988, 311).

player. The very rationale for macrodynamics, to account for dynamic implications of structure and the complex interplay of its components, has disappeared. In the meantime, the meaning of *endogenous theory* has changed. I believe there was an alternative, and that it is still there, though my rational reconstruction of the preceding pages shows recent developments as the necessary consequence of earlier failures.

The most recent, exciting but so far only promising developments of nonlinear macro-econometrics seem to be once again addressing that relentless demand for a unified framework, which has motivated the intellectual cycle described thus far. The nonlinear formulation and its conjugation with quantitatively oriented theorizing seem to be the up-to-date and, hopefully, finally adequate response to the long search of business cycle research.

It is already time to assess such advances (see Durlauf, this volume, and the references therein). In any case, a question arises: have we ourselves been trapped in an intellectual limit cycle of some sort?

Any project to progress farther in macrodynamics should probably try to find a way out of the dichotomy of equilibrium versus disequilibrium approaches. *Real life* dynamics is probably the result of the interaction of adjustment and structural dynamics, of growth and development and fluctuations, and this interaction has to be tackled directly, if possible, once and for all. We have to accept the implied challenge: this attempt can be framed only in a highly disaggregated setting where the internal wiring of the economy is made explicit and enormous mathematical complications arise. These latter can be handled, if at all, only by a computational approach.

History is our other support in this enterprise, as we are told by Steven Durlauf and, of course, by the central figure in this conference, Robert Solow.

References

Besomi, D. 1999. *The Making of Harrod's Dynamics.* London: Macmillan.
———. 2001. Harrod's Dynamics and the Theory of Growth: The Story of a Mistaken Attribution. *Cambridge Journal of Economics* 25.1:79–96.
Domar, E. 1946. Capital Expansion, Rate of Growth, and Employment. *Econometrica* 14.2:137–47.
Durlauf, S. N. 2001. Manifesto for a Growth Econometrics. *Journal of Econometrics* 100:65–69.
Frisch, R. 1933. Propagation Problems and Impulse Problems in Dynamic Economics. In *Economic Essays in Honour of Gustav Cassel.* London: Allen and Unwin.

Goodwin, R. M. 1946. Innovations and the Irregularity of Economic Cycles. *Review of Economic Statistics* 28.2:95–104.

———. 1947. Dynamical Coupling with Especial Reference to Markets Having Production Lags. *Econometrica* 15.3:181–204.

———. 1950. A Non-linear Theory of the Cycle. *Review of Economics and Statistics* 32.4:316–20.

———. 1951a. Econometrics in Business Cycle Analysis. In *Business Cycles and National Income*, edited by A. H. Hansen. London: Allen and Unwin.

———. 1951b. The Non-Linear Accelerator and the Persistence of the Business Cycle. *Econometrica* 19.1:1–17.

———. 1953. The Problem of Trend and Cycle. *Yorkshire Bulletin of Economic and Social Research* 5.2.

———. 1955. A Model of Cyclical Growth. In *The Business Cycle in the Post War World*, edited by E. Lundberg. London: Macmillan.

———. 1982. *Essays in Economic Dynamics*. London: Macmillan.

———. 1985. A Personal Perspective on Mathematical Economics. *Banca Nazionale del Lavoro Quarterly Review* 152:3–13.

Hahn, F. H., and R. C. O. Matthews. 1964. The Theory of Economic Growth: A Survey. *Economic Journal* 74.296:779–902.

Hansen, A. H. 1937. Harrod on the Trade Cycle. *Quarterly Journal of Economics* 51.3:509–31.

Harrod, R. F. 1936. *An Essay on the Trade Cycle*. Oxford: Clarendon.

———. 1939. An Essay in Dynamic Theory. *Economic Journal* 49.193:14–33.

———. 1948. *Towards a Dynamic Economics*. London: Macmillan.

Hartley, J. E., K. D. Hoover, and K. D. Salyer. 1998. *Real Business Cycles: A Reader*. London: Routledge.

Hicks, J. R. 1950. *A Contribution to the Theory of the Trade Cycle*. Oxford: Clarendon.

———. 1965. *Capital and Growth*. Oxford: Clarendon.

Jolink, A. 1995. "Anecdotal Myths": Tinbergen's Influence on Harrod's Growth Theory. *European Journal of the History of Economics Theory* 2.2:434–49.

Kaldor, N. 1940. A Model of the Trade Cycle. *Economic Journal* 50.197:78–92.

———. 1954. The Relation of Economic Growth and Cyclical Fluctuations. *Economic Journal* 64.253:53–71.

Leontief, W. 1934. Verzögerte Angebotsanpassung und partielles Gleichgewicht. *Zeitschrift für Nationalökonomie*.

Louçã, F. 2004. Doctor Lucas and Foes. *HOPE* 36.4:689–734.

Mankiw, N. G. 1989. Real Business Cycle: A New Keynesian Perspective. *Journal of Economic Perspectives* 3.3:79–90.

Morgan, M. S. 1990. *The History of Econometric Ideas*. New York: Cambridge University Press.

Punzo, L. F. 1988. Harrodian Macrodynamics in Generalised Coordinates. In *Growth, Cycles, and Multisectoral Economics*, edited by R. Ricci and K. Velupillai. Heidelberg: Springer Verlag.

———. 2006. Towards a Disequilibrium Theory of Structural Dynamics: Goodwin's Contribution. *Structural Change and Economic Dynamics* 17.34:382–99.

Solow, R. 1956. A Contribution to the Theory of Economic Growth. *Quarterly Journal of Economics* 70.1:65–94.

———. 1988. Growth Theory and After. *American Economic Review* 78.3:307–17.

———. 1992. *Siena Lectures on Growth Theory.* Siena: University of Siena.

———. 1994. Perspectives on Growth Theory. *Journal of Economic Perspectives* 8.1:45–54.

Tinbergen, J. 1937. Review of Harrod, R. F. *The Trade Cycle. Weltwirtschaftliches Archiv* 45:89–91.

Weintraub, E. R. 1991. *Stabilizing Dynamics: Constructing Economic Knowledge.* New York: Cambridge University Press.

Young, W. 1989. *Harrod and His Trade Cycle Group: The Origins and Development of the Growth Research Programme.* London: Macmillan.

Trevor Swan and the Neoclassical Growth Model

Robert W. Dimand and Barbara J. Spencer

Addressing an American Economic Association session celebrating the fiftieth anniversary of his 1956 "Contribution to the Theory of Economic Growth," Robert Solow (2007, 3) issued a pointed reminder to his audience: "If you have been interested in growth theory for a while, you probably know that Trevor Swan—who was a splendid macroeconomist—also published a paper on growth theory in 1956. In that article, you can find the essentials of the basic neoclassical model of economic growth. Why did the version in my paper become the standard, and attract most of the attention?" The text of Solow's address was published in the *Oxford Review of Economic Policy* in a special issue: "The Solow Growth Model." The inattention that Trevor Swan's model has suffered is underscored not so much by the title of the special issue, or the title of the present volume (which also refers only to Solow), but by the striking fact that neither the editorial preface nor any of the other seven articles cite Trevor Swan.

Some prominent publications provide notable exceptions.[1] In particular, two leading textbooks, Barro and Sala-i-Martin 2004 and Aghion and Howitt 1998, both refer to the "Solow-Swan" model (and not the "Solow" model) in their index section with sixty-one and twelve citations, respectively. Both Solow 1956 and Swan 1956 are included in the references. David Romer's 2006 textbook is less generous to Swan, but he still

Barbara Spencer is Trevor Swan's daughter.
    1. We would like to thank Steve Dowrick and Robert Dixon for these exceptions.

History of Political Economy 41 (annual suppl.) DOI 10.1215/00182702-2009-019

manages to mention the Solow-Swan model and Swan 1956 in a foot-note (on page 7). In his introduction to the Penguin readings on growth economics, Amartya Sen (1970, 21, 30) refers to the Solow-Swan model and cites Swan 1956.[2] An indication of the relative prominence of Swan 1956 and Solow 1956 in the economic literature more generally is pro-vided by a cited-reference search of the ISI Web of Science. As of March 2009, 401 publications cite Swan 1956 and 1,718 cite Solow 1956. Publi-cations in the year 2000 or later represent 40 percent of Swan's citations (160 cites) and 46 percent of Solow's citations (798 cites). Apart from highlighting the current importance of growth theory, these numbers sug-gest that there has been only a small decline in the relative citation of Swan 1956 over time.

Swan's contribution initially won international academic recogni-tion. He was a visiting professor at MIT in 1958, Irving Fisher Professor at Yale in 1962–63, and Marshall Lecturer at Cambridge in 1963.[3] Swan 1956 was reprinted in Newman 1968, Williams and Huffnagle 1969, Stig-litz and Uzawa 1969, and, in part, Harcourt and Laing 1971. Nonetheless, and despite the generous efforts of Robert Solow himself (see, for instance, Solow 1997), Swan's work on growth theory has been overshadowed, at least outside Australia, by Solow's. Textbooks and classroom presenta-tions typically discuss the steady-state equilibrium path of the neoclassical growth model in terms of the capital-labor ratio, as in Solow 1956, rather than the output-capital ratio, as in Swan 1956.

Who was Trevor Swan, what was his contribution to neoclassical growth theory, and how did it come to be eclipsed? Section 1 discusses Swan's background and early work, including his initial work on a growth model in 1950. Section 2 examines why Solow 1956 and Swan 1956 are viewed as independent contributions. Section 3 describes the Swan growth dia-gram. Section 4 discusses why Swan's work, including his diagram, has received less attention. Section 5 contains concluding remarks.

1. Swan's Way

Born in Sydney in 1918, Trevor Swan was a part-time student at the Univer-sity of Sydney while working from 1936 to 1939 as a bank officer with the Rural Bank of New South Wales (see Butlin and Gregory 1989, Swan 2006,

2. Swan 1956 is referenced in two of the reprints in Sen 1970. Swan 1964 is reprinted, but does not reference Swan 1956 or Solow 1956.

3. Robert Solow gave the Marshall Lectures in the subsequent 1963–64 academic year.

and King 2007, 271–75 for biographical material, and Groenewegen and McFarlane 1990 for Australian economic thought). Despite the distraction of a full-time job, Swan received his bachelor of economics in 1940 with First Class Honours and with the University Medal and was appointed an assistant lecturer at the University of Sydney. At the age of only twenty-two, he immediately began publishing in the *Economic Record* on Australian war finance and banking policy (Swan 1940) and on the loanable funds–liquidity preference controversy over how the interest rate is determined (Swan 1941).

Wartime and postwar government service halted this promising early start on scholarly publication. From 1942, Swan was successively an economist in the Department of War Organization of Industry, secretary to the War Commitments Committee, chairman of the Food Priorities Committee, joint secretary of the Joint Administrative Planning Sub-Committee of the Defence Committee, chief economist of the Department of Post-War Reconstruction, and, from 1949, chief economist of the Department of the Prime Minister. Along the way, he was seconded to the UK Cabinet Office in 1947–48 (writing such memoranda as "Hicks on Budgetary Reform" and "The Theory of Suppressed Inflation," plus three appendixes to "United Kingdom National Income, Output and Employment") and to the U.S. Council of Economic Advisors in 1948–49 (where he wrote a series of memoranda on the supposed dollar shortage). He also accompanied Prime Minister Robert Menzies to London and Washington in 1950, negotiating a World Bank loan. As part of a group of experts appointed by the secretary-general of the United Nations, Swan helped write a 1951 report, "Measures for International Economic Security."

Despite this heavy workload of public service, Swan managed to find time to write substantial review articles for the *Economic Record* on Oskar Lange's Cowles monograph, *Price Flexibility and Employment* (Swan 1945, 1946), and on J. R. Hicks on the trade cycle (Swan 1950b). Even after leaving the Department of the Prime Minister in June 1950 to be the first holder of the chair in economics at the Australian National University's Research School of Social Sciences,[4] Swan served on the prime minister's Committee of Economic Advice in 1955 and 1956 (and on the Board of the Reserve Bank of Australia from 1975 to 1985). Certain distinctive characteristics of Swan's career are discernible: an economist fully engaged with cutting-edge macroeconomic theory but concerned about

4. See Cornish 2007 for details on the process of Swan's appointment.

relevance to public policy, deeply rooted in Australian public life and academic discourse (he never published in a journal outside Australia) yet fully aware of developments in Britain and America (and in developing countries, taking part in a World Bank mission to Malaya that published its report in 1955 and leading the MIT–Ford Foundation mission to assist India's five-year plan in 1958), and an economist who wrote more than he published.

In 1945, around the time of the Australian White Paper on Employment Policy, Swan wrote "The Principle of Effective Demand—a 'Real Life' Model" (published posthumously in 1989). This paper laid out the first macroeconomic model of the Australian economy. Characteristically, Swan opened his exploration of the inner workings of his Keynesian model with a quotation from Edgar Allan Poe's "Maelzel's Chess Player," beginning with, "The interior of the figure, as seen through these apertures, appears to be crowded with machinery." Solow (1997, 594–95) hails Swan's 1945 paper as "a truly remarkable, precocious and pioneering exercise in empirical Keynesianism. . . . Apart from the *General Theory*, Swan's guides are Lange's 1938 translation into equations, Kalecki's 1939 *Essays . . .* , Kaldor's 1940 model of the trade cycle and even Pigou's *Employment and Equilibrium*, but he puts them all to shame by virtue of the clarity of his thinking and his use of the macroeconomic data of the Australian economy, 1928–39, to give empirical substance to the analytical structure. . . . This combination of equilibrium thinking and sequence analysis is child's play now. For the time, its 26-year-old author is producing a virtuoso performance. The model works and Swan's commentary on it is very sophisticated."

Solow (1997, 594) regards the Keynesianism of Swan 1989 and the neoclassical growth model of Swan 1956 "as a reminder that one can be a Keynesian for the short run and a neoclassical for the long run, and this combination of commitments may be the right one." He reminds us that Swan (1956, 334) ended the opening paragraph of his neoclassical growth article by affirming, "When Keynes solved 'the great puzzle of Effective Demand,' he made it possible for economists once more to study the progress of society in long-run classical terms—with a clear conscience, 'safely ensconced in a Ricardian world.'" Without rejecting the short-run Keynesian concerns of his 1945 paper (Swan 1989), Swan (1956, 335) assumed that "effective demand is so regulated (*via* the rate of interest or otherwise) that all savings are profitably invested, productive capacity is fully utilized, and the level of employment can never be increased merely by raising the level of spending." Already in 1950, Swan (1950a) was prepared to assume full employment to analyze questions related to long-run growth. Also, in his policy advice in the early 1950s, Swan focused on problems of inflation and the balance of payments rather than unemployment, a concern illustrated by his opposition to import restrictions.[5]

While still chief economist in the Department of the Prime Minister, Swan (1950a) made his first venture into trying to reach some understanding of "the theory underlying any policy of economic development" with a sixteen-page memorandum titled "Size and Composition of Investment, and the Industrial Distribution of Labour in a Closed Progressive Economy." Swan (1950a, 1) writes, "It cannot of course be proved that it is vital to understand the fundamental principles of our current actions—it may be quite sufficient in practice (and it is certainly easier) to tackle symptoms in an empirical commonsense sort of way—but there can be no harm in doing both. So far as I know, practically nothing has been done so far in this branch of theory [economic development]. The mathematicians have, I suggest, done something incidentally to enquiries which overlap this field, but if so I cannot understand them. A mathematician should, obviously, do this, but as none seems to have tried yet—I look you straight in the eyes—it may, as a very second best, be worthwhile to make a first shot of it in prose, with all the muddles and inaccuracies that involves."

Although no formal mathematical model was written down, the discussion involved several formal assumptions, including "savings a constant proportion of income and unaffected by the rate of interest," "complete mobility of labour," "constant physical returns from land," "full employment," and "no inventions," which were all included, at least as initial simplifying assumptions, in Swan 1956. Setting savings equal to investment, Swan (1950a, 5) reasoned using a simple numerical example that if capital and population is increasing at the same rate, then "the population increase will wholly exhaust net investment," and capital and output per head will remain constant.[6] In this case, the "increment of consumption

5. Swan (1951, 2–3) writes, "If we bring about this reduction [in consumption and investment] by directly restricting the *supply* of imports (by imposing quotas etc. . . .), the inflationary pressure of internal demand will be revived and increased. Without the safety valve hitherto provided by supplies from overseas, the whole economy might then blow up." Later, Swan (1955, 2–3) writes: "Now they [import restrictions] imply acute problems of allocation, unofficial rationing, black-marketing, and some transitional unemployment for lack of materials."

6. The capital stock is assumed to start at four times national income, which with a savings and net investment rate of 10 percent implies an initial 2.5 percent growth rate of capital (Swan 1950a, 2, 5).

demanded is an increment in the existing 'average' consumption in proportion to the rate of population increase" (5), but most of the analysis is concerned with a more complicated, but policy relevant case, in which marginal consumption as real income rises is biased toward specific uses, such as housing. Swan was concerned with the implications for living standards of the high allocation of capital to housing implied by a high rate of immigration to Australia.

Consumption goods were divided into three categories: houses, produced with capital alone; manufactures, produced with current labor and capital (in the form of machinery); and services, produced with current labor alone. The capital used to produce housing and manufactures embodies past labor services. Capital and labor are substitutable in the production of manufactures.[7] However, given the difficulties of verbal analysis, it is not surprising that the general equilibrium effect of an increase in capital on relative factor prices and hence on the proportions of labor and capital in manufacturing is ignored.

In conclusion, Swan (1950a, 15) argues the approach in the paper "ought to provide a logical basis for analyzing the changes in industrial structure that we would wish to see today in Australia." If researchers could determine basic magnitudes, such as "the ratios of capital to income, the precise investment requirements of population increase . . . we would know what industries (assuming constant prices and perfect mobility) we would wish to expand and how much and what industries ought to contract" (Swan 1950a, 15–16). His specific conclusion is of less interest than the fact that as early as January 1950, while still chief economist in the prime minister's department, Swan was already experimenting with models of a growing economy with a given average (and marginal) propensity to save and mobile labor that is released into other sectors because of the substitution of capital for labor in manufacturing.

2. 1956 and All That

For those who knew Trevor Swan there is no doubt that he and Robert Solow each independently pioneered the neoclassical growth model. In

7. If the constant population desires only more manufactures, then all next investment is in machines, and "capital per head will rise steadily in manufactures, which will have constant current labor." If it is services that people desire marginally, then all net investment is in machinery for manufactures, but the increase in capital per head and output per head in manufactures "means that manpower must be released from manufactures" to the production of services (Swan 1950a, 4).

particular, from Arrow, Chenery, Minhas, and Solow 1961 onward, Solow has repeatedly cited Swan's contribution to the neoclassical growth model, always treating Swan 1956 as an independent contribution (e.g., Solow 1997, 2007). Solow 1956 was published in February and Swan 1956 was published in December, giving Solow priority in terms of date of publication.

Swan first presented his growth model in an interdisciplinary seminar at the Research School of Social Sciences at the Australian National University (ANU) in June or early July 1956, circulating postseminar notes on 23 July with the title "Economic Growth," which were published posthumously as Swan 2002. According to John Pitchford, who had Swan as his PhD supervisor at the time, the seminar's official purpose was to discuss W. Arthur Lewis's *Theory of Economic Growth* (1955). Pitchford (2002, 382) reports that Swan was "rumoured to be working on something of significance on growth" and was asked to discuss Lewis's material on capital. "However, Trevor's responses to such requests were not always conventional." Instead, the economic historian Noel Butlin reluctantly gave a talk on determinants of saving and investment, and estimates of average capital-output ratios. "When Butlin had finished speaking Swan stood up and, by way of comment on Butlin's talk, gave us a version of his economic growth model." James Meade, who was a visitor at the ANU from May to September 1956, pronounced that "what we had just heard from Swan was a significant and original advance on received growth theory."

When did Swan become aware of Solow 1956? Pitchford (2002, 383) states that there was no mention by Meade or Swan of Solow 1956 during the 1956 seminar, and "the presumption from this must be that both were unaware of this paper at the time of the seminar." This view of the seminar and the independence of Swan's work is supported by Butlin and Robert G. Gregory (1989, 373–74), who refer to the model as the "Swan-Solow" model and also point out that as late as 1970 the growth model was taught at Yale as simply the "Swan Model." The journal issue with Solow's article reached Canberra in April 1956 (Pitchford 2002, 383n), but from 1955 through to the 1956 seminar, Swan was acting as a main economic adviser and close confident of Prime Minister Menzies, so he could have easily missed it. With the positive response to his presentation, Swan would have been motivated to work further on his paper, which would naturally involve a check of the most recent literature. In postseminar notes, dated 23 July 1956, Swan (2002, 375n) mentions Solow 1956 in a footnote. Pitchford (2002, 383) recalls that these notes were produced some weeks after the seminar.

Solow became aware of Swan 1956 likely in March 1957. In a letter to Swan dated 1 April 1957, Solow writes, "I have just finished reading the article [Swan 1956] you so kindly sent me, and I must tell you that I can't remember when I have enjoyed a piece of economics so much. It was sheer pleasure."[8] Swan's visit to MIT in 1958 to lead the MIT–Ford Foundation mission to assist India's five-year plan must have been arranged soon after that letter. Although we know of no direct documentation, Solow's high opinion of Swan 1956 presumably influenced the invitation to Swan.

Although Solow and Swan each developed the essentials of what became known as the neoclassical growth model, their contributions were not identical. Indeed the very differences in their approaches help establish the independence of their contributions. There are a number of parallels in the history of the profession. Edward Chamberlin insisted that his monopolistic competition differed from Joan Robinson's imperfect competition (see the introductions and appendixes to any later edition of Chamberlin 1933). The pamphlets that Thomas Robert Malthus, Sir Edward West, and David Ricardo published in February 1815 about rent and the Corn Laws were not identical (Malthus stressed the intensive margin, Ricardo the extensive margin of cultivation). There were distinctions among the marginal utility theorists of the early 1870s—William Stanley Jevons, Carl Menger, and Léon Walras—as displayed by William Jaffé (1976). Evsey Domar (1946) had an exact counterpart to the warranted rate of growth of Roy Harrod (1939), but not to Harrod's natural rate of growth (Ahmad 1991, 87). Yet it is still meaningful to speak of the imperfect competition revolution of 1933, the classical theory of rent, the rise of marginalism in 1871–74, or Harrod-Domar growth theory.

The two pioneers of the neoclassical growth model, although finding much to admire in each other's contributions, did not completely endorse every aspect of each other's work: Solow (2007, 4) states that his 1956 article "didn't get lost in the complications and blind alleys that beset Trevor Swan's approach," while the first footnote of Swan's (2002, 375n) postseminar notes concludes: "Warning: Solow's article is in several respects misleading." Pitchford (2002, 385) explains that "'misleading' in this context is a matter of approach, one might even say of taste in that

---

8. Solow goes on to praise Swan's appendix, "Notes on Capital," and also states that he has two minor reservations about the first part of the paper, arising from the lack of generality of the Cobb-Douglas production function. We are indebted to Will Hansen at the Rare Book, Manuscript, and Special Collections Library at Duke University for this letter.

one's own expositional devices seem easier to work with, and of course did not imply that Swan thought Solow was wrong."[9] Barbara Spencer recalls that one concern of her father was that subsequent researchers might use Solow 1956 to derive naive empirical estimates that were misleading as to appropriate policy.[10] Swan (1956) also applied the term "misleading" to claims that Harrod's growth theory had a "knife-edge" equilibrium, and quoted Harrod (1948) on the progressive decline of the interest rate (and hence the marginal product of capital, as capital intensity rose) until the warranted growth rate equals the natural growth rate. Swan references Robinson (1956, 405) here, but not Solow, which suggests that he had written this material prior to reading Solow 1956.[11]

Harrod 1939 and Domar 1946 were interpreted by Solow (1956) and many others (but not by Swan 1956) as assuming fixed-coefficient production technologies that gave their models knife-edge equilibria (also referred to as "razor-edge" equilibria), with the implausible implication that any deviation at all from equilibrium would cause the model to diverge farther and farther away from equilibrium. One possible solution, proposed by Nicholas Kaldor (1955–56), was to allow the aggregate propensity to save to adjust by making it depend on the distribution of income between labor and capital. An alternative was to allow substitution between labor and capital, as Solow and Paul Samuelson (1953; Samuelson and Solow 1956) did for multisector growth models, and as Harold Pilvin (1953) did for a one-commodity model (see Ahmad 1991, 87–90).[12] By making production coefficients variable, Solow and Samuelson (1953) resolved

9. However, in an editorial comment at the end of their facsimile reprint of Solow 1956, Stiglitz and Uzawa (1969, 87) correct errors and typos in equations on pages 84, 85, 86, 87, 90.

10. Swan (1956) draws attention to real-world complexities such as the role of technical progress when there are diminishing returns because of a fixed supply of land or the interaction between investment and technical progress. Swan's concern that growth models do not capture enough of reality to provide direct prescriptions for growth is shown by his introduction to Swan 1964: "In this paper I intend to ask more questions than I can answer, and mainly to urge that economists need to consider very closely what it is that theories of economic growth are about, what questions they are trying to answer, if economic theory is not merely jejune mathematics."

11. Pitchford (2002, 383) mentions that prior to the seminar, Swan was reading Robinson 1956.

12. Ahmad (1990, 112 n. 20) reports, "In a recent personal communication, Professor Solow agrees that Pilvin's contribution (1953) deserves recognition, but . . . rightly draws our attention to the treatment of the non-steady-state path in his model (1956). The main difference is that Solow traces the path of capital intensity in the non-steady state, Pilvin the path of income." Solow (1956, 83) cites John Chipman's published comment on Pilvin 1953, but gives no indication of having read Pilvin 1953.

the problem that, with fixed coefficients, the multisector growth model of John von Neumann (1945–46) was overdetermined. Thus the original contribution of Solow (1956) and Swan (1956) was not the elimination of the Harrod-Domar knife-edge by making the output-capital and capital-labor ratios endogenous, because that had been done by Pilvin (1953) and Solow and Samuelson (1953). Rather, Solow and Swan created a simple, convenient, and powerful apparatus for finding the steady-state growth path of a one-commodity world. In addition, Swan demonstrates the importance of technical progress for long-run growth. Technical progress is considered by Solow, but Solow's fundamental contribution is not until Solow 1957.[13]

Rather than addressing the knife-edge problem, Swan 1956 could be viewed as trying to sort out the differences between classical and neoclassical approaches to growth. Swan considers the role of technical progress in a classical setting in which there are diminishing returns because of a fixed supply of a third factor, land. A main question is the rate of technical progress that is necessary to prevent population pressure from moving the economy to a Malthusian outcome. A higher savings rate (and a faster accumulation of capital) raises the growth rates at every point, but only temporarily interrupts the inevitable progress toward the stationary state determined by technical progress and the rate of growth of the labor supply. In the words of Solow (1997, 596),

> Swan notices that the model makes technical progress a powerful way of improving the standard of living and capital accumulation a disconcertingly weak reed. He looks for an answer to "this anti-accumulation, pro-technology line of argument" and mentions two possibilities. One is very classical: if higher output per head will induce faster growth of the labor force, then something like Arthur Lewis's unlimited supply of labor is present, and additional capital accumulation becomes much more powerful. His second idea is that "the rate of technical progress may not be independent of the rate of accumulation of capital, or . . . accumulation may give rise to external economies, so that the true social yield of capital is greater than any 'plausible' figure based on common private experience. This point would have appealed to Adam Smith, but it will not be pursued here." Of course that point is now being pursued by an army of economists.

13. Swan (1956) and Solow (1956) both assume "neutral" technical progress, but an error prevents Solow from showing that the capital-output ratio is constant in equilibrium (see Dixon 2003).

Growth Rates

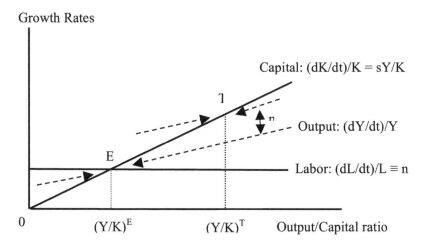

Figure 1 The Swan diagram

3. The Swan Diagram

At a fundamental level the growth models of Solow 1956 and Swan 1956 are the same. A main difference is expository: Solow's diagrams focus on the capital-labor ratio, whereas Swan's diagrams focus on the output-capital ratio and rates of growth. Figure 1 illustrates the basic Swan diagram with the output-capital ratio (denoted Y/K) on the horizontal axis and growth rates on the vertical axis.

In the simplest version of Swan 1956, the growth rate of labor, shown as $(dL/dt)/L \equiv n$ in figure 1, is exogenous and hence is represented by a horizontal line.[14] Since investment is equal to savings and saving is a fixed proportion, s, of income, it follows that $dK/dt = sY$. The rate of growth of capital, shown as $(dK/dt)/K = sY/K$ in figure 1, is simply a straight line through the origin with slope s. With constant returns to scale and no technical progress, the rate of growth of output, $(dY/dt)/Y$, is intermediate between (or equal to) the rates of growth of capital and labor as shown by the lower-level dotted arrows in figure 1.[15] Equilibrium is at E, where the

14. Swan later relaxes this assumption to consider the response of labor supply to changes in income.

15. For a Cobb-Douglas production function, $Y = K^\alpha L^\beta$ with $\alpha + \beta = 1$, Swan (1956) obtains $(dY/dt)/Y = \alpha sY/K + \beta n$. For a linearly homogeneous production function used by Swan (2002) in postseminar notes the equation is the same except that α and β are no longer constant (see Pitchford 2002, 385).

rates of growth of capital, labor, and output coincide. Anywhere to the left of point E, output is growing faster than capital, so Y/K rises toward $(Y/K)^E$. Anywhere to the right of E, output is growing more slowly than capital, so Y/K falls.

Exogenous technical progress at rate m shifts up the growth rate of output by m, leading to a new equilibrium at T in figure 1 with a higher output-capital ratio, $(Y/K)^T$. While Solow's diagram highlights the substitution between labor and capital, Dixon (2003) points out that the Swan diagram has the advantage of directly showing the effects of technical progress. For any given rate of technical progress, Y/K is constant in equilibrium, whereas the K/L ratio used by Solow needs to be redefined in efficiency units for it to remain constant.

4. Why the Solow Diagram Rather Than the Swan Diagram?

Any look at recent textbooks will show that the economics profession eventually adopted Solow's 1956 diagram for analyzing steady-state growth (for a given technology) in terms of the capital-labor ratio and his 1957 growth accounting equation (with technical progress measured as the "Solow residual"), rather than Swan's 1956 diagram. Why? Solow (2007, 3) cites "a collection of reasons of different kinds, none individually of very great importance."

The first reason cited by Solow is that "Swan worked entirely with the Cobb-Douglas function; but this was one of those cases where a more general assumption turned out to be simpler and more transparent" (3). Solow (1997, 596) also remarks that

> [Swan's] model works exclusively in Cobb-Douglas terms (mostly with constant returns to scale). This allows an exposition entirely in terms of growth rates. Although this formulation fits in well with the literature of the time, it obscures the general-equilibrium character of the model. Between them, the limited generality and the preoccupation with growth rates may account for the fact that Swan's mode of exposition did not catch on.

Swan's December 1956 *Economic Record* article did indeed use the convenient Cobb-Douglas production function (used decades before Charles Cobb and Paul Douglas by Knut Wicksell and familiar to Swan from Wicksell 1934, 1:274–99, a book he much admired). Solow (1956,

1957) based his main analysis on a general production function, although textbook exercises with the growth accounting equation of Solow 1957 often use Cobb-Douglas, the student's friend. But Swan's analysis was based on a general, constant returns to scale (linearly homogeneous) production function in his 1956 presentation of his growth model at the previously mentioned ANU seminar and in his 23 July 1956 postseminar notes. Pitchford (2002, 383) recalls that during the seminar, "Conrad Leser . . . made the suggestion that Swan should consider using the Cobb/Douglas production function to exposit his model."[16] Also, Geoffrey Sawer, a professor of law and then director of ANU's Research School of Social Sciences, commented that Swan's diagram would be clearer with percentage rates of growth instead of units of output on the vertical axis. The eventual publication of Swan's postseminar notes as Swan 2002 was much too late to alter the widespread identification of Swan's analysis with a specific functional form.

Swan was also involved in developing the constant elasticity of substitution production function, of which Cobb-Douglas (elasticity of substitution equal to one) and Leontief fixed-coefficients technology (zero elasticity of substitution) are special cases. Arrow et al. (1961, 143n) remark in a footnote, "We note that Trevor Swan has independently deduced the constant elasticity of substitution property of [their equation 11, the CES production function]. The function itself was used by Solow (1956, p. 77) as an illustration." They (Arrow et al. 1961, 154) also observe that Swan's doctoral student, Pitchford (1960),[17] "considers the introduction of a CES production function into a macroeconomic model of economic growth and concludes that at least in some cases this amendment restores to the saving rate some influence on the ultimate rate of growth." However, the literature generally overlooks these mentions of Swan and Pitchford (and of Solow 1956, 77), so that, for example, Ahmad (1991, 24) refers to "the general form of the constant elasticity of substitution production function, originally examined in some detail by Arrow, et al. (1961)."

16. Leser was an economist working at the Canberra University College, which in 1960 became the School of General Studies within the ANU.

17. Other Australian contributions to capital and growth theory in the wake of Swan 1956 include Pitchford and Hagger (1958) on the conditions for uniqueness of the internal rate of return and Warren Hogan (1958), who corrected a calculation error in Solow 1957. W. E. G. Salter (1959, 1960) published on embodied technical change and vintage capital, but this work arose from a 1955 Cambridge PhD dissertation predating Swan 1956 (see Swan's 1963 obituary of Salter).

Swan published his papers after long reflection, if at all: "Economic Control in a Dependent Economy" was presented in a seminar, "Social Control," on 30 June 1953 but not published until March 1960. His best-known paper outside growth theory, "Longer Run Problems of the Balance of Payments" (Swan [1963] 1968), was mimeographed and circulated in May 1955, eight years before publication. His 1945 paper, "The Principle of Effective Demand," appeared posthumously as Swan 1989. So until 2002 it appeared incorrectly (thanks to Swan's acceptance of Leser's suggestion about simplicity of exposition), that Swan's 1956 analysis of steady-stage growth was, unlike Solow's analysis, limited to the Cobb-Douglas functional form (notwithstanding the footnote in Arrow et al. 1961 acknowledging Swan's independent statement of CES).

Barbara Spencer believes that her father's reluctance to publish was mainly due to an extremely high standard that he set for his own work and to an inherent modesty as to the value of his academic contributions. For example, Swan (1956, 334, 342) claims very little with respect to the paper's contribution to the literature: "The aim of this paper is to illustrate with two diagrams a theme common to Adam Smith, Mill, and Lewis, the theory of which is perhaps best seen in Ricardo," and "the model used above differs from Harrod's model of economic growth only in that it systematizes the relations between the 'warranted' and 'natural' rates of growth, and introduces land as a fixed factor." In deciding on the contribution of economic analysis (whether theory or econometric estimation), Swan placed a huge weight on the importance of the work for economic policy in addition to requirements for originality and rigor. Swan 1964, "Growth Models: Of Golden Ages and Production Functions," prepared for the roundtable conference (1960) in Japan,[18] explains some of the inadequacies of growth models for practical development. It is also likely that Swan's interest in further contributions to the growth literature was reduced by the frustrations of dealing with bureaucracy while working on India's five-year plan in 1958.[19]

According to Solow (2007, 4): "A second and more substantial reason (for the adoption of Solow's approach) was that Swan saw himself as responding to Joan Robinson's complaints and strictures about capital and growth, while I was thinking more about finding a way to avoid the

18. We thank Aiko Ikeo for pointing out that the International Economic Association's roundtable conference held at Gamagori (near Nagoya) in April 1960 was the first international conference in economics held in Japan.
19. For the difficulties that Swan faced in India, see Rosen 1985.

implausibilities of the Harrod-Domar story." Some indication that Swan 1956 was regarded that way is provided by Geoffrey Harcourt in his introduction to Harcourt and Laing 1971, where he refers to the "model which Swan used in the famous article (1956) which preceded his even more famous appendix, the latter being designed to keep off 'the index number birds and Joan Robinson herself'" (12).[20] Only the appendix, "Notes on Capital," was reprinted in Harcourt and Laing 1971, not the main part of the article, placing Swan's appendix squarely in the context of the Cambridge capital controversies (on which, see Bliss, Cohen, and Harcourt 2005).

Swan's appendix defended those who, like Swan and Solow, used aggregate capital and an aggregate production function in their growth theorizing, against the criticism of Robinson (1954, 1956). Such a defense was the motivation for the appendix, not the motivation for the growth theory itself. There is only a brief mention of Robinson and the capital-theoretic issues she raised in Swan's (2002, 376) postseminar notes, which was the preliminary version of the main body of Swan 1956. Swan's growth model was certainly read by many separately from his appendix. For example, as pointed out by a referee, Mordecai Kurz (1963) extended Swan's growth model to a two-sector framework, and W. Max Corden (1971) based his extension of the neoclassical growth model to an open economy on the Swan diagram.

Solow (1955–56) also replied to Robinson in an article that attracted sufficient notice to be reprinted by Stiglitz and Uzawa 1969, with the opening salvo, "Mrs. Robinson was annoyed at many of the practices of academic economists. We have reason to be grateful for her annoyance, for she seems to have written her article [Robinson 1953–54] in the way that an oyster makes pearls—out of sheer irritation." The oyster making pearls out of sheer irritation is an image as striking and memorable as the scarecrow keeping away the index-number birds. To the extent that Swan 1956 lost attention as the Cambridge capital controversies lost the profession's interest, why did the same not apply to Solow 1956? Swan tacked on his response to Robinson as an appendix to his growth model, while Solow published his response separately as a comment in the same journal in which Robinson (1953–54) had appeared, the *Review of Economic Studies.*

---

20. Swan's appendix (1956, 343) opens with the following, "If we had to put up a scarecrow (as Joan Robinson calls it) to keep off the index-number birds and Joan Robinson herself, it would look something like this."

The difference is as much an accident as Swan's acceptance of Leser's suggestion of using a Cobb-Douglas production function for a more accessible exposition, but such accidents can matter in how a contribution is received by the profession.

Solow (2007, 4) suggested, "A third reason is that Swan was an Australian writing in the *Economic Record*, and I was an American writing in the *Quarterly Journal of Economics*." As a matter of course (and perhaps of patriotism), Swan published all his papers in Australia, and all but one (a 1986 book review) in the *Economic Record*—indeed, it was "known that Dick Downing (the then editor of the *Economic Record*) was supposed to be holding an issue of the *Economic Record* in anticipation of publishing Swan's [growth] model" (Pitchford 2002, 386). Swan 1956 was reprinted several times in North America (in Newman 1968, Williams and Huffnagle 1969, Stiglitz and Uzawa 1969), and in the years following its publication Swan was invited to visit MIT, Yale, and Cambridge. His work did not face any language barrier of the sort that delayed the discovery by anglophone economists that Maurice Allais (1947) had published the overlapping-generations model of money eleven years before Samuelson, the square-root rule for the transactions demand for money before Baumol and Tobin, and the golden rule of capital accumulation fifteen years before Edmund Phelps. Even so, economists, like other academics, can be parochial, and impact depends on place of publication. International communication was slower then: journals traveled to Australia by sea mail, with the February 1956 issue of the *Quarterly Journal of Economics* arriving at Canberra in April. Still, Canberra was not that isolated: indeed, as previously mentioned, Swan's seminar presentation in 1956 was attended by no less a luminary than James Meade.

5. Conclusion: Neoclassical Growth in the Antipodes

Trevor Swan (1956, 2002) independently developed the standard neoclassical growth model. Swan 1956 was published ten months after Solow 1956 but included a more complete analysis of technical progress, which Solow treated separately in Solow 1957. Solow's 1956 diagram highlights the substitution between labor and capital. By relating the output-capital ratio to rates of growth, Swan's diagram is able to directly illustrate the effects of variations in the rate of technical progress. But Swan's article was ultimately overshadowed by Solow's, partly because Solow's article appeared first, but also because of accidental factors. Comments by Leser on Swan's 1956 seminar presentation led Swan to adopt an exposition in terms of the Cobb-Douglas production function, even though his original version (not published until 2002) had a general functional form. Solow (1955–56) published his response to Robinson 1953–54 separately, as a comment in the same journal that had published Robinson's article, while Swan appended his response to Robinson to his article on the neoclassical growth model. Consequently, Swan 1956, but not Solow 1956, may have been perceived as an episode in the Cambridge capital controversies, of which the economics profession grew tired. The infrequency of Swan's subsequent publication also cost him attention and left him out of the later expansion of the literature on growth theory: Swan 1964 demonstrated that steady-state growth requires technical change to be Harrod-neutral, but his Fisher Lecture at Yale in 1962–63 and his Marshall Lecture at Cambridge in 1963 were not published and do not even survive among his papers. Information about his Giblin Lecture, "Structure and Stress," delivered to the Australian and New Zealand Association for the Advancement of Science (ANZAAS) in 1967 is limited to three pages of shorthand notes. Of his 1977 presidential address, "Population Growth and Economic Development" to section G of ANZAAS, all that exists in his papers are two pages of notes taken by Heinz Arndt. These factors let Swan 1956 be overshadowed, so that his mode of exposition did not catch on, but that cannot detract from the remarkable achievement that Solow (1997, 594) describes as "Swan's independent version of the standard neoclassical growth model."

References

Aghion, Philippe, and Peter Howitt. 1998. *Endogenous Growth Theory.* Cambridge: MIT Press.

Ahmad, Syed. 1991. *Capital in Economic Theory: Neo-Classical, Cambridge, and Chaos.* Aldershot, U.K.: Elgar.

Allais, Maurice. 1947. *Économie et intérêt.* Paris: Imprimerie National.

Arrow, Kenneth J., Hollis B. Chenery, B. S. Minhas, and Robert M. Solow. 1961. Capital-Labor Substitution and Economic Efficiency. *Review of Economics and Statistics* 43:225–48. Excerpted in Harcourt and Laing 1971.

Barro, Robert J., and Xavier Sala-i-Martin. 2004. *Economic Growth.* 2nd ed. Cambridge: MIT Press.

Bliss, Christopher, Avi Cohen, and Geoffrey C. Harcourt, eds. 2005. *Capital Theory.* 3 vols. Cheltenham, U.K.: Elgar.

Butlin, Noel G., and Robert G. Gregory. 1989. Trevor Winchester Swan, 1918–1989. *Economic Record* 65.4:369–77.

Chamberlin, Edward H. 1933. *The Theory of Monopolistic Competition.* Cambridge: Harvard University Press.

Corden, W. M. 1971. The Effects of Trade on the Rate of Growth. In *Trade, Balance of Payments, and Growth: Essays in Honour of Charles P. Kindleberger,* edited by Jagdish Bhagwati. Amsterdam: North-Holland.

Cornish, Selwyn. 2007. The Appointment of ANU's First Professor of Economics. *History of Economics Review* 46:1–18.

Dixon, Robert. 2003. Trevor Swan on Equilibrium Growth with Technological Progress. *Economic Record* 79.247:489–92.

Domar, Evsey D. 1946. Capital Expansion, Rate of Growth, and Employment. *Econometrica* 14.2:137–47.

Groenewegen, Peter, and Bruce McFarlane. 1990. *A History of Australian Economic Thought.* London: Routledge.

Harcourt, G. C., and N. F. Laing, eds. 1971. *Capital and Growth.* Harmondsworth, U.K.: Penguin.

Harrod, Roy F. 1939. An Essay in Dynamic Theory. *Economic Journal* 49.193:14–33.

———. 1948. *Towards a Dynamic Economics.* London: Macmillan.

Hogan, Warren P. 1958. Technical Progress and the Production Function. *Review of Economics and Statistics* 40:407–11.

Jaffé, William. 1976. Jevons, Menger, and Walras Dehomogenized. *Economic Inquiry* 14:511–24.

Kaldor, Nicholas. 1955–56. Alternative Theories of Distribution. *Review of Economic Studies* 23:83–100.

King, John E. 2007. Trevor Winchester Swan (1918–1989). In *A Biographical Dictionary of Australian and New Zealand Economists,* edited by J. E. King. Cheltenham, U.K.: Elgar.

Kurz, Mordecai. 1963. A Two-Sector Extension of Swan's Model of Economic Growth: The Case of No Technical Change. *International Economic Review* 4.1:68–79.

Lewis, W. Arthur. 1954. Economic Development with Unlimited Supplies of Labour. *Manchester School* 22.2:139–91.

———. 1955. *The Theory of Economic Growth.* London: Allen and Unwin.

Newman, Peter, ed. 1968. *Readings in Mathematical Economics.* Vol. 2 of *Capital and Growth.* Baltimore, Md.: Johns Hopkins University Press.

Pilvin, Harold. 1953. Full Capacity versus Full Employment Growth. *Quarterly Journal of Economics* 67:545–52.

Pitchford, John D. 1960. Growth and the Elasticity of Factor Substitution. *Economic Record* 36:491–500.

———. 2002. Trevor Swan's 1956 Economic Growth "Seminar" and Notes on Growth. *Economic Record* 78.243:381–87.

Pitchford, John D., and A. Hagger. 1958. A Note on the Marginal Efficiency of Capital. *Economic Journal* 68:597–600.

Robinson, Joan. 1954. The Production Function and the Theory of Capital. *Review of Economic Studies* 21.2:81–106.

———. 1956. *The Accumulation of Capital*. London: Macmillan.

Romer, David. 2006. *Advanced Macroeconomics*. 3rd ed. New York: McGraw-Hill.

Rosen, George. 1985. *Western Economists and Eastern Societies: Agents of Change in South Asia, 1950–1970*. Baltimore, Md.: Johns Hopkins University Press.

Salter, W. E. G. 1959. The Production Function and the Durability of Capital. *Economic Record* 35:47–66.

———. 1960. *Productivity and Technical Change*. Cambridge: Cambridge University Press.

Samuelson, Paul A., and Robert M. Solow. 1956. A Complete Capital Model Involving Heterogeneous Capital Goods. *Quarterly Journal of Economics* 70:537–62.

Sen, Amartya K., ed. 1970. *Growth Economics*. Harmondsworth, U.K.: Penguin.

Solow, Robert M. 1955–56. The Production Function and the Theory of Capital. *Review of Economic Studies* 23.2:101–8.

———. 1956. A Contribution to the Theory of Economic Growth. *Quarterly Journal of Economics* 70.1:65–94.

———. 1957. Technical Change and the Aggregate Production Function. *Review of Economics and Statistics* 39:312–20.

———. 1958. Reply to Hogan 1958. *Review of Economics and Statistics* 40:411–13.

———. 1997. Swan, Trevor W. In *An Encyclopedia of Keynesian Economics*, edited by Thomas Cate. Cheltenham, U.K.: Elgar.

———. 2007. The Last 50 Years in Growth Theory and Next 10. *Oxford Review of Economic Policy* 23.1:3–14.

Solow, Robert M., and Paul A. Samuelson. 1953. Balanced Growth under Constant Returns to Scale. *Econometrica* 21.3:412–24.

Stiglitz, Joseph, and Hirofumi Uzawa, eds. 1969. *Readings in the Modern Theory of Economic Growth*. Cambridge: MIT Press.

Swan, Peter L. 2006. Trevor Winchester Swan AO, ANU Inaugural Trevor Swan Distinguished Lecture, mimeo.

Swan, Trevor W. 1940. Australian War Finance and Banking Policy. *Economic Record* 16.30:50–67.

———. 1941. Some Notes on the Interest Controversy. *Economic Record* 17.33:153–66.

———. 1945. Price Flexibility and Employment. *Economic Record* 21.41:236–53.

———. 1946. Price Flexibility and Employment: Rejoinder. *Economic Record* 22:282–84.

———. 1950a. Size and Composition of Investment, and the Industrial Distribution of Labour in a Closed Progressive Economy. Unpublished manuscript, Canberra, 10 January.

———. 1950b. Progress Report on the Trade Cycle. *Economic Record* 26.51:186–200.

———. 1951. Seminar on Social Control. Unpublished notes, November.

———. 1955. Why Economists Don't Know. Unpublished partial summary of a public lecture by T. W. Swan, 14 September.

———. 1956. Economic Growth and Capital Accumulation. *Economic Record* 32.63:334–61.

———. 1960. Economic Control in a Dependent Economy. *Economic Record* 36.73:51–66.

———. 1962. Circular Causation. *Economic Record* 38:421–26.

———. 1963. Obituary: Wilfred Edward Graham Salter, 1929–1963. *Economic Record* 39.88:486–87.

———. 1964. Growth Models: Of Golden Ages and Production Functions. In *Economic Development with Special Reference to South East Asia*, edited by K. Berrill. London: Macmillan for the International Economic Association.

———. [1963] 1968. Longer-Run Problems of the Balance of Payments. In *The Australian Economy*, edited by H. W. Arndt and W. Max Corden. Sydney: Cheshire. Reprinted in *Readings in International Economics*, edited by Richard E. Caves and Harry G. Johnson. Homewood, Ill.: Irwin for the American Economic Association.

———. 1989. The Principle of Effective Demand—a "Real Life" Model. *Economic Record* 65:378–98.

———. 2002. Economic Growth. *Economic Record* 78.243:375–80.

Von Neumann, John. 1945–46. A Model of General Economic Equilibrium, translated by G. Morton. *Review of Economic Studies* 13.1:1–9.

Wicksell, Knut. 1934. *Lectures on Political Economy*. 2 vols. London: Routledge.

Williams, Harold R., and John D. Huffnagle, eds. 1969. *Macroeconomic Theory: Selected Readings*. Englewood Cliffs, N.J.: Prentice-Hall.

Dynamizing Stability

Marcel Boumans

> I can not tell you why I thought first about replacing
> the constant capital-output (and labor-output) ratio by a
> richer and more realistic representation of the technology.
> —Robert Solow, "Growth Theory and After" (1988)

This article aims to show the mathematical context out of which Robert Solow's 1957 article, "Technical Change and the Aggregate Production Function," emerged. In particular, it aims to provide some understanding of its (to me) most striking feature, namely, the highly aggregate level on which technical change is discussed and the simple way in which it is represented:

> If Q represents output and K and L represent capital and labor inputs in "physical" units, then the aggregate production function can be written as:
>
> $$Q = F(K, L; t). \tag{1}$$
>
> The variable t for time appears in F to allow for technical change. . . .
> It is convenient to begin with the special case of *neutral* technical change. . . . In that case the production function takes the special form
>
> $$Q = A(t)f(K, L) \tag{1a}$$
>
> and the multiplicative factor $A(t)$ measures the cumulated effect of shifts over time. (Solow 1957, 312)

History of Political Economy 41 (annual suppl.) DOI 10.1215/00182702-2009-020

One should, for example, compare this simple presentation with Herbert Simon's (1951) account of technological change, which is very much on a disaggregate level.[1] It is even more striking when one realizes that Solow was a student of Wassily Leontief, the designer and builder of large and detailed input-output tables.[2] It seems that Solow himself did not take this high level of aggregation for granted, as witnessed by the opening lines of his 1957 article:

> In this day of rationally designed econometric studies and super-input-output tables, it takes something more than the usual "willing suspension of disbelief" to talk seriously of the aggregate production function. (312)[3]

A crucial part of the explanation for Solow's aggregate approach to technical change can simply be captured by one name: Paul Samuelson.

> M.I.T. hired me primarily to teach courses in statistics and econometrics. In the beginning I fully intended to make my career along those lines. It did not turn out that way, probably for a geographical reason. I was given the office next to Paul Samuelson's. Thus began what is now almost 40 years of almost daily conversations about economics, politics, our children, cabbages and kings. This has been an immeasurably important part of my professional life. (Solow 1987)

The approach in the present article is similar to E. Roy Weintraub's (1991) mathematical contextualization of Samuelson's *Foundations of Economic Analysis* (1947), but it will develop the mathematical contexts in which Solow's 1957 article can be located. As I will show, Samuelson's concepts of stability provided Solow the tools for the aggregation of technical change. However, Samuelson's concepts were defined in relation to

1. In his review of *Activity Analysis* (Koopmans 1951), in which Simon 1951 appeared, Solow (1952c), remarkably, does not spend one line on Simon's contribution.

2. See, for example, his autobiography, written when he received the Nobel Prize: "Upon returning to Harvard in 1945, . . . I chose, almost casually, to go on with economics. By a piece of good luck, Wassily Leontief became my teacher, guide and friend. I learned from him the spirit as well as the substance of modern economic theory. He was responsible for my introduction to empirical work: as his research assistant I produced the first set of capital-coefficients for the input-output model" (Solow 1987). In the "Technical Change" article, besides William Fellner and Theodore Schultz, Leontief is thanked for his "stimulating suggestions."

3. This ambivalence was reaffirmed in his Nobel Prize lecture: "The first few paragraphs of my 1957 article are thoroughly ambivalent, not about the method but about the use of aggregate data on inputs and output. After expressing my doubts I went ahead in a pragmatic spirit" (Solow 1988, 313).

static equilibrium and not to growth. To arrive at his 1957 representation of technical change, Solow successfully applied P. H. Leslie's concepts and tools of population mathematics.

The main mathematical concepts around which this development of a static type of stability to a dynamic type is described are *eigenvalue* and *eigenvector*. It is by the use of these two concepts that "aggregation" of input-output tables was made feasible. For a square and nonsingular matrix a, a unique solution of the equation $ax = b$ exists for any arbitrary b.[4] Equations of this form arise frequently when analyzing the static behavior of economic systems and often represent the response of a system to a particular set of stimuli embodied in the vector b. If, however, we wish to investigate the dynamic behavior of such systems, it is more comprehensible to use the eigenvalues of matrix a, that is, those values of a scalar λ for which $| a - \lambda I | = 0$. Connected to these eigenvalues are the eigenvectors. These are the non-null vectors ψ such that $(a - \lambda I)\psi = 0$. These eigenvalues λ and associated eigenvectors ψ represent the innate properties of the system a under investigation and as such are independent of applied stimuli. This feature makes the scalars λ most appropriate to describe the aggregate characteristics of a matrix, like its stability. This is in marked contrast to the use of the solution of the related set of linear equations $ax = b$ to describe the key properties of a.

The first section gives an exposition of Samuelson's definitions of stability as presented in his *Foundations of Economic Analysis*. Solow applied this framework to show that the existence of a meaningful static equilibrium is equivalent to the stability of a dynamic system. He showed this connection by a clever use of eigenvalues and eigenvectors. However, this concept of stability, defined in terms of a static equilibrium position, was not very helpful to assess whether a growth path is stable or not. Section 2 shows that Solow and Samuelson arrived at such a stability concept for growth by applying the mathematics of population growth used in ecology. In this kind of mathematics, stability is defined in terms of eigenvectors and growth in terms of eigenvalues. Solow and Samuelson used this concept of stability to define balanced growth, that is, when an economy changes only in scale (defined by the eigenvalues), but not in composition (defined by the eigenvectors). The applications of this mathematics of eigenvalues showed that for the discussion of the characteristics of a dynamic system one does not need to take the whole matrix into account,

---

4. A square matrix a is called nonsingular if $| a | \neq 0$.

but one could restrict oneself to a limited number of scalars. Section 3 shows that from this perspective, according to Solow, there is not so much difference in structure between Leontief's input-output tables and Harrod's and Domar's dynamic models. Technology, originally represented by the input-output matrix, can now be "aggregated" by its eigenvalues. The fourth section shows that, as a result, shifts in technology can easily be represented by increases of this scale factor, leaving the input proportions unchanged. These shifts were called neutral technical changes. Section 5 discusses the similarity between Solow's approach and Jan Tinbergen's work on trends in the early 1940s.

1. Samuelson's Concepts of Stability

Samuelson's view on mathematics is made quite explicit by the epigraph at the beginning of his *Foundations of Economic Analysis*:

> "Mathematics is a Language."—J. Willard Gibbs

To be accurately used, a language needs a dictionary, and so the foundations of the mathematical analysis of economics are laid down by the definitions of the key concepts for this analysis. One key concept, which will appear at the center of this history, is stability. Part 2 of *Foundations* is actually an elaborate treatment of stability, where different kinds of stability were defined. This treatment was the starting point of Solow's early work on equilibrium systems.

The main concept of his account on stability was that of "perfect stability of the first kind," which Samuelson (1947, 261) defined as follows:

> The equilibrium position possesses *perfect stability of the first kind* if from any initial conditions all the variables approach their equilibrium values in the limit as time becomes infinite; i.e., if
>
> $$\lim_{t \to \infty} x_i\,(t) = x_i^0,$$
>
> regardless of the initial conditions.

In other words, an equilibrium is stable (of the first kind) if a displacement from equilibrium is followed by a return to equilibrium. Stability of the first kind is called stability of the first kind *in the small* if for sufficiently small displacements the equilibrium is stable. Another kind of stability, *stability of the second kind*, which is of no further interest here, appears when a system oscillates endlessly around the position of a stable equilibrium.

Foundations also provided sufficient conditions for stability of equilibrium systems. Conditions were given for several types of systems of equations: linear and nonlinear, differential and difference equations. For the subject of the present article, we need only to have a closer look at systems of linear difference equations in n variables:

$$x(t + 1) = ax(t),$$

where $x(t)$ is a vector of n variables, and a an $n \times n$ matrix, representing the dynamic system. These conditions are given in terms of the "latent roots" of a. Latent roots λ_i ($i = 1, \ldots, n$) are defined as the roots of the characteristic equation $| a - \lambda I | = 0$. In other words, *latent root* is a synonym for *eigenvalue*; see above.[5] The system will be said to have first-order stability if $|\lambda_i| < 1$ ($i = 1, \ldots, n$), since this will imply damped motion (exponential or harmonic). Then, the following theorem could be derived:

> For a difference-equation system first-order stability is a sufficient condition for stability in the small, and the absence of first-order instability is a necessary condition. (Samuelson 1947, 308)

One of Solow's first papers, "On the Structure of Linear Models" (1952b), can be considered as an application (or extension, if you like) of Samuelson's stability framework to linear systems.[6] The paper studies the relationship between the existence of economically meaningful solutions in the static case and the stability of the dynamic version. The general structure of the static case is

$$(I - a)x = b, \tag{1}$$

where a and x are as defined above, I the identity matrix, and b a vector of n components. This static case can be considered as the static solution of the dynamic system

$$x(t + 1) - ax(t) = b \tag{2}$$

and is obtained by putting $x(t + 1) = x(t) = x$. One of the considered linear models is an open-end Leontief system. For these kinds of systems, it is assumed that a is a nonnegative matrix.

5. The terminology throughout the literature discussed here is not stable: another synonym for *eigenvalue* besides *latent root* is *characteristic root* (see below).
6. His indebtedness to Samuelson was emphasized by a footnote: "My interest in these problems was stimulated by reading an unpublished paper by Professor Paul A. Samuelson. It would be impossible for me to note in the text every point that is actually the joint product of innumerable conversations with him; there are many such" (Solow 1952a, 29).

The close relationship between the solution of the static case (1), which is

$$x = (I - a)^{-1}b, \tag{3}$$

and the stability of the dynamic case (2) can be easily seen from the solution of the latter case, which can, by iteration, be represented as

$$x(t) = a^t x(0) + (I + a + a^2 + \ldots + a^{t-1})b.$$

This solution will converge to the stationary solution (3) if and only if all the latent roots (characteristic roots, as called by Solow) of the matrix a are less than one in modulus ($|\lambda_i| < 1$), in which case the infinite series $I + a + a^2 + \ldots$ converges to the matrix $(I - a)^{-1}$ and a^t tends to the null matrix. If this is so, clearly all components of the equilibrium output vector $x = x(\infty)$ will be nonnegative. From results already obtained by Lloyd Metzler (1950) and David Hawkins and Herbert A. Simon (1949), it follows that for a nonnegative matrix a, $(I - a)^{-1}$ will have no negative elements if and only if all the characteristic roots of a are less than one in modulus. Hence the stability of the dynamic system (2) and the existence of a meaningful solution of the static case are interconnected.

The innovative contribution of Solow's paper to investigating the relationship between the existence of an equilibrium and the stability of a dynamic system is that Solow applied efficiently the mathematics of eigenvalues and eigenvectors, instead of the more laborious application of principal minors,[7] as Metzler and Hawkins and Simon did.[8] To do so, Solow first needed to introduce the idea of decomposable systems. The definition was taken from the theory of Markov chains (Solow 1952b, 33). Before this definition is introduced, it is of interest to note that this combination of the mathematics of eigenvalues and eigenvectors and the concept of decomposability were also the basic tools of Simon's later work on complexity, which was first elaborated in his 1961 "Aggregation of Vari-

---

7. A principal minor of a matrix a is a square submatrix of a, which is obtained by deleting certain rows and the same numbered columns of a.

8. This was, however, not the first publication in which the dynamics of a system was explored by applying the mathematics of eigenvalues and eigenvectors. Richard M. Goodwin, another Harvard colleague, published two papers (Goodwin 1949, 1950) on whether the multiplier mechanism represented by a matrix would give rise to oscillations. Remarkably, for the central result of the first paper, namely, that a matrix multiplier mechanism does exhibit oscillations, Goodwin (1949, 550) acknowledges Solow: "I am indebted to Mr. Robert Solow for receiving this remarkable result." In his second (1950) paper, he referred to a publication of Frobenius, from which he took a theorem today better known as the Perron-Frobenius theorem.

ables in Dynamic Systems" and was actually an account of how to simplify large Walrasian systems (see Boumans 2001).

Consider a nonnegative $n \times n$ matrix, $a = [a_{ij}]$. A collection of indices selected from $1, 2, \ldots, n$ will be called a closed set if $a_{pq} = 0$ for any q in the set and any p not in the set. The matrix is said to be indecomposable if there is no closed set other than the set of all indices $1, 2, \ldots, n$. Otherwise a is decomposable. A decomposable matrix can be partitioned (after renumbering) in the form

$$a = \begin{bmatrix} A_1 & R & \ldots & S \\ 0 & A_2 & \ldots & T \\ \ldots & \ldots & \ldots & \ldots \\ 0 & 0 & \ldots & A_m \end{bmatrix}.$$

For indecomposable matrices, Solow (1952b, 36) derived the following "theorem":

> If a is a nonnegative, indecomposable matrix none of whose column sums is greater than one, and at least one of whose column sums is less than one, then all the characteristic roots of a have a modulus less than one.

Or, in other words, these systems have "perfect stability" (37).

One result of this approach is that one can discuss the properties of a linear complex system in a much more simplified way. The paper shows that the conditions for properties like stability or nonnegativity "depend in only a simple way on the numerical values of the a_{ij} input coefficients," namely, "a good deal depends on the row- or column sums of a" (41). Moreover, the properties of being decomposable or not are "topological" in nature. "Indecomposability in particular is essentially a property of connectedness." These properties "can be investigated with no knowledge of the values of the a_{ij} other than which ones are zero and which are not" (41).[9]

2. Balanced Growth

Samuelson's concept of stability was defined and applied with respect to static equilibrium systems, and gave no clue how to expand this concept to

---

9. In his early work on causality, Simon (1953) showed that the causal ordering and identifiability are "topological properties" in the same sense: it only matters whether the values of a_{ij} are zero or not. Instead of "indecomposable matrix," however, Simon used "self-contained structure."

make it applicable to growth models. However, in the same period in which Solow (in close cooperation with Samuelson) worked on stability of equilibrium systems, he also developed, again with Samuelson, ideas about stability properties of growth systems. These properties appeared, however, under a different label: balanced growth. To show that the idea of balanced growth is in fact a stability concept, we first have to discuss a classic article in population statistics, written by P. H. Leslie.[10] This article formed the main context for the development of this new concept of stability.

In 1945 Leslie published "On the Use of Matrices in Certain Population Mathematics," on a discrete and age-structured matrix of population growth, which became very popular in population ecology and is today named after him: the Leslie matrix. The matrix describes the growth of populations and their projected age distributions, in which a population is closed to migration and where only one sex, female, is considered. For the present discussion, however, it is not the matrix that is of interest but its "use."

To simplify the discussion of the dynamics of age distributions, Leslie (1945, 191) introduced the concept of a "stable vector": ψ is a stable vector appropriate to a matrix a if

$$a\psi = \lambda\psi,$$

where λ is an algebraic number. In fact, the scalars for which a "stable ψ" can be found are the latent roots of a.[11] Thereupon, Leslie discussed the properties of the stable vectors for the simple case that

$$a_L = \begin{bmatrix} A & B & C & D \\ 1 & 0 & 0 & 0 \\ 0 & 1 & 0 & 0 \\ 0 & 0 & 1 & 0 \end{bmatrix},$$

which is a generalization of his population matrix. For this matrix, Leslie showed that only one of the latent roots will be real and positive, and the modulus of this root (λ_1) is greater than any of the others,

$$|\lambda_1| > |\lambda_2| > |\lambda_3| > \ldots,$$

10. P. H. ("George") Leslie was a staff member at the Bureau of Animal Population, Oxford University, from 1935 to 1967. He died in 1972. "Leslie had graduated in physiology and had been prevented from completing a medical degree by illness. He began by working on *Salmonella*, which was being considered as a causal factor in rodent cycles, but soon his remarkable flair for mathematics came to be realized, and at age thirty-five he began his career in statistical theory and population dynamics" (Crowcroft 1991, 18).

11. In the literature whenever the latent roots are called eigenvalues, these "stable vectors" are better known as eigenvectors; see also footnote 5.

thus the remaining roots being either negative or complex. This dominant latent root λ_1, which will be $>$, $=$, < 1, according to whether the sum of the elements in the first row of a_L is $>$, $=$, < 1, is the one that is principally of interest. Since it is real and positive, it is the only root that will give rise to a stable vector consisting of real and positive elements. It is this stable ψ_1 associated with the dominant root λ_1 that is ordinarily referred to as the stable age distribution appropriate to the given age-specific rates of fertility and mortality. If at a given moment a transformed population has an arbitrary age distribution x, and the sequence $a_L x$, $a_L^2 x$, $\ldots$, $a_L^t x$ is formed, it can be shown that when t is large, we have approximately

$$a_L^t x = c\lambda_1^t \psi_1,$$

where c is an arbitrary constant. Thus a population with any arbitrary age distribution tends ultimately to approach the stable form appropriate to the given rates of fertility and mortality, provided that these age-specific rates remain constant.

As I show below, in "Balanced Growth under Constant Returns to Scale" (Solow and Samuelson 1953), it is this use of stable vectors that changed the focus of where stability should be located. Solow read an earlier version of this paper at the Santa Monica meeting of the Econometric Society in August 1951. To my knowledge, the first published introduction of the idea of balanced growth appeared in the abstract of that paper: "Balanced growth is defined as proportionate increase or decrease of all outputs, with the relative composition remaining unchanged" (Solow 1952a, 87). The paper was published the year after, in which a more elaborate definition was given:

> By balanced growth (or decay) we mean a state of affairs in which the output of each commodity increases (or decreases) by a constant percentage per unit of time, the mutual proportions in which commodities are produced remaining constant. The economy changes only in scale, but not in composition. (Solow and Samuelson 1953, 412)

The usual assumption of fixed proportions was replaced by a more general one that the production functions are homogeneous of first degree.[12] Thus the production functions retain constant returns to scale, but permit continuous substitution of inputs. Moreover, the system was presented as a

---

12. A function $f(x)$ is homogeneous of first degree if $f(\alpha x) = \alpha f(x)$, where x is a vector. In economics, this feature is called constant returns to scale.

more general system of production functions H^i, which need not necessarily be linear ($i = 1, \ldots, n$):

$$x_i(t + 1) = H^i[x_1(t), x_2(t), \ldots, x_n(t)], \tag{4}$$

where $x_i(t)$ is the output of the ith commodity in period t, and H^i is homogeneous of first degree.

When Solow and Samuelson presented this system, the link with Leslie's work was made explicit: they referred to his work but also gave the above system an interpretation of population age distributions:

> This is not the only interpretation which can be given to the fundamental difference equations [4]. Another possibility is to think of $x_i(t)$ as the size of a population in the ith age (or other) group. The increasing functions H^i would then represent combined fertility-mortality schedules.[13] (Solow and Samuelson 1953, 413–14)

Balanced growth has been defined to mean $x_i(t + 1) = \lambda x_i(t)$ for each i and for some positive constant λ. This in turn implies, by iteration, that

$$x_i(t) = x\lambda^t V_i, \tag{5}$$

and since the $x_i(t)$ have to be positive, one must be able to choose the x, $V_1, \ldots, V_n$ all positive. Inserting (5) in (4) and using the homogeneity of H^i gives

$$\lambda V_i = H^i(V_1, \ldots, V_n). \tag{6}$$

The constant x is adjusted to ensure that

$$\sum_{j=1}^{n} V_j = 1.$$

Thus finding a balanced growth solution (5) to the difference equations is reduced to solving the "eigenvector problem" (6) with positive λ, $V_1, \ldots$, V_n. This will determine the eigenvector $V^* = (V_1{}^*, V_2{}^*, \ldots V_n{}^*)$, the proportions in which output may grow or decay steadily.

In the subsequent sections of their paper, Solow and Samuelson proved the existence of a balanced growth path (using Brouwer's fixed-point theorem), the uniqueness of this growth rate, and the uniqueness of the proportions. So, in the case of constant returns to scale, the dynamics of the entire structure of the system is fully characterized by the factor λ.

---

13. A lowercase x replaces the original uppercase X to make the discussion of the literature uniform.

Our result so far is that under the assumption of strict monotonicity of the functions H^i, there is only one possible rate of geometric growth or decay, and only one composition of output capable of growth or decay at this constant geometric rate. This uniqueness of the magnification factor λ means, disregarding the razor's edge of a stationary system, that a system is capable either of balanced growth or of balanced decay but never of both. (Solow and Samuelson 1953, 417)

The remaining sections discuss another "important circle of questions," namely, the stability of the balanced growth solution. From Samuelson's *Foundations*, one already knew that a sufficient condition for "stability in the small" of the solution (5) is that all characteristic roots of $J'J$ be less than one, where J is the Jacobian matrix of system $H : J = [\partial H^i(V)/\partial V_j]$; see appendix 1. However, this condition for stability was "not much of an advance":

Smallness of the characteristic roots of $J'J$ will tend to be associated with smallness of the roots of J, and therefore . . . with balanced decay. Hence the case of balanced growth cannot be fruitfully handled by the above condition. (Solow and Samuelson 1953, 418)

To clarify that this kind of stability was not the one that would be helpful to understand balanced growth, again a reference was made to Leslie's article on population mathematics:

This is especially clear if, as suggested earlier, we think of $x_i(t)$ as being the size of a population in the ith age group. Now suppose one mother had been subtracted from the population many generations ago. If the population is expanding geometrically in the Malthusian manner, the number of potential descendants would also be increasing approximately geometrically. The loss in potential population attributable to the past disturbance would be increasing, not decreasing. The steady-growth solution cannot be stable in the absolute sense that changes in initial conditions have effects ultimately damping to zero. (418–19)

What they showed instead was that the system (4) has *relative stability in the large*, that is, "from any arbitrary positive initial conditions, the equations [4] eventually generate steady growth in the unique proportions V^* and rate λ" (419).

What we might expect, however, is that the equilibrium *relative* age distribution might tend to reestablish itself; that the population might tend to resume its geometrical expansion at the rate λ. In our notation, we might expect that the proportions $V_1^*: V_2^*: \ldots V_n^*$ will be asymptotically regained and the system will asymptotically again expand at the rate λ, as a result of some initial conditions other than the original ones. (419)

In mathematical terms, they showed that

$$\lim_{t \to \infty} \frac{x_i}{\lambda^t V_i^*} = \text{constant} = x,$$

where x is a constant depending on the initial conditions or last arbitrary displacement, but independent of i; see equation (5).

3. Leontief = Harrod = Domar

Before I explore the last step of arriving at aggregate neutral technical change, I first have to identify Leontief's input-output system with Harrod's and Domar's dynamic models. This connection was, conveniently, made explicit by Solow himself in "A Note on the Price Level and Interest Rate in a Growth Model" (1953–54), using the following dynamic version of Leontief's system:

$$(I - a)x_t = b(x_t - x_{t-1}). \tag{7}$$

By presenting it in this way, the identification was easily made:

> Now banish the thought that a and b are matrices and x_t is a vector and think of these quantities as ordinary numbers. Then equation [7] looks suspiciously like Mr. Harrod's system. In fact, deep down, it *is* Mr. Harrod's system. (Solow 1953–54, 74)

In a footnote to this remark, Solow made the connection with Domar's work:

> The same kind of theoretical system was formulated quite explicitly by Evsey Domar in "Capital Expansion, Rate of Growth, and Employment," *Econometrica*, April, 1946, p. 137, and subsequent papers, where the treatment is even more clear-cut than Harrod's. I refer to Harrod instead only because I here follow Harrod in the use of discrete time periods. (74)

To settle the comparison, Solow gave the following interpretations of the variables: x is a measure of real output or income. The coefficient b measures the quantity of real commodities needed as capital per unit of current output; it is an acceleration coefficient, both in the Leontief and Harrod formulations. The interpretation of a was a little bit more complicated. In the input-output model a represents current input requirements per unit of output, a technological datum. In the Harrod model a would be the average propensity to consume and $1 - a$ the savings ratio.

> But a man from Mars observing a Harrod economy in operation, and ignorant of the social organization underlying it, would see only that a fraction a of each period's output was always consumed. It would look to him quite as if the consumption of ax were *required* for the production of the remaining $(1 - a)x$ of output, perhaps as subsistence for the population. (74)

If consumption plans are always realized so that a constant fraction of output produced is consumed, it is as if we were to regard the saved-invested portion of output as being produced from consumption and the services of capital. "The two interpretations of the coefficient a collapse into one" (74).

Solow also mentioned another aspect with respect to the identification of Leontief's and Harrod's dynamic models. They both were only representations of equilibrium systems: "Neither model has anything to say about the actual time-path that will be followed by any economic system starting from arbitrary initial conditions. Neither model contemplates in any detail the possibility or consequences of a disequilibrium situation" (75). Harrod did, of course, discuss the consequences of departure from an equilibrium path, but he did not provide an "explicit causal dynamics" (75).

As is well known, Solow provided this causal dynamics in his Nobel Prize–winning article, "A Contribution to the Theory of Economic Growth" (1956). This growth model departs from the Harrod and Domar kind of models by releasing the assumption that production takes place under conditions of fixed proportions, the assumption that was responsible for the "knife-edge notion of unstable balance." The paper shows that, with constant returns to scale, "whatever the initial value of the capital-labor ratio, the system will develop *toward* a state of balanced growth at the natural rate" (Solow 1956, 70).

4. Neutral Technical Change

Solow's 1956 growth model does not incorporate technological change. Technological possibilities are represented by the production function

$F(K, L)$, which does not allow the representation of changes of technology. The first proposed extension to this model, discussed at the end of the article, however, was to incorporate "neutral technological change": "Perfectly arbitrary changes over time in the production function can be contemplated in principle, but are hardly likely to lead to systematic conclusions. An especially easy kind of technological change is that which simply multiplies the production function by an increasing scale factor" (Solow 1956, 85). In other words, production function $F(K, L)$ was altered to read $A(t)F(K, L)$.

This altered production function was the theoretical basis of his 1957 paper on technical change. The term *technical change* was meant as "a shorthand expression for *any kind of shift* in the production function. Thus slowdowns, speedups, improvements in the education of the labor force, and all sorts of things will appear as 'technical change'" (Solow 1957, 312). Shifts in the production function are defined as neutral if they leave marginal rates of substitution untouched but simply increase or decrease the output attainable from given inputs: "I have defined neutrality to mean that the shifts were pure scale changes, leaving marginal rates of substitution unchanged at given capital/labor ratios" (316).

For the general case when the production function is $Q = F(K, L; t)$, it can be shown that if $\dot{F}/F$ is independent of K and L, the general production function has the special form $Q = A(t)f(K, L)$, and technical shifts are neutral (see appendix 2). Moreover, in the case of constant returns to scale, $\dot{F}/F$ needs only to be independent of K/L to have neutral shifts.

5. Tinbergen: Missing Link?

According to Zvi Griliches (1996), two traditions came together in Solow's (1957) article on technical change. The first developed out of the national income measurement tradition, based largely on the work of the National Bureau of Economic Research and what was later to become the Bureau of Economic Analysis. This tradition, together with the development of Keynesian economics, also contributed to the rise of growth theory in the works of Harrod and Domar. The second tradition was influenced by Paul Douglas's work on production functions. This tradition had a more econometric background.

In this latter tradition, Tinbergen, in a 1942 paper, published in German, generalized the Douglas production function by adding a geometric trend to it, intended to represent various "technological developments":

$$Q = A^t L^{\frac{3}{4}} K^{\frac{1}{4}}$$

Thus we take into account the possibility of an increasing (perhaps also decreasing) effectiveness of the production process in time and we have the possibility of including the element of technical development in our model. (Tinbergen [1942] 1959, 193)[14]

To compute the "rate of growth of efficiency," Tinbergen derived the following formula:

$$\frac{\dot{Q}}{Q} = \ln A + \frac{3}{4}\frac{\dot{L}}{L} + \frac{1}{4}\frac{\dot{K}}{K}.$$

Before Tinbergen measured "efficiency," he first simplified this formula by assuming that A deviated only slightly from one, so $\ln A \equiv \ln (1 + A') \approx A'$, and to substitute the number 1 for the values of Q, L, and K in the middle of the period under review, 1870–1914. This simplifies the above formula to

$$A' = \dot{Q} - \tfrac{3}{4}\dot{L} - \tfrac{1}{4}\dot{K}.$$

With this formula he measured the rate of growth of efficiency in Germany, Great Britain, France, and the United States.

Though the similarity with Solow's 1957 article is striking, one can doubt whether Solow had seen Tinbergen's German-language paper at that time. As usual, the articles in *Weltwirtschaftliches Archiv* had summaries in four languages, including English. Although the English summary mentions that "a theory of trend movements has to explain how the economy develops under influence of population growth, technical development and capital formation" (Tinbergen [1942] 1959, 547), it does not describe how to measure technical development.

Griliches (1996, 1326) assumes that "nobody seems to have been aware of Tinbergen's paper in the U.S. until much later." In a footnote to this remark, Griliches notes that Stefan Valavanis-Vail (1955), to whom Solow refers in his 1957 article, mentions Tinbergen, but without any bibliographic reference. The only reference to Tinbergen's work is in one of the first sentences: "This model adds to the short list of long-term estimating models (other such: Tinbergen, Kalecki)" (Valavanis-Vail 1955, 208). According to Griliches, from the context of that paper, it is obviously not Tinbergen's 1942 article.

---

14. Page numbers refer to the 1959 English translation. To make the discussion of the literature uniform, some of Tinbergen's symbols are replaced by Solow's.

Presumably, Valavanis-Vail had another one of Tinbergen's papers in mind, namely, the probably better-known English paper "Professor Douglas' Production Function," published in 1942 in *Revue de l'institut international de statistique*. This paper was a critical assessment of statistical investigations based on the Cobb-Douglas function. Tinbergen (1942, 37) was interested in this subject because, "for the study of technical development and its influence on employment, the knowledge of the production function is obviously of great importance." In the last section of this paper, Tinbergen discusses suggestions for "alternative production functions," of which the first was "to introduce time as an additional variable in the function" (46). This would lead to the "generalised function":[15]

$$Q = A^t L^\alpha L^{1-\alpha}.$$

In contrast with his "On the Theory of Trend Movements" ([1942] 1959) paper, Tinbergen (1942), however, does not ascribe any economic meaning to the symbol A.

Without any direct evidence, this part of the history is rather speculative. Probably by sheer coincidence, there is a striking mathematical similarity in Solow's and Tinbergen's work of how technical development is represented, namely, by this geometrical term A^t. It very much looks like the technical development as described by eigenvalues. If Solow had seen one of these two papers by Tinbergen, it might have brought him to the idea of adding the factor representing neutral technical change to the Cobb-Douglas production function.

6. Conclusions

When Tinbergen's 1942 article was reprinted in English, it was reviewed by William Fellner in *Econometrica*. While Fellner considered Tinbergen's idea of imputing part of the total growth observable in a country to technological progress as definitely pioneering, he also pointed at an essential difference between Tinbergen's and Solow's approach:

> Solow, for example, starts out by establishing the proposition that the foregoing type of production function applies only to neutral innovations, and thus to conditions where relative factor-shares stay *unchanged*; yet Tinbergen presents data on rates of change of wage rates on the one hand, and of the average productivity of labor on the other, and the sig-

15. Again, the symbols are adjusted to make the discussion uniform.

nificant discrepancies between these two rates of change shows clearly that according to his data relative factor-shares *changed appreciably.* (Fellner 1961, 90)

The crucial difference between these two approaches is the neutrality of technical change, leaving relative factor-shares unchanged.

So, although the ultimate mathematical forms were equal, the routes along which these concepts were developed were quite different. The present article has described the contexts in which Solow arrived at the concept of "neutral technological change."

The main context is Samuelson's *Foundations of Economic Analysis*, in which an equilibrium is defined as "perfectly stable" if a displacement from equilibrium, x_0, is followed by a return to equilibrium, $\lim_{t \to \infty} x_t = x_0$. He also described sufficient conditions for a dynamic system, $x_{t+1} = ax_t$, to be stable, namely, the eigenvalues of a should be less than one in modulus: $|\lambda| < 1$.

The other important context is Leslie's use of population matrices, in which he defined a stable vector ψ as the eigenvector of a matrix a: $a\psi = \lambda\psi$. Both concepts of eigenvalue and stable vector were used to indicate what is meant by stable growth, that is, growth in which the relative proportions of the elements do not change: $a^t x = c\lambda^t \psi$.

These were the two contexts in which Solow, together with Samuelson, developed the concept of "balanced growth": steady growth in the unique proportions ψ and rate λ: $a^t x = c\lambda^t \psi$. This kind of growth was shown to be "relatively stable": $\lim_{t \to \infty} \frac{x_t}{\lambda^t \psi} = c$. By equating Harrod's and Domar's dynamic models with Leontief's input-output system, a came to denote the production function. Because in the case of balanced growth, the factor shares ψ and growth rate λ can be separated, changes in λ are "neutral" and can be measured independently from changes in factor shares.

Appendix 1

Euler's theorem states that if a function f is homogeneous of first degree then

$$f(x_1, x_2, \ldots, x_n) = x_1 \cdot [\partial f/\partial x_1] + x_2 \cdot [\partial f/\partial x_2] + \ldots + x_n \cdot [\partial f/\partial x_n].$$

An alternative characterization of the eigenvalue problem can found by using Euler's theorem in (6) to obtain

$$\lambda V_i = \sum_{j=1}^{n} \left[\partial H^i(V) / \partial V_j \right] V_j,$$

so that λ is the eigenvalue of the Jacobian $J = [\partial H^i(V)/\partial V_j]$.

At the end of the "Mathematical Appendix B" of his *Foundations* (1947, 438), Samuelson listed a few theorems without proof. The one of interest here is Theorem 3, stating that if $a'a - I$ is negative definite, then $x_{t+1} = ax_t$ is stable ($\lim_{t \to \infty} x_t = 0$), and the eigenvalues of a have a modulus less than one. A negative definite matrix is a symmetric matrix all of whose eigenvalues are negative. But the assumption $a'a - I$ is negative definite is equivalent to the assumption that all eigenvalues of $a'a$ are less than one.

Appendix 2

Let

$$Q = F(K, L; t). \tag{8}$$

Differentiate (8) totally with respect to time and divide by Q, and one obtains

$$\frac{\dot{Q}}{Q} = \frac{\dot{F}}{F} + w_K \frac{\dot{K}}{K} + w_L \frac{\dot{L}}{L}, \tag{9}$$

where w_K and w_L are the relative shares of capital and labor. If $\dot{F}/F$ is independent of K and L, then it can be represented as a function of only time: $\dot{A}(t)/A(t)$. Integrating (9) leads to the following expression:

$$\ln Q = \ln A + w_K \ln K + w_L \ln L + \text{Constant.}$$

Thus

$$Q = AK^{w_K}L^{w_L},$$

where the constant is taken up by A. For this production function, the marginal rate of substitution is $\frac{w_L}{w_K}\frac{\dot{K}}{\dot{L}}$. With any shift in A, this rate remains unchanged at a given capital-labor ratio.

References

Boumans, Marcel. 2001. A Macroeconomic Approach to Complexity. In *Simplicity, Inference, and Modelling*, edited by Arnold Zellner, Hugo A. Keuzenkamp, and Michael McAleer. Cambridge: Cambridge University Press.

Crowcroft, Peter. 1991. *Elton's Ecologists: A History of the Bureau of Animal Population*. Chicago: University of Chicago Press.

Fellner, William. 1961. Review of *Jan Tinbergen: Selected Papers*. *Econometrica* 29.1:89–91.

Goodwin, Richard M. 1949. The Multiplier as Matrix. *Economic Journal* 59.236:537–55.

——. 1950. Does the Matrix Multiplier Oscillate? *Economic Journal* 60.240:764–70.

Griliches, Zvi. 1996. The Discovery of the Residual: A Historical Note. *Journal of Economic Literature* 34.3:1324–30.

Hawkins, David, and Herbert A. Simon. 1949. Note: Some Conditions of Macroeconomic Stability. *Econometrica* 17.3–4:245–48.

Klaassen, L. H., L. M. Koyck, and H. J. Witteveen, eds. 1959. *Jan Tinbergen: Selected Papers*. Amsterdam: North-Holland.

Koopmans, Tjalling C., ed. 1951. *Activity Analysis of Production and Allocation*. Cowles Foundation Monograph 13. New Haven, Conn.: Yale University Press.

Leslie, P. H. 1945. On the Use of Matrices in Certain Population Mathematics. *Biometrika* 33.3:183–212.

Metzler, Lloyd A. 1950. A Multiple-Region Theory of Income and Trade. *Econometrica* 18.4:329–54.

Samuelson, Paul A. 1947. *Foundations of Economic Analysis*. Cambridge: Harvard University Press.

Simon, Herbert A. 1951. Effects of Technological Change in a Linear Model. In *Activity Analysis of Production and Allocation*, edited by T. C. Koopmans. New Haven, Conn.: Yale University Press.

——. 1953. Causal Ordering and Identifiability. In *Studies in Econometric Method*, edited by W. C. Hood and T. C. Koopmans. Cowles Foundation Monograph 14. New York: Wiley.

Simon, Herbert A., and Albert Ando. 1961. Aggregation of Variables in Dynamic Systems. *Econometrica* 29.2:111–38.

Solow, Robert M. 1952a. Balanced Growth under Constant Returns. Report of the Santa Monica Meeting, 2–4 August 1951. *Econometrica* 20.1:87.

——. 1952b. On the Structure of Linear Models. *Econometrica* 20.1:29–46.

——. 1952c. Review of *Activity Analysis of Production and Allocation*, by Tjalling C. Koopmans. *American Economic Review* 42.3:424–29.

——. 1953–54. A Note on the Price Level and Interest Rate in a Growth Model. *Review of Economic Studies* 21.1:74–79.

——. 1956. A Contribution to the Theory of Economic Growth. *Quarterly Journal of Economics* 70.1:65–94.

——. 1957. Technical Change and the Aggregate Production Function. *Review of Economics and Statistics* 39.3:312–20.

——. 1987. Autobiography. http://nobelprize.org/nobel_prizes/economics/laureates/1987/solow-autobio.html.

——. 1988. Growth Theory and After. *American Economic Review* 78.3:307–17.

Solow, Robert M., and Paul A. Samuelson. 1953. Balanced Growth under Constant Returns to Scale. *Econometrica* 21.3:412–24.

Tinbergen, J. 1942. Professor Douglas' Production Function. *Revue de l'institut international de statistique* 10.1–2:37–48.

———. [1942] 1959. Zur Theorie der langfristigen Wirtschaftsentwicklung. *Welt-wirtschaftliches Archiv* 55:511–49. Reprinted in translation as *On the Theory of Trend Movements* in Klaassen, Koyck, and Witteveen 1959.

Valavanis-Vail, Stefan. 1955. An Econometric Model of Growth: U.S.A., 1869–1953. *American Economic Review* 45.2:208–21.

Weintraub, E. Roy. 1991. *Stabilizing Dynamics*. Cambridge: Cambridge University Press.

Part 3
Spread and Consolidation

More Cobwebs?
Robert Solow, Uncertainty,
and the Theory of Distribution

William Darity Jr.

At the close of his (justifiably) famous 1956 *QJE* paper, Robert Solow referred to a set of qualifications for the model he had just presented in the preceding pages. The model was, of course, the well-known framework of steady-state, full-employment growth featuring an aggregate production function in intensive form with substitutability between the two factors, capital and labor, under constant returns to scale. It is often called the neoclassical theory of economic growth—Solow himself characterized it as such in the 1956 paper—and his intensive form of the aggregate production function has been borrowed by scores of subsequent economists—including myself (e.g., Darity 1981)—in a still-growing array of papers.

The limitations on the model that Solow (1956, 91) highlighted included "some of the more elementary obstacles to full employment." Among the obstacles highlighted by Solow were wage rigidity, the liquidity trap and its counterpoint, insensitivity of investment to the interest rate, and uncertainty (91–94). At the end of the paper, Solow observed, "All these cobwebs and some others have been brushed aside throughout this essay" (94).

Ironically, "these cobwebs" constituted the core of Solow's subsequent research program. It was Solow in tandem with Paul Samuelson who reinterpreted the Phillips curve as positing a stabilization policy

I am grateful to Steven Durlauf for several extremely helpful suggestions, including suggestions for several valuable references.

History of Political Economy 41 (annual suppl.) DOI 10.1215/00182702-2009-021

trade-off between unemployment and inflation (Samuelson and Solow 1960; Solow 1978). Solow was instrumental in the emergence of the New Keynesian school in economics that sought to explain the existence of wage stickiness—or price stickiness in general—on the basis of the collective consequences of autonomous rational optimizing behavior on the part of economic actors, rather than interference by the state or other monopolistic coalitions (e.g., trade unions, cartels). Price stickiness, in turn, constituted the New Keynesian explanation for the occurrence of unemployment. Solow (1980) covered virtually the entire terrain of New Keynesian arguments about the sources of unemployment in his presidential address to the American Economic Association.

It is paradoxical that we now refer to this approach in macroeconomics as "new" Keynesian. The sticky or rigid wage explanation for unemployment was precisely the type of argument predicated on systemic friction that John Maynard Keynes rejected as the core explanation for unemployment.[1] Specifically, Keynes (1935, 35) positioned himself "on the other side of the gulf" from "those who believed that the existing economic system is in the long-run self-adjusting, though with creaks and groans and jerks, and interrupted by time-lags, outside interference and mistakes." For Keynes, the economic system was not predisposed to self-adjust to full employment even under a regime of complete wage and price flexibility (see, e.g., Darity and Goldsmith 1995). In his view, the frictionless capitalistic economic system still would be defective.

The "cobwebs" that I want to consider in some detail here are associated with (1) the neoclassical theory of distribution—the marginal productivity theory of distribution—and (2) the treatment of uncertainty. With respect to the first cobweb, the marginalist approach to distribution is what the late Martin Bronfenbrenner (1971) playfully referred to as the "good ol' theory." Somewhat "old" it is; "good" it is not. In fact, a still-older tradition of thinking about distribution is more general and more theoretically sound. That older tradition dates at least to the period of classical political economy, and I will refer to it as the surplus approach. It is the

---

1. Solow's (1980) American Economic Association presidential address on sticky wage explanations for unemployment, which is the cornerstone for New Keynesian economics, owed much more to A. C. Pigou than to Keynes. Wage rigidity was due not to government interference in markets in Solow's framework but instead to the rational optimizing behavior of economic actors. Solow's preference for Pigou over Keynes is very much in evidence as early as the 1956 essay. Perhaps the neoclassical theory of economic growth is also the neo-Pigovian theory of economic growth.

theory of distribution implicitly or explicitly presented in a tradition in economics that stretches roughly from David Ricardo to Piero Sraffa (1960). Solow consistently has aligned himself with the marginalists in opposition to this alternative tradition.

Increasing Returns

In the 1956 paper Solow asserts that "in a competitive economy the real wage [of labor] and real rental [on capital] are determined by the traditional marginal-productivity equations" (79). In Solow's single-sector world, remuneration for each of the factors was equal to their physical marginal products. And, of particular importance, under marginal product factor pricing, total factor payments under Solow's assumption of constant returns to scale would exactly match the total output of the economy. Labor and capital appear to be distinguished here by their respective mechanisms of accumulation. Labor grows at an autonomous "natural" rate, while capital grows in response to savings at a fixed rate out of income at each instant in time.

One of Solow's major goals in the 1956 paper was to overcome the so-called knife-edge instability problem associated with Roy Harrod's (1939) dynamic model. While Solow simply assumed away the instability problem that Harrod posed between the warranted and actual rates of growth by eliminating any distinction between saving and investment (by claiming the world is always in an "*ex post*" state of affairs), any discrepancy between the actual and natural rates was removed by the introduction of a production technology with substitutability between capital and labor and factor price flexibility.[2]

In the process, though, Solow introduced a new knife-edge that preserves the unity of his model. Long-run stability and the neat distributional properties of the system hinge on the knife-edge assumption that technology lies precisely between conditions of diminishing returns to scale and increasing returns to scale. Otherwise there must be a surplus

---

2. Immediately after Solow 1957 appeared, Robert Eisner (1958) published a challenge to Solow's fixed-coefficients interpretation of the Harrod model. Eisner argued that the Harrod model could be understood in the context of more general assumptions about the nature of the production technology *and* a world with flexible prices. In Eisner's framework a problem still would exist in bringing the natural and warranted rates into conformity. Eisner did not address the concern expressed here, that Solow renders invisible the problem of the potential disjuncture between the actual and warranted rates attributable to the investment process.

above and beyond the remuneration of the factors, or at least one factor must receive less than the value of its marginal product in payment.

This is simply recognition of the old "adding up" problem, as Paul Samuelson (1958) labeled it a half-century ago. Under decreasing returns to scale, if all factors are paid their marginal products, there will be some portion of total output that remains—a "surplus." Under increasing returns, payment of all factors at their marginal products will mean a factor bill in excess of the total output. A feasible distribution of income will necessitate at least one factor receiving less than its marginal product. In principle, in the aggregate labor could receive its marginal product, but there must be some factor somewhere that receives less than its marginal product. In neither case can marginal productivity theory fully explain the distribution of income. Only in the knife-edge case of constant returns to scale can the "good ol' theory" potentially comprehensively explain the distribution of income.

In a multisector world under the terms of the good ol' theory, presumably the value of the marginal product of capital must equalize across sectors. But the existence of a regime where returns to capital conform to marginal productivity theory again is dependent on a universe of sectors characterized by constant returns to scale.

Of course, empirically the deviation from constant returns to scale is more likely to be in the direction of increasing returns rather than decreasing returns to scale. Solow's next most influential paper, the 1957 paper that introduced us to the "Solow residual" and the importance of total factor productivity, points directly toward evidence of increasing returns (Easterly and Levine 2001). Certainly Solow now acknowledges the empirical relevance of increasing returns. In reassessing growth theory almost forty years after his 1956 paper, Solow (1994, 48) said that "modelling of imperfect competition was made necessary by the appearance of increasing returns to scale." In the same article he made the following comment about the significance of constant returns:

> The assumption of constant returns to scale is a considerable simplification, both because it saves a dimension by allowing the whole analysis to be conducted in terms of ratios and because it permits the further simplification that the basic market-form is competitive. But it is not essential to the working of the model nor even overwhelmingly useful in an age of cheap computer simulation. (48)

Indeed, it is not even essential for treating "the basic market-form" as "competitive." If one assumes that increasing returns take the form of scale economies internal to the industry but external to the firm, the familiar neoclassical competitive imputation is sustainable. Sraffa (1926, 540) once observed caustically, "The only economies which could be taken into consideration would be such as occupy an intermediate position between these two extremes; but it is just in the middle that nothing, or almost nothing is to be found."

Much of the "new" decreasing costs trade theory is grounded on Sraffa's "middle" (Helpman and Krugman 1985, 1989) where "nothing, or almost nothing is to be found." When the gambit shifts to modeling trade with decreasing returns to an environment of imperfect competition (again see Helpman and Krugman 1985, 1989), the applicability of the marginal productivity theory as a general theory of distribution no longer can be upheld.

Constant returns are essential for distribution to be explained fully on the basis of marginal productivity. If we are not in a world of generalized constant returns to scale, marginal product pricing for all factors is untenable. If it is not sustainable at the macroeconomic level, it would require some major—and unpersuasive—mental gymnastics to justify its existence at the microeconomic level. If macrodistribution is incompatible with the good ol' theory, then it is not reasonable to postulate, as most economists so blithely proceed to do, that each individual's wage is equal to his or her marginal product. Macrofoundations would mandate a different microeconomics of distribution for logical consistency.

There also are reasons to be hesitant about the validity of the marginal productivity theory of distribution when we move in the reverse direction—from the micro level to the macro. Discrimination and its opposite, nepotism, in labor markets lead to conditions where phenotypically (or otherwise superficially) differentiated workers with equivalent capabilities receive markedly different returns to their labor (see Darity and Mason 1998). Both sets of workers cannot be receiving their marginal products; perhaps neither is receiving its marginal products. Perhaps a weighted average of their wages would amount to a general marginal product wage, but under a regime where discrimination and nepotism are persistent practices there is no clear mechanism that would produce such a (knife-edge?) result.

Furthermore, quantifiable uncertainty when compensation seems to be linked to future performance, for example, rookie professional athletes who have yet to play a minute at that level of competition, could justify their wage being equivalent to some type of expected marginal product. But if the uncertainty is unquantifiable—if it is Keynes's (1936, esp. chap. 12)

deep subjective uncertainty—then at best the rookie contract is predicated
on rules of thumb, including precedents established in the past for the sal-
ary standards.

The Surplus Approach

At the macro level, Solow has been silent about the implications of increasing returns for the theory of distribution. Luigi Pasinetti (2000), in contrast, suggests that the good ol' theory runs into deep trouble outside the
boundaries of constant returns and that there is a viable alternative in the
surplus approach.

The surplus approach attained its formal apex in Sraffa's *Production of Commodities by Means of Commodities* (1960). For Sraffa, profit
is the surplus above and beyond remuneration of the factors, which may
or may not be paid their marginal products. In classical/Ricardian equilibrium, output prices are determined and profit/surplus is allocated in
a manner consistent with equalization of the rate of profit across all
sectors. The Sraffian/classical equilibrium is a snapshot condition where
relative prices of factors and products align with a uniform rate of
profit.[3]

The tendency toward profit-rate equalization is most easily fulfilled
if investment in sectors with higher rates of profit lowers profitability,
and disinvestment in sectors with lower rates of profit raises profitability.
No particular assumption must be made about the laws of returns, production conditions (i.e., fixed coefficients or substitutability of factors),
or market structure in any sector. A key question that remains is what
determines the general rate of profit that functions as the reference point
for the direction of investment flows. Sraffa (1960), intriguingly, proposed
that the monetary rate of interest, determined by financial processes,
might set the standard for the general rate of profit—a position quite similar to Keynes's (1936) claim in chapter 17 of the *General Theory* about the
decisive role of the rate of interest on money.

As Pasinetti (2000, 22) commented, "Sraffa's most important contribution was to open up the issue of the determination of the rate of profits—

---

3. Unlike Michael Mandler (1999), who has written a fascinating assessment of the state of
economic theory, I do not interpret the Sraffian system as a world of linear activities or fixed
coefficients. The input-output ratios in Sraffian systems are those that prevail in equilibrium,
not a general characterization of the technical conditions of production. Mandler also argues for
the lack of generality of the marginal productivity theory on grounds that general equilibrium
systems generate factor price indeterminacy when production functions are not differentiable.

and, with it, the whole problem of income distribution—to an investigation that did not stop short at purely economic considerations but would go beyond them, up to including the entire institutional organisation of an economic system, as a subject of analysis . . . to achieve a satisfactory explanation of the phenomenon of income distribution. Unfortunately, after an initial period—possibly even excessive—enthusiasm, Sraffa's formulations concerning income distribution were . . . either forgotten or left on the sideline of the economists' attention."

In a suitably clever paper, Amartya Sen (1963) displayed the surplus model in action in a one-sector model with constant returns to scale. Sen proposed that under each of two regimes, unemployment is a normal outcome of the model, but in one of the regimes the wage rate is equal to the marginal product of labor, while it is not in the other. In either case, profit was the surplus after the wage bill had been met. Sen proceeds to construct a world where the existence of constant returns to scale is not necessarily associated with general marginal product factor pricing.

The surplus approach is given pride of place as the more general theory of distribution; complete marginal product factor pricing is, de facto, a special case where the surplus is zero. The elaboration and development of the surplus approach could have led to a rich research program, but such a program has not been pursued avidly and widely by the economics profession at large.[4]

Uncertainty

Next, I turn to a second cobweb, the issue of uncertainty, with a further look at Harrodian instability. To begin this reconsideration it is necessary to begin with Keynes, specifically the Keynes of the period of the *General Theory*. Keynes's departures from what is best termed pre-Keynesian economics rest on his claims that the economic system does not self-adjust to full employment; that the failure to self-adjust is not due to lags, leaks, frictions, or price stickiness; and that money is not neutral in any run (see Keynes 1935, 1936). These are also key points of departure from both the new classical and New Keynesian economists.

4. One notable early exception would be Nicholas Kaldor (1955), whose aggregate growth model was consciously construed as emerging out of the "surplus" rather than the "neoclassical" theory of distribution. Duncan Foley and Thomas R. Michl (1999) explored related territory more than forty years later. For the most part, though, the profession marches to the tune of marginal factor pricing without a critical glance backward—neither in preparing new papers nor in refereeing them.

Critical to Keynes's construction of the operation of the economy were his concepts of the state of long-term expectation and the long period. The long period for Keynes was not the conventional notion of the "long run" when all factors of production can be altered, thereby overcoming some type of sheer physical rigidity associated with the locking down of equipment and machinery. Nor is it necessarily a Friedmanite long run where expectations are fully mirrored by the actual performance of the economic system.

The state of long-term expectation are those beliefs held by entrepreneurs—those persons who invest in physical capital—about prospective yield (any capital asset for Keynes has three properties: a prospective yield, a carrying cost, and a liquidity premium). These beliefs, according to Keynes (1936, chap. 12), include those concerning "future changes in the type and quantity of the stock of capital-assets and the tastes of consumers, the strength of effective demand and the change in the wage-unit." The long period, or the (generally an underemployment) equilibrium condition in Keynes's system, is connected explicitly to the state of long-term expectation. Keynes writes:

> If we suppose a state of expectation to continue for a sufficient length of time for the effect to have worked itself out so completely that there is, broadly speaking, no piece of employment going which would not have taken place if the new state of expectation had always existed, the steady level of employment may be called the long-period employment corresponding to that state of expectation. It follows that, although expectation may change so frequently that the actual level of employment has never had time to reach long-period employment corresponding to the state of expectation, nevertheless every state of expectation has its definite corresponding level of long-period employment. (chap. 5)

Thus the state of long-term expectation influences the prevailing level of employment, but it can fully determine the prevailing level of employment only if sufficient time has elapsed for a specific state of long-term expectation to have its effects fully worked out. The sustainability of a particular level of employment is contingent on the sustainability of a particular state of long-term expectation. There is no reason for a level of employment that corresponds to a given state of long-term expectation to match the full-employment level (a word of caution here as well—Keynes's concept of full employment has little or nothing to do with whether markets clear; they can all clear at less than full employment [see, e.g., Darity and Goldsmith 1995]). There is no reason for a given state of long-term expectation to be maintained; for Keynes the operation of financial markets and speculation renders each state of long-term expectation inherently fragile. This is the context for Keynes's famous description of the importance of entrepreneurs' "animal spirits."

This also is the context in which it is best to understand Harrod's (1939) notion of the warranted rate of growth. It is intimately connected to Keynes's long period and the associated force of subjective uncertainty (yes, the door is wide open for the brilliant madman, G. L. S. Shackle, e.g., 1992).

Harrod (1939, 16) writes in his famous paper advancing his dynamic model of the economy:

> The warranted rate of growth is taken to be that rate of growth, which, if it occurs, will leave all parties satisfied that they have produced not more nor less than the right amount. Or, to state the matter otherwise, it will put them into a frame of mind which will cause them to give such orders as will maintain the same rate of growth.

It is transparent that there is no reason for the actual and warranted rates of growth to converge unless a given state of long-term expectation can be maintained long enough for the system to reach the corresponding long-period employment level.

And, again, that level of employment need not be full employment. In general, it will not be.

Solow's (1956) neoclassical model obscures this central issue, thereby brushing aside the cobweb of uncertainty. The warranted rate and the actual rate are collapsed onto one another by Solow's decision to eliminate an investment function independent of saving activity, a point that Sen (1963) makes clear. This is an exit from the world of growth that Harrod was struggling to depict where investment activity is the critical source of instability in a capitalist economy. There is no discrepancy between the warranted rate and the actual rate to be resolved in Solow's world. It is erased at the start of his exercise. In Solow's cobweb-free world, without an independent investment function there is no role for entrepreneurial expectations to affect economic performance. Uncertainty is rendered irrelevant. In a new classical or New Keynesian world characterized by rational expectations, actions taken by economic actors predicated on their model-specific beliefs about the future do not affect the model. The model is not a moving target. Uncertainty is rendered impotent.

Harrod, although lacking the mathematical ammunition to present the argument systematically, seems to have had in mind a model where entrepreneurial beliefs affect the model itself. The model is a moving target with an "endogenous" and reciprocal relationship between expectations of economic actors and the structure of the model itself. If the model changes in an unpredictable way, there can be uncertainty about the model itself. In a world where there are multiple models that could be true, model-specific optimal rules for action are lost (Brock et al. 2007). Uncertainty regains its authority.

Conclusions

Solow's (1956) focus in his neoclassical growth model is on achieving balanced growth by bringing the actual rate into conformity with the natural rate. Thus the problem of capitalist instability is rendered a matter of whether there is a nonzero elasticity of substitution between factors of production and the degree of price flexibility. The gigantic endemic problems of instability associated with uncertainty, investment, finance, and speculation are cast into the ranks of the disappeared. Indeed, the presence of finance—with borrowing and indebtedness and even the recent transformation of the residential housing market into a casino—raises the question of whether a new act of personal saving is necessary to support a new act of investment. A "real" growth model of the neoclassical type masks the potential for real-world economic traumas.

In addition to the absence of uncertainty, investment, finance, and speculation, there are two other key dimensions of the Solow 1956 model that are important to its construction of steady-state, full-employment growth that often are underestimated: the one-sector nature of the model and the assumption of a fixed labor supply that is insensitive to relative prices at each moment in time. The simple modeling expedient of having separate physical capital and consumer goods–producing sectors immediately complicates the story of smooth growth. If labor supply is sensitive to real wages, interest rates, and wealth, the position of full employment cannot be situated by labor market clearing. For early hints at all of these problems, consider the appendix to chapter 19 of the *General Theory*.

Recently, Avi Cohen and Geoffrey Harcourt (2003) have asked whatever happened to the Cambridge-Cambridge debate over the conceptualization and measurement of capital, a squabble that for a time took central stage across the Atlantic. It was really a surface manifestation of the fundamental breach between the marginalist and surplus perspectives on distribution. Cohen and Harcourt think that debate will "erupt" again because the issues raised still lurk beneath the developments in endogenous growth theory and business cycle theory. I think they are incorrect about the inevitability of an eruption. If the vast majority of economists can proceed, unquestioningly, to use a theory of distribution that is fundamentally flawed and to treat uncertainty as if it is a beast that has been tamed, they can continue to construct theories of growth and the business cycle without paying attention to cracks in the foundation. Only if the cobwebs are brought to center stage can we construct an economic theory that is wholly relevant to the crisis-prone world in which we live.

References

Brock, William A., Steven N. Durlauf, James M. Nason, and G. Rondina. 2007. Simple versus Optimal Rules as Guides to Policy. Working Paper 2007–7, Federal Reserve Bank of Atlanta. April.

Bronfenbrenner, Martin. 1971. *Income Distribution Theory*. Chicago: Akline-Atherton.

Cohen, A. I., and G. Harcourt. 2003. Retrospectives: Whatever Happened to the Cambridge Capital Theory Controversies? *Journal of Economic Perspectives* 17.1:199–214.

Darity, W. A., Jr. 1981. The Simple Analytics of Neo-Ricardian Growth and Distribution. *American Economic Review* 71.5:978–93.

Darity, W. A., Jr., and A. H. Goldsmith. 1995. Mr. Keynes, the New Keynesians, and the Concept of Full Employment. In *Post-Keynesian Economic Theory*, edited by Paul Wells. Boston: Kluwer Academic Publishers.

Darity, W. A., Jr., and P. L. Mason. 1998. Evidence on Discrimination in Employment: Codes of Color, Codes of Gender. *Journal of Economic Perspectives* 12:63–90.

Easterly, W., and R. Levine. 2001. What Have We Learned from a Decade of Empirical Research? It's Not Factor Accumulation: Stylized Facts and Growth Models. *World Bank Economic Review* 15.2:177–219.

Eisner, Robert. 1958. On Growth Models and the Neoclassical Resurgence. *Economic Journal* 68.272:707–21.

Foley, Duncan, and Thomas R. Michl. 1999. *Growth and Distribution*. Cambridge: Harvard University Press.

Harrod, R. F. 1939. An Essay in Dynamic Theory. *Economic Journal* 49:14–33.

Helpman, Elhanan, and Paul Krugman. 1985. *Market Structure and Foreign Trade*. Cambridge: MIT Press.

———. 1989. *Trade Policy and Market Structure*. Cambridge: MIT Press.

Kaldor, Nicholas. 1955. Alternative Theories of Distribution. *Review of Economic Studies* 2.2:83–100.

Keynes, J. M. 1935. A Self-Adjusting Economic System? *New Republic*, 20 February, 35–37.

———. 1936. *The General Theory of Employment, Interest, and Money*. London: Macmillan.

Mandler, Michael. 1999. *Dilemmas in Economic Theory: Persisting Foundational Problems in Microeconomics*. New York: Oxford University Press.

Marx, K. 1977. *Capital: Volume 1*. New York: Vintage Books.

Pasinetti, L. 2000. Critique of the Neoclassical Theory of Growth and Distribution. *Banca Nazionale del Lavoro Quarterly Review* 53:383–431.

Samuelson, P. A. 1958. *Economics: An Introductory Analysis*. New York: McGraw-Hill.

Samuelson, P. A., and R. M. Solow. 1960. Analytical Aspects of Anti-Inflation Policy. *American Economic Review* 50.2:177–94.

Sen, A. K. Y. 1963. Neo-Classical and Neo-Keynesian Theories of Distribution. *Economic Record* (March): 53–64.

Shackle, G. L. S. 1992. *Epistemics and Economics: A Critique of Economic Doctrines*. New Brunswick, N.J.: Transaction Publishers.

Solow, R. M. 1956. A Contribution to the Theory of Economic Growth. *Quarterly Journal of Economics* 70.1:65–94.

———. 1957. Technical Change and the Aggregate Production Function. *Review of Economics and Statistics* 39.3:312–20.

———. 1978. Down the Phillips Curve with Gun and Camera. In *Readings in Money, National Income, and Stabilization Policy*. New York: McGraw-Hill.

———. 1980. On Theories of Unemployment. *American Economic Review* 70 (March): 1–11.

———. 1994. Perspectives on Growth Theory. *Journal of Economic Perspectives* 8.1:45–54.

Sraffa, P. 1926. The Laws of Returns under Competitive Conditions. *Economic Journal* 86:535–50.

———. 1960. *Production of Commodities by Means of Commodities*. Cambridge: Cambridge University Press.

The Growing of Ramsey's Growth Model

Pedro Garcia Duarte

Frank Ramsey's "A Mathematical Theory of Saving" was published in 1928, but according to several economists, thirty-odd years had to pass before the paper and the model it contained had an impact on economics. The delayed recognition is normally attributed to the sophisticated mathematics that Ramsey used in the paper, which was out of reach of his contemporaries. Only during the 1960s, when economists became more mathematically literate, was the "generalization of Ramsey's study . . . made independently and more or less simultaneously" by David Cass (1965, 1966), Tjalling Koopmans (1965), and others (Koopmans 1967, 6).[1] Ramsey's "classic" article was "several decades ahead of its time," Robert Barro and Xavier Sala-i-Martin (2003, 16–17) wrote in their conventional graduate textbook on economic growth; "the economics profession did not . . . accept or widely use Ramsey's approach until the 1960s."

This article is partly based on my PhD dissertation (Duarte 2007a, chap. 4). I am very grateful to participants at the 2008 *HOPE* and 2008 HISRECO conferences for comments on a previous draft, especially Wade Hands, Tiago Mata, Roger Backhouse, and Philippe Fontaine. I also thank the editors of this volume and two anonymous referees for the suggestions they made. The usual disclaimer applies.

    1. Ramsey's 1928 model had no population growth and, thus, in it the capital-labor ratio approaches a stationary state until capital accumulation ceases. Cass and Koopmans introduced exogenous population growth making per capita variables constant in that equilibrium.

History of Political Economy 41 (annual suppl.) DOI 10.1215/00182702-2009-022

The portrait of Ramsey as a genius ahead of his time appeared as early as the 1930s, mainly after his untimely death.[2] In the obituary note published in the *Economic Journal* in 1930, John Maynard Keynes ([1933] 1972, 335–36) stressed the image of Ramsey as both a genius and an outsider to economics, and praised Ramsey's contribution to economic growth as "one of the most remarkable contributions to mathematical economics ever made," despite being "terribly difficult reading for an economist."

After Keynes's death, Paul Samuelson (1946, 196) criticized "the importance which Keynes attached to [Ramsey's 1928 growth model]" as being "actually exaggerated" and that it "can be accounted for only in terms of his paternal feeling toward Ramsey, and his own participation in the solution of the problem."[3] But even Samuelson came around in time: in a 1970 article published in the *Journal of Political Economy*, Samuelson (1970, 1372) proclaimed his admiration for Ramsey and his growth model, calling the model "a strategically beautiful application of the calculus of variations to define how much an economy should invest." Samuelson, along with Keynes, helped popularize the romantic image of Ramsey in economics, particularly with respect to another contribution of Ramsey's, his 1927 paper on optimal taxation (Duarte 2008a).

The portrayal of Ramsey as a sleeping giant in the economic growth literature was, because of the advanced mathematics he used, already common by the time his 1928 model was incorporated into neoclassical economics, in the 1960s.[4] For example, Richard Stone (1966, 59–60) asserted that Ramsey's "model and the technique which it employs, the calculus of variations, have attracted remarkably little attention among economists despite an excellent introduction to both by Allen (1938). The technique in a form suitably modified for computing is only now coming to its own in the work of the dynamic programmers, well exemplified by [Richard]

2. Duarte 2009 presents Ramsey's biographical information and explores the creation of his image as a Cambridge genius, which parallels the emergence of the romantic image of a mathematician genius (a young prodigy who challenges the established mathematicians with groundbreaking contributions that are rejected by the latter) discussed by Amir Alexander (2006).

3. Samuelson (1953, 577 n. 26) also criticized the heroic assumptions made by Ramsey (1928), but demonstrated admiration for the "brilliant short-lived philosopher-protégé of Keynes," as he did in Samuelson 1937, 159 n. 1, and in Samuelson 1943, 67. In contrast to Ramsey's growth model, Samuelson did not think his paper on taxation was very good until 1948 (Duarte 2008a, 1).

4. This view is implicitly held by J. Black (1962, 360), who offers a "Ramsey without tears" by treating Ramsey's subject "with a set of mathematical tools more within the grasp of plain economists."

Bellman." In reviewing Stone's 1966 book, Roy Allen (1966, 858) stated that "the Ramsey theory, only recently recognised as basic after more than thirty years of neglect, is an exercise in optimalisation over time by the calculus of variations, now in process of being freed from its classical limitations by the dynamic programmers and by Pontriagin's maximum principle."[5] Along those same lines, Maurice Peston (1969, 211) puzzled over why the field of optimal growth was neglected for thirty years. He asserted that in the case of both Ramsey's and John von Neumann's growth models, "mathematics appears as much more of a help than a hindrance" and concluded that "it was the ignorance (I am tempted to write wilful ignorance) of the nonmathematical theorists which caused such waste of effort."

Kenneth Arrow (1974, 1103; 1980, 637) argued that the use of the calculus of variations was not accepted by economists during the early 1930s, and this was why his professor, Harold Hotelling, had a paper rejected by the *Economic Journal* in 1931:[6]

> [The] delayed recognition [of Ramsey's papers on economic growth and on optimal taxation] is indeed a problem in *Dogmengeschichte*. The paper on optimal savings made use of calculus of variations, a technique regarded as beyond the pale of decent usage in economics; Harold Hotelling's famous piece on exhaustible resources, also using the calculus of variations, was rejected as incomprehensible by the Economic Journal before publication in this journal [*Journal of Political Economy*, in the same year]. (Presumably, Ramsey's patron, Keynes, smoothed the way for him.) (Arrow 1980, 637)[7]

5. Allen (1967, 405) repeated similar words. A comparable statement is found in Werin and Jungenfelt 1976, 95, and, much later, in Gaspard 2003, 413, and Faria 2005, 104.

6. In fact, the 1974 piece ("In Memoriam") is an unsigned note. However, Arrow was the president of the American Economic Association in 1973, the year that Hotelling died, and a draft of this note can be found in the Arrow Papers at Duke University. Moreover, practically the same text constitutes Arrow's 1987 entry to the *New Palgrave*.

7. In 1974 Arrow started working on a memorial article on Hotelling, to be published in *Econometrica* (Arrow 1973), but he never published it (Arrow 2008). In 1986 he wrote to the editor of Hotelling's collected works: "One thing you might check on in England: Hotelling told me, when I was a student, that his paper was rejected by the Economic Journal, on the ground that its mathematics made it unintelligible to the readers. It was not until later that I realized that Ramsey's paper on savings, which also uses the calculus of variations, had been published in the E.J. a few years earlier. I am not surprised at the idea that Keynes would treat a Cambridge colleague and protege differently from an uncouth American, but perhaps the records of the E.J. would cast some light on this episode" (Arrow 1986). Apparently Darnell (1990, 13) could not find any evidence of this episode, which was again mentioned later by Arrow and Lehmann (2005, 6–7).

As we shall see, Hotelling (1931) was one of the first to cite Ramsey's contribution to economic growth.

My main goal here is to appraise the portrait of Ramsey as a slumbering titan and not just for the sake of straightening out the historical record. Accounts are interpretations, and that of Ramsey as a genius ahead of his time is one well entrenched among postwar economists. The romantic view of Ramsey fits well with the popular perception that scientists, like artists, are those gifted with privileged access to a higher reality (to use Alexander's [2006, 726] words). Instead, the purpose of the present article is to challenge such a view in order to better understand how Ramsey (1928) became stabilized in mainstream economics in the postwar period, which happened only after the stabilization of the so-called neoclassical synthesis.[8] Ramsey's model combines mathematical formalism, utility-maximizing agents, and aggregate-level control with clear normative content. These three key features were at the core of the neoclassical synthesis and became criteria for judging which are and which are not acceptable models. In particular, the latter two aspects were considered to be mutually exclusive prior to the 1950s, and such incompatibility is also behind the delayed recognition of Ramsey's 1928 analysis among economists.

The effort of combining utility-maximizing agents with aggregate-level control (either in the context of a planner's problem or in an allocation reached through decentralized markets) is the hallmark of the optimal growth literature that emerged in the 1960s, in which Ramsey 1928 was canonized. This literature was composed of exercises in dynamic welfare economics, generally in an efficient (Pareto-optimal) context. By surveying the growing acceptance of Ramsey's model from the early 1930s onward, I intend to shed some light on important issues behind its rediscovery and on how the calculus of variations was increasingly used in the optimal growth literature. I will explore the changes both in welfare and in dynamic economics that occurred during the period of dormancy that ultimately set the stage for the front-door entry of Ramsey's model in the growth literature after World War II. More broadly, this episode helps us characterize how the economists who rediscovered Ramsey understood "the enterprise of making economics more mathematical" (Weintraub 2002, 37).

To analyze the iconic view of Ramsey and the alleged dormancy of his growth model, I trace references to him in the economics and finance journals available in JSTOR. I also complement this information with citations

---

8. *Stabilize* here refers to attempts "by members of a particular community to narrow the possibilities for disagreement among community members" (Weintraub 1991, 120).

in a few influential books. The analysis focuses on the period after the publication of Ramsey's growth model and up to the early 1980s, the time when he was already a patron saint of the economic growth literature.

Uncovering Ramsey's Growth Model

To track references to Frank Ramsey, I searched all economics and finance journals available in JSTOR (forty-four and six, respectively) for the word *Ramsey*, including all possible fields, languages, and types (article, review, editorial, and other).[9] I then checked each item to verify whether it in fact referred to Ramsey. The search period started in the beginning of 1928, and it included the fifty-five subsequent years (i.e., until the end of 1982).

Three other things about the search are worth mentioning. First, I was able to include a few misspelled references to Frank Ramsey (as "Ramsay").[10] Second, I classified all references to Ramsey under four headings: economic growth (although this became a clear research area only in the postwar period), taxation, subjective probability and/or expected utility, and other (which includes things like Ramsey's obituary written by Keynes, Arthur C. Pigou's acknowledgment of Ramsey's help in some of his papers, and any allusion to Ramsey not in the specific context of any of the first three categories). Third, I also included references to Ramsey in a

9. The economics journals included the *American Economic Review*, the *American Journal of Agricultural Economics*, the *American Journal of Economics and Sociology*, *Annals of the American Academy of Political and Social Science*, *Brookings Papers on Economic Activity*, *Business History Review*, the *Canadian Journal of Economics*, the *Canadian Journal of Political Science*, *Canadian Public Policy*, *Desarrollo Economico*, *Econometric Theory*, *Econometrica*, *Economic Development and Cultural Change*, *Economic Geography*, *Economic History Review*, the *Economic Journal*, *Economic Policy*, *Economica*, the *European Journal of Health Economics*, the *International Economic Review*, the *Journal of Applied Econometrics*, the *Journal of Business and Economic Statistics*, the *Journal of Economic History*, the *Journal of Economic Literature* (*Journal of Economic Abstracts*), the *Journal of Economic Perspectives*, the *Journal of Industrial Economics*, the *Journal of Labor Economics*, the *Journal of Money, Credit and Banking*, the *Journal of Political Economy*, *Land Economics*, the *NBER Macroeconomics Annual*, the *Oxford Economic Papers*, the *Quarterly Journal of Economics*, the *RAND Journal of Economics* (*Bell Journal of Economics*, *Bell Journal of Economics and Management Science*), the *Review of Agricultural Economics*, the *Review of Economic Studies*, the *Review of Economics and Statistics*, the *Revue économique*, the *Scandinavian Journal of Economics* (*Swedish Journal of Economics*), and the *Southern Economic Journal*. The finance journals included the *Journal of Finance*, the *Journal of Business*, the *Journal of Financial and Quantitative Analysis*, the *Journal of Risk and Insurance*, the *Review of Financial Studies*, and *Business History Review*.

10. In the text I use the words *reference* and *citation* interchangeably, both meaning any time Ramsey was mentioned in a work in a favorable way or not. It may or may not be accompanied by a (complete or partial) bibliographic citation of Ramsey's papers.

Table 1   References to Frank Ramsey, 1928–82

	All Items (Articles, Book Reviews, etc.)	All Items Excluding Book Reviews
Economic growth	332	268
Taxation	114	105
Subjective probability/ expected utility	58	47
Other	29	22
Total	533	442

few journals other than the fifty mentioned through the abstracts published in journals available in JSTOR.[11]

As shown in table 1, Ramsey was mentioned 533 times in those fifty-five years, of which 62 percent are references to his growth model, 21 percent to his contribution to taxation, and 11 percent to subjective probability. The data include references in book reviews; many books on growth were published during the 1960s, and they were frequently reviewed. If a book gave Ramsey prominence, it is likely that many of its reviews would mention him, and this would therefore inflate the number of references. To check this, I also computed the overall number of references to Ramsey excluding all book reviews. In the second column of table 1, we observe the same pattern as with the book reviews: approximately 61 percent of the 442 citations were of Ramsey on economic growth, 24 percent on taxation, and 11 percent on subjective probability.

Since the pattern of references to Ramsey does not change much qualitatively by including or excluding book reviews, all the results reported hereafter are based on references to Ramsey that appeared in economics and finance journals including book reviews.[12]

11. These cases were recorded according to the date of their publication in the JSTOR journals, not in their original journal. I included an abstract only if it was not of a paper already selected in my search.

12. The same similarity between references with and without book reviews is observed in the yearly data. Moreover, it is not completely clear that including book reviews may distort the portrait if the interest is to see whether Ramsey was mentioned in the professional economics literature. Similarly, after examining the references to Ramsey only in economics journals, I concluded that it was qualitatively akin to the pattern of references in economics and finance journals I present here.

Table 2 References to Ramsey 1928, by Author and Journal, 1928–82

	Top-5 Authors	(t; p)	Top-5 Journals	(t; p)
Total citations	P. Samuelson	(38; 7%)	*Econometrica*	(72; 14%)
	E. Phelps	(9; 2%)	*AER*	(69; 13%)
	R. Solow	(8; 2%)	*Rev. Econ. Studies*	(67; 13%)
	F. Hahn/	(7; 1%)	*Economic Journal*	(52; 10%)
	M. Feldstein/			
	J. Stiglitz/		*JPE*	(27; 5%)
	K. Arrow			
Economic growth	P. Samuelson	(22; 7%)	*Rev. Econ. Studies*	(56; 17%)
	E. Phelps/R. Solow	(8; 2%)	*Econometrica*	(50; 15%)
	F. Hahn	(7; 2%)	*Economic Journal*	(37; 11%)
	P. Dasgupta/	(4; 1%)	*QJE/*	(16; 5%)
	K. Shell/		*Intern. Econ. Rev./*	
	S. Chakravarty		*JPE*	

Note: (*t*; *p*) indicate respectively the total number of references by an author or in a journal and as a percentage of the corresponding total. Thus, Samuelson cited Ramsey in 38 articles (22 of which cited Ramsey's growth model); those 38 articles make up 7 percent of all articles (whether by Samuelson or not) that cite Ramsey (the 22 articles also make up 7 percent of all articles that cite Ramsey's growth model). If a row has multiple entries, those entries correspond to each author or journal in it and not to their sum.

Another aspect worth exploring is the question of who mentioned Ramsey the most and in which journals. As table 2 demonstrates, even though there was a single author (Samuelson) who led the references to Ramsey, they were evenly spread throughout many journals.

So the next question to consider is whether Ramsey was mentioned by economists at all in the period 1928–50s. The answer is yes, he was, but not as frequently as in the boom observed since the 1950s. As figure 1 illustrates, we see the line of total references to Ramsey as a percentage of economics and finance articles published per year and vertical bars decomposing them into the categories mentioned before.

From figure 1, we see that from the 1930s up to the early 1950s Ramsey was mostly mentioned with respect to his growth model, at a level generally below 0.1 percent of the total articles published in economics and finance. Even though the relative importance of Ramsey in the 1930s was practically the same as that of the early 1950s, from roughly 1955 onward this number increased substantially.

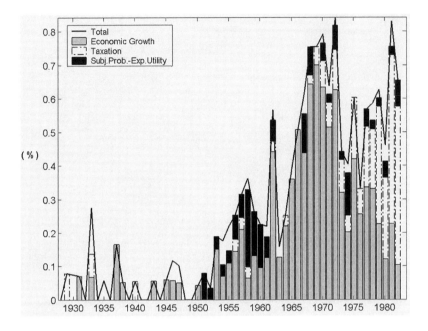

Figure 1 References to Ramsey by category over time (1928–82)

We can identify three different waves of "rediscoveries" of Ramsey. First, the references to Ramsey's discussion of subjective probability and expected utility appeared in the 1950s and early 1960s in the journals available at JSTOR (about 40 percent of the 61 references to Ramsey in 1951–60 were on subjective probability, while this share was not greater than 8 percent in the following decades).[13] Second, from the late 1960s onward, there was an important movement in public economics (and a bit later in monetary economics) of rediscovering Ramsey's 1927 contribution to optimal taxation (about 40 percent of the 252 references to Ramsey from 1971 to 1982 were on taxation, the highest mark after the 15 percent level registered in 1928–50s).[14] Third, the wave in the growth literature references to Ramsey's growth model boomed from the mid-1950s until the early 1970s, reaching a maximum in the late 1960s (85 percent of the

13. This finding needs to be understood with care, as it is limited to JSTOR journals and does not include publications of the Cowles Commission or the RAND Corporation on subjective probability and game theory, where Ramsey may have been mentioned.
14. See Duarte 2007b for a discussion of Ramsey in monetary economics.

200 references to Ramsey in 1961–70 were on economic growth).[15] From the mid-1960s (intensified mostly from the mid-1970s onward), Ramsey's growth model was incorporated into the literature of the economics of conservation and exhaustible resources.[16] From the 1970s references to Ramsey's growth model gradually decreased and by the early 1980s had reached the prewar levels.

Why are these waves relevant? Because the fact that Ramsey became a patron saint in the subjective probability literature, for instance, may have helped his later canonization in the growth literature. This is particularly important when we observe that a few economists were engaged in some or all of these branches, such as Samuelson, who was the leading author citing Ramsey in three out of the four categories I considered (economic growth, expected utility, and other).

What do the data presented in figure 1 say about the neglect of Ramsey from 1928 to the late 1950s? Clearly, the pattern observed up to 1950 is different from the citations Ramsey's growth paper received afterward. If having an impact on economics means observing the number of relative references above 0.2 percent of the total, it is indeed correct to state that Ramsey was neglected until the 1960s. Despite the different patterns observed before and after 1950, I would argue that it is too strong to claim that Ramsey 1928 did not have an immediate impact on economics.

As Marion Gaspard (2003, 313–14) has argued, the "*à la* Ramsey" model that emerged in the postwar growth economics was, not surprisingly, substantially different from Ramsey's original contribution. The Ramsey-Cass-Koopmans model is a (stochastic) model based on a representative agent who discounts future utility at a constant rate, which is quite different from Ramsey's model with an ambiguity regarding both time discounting and whose utility function it is, besides having no uncertainty.[17] What happened in the 1950s and 1960s was the emergence of the optimal growth literature, which incorporated and generalized Ramsey's contribution.

---

15. This pattern also reflects the emergence of the economic growth literature. It is hard to get from JSTOR a meaningful indicator of the references to Ramsey 1928 as a percentage of economic growth articles.

16. The main goal of this literature was to discuss optimal-growth paths when there are exhaustible resources. See Erreygers, this volume, for a historical analysis of this branch of economics.

17. Duarte (2008b) discusses the stabilization of the time-discounting practice. On Ramsey's ambiguity about whose utility function he analyzed, whether of a social planner or of some sort of a representative agent, Duarte (2008a) argues that Ramsey may have had in mind a representative agent similar to the way macroeconomists think of it nowadays.

Table 3   First References to Ramsey 1928 in JSTOR Journals

Author	Title	Journal	Year	Reference
H. Hotelling	"The Economics of Exhaustible Resources"	*JPE*	1931	Y
H. Dickinson	"Price Formation in a Socialist Community"	*EJ*	1933	Y
P. Samuelson	"A Note on Measurement of Utility"	*RES*	1937	Y
H. Smith	"Marx and the Trade Cycle"	*RES*	1937	Y
N. Kaldor	"Prof. Pigou on Money Wages . . ."	*EJ*	1937	Y
R. Harrod	"Scope and Method of Economics"	*EJ*	1938	N
P. Samuelson	"Dynamics, Statics, and the Stationary State"	*RESt*	1943	Y
J. Meade	"Mr. Lerner on 'The Economics of Control'"	*EJ*	1945	Y
P. Samuelson	"Lord Keynes and the General Theory"	*Ecm*	1946	Y
A. Pigou	"Economic Progress in a Stable Environment"	*Ecn*	1947	Y
J. Graaf	"Mr. Harrod on Hump Saving"	*Ecn*	1950	Y

Note: The last column indicates if the article gives the bibliographic reference of Ramsey 1928 (Y = yes, N = no). Journal codes: *Journal of Political Economy (JPE)*, *Economic Journal (EJ)*, *Review of Economic Studies (RES)*, *Review of Economics and Statistics (RESt)*, *Econometrica (Ecm)*, *Economica (Ecn)*.

The fact that such generalization happened only during that period does not mean that Ramsey's 1928 article was entirely neglected, as the JSTOR data indicate.

A look at the articles citing Ramsey 1928 during the period 1928–50s (see table 3) shows that different economists discussed different aspects of Ramsey's analysis. For instance, his notion of a utility saturation level (which he calls "Bliss," a trick he used to guarantee that the improper integral of undiscounted flows of instantaneous utilities over the infinite future has an upper bound); the so-called Ramsey rule, which gives the optimal saving rate; issues of savings in a planned economy; and the problem of discounting future utilities were all examined in the period before 1950. This shows that Ramsey's ideas were actually understood and explored by some (although less than in the postwar period), even though generalizations of his method and mathematical tools appeared later.

To strengthen my claim that Ramsey's growth model was appreciated to some degree in the period following its publication (1928–50s), I would like to mention some important books that cited his paper, as additional evidence to the JSTOR article search analyzed above. Pigou was the first to cite Ramsey 1928, in the second edition of his book *A Study in Public Finance*, published in 1929 (123).[18] This was an important book throughout the 1930s. In 1930 Keynes cited Ramsey twice: in his *Treatise on Money*, when discussing the rate of investment and its fluctuations, and in Ramsey's obituary note published in the *Economic Journal*. In 1936 James Meade cited Ramsey 1928 in his book *Economic Analysis and Policy*.[19] In this same year, Roy Harrod ([1936] 1965, 106–9), who had been a friend of Ramsey and had discussed with him some of the ideas of his 1928 article (Duarte 2009), discussed how to justify that "people tend to save a larger proportion of a large income" and examined Ramsey's ideas (with full reference to his article) as one out of three motives for savings. Later, Ramsey 1928 is cited, discussed, and used as an application in economics of the calculus of variation by Allen (1938, 536–40), a prominent book on mathematical economics of the first half of the twentieth century.[20] Pigou (1941, 105) again cites Ramsey 1928 when explaining the optimal saving condition: "This is a well-known proposition. Anyone to whom it is not apparent is referred to Frank Ramsey's article." A few years later, Harrod (1948, 40) refers again to Ramsey 1928 in discussing the distinction between the law of diminishing utility and pure time preference in determining the intertemporal allocation of consumption. Finally, Abram Bergson (1948, 422) cites Ramsey 1928 in a book published for the American Economic Association, aiming "to provide to the economist outside a particular field an intelligible and reliable account of its main ideas . . . which have evolved during the last ten or fifteen years."[21]

18. Duarte (2009) shows that Ramsey and Pigou interacted very closely and argues that Ramsey's papers on taxation and on growth emerged out of this relation.

19. Meade's 1936 book was perceived as providing an explanation of Ramsey 1928: Dennis Robertson (1958, 89 n. 1), who interacted with Meade in 1930–31, had exactly this view, as well as Samuelson (1953, 577 n. 26). Meade (1955, 93–101), and in the accompanying Mathematical Supplement, also discussed Ramsey's ideas on optimal growth and referred to "Mr. Ramsay's [*sic*] well-known article."

20. Remember that Allen (1966, 1967) himself argued later that Ramsey 1928 was neglected for more than thirty years after its publication. He can be understood as saying that "thirty years went by before a generalization of Ramsey's study was made," as Koopmans (1967, 6) writes about Ramsey. As indicated before, my claim is that having no generalization is not synonymous with having no substantial immediate impact.

21. Preface to the book (v) written by Howard Ellis.

After World War II, Robert Dorfman, Samuelson, and Robert Solow (1958), following Samuelson and Solow 1956, presented "the Ramsey model" as an intertemporal optimal one-sector (linear) growth model. The model's main characteristic was to have a single good and therefore to serve as a benchmark for the multisector models of the time. At this time, we find in the literature different labels used to designate the one-sector model: the "Ramsey-Solow model," "Clark-Ramsey parable," or even "Clark-Ramsey-Solow-Swan-Meade model" (but never "Harrod-Domar-Ramsey," despite Harrod-Domar's being a single-good model). Later, the key distinction came between the two strands of the neoclassical growth model: the behaviorist, represented by the Solow model, and the optimizing, characterized by the Ramsey model. It was at this moment that the Ramsey model became also known as the Ramsey-Cass-Koopmans model (as in Sato 1971 and much later in Romer 1996, chap. 2, pt. A). It was the optimizing Ramsey model with explicit microfoundations that became the core of many areas of modern economics, as suggested by Barro and Sala-i-Martin (2003, 16–17). It is worth mentioning that Solow (1953) was aware of Ramsey's contribution prior to publishing his two major articles on growth, in 1956 and 1957 (when discussing how to couple, contrary to the Harrod model, prices and output equilibrium dynamics).[22]

Before concluding, I want to stress that Harrod and Meade, two key figures in the development of growth theory, knew and cited Ramsey's growth model. Harrod ([1936] 1965) initially saw Ramsey's contribution as a possible foundation for his exogenous saving function. Harrod (1960, 280–81) stated that the ideas he developed in chapter 2 of his 1948 book were "much influenced" by Ramsey. However, over time he broke away from Ramsey to the point of repudiating his utilitarian analysis in 1960 (Young 1989, 183). Meade ("The Last Great Utilitarian," according to Solow 1987, 986) was important in explaining Ramsey's analysis and connecting it with his discussion on the optimal population size (combining arguments of efficiency and equity). Meade came to discuss welfare economics and the optimal population problem with Koopmans while both were at the League of Nations in 1938–40 (Koopmans [1975] 1992). Finally, Solow was also familiar with Ramsey's contribution in the 1950s, which he understood as an additional normative chapter to his own positive growth theory.

22. Solow (1987, 986–87) suggests that in the 1950s he was working on a Ramsey problem with population growth. He scrapped it after seeing that Meade (1955) had discussed this.

**Understanding the Growing Uses
of Ramsey 1928**

The conclusion that Ramsey had some impact on economics raises questions about why Ramsey happened to be so popular in the postwar period. The usual explanation among contemporary economists is, as noted above, that Ramsey's mathematics was too sophisticated for, and not well received by, the economists of his time. However, we can better understand this by analyzing how the three ingredients of his model (mathematical formalism, utility-maximizing agents, and aggregate-level control with clear normative content) became central to the growth literature that emerged in the postwar period.

It is a very apt description of the optimal growth literature that emerged in the 1960s to say that it "carries the imprint: 'Economics by Ramsey; Mathematics by Pontryagin'" (Intriligator 1969, 117). Thus the Hamiltonian formalism, from its origins in the energy physics of the mid-nineteenth century to its transformation into the modern control theory of Pontryagin during the postwar period (Wulwick 1995), is one important cause behind the explosion of references to Ramsey 1928 after World War II. More broadly, the mathematization of economics during the second half of the twentieth century and the widening use of optimal control theory and stochastic dynamic methods in this period—from military needs to the broader audience of social scientists, government officials, mathematicians, engineers, and businessmen involved in nonmilitary problems—set the stage for making Ramsey a giant in the optimal growth literature by generalizing his analysis.

The expanding use of some of the tools employed by Ramsey 1928 was part of the move from interwar pluralism to postwar neoclassicism (Morgan and Rutherford 1998). Here a comparison between Ramsey (a British mathematician) and Griffith C. Evans (a North American mathematician) illustrates why the former, and not the latter, became a venerated figure in economics even though both employed calculus of variations techniques to economic problems. While Evans published several papers on economic problems in mathematics journals, Ramsey 1928 was published in one of the most important economics journals, and his contribution was quickly praised by Pigou and Keynes. More important, Evans was dismissive of the subjective theory of value and utilitarian framework of welfare analysis, while Ramsey applied the type of mathematics that came to be appreciated by economists during the postwar period in utility-maximizing models (Evans does not cite Ramsey in his 1930 book

Mathematical Introduction to Economics).[23] This partially explains why Lawrence Klein (1951, 450), who was linked to Evans (Weintraub 2002, 71), was harsh with both Keynes and Ramsey:

> Keynes really cannot have appreciated mathematical economics, to judge from his published comments on it, and one of his main positive statements in print praising Ramsey's article on savings is surely a mistaken view. Ramsey's article is competent and interesting but hardly deserving of very special notice or comment that is not equally well due to numerous other articles in mathematical economics of the same period. Ramsey's methods and results are not especially novel.

Besides the issue of the tools employed, there are other important changes occurring in economics in the interwar period that opened the door for Ramsey's induction into the economist hall of fame. Since optimal growth theory can be seen as dynamic welfare economics, its way was paved by other developments in welfare and dynamic economics during the 1960s. The general move was from partial to a formal general equilibrium framework, with normative statements following the scientific ethic of new welfare economics (Duarte 2008a): that of an ordinal welfare economics that sidestepped interpersonal comparison of utilities. Economics during the 1930s and early 1940s had not completed these general moves. In this period, few English-speaking economists knew the work of Vilfredo Pareto, and those interested in mathematical economics formed a very small community (Weintraub 2002, esp. chap. 5). Neil De Marchi (2003) analyzes how Samuelson struggled from 1938 to 1962 to find an appropriate graphical representation of a Paretian argument about gains of trade (and answer the subtle challenge brought by the new welfare economics to the economists' identification of "being on a higher indifference curve" with "is preferable to"). Moreover, Ramsey 1928 was not employed in any of the efforts to develop a general equilibrium analysis during the 1930s and 1940s: von Neumann (1945–46) does not mention Ramsey in his general equilibrium growth model. The same is true about Abba Lerner's discussion of the determination of investment in a controlled economy (in his 1944 book *The Economics of Control*). Lerner's neglect of Ramsey's analysis was criticized by Meade in 1945 (table 3).

---

23. See Weintraub 2002, chap. 2, for an analysis of "the marginalization of Evans's ideas in the postwar period in economics," which happened "not because [Evans's ideas] were mathematically unsophisticated [or because he was] disconnected from the disciplinary networks that validate acceptable contributions to the discipline" (42).

With respect to dynamics, Weintraub (1991, esp. chap. 2) discusses how economists of the 1930s had a diverse and complex understanding of equilibrium and dynamic theory. Samuelson, in his *Foundations* (1947), "set out the issues of statics and dynamics and equilibrium in economic theory" (Weintraub 1991, 39), while in 1948, based on a series of lectures composed during the autumn of 1946, Harrod (1948, 1–2) wrote that despite the increasing use of the terms *static* and *dynamic* in economics, "we have lacked a full methodological consideration of their proper application. Failing this, their use may tend to make confusion worse confounded."

The variety of dynamic methods and concepts also explains in part the delay of bringing Ramsey's growth model to the core of this literature. As late as 1969 we find Michio Morishima aiming to make a contribution to the theory of dynamic general equilibrium:

> The general theory of static equilibrium was nearing completion as early as 1874 [with the work of Léon Walras], but, in spite of our keen desire and constant effort, it is taking a long time to obtain its dynamic counterpart. It seems to me that this is mainly due to the lack of an established concept of "dynamic" or "moving" equilibrium. It is true that a number of definitions of dynamic equilibrium have been presented. But we have not yet been provided with a generally accepted one which can serve as the core of the theory. (v)

Along with the issues associated with the mathematical tool that Ramsey employed and the changes taking place in welfare and dynamic economics during the 1930s and 1940s, the late reception of Ramsey's utility-maximizing analysis in economics may also be explained by three other factors.[24] First, his death in 1930 obviously prevented him from extending his model by enlisting economists to a utilitarian growth agenda or by training his own pupils—of course assuming that Ramsey would wish to develop further his growth model, despite the turbulent years from the Great Depression to World War II.

Second, the Great Depression came a year after the publication of Ramsey's paper. This meant that the economy was perceived to be far

---

24. It was the utilitarian perfect-knowledge framework in which Ramsey worked that led G. L. S. Shackle (1967, 5) not to include him in the "new generation of students, which went seriously to college only in 1919" that generated "an immense creative spasm which . . . has completely altered the orientation and character of economics." Ramsey is mentioned nowhere in Shackle's book. His economics was presumably part of the economic theory at the opening of the 1930s that "still rested on the assumption of a basically orderly and tranquil world" (5).

from things like a bliss point and to be potentially unstable. Moreover, several economists, including Keynes, saw excessive savings as one cause of the Depression. Koopmans (1967, 3) went to the extreme of blaming solely the Great Depression, and not the calculus of variations, for the dormancy of Ramsey's growth model until the 1960s: "Had not these events intervened and deflected economists from following up Ramsey's powerful ideas, the optimal growth literature of the sixties might and indeed could have been written in the thirties." Another aspect of the Great Depression is that it may have made some economists very skeptical about assumptions that individuals decide how much to consume and to save by solving an intertemporal utility maximization problem. A by-product of such reasoning would be the claim that Keynesian economists did not leave much room for a conception of optimizing economic agents. These arguments may partially explain Ramsey's late receptivity if taken a step forward, beyond what has been pursued here: it is necessary to unravel the network in which these arguments operated, what economists subscribed to and disseminated them, what arguments were used by their critics, and so on.[25]

Finally, we can appreciate why three decades separated Ramsey's original paper from its later popularity by also paying attention to the reasons behind the emergence of the optimal growth literature in the 1950s (see Chakravarty 1987). Economists concerned with problems of development planning in low-income countries redirected their attention exactly to the question Ramsey asked: how much of its income should a nation save?

Another element of the rise of the optimal growth literature pointed out by Sukhamoy Chakravarty (1987, 731) was that it provided theoretical advice to the government about optimal savings. As Jan Tinbergen (1956, 603) had argued, the choice of the rate of savings in developing economies "has been made . . . on rather arbitrary grounds." This choice also had no theoretical foundations both in the Russian planned economy and in the Western democracies after World War II where savings "was controlled to a large extent by the governments." "Since the choice is of such far-reaching impact on the economy, the question seems in place whether a more rational basis can be given to such a choice" (603). A bit later, the literature on "golden rule" growth discussed how to obtain a steady-state solution in Solow's model where consumption per capita is the highest pos-

---

25. Something in the line of Kyun Kim (1989), who shows how different business cycle theories of the interwar period were dominated by Keynesian economics.

sible. This solution was a possible answer to Ramsey's question, although not necessarily using his formal utility-maximizing framework (see Phelps 1966 and references therein).

Concluding Remarks

Frank Ramsey's important 1928 contribution to economic growth became very popular in economics in the late 1950s. Economists engaged in this literature portray Ramsey as a sleeping giant: a mathematician who had almost no impact on the economics profession prior to the late 1950s because his mathematical analysis was out of reach for the typical economist of his time.

My goal in this article was to challenge this view in order to understand how Ramsey's growth model became part of the neoclassical economic growth literature during the 1950s and 1960s and how Ramsey came to be viewed as a patron saint of this field. I analyzed the stabilization of Ramsey's growth model in postwar economics through a JSTOR search for the period 1928–82 and also important book references up to the 1950s. Based on this data set, I concluded that Ramsey was in fact recognized in economics before 1950. What happened after 1950 was a series of generalizations of Ramsey's growth model, which generated a very different pattern of references to the Cambridge mathematician's contribution.

It is clear that the Ramsey-Cass-Koopmans model that emerged in the postwar period was different from Ramsey's original contribution and provided a flexible framework of analysis because it combined mathematical formalism with utility-maximizing agents and aggregate-level control. The postwar growth models carried the imprint: economics by Ramsey, mathematics by Pontryagin. This literature was a result of developments in economics and the associated tools such as control theory. As Koopmans (1957, 170) explained, "Changes in tools and changes in emphasis on various problems go together and interact."[26]

The crucial point for historians is to provide a context for understanding the delayed recognition of Ramsey. It was a consequence not only of the mathematical tools he employed and his utility-maximizing framework but also of the variety of notions of dynamic equilibrium that existed in the 1930s and 1940s, the uneasiness of the economists of this period

---

26. Pickering (1995, 7) characterizes this as a dialectic resistance and accommodation among human and material agencies.

with Paretian arguments and the discussions about the role of normative statements in scientific economics, the call for a dynamic general equilibrium framework, and the factors that led development economists during the 1950s to ask the same question addressed by Ramsey.

Only by examining all these elements can we place the progression of logical improvements stressed by Solow ([1970] 2000) to explain the development of growth theory (from Harrod-Domar's unstable equilibrium, to Solow's smooth and self-limiting fluctuations based on a Keynesian ad hoc savings function, to the Ramsey-Cass-Koopmans model of optimizing savings, and later to the endogenous growth literature) in a context that helps us understand how economists transported Ramsey from the Cambridge milieu of the 1920s to the North American economics of the postwar period.

References

Alexander, A. R. 2006. Tragic Mathematics: Romantic Narratives and the Refounding of Mathematics in the Early Nineteenth Century. *Isis* 97.4:714–26.

Allen, R. G. D. 1938. *Mathematical Analysis for Economists.* London: Macmillan.

———. 1966. Review of "Mathematics in the Social Sciences and Other Essays," by R. Stone. *Economic Journal* 76.304:857–59.

———. 1967. A Simple Approach to Macro-Economic Dynamics. *Economica* 34.136:395–407.

Arrow, K. J. 1973. Box 22, folder "Hotelling Obituary (1)." Arrow Papers, Rare Book, Manuscript, and Special Collections Library, Duke University.

———. 1974. In Memoriam: Harold Hotelling, 1895–1973. *American Economic Review* 64.6:1102–3.

———. 1980. Review of "Foundations: Essays in Philosophy, Logic, Mathematics and Economics," by F. P. Ramsey, edited by D. H. Mellor. *Journal of Political Economy* 88.3:636–38.

———. 1986. Letter to Adrian Darnell, 14 July. Arrow Papers, Rare Book, Manuscript, and Special Collections Library, Duke University.

———. 1987. Harold Hotelling. In *The New Palgrave: A Dictionary of Economics*, edited by J. Eatwell, M. Milgate, and P. Newman. London: Macmillan.

———. 2008. E-mail to the author, 27 May.

Arrow, K. J., and E. L. Lehmann. 2005. Harold Hotelling 1895–1973, A Biographical Memoir. In *Biographical Memoirs* 87. Washington, D.C.: National Academy of Sciences.

Barro, R. J., and X. Sala-i-Martin. 2003. *Economic Growth.* 2nd ed. Cambridge: MIT Press.

Bergson, A. 1948. Socialist Economics. In *A Survey of Contemporary Economics*, edited by H. S. Ellis. Philadelphia: Blakiston.

Black, J. 1962. Optimum Savings Reconsidered, or Ramsey without Tears. *Economic Journal* 72.286:360–66.

Cass, D. 1965. Optimum Growth in an Aggregate Model of Capital Accumulation. *Review of Economic Studies* 32.3:233–40.

———. 1966. Optimum Growth in an Aggregate Model of Capital Accumulation: A Turnpike Theorem. *Econometrica* 34.4:833–50.

Chakravarty, S. 1987. Optimal Savings. In *The New Palgrave: A Dictionary of Economics*, edited by J. Eatwell, M. Milgate, and P. Newman. London: Macmillan.

Darnell, A. C., ed. 1990. *The Collected Economics Articles of Harold Hotelling*. New York: Springer-Verlag.

De Marchi, N. 2003. Visualizing the Gains from Trade, Mid-1870s to 1962. *European Journal of the History of Economic Thought* 10.4:551–72.

Dorfman, R., P. A. Samuelson, and R. M. Solow. 1958. *Linear Programming and Economic Analysis*. New York: McGraw-Hill.

Duarte, P. G. 2007a. Constructing Concepts of Optimal Monetary Policy in the Postwar Period. PhD diss., Duke University.

———. 2007b. Visiting Frank P. Ramsey: The Public Finance Concept of Optimal Monetary Policy. Unpublished manuscript, http://ssrn.com/abstract=985331.

———. 2008a. Another Chapter in the History of Ramsey's Optimal Feasible Taxation. Unpublished manuscript, Department of Economics, University of São Paulo (FEA-USP).

———. 2008b. A Path through the Wilderness: Time Discounting in Growth Models. Unpublished, Department of Economics, University of São Paulo (FEA-USP).

———. 2009. Frank P. Ramsey: A Cambridge Economist. *HOPE* 41.3:445–70.

Faria, J. R. 2005. The Contributions of Ramsey to Economics. In *F. P. Ramsey— Critical Reassessments*, edited by M. J. Frápolli. London: Continuum.

Gaspard, M. 2003. Ramsey's Theory of National Saving: A Mathematician in Cambridge. *Journal of the History of Economic Thought* 25.4:413–35.

Harrod, R. F. 1948. *Towards a Dynamic Economics*. London: Macmillan.

———. 1960. Second Essay in Dynamic Theory. *Economic Journal* 70.278:277–93.

———. [1936] 1965. *The Trade Cycle*. New York: Kelley.

Hotelling, H. 1931. The Economics of Exhaustible Resources. *Journal of Political Economy* 39.2:137–75.

Intriligator, M. D. 1969. Review of "Essays on the Theory of Optimal Economic Growth," edited by K. Shell. *Journal of Business* 42.1:116–17.

Keynes, J. M. 1930. *A Treatise on Money*. Vol. 2. London: Macmillan.

———. [1933] 1972. *Essays in Biography*. Vol. 10 of *The Collected Writings of John Maynard Keynes*, edited by D. Moggridge. London: Macmillan.

Kim, K. 1989. *Equilibrium Business Cycle Theory in Historical Perspective*. Cambridge: Cambridge University Press.

Klein, L. R. 1951. The Life of John Maynard Keynes. *Journal of Political Economy* 59.5:443–51.

Koopmans, T. C. 1957. *Three Essays on the State of Economic Science*. New York: McGraw-Hill.

———. 1965. On the Concept of Optimal Economic Growth. In *The Econometric Approach to Development Planning*. Amsterdam: North-Holland.

———. 1967. Objectives, Constraints, and Outcomes in Optimal Growth Models. *Econometrica* 35.1:1–15.

———. [1975] 1992. Autobiography. In *Nobel Lectures, Economics 1969–1980*, edited by A. Lindbeck. Singapore: World Scientific.

Meade, J. E. [1936] 1937. *An Introduction to Economic Analysis and Policy*. 2nd ed. Oxford: Oxford University Press.

———. 1955. *Trade and Welfare*. Vol. 2. Oxford: Oxford University Press.

Morgan, M., and M. Rutherford, eds. 1998. *From Interwar Pluralism to Postwar Neoclassicism*. Supplemental issue of vol. 30 of *HOPE*. Durham, N.C.: Duke University Press.

Morishima, M. 1969. *Theory of Economic Growth*. Oxford: Clarendon.

Peston, M. 1969. Review of "Precursors in Mathematical Economics: An Anthology," edited by W. Baumol and S. Goldfeld. *Economica* 36.142:210–11.

Phelps, E. S. 1966. *Golden Rules of Economic Growth*. New York: Norton.

Pickering, A. 1995. *The Mangle of Practice: Time, Agency, and Science*. Chicago: University of Chicago Press.

Pigou, A. C. 1929. *A Study in Public Finance*. 2nd ed. London: Macmillan.

———. 1941. *Employment and Equilibrium*. London: Macmillan.

Ramsey, F. P. 1927. A Contribution to the Theory of Taxation. *Economic Journal* 37.145:47–61.

———. 1928. A Mathematical Theory of Saving. *Economic Journal* 38.152:543–59.

Robertson, D. H. 1958. *Lectures on Economic Principles*. Vol. 2. London: Staples.

Romer, D. 1996. *Advanced Macroeconomics*. New York: McGraw-Hill.

Samuelson, P. A. 1937. A Note on Measurement of Utility. *Review of Economic Studies* 4.2:155–61.

———. 1943. Dynamics, Statics, and the Stationary State. *Review of Economics and Statistics* 25.1:58–68.

———. 1946. Lord Keynes and the General Theory. *Econometrica* 14.3:187–200.

———. 1947. *Foundations of Economic Analysis*. Cambridge: Harvard University Press.

———. 1953. Full Employment versus Progress and Other Economic Goals. In *Income Stabilization for a Developing Democracy*, edited by M. F. Millikan. New Haven, Conn.: Yale University Press.

———. 1970. What Makes for a Beautiful Problem in Science? *Journal of Political Economy* 78.6:1372–77.

Samuelson, P. A., and R. M. Solow. 1956. A Complete Capital Model Involving Heterogeneous Capital Goods. *Quarterly Journal of Economics* 70.4:537–62.

Sato, R. 1971. Review of "Mathematical Theories of Economic Growth," by E. Burmeister and A. R. Dobell. *Journal of Economic Literature* 9.2:482–84.

Shackle, G. L. S. 1967. *The Years of High Theory*. Cambridge: Cambridge University Press.

Solow, R. M. 1953. A Note on the Price Level and Interest Rate in a Growth Model. *Review of Economic Studies* 21.1:74–79.

———. 1987. James Meade at Eighty. *Economic Journal* 97.388:986–88.

———. [1970] 2000. *Growth Theory: An Exposition.* 2nd ed. Oxford: Oxford University Press.

Stone, R. 1966. Three Models of Economic Growth. In *Mathematics in the Social Sciences and Other Essays*, edited by R. Stone. Cambridge: MIT Press.

Tinbergen, J. 1956. The Optimum Rate of Saving. *Economic Journal* 66.264:603–9.

Von Neumann, J. 1945–46. A Model of General Economic Equilibrium. *Review of Economic Studies* 13.1:1–9.

Weintraub, E. R. 1991. *Stabilizing Dynamics.* Cambridge: Cambridge University Press.

———. 2002. *How Economics Became a Mathematical Science.* Durham, N.C.: Duke University Press.

Werin, L., and K. G. Jungenfelt. 1976. Tjalling Koopmans' Contribution to Economics. *Scandinavian Journal of Economics* 78.1:81–102.

Wulwick, N. J. 1995. The Hamiltonian Formalism and Optimal Growth Theory. In *Measurement, Quantification, and Economic Analysis*, edited by I. H. Rima. London: Routledge.

Young, W. 1989. *Harrod and His Trade Cycle Group.* New York: New York University Press.

James Tobin and Growth Theory: Financial Factors and Long-Run Growth

Robert W. Dimand and Steven N. Durlauf

James Tobin, while universally acknowledged as one of the leading macro-economists of the twentieth century, is less well remembered as a growth economist, despite his continuing interest in growth throughout his career. His early work placed him near the origins of modern growth economics. Robert Solow (2004, 657) recalls that Tobin "published 'A Dynamic Aggregate Model' at just the time when I was working on economic growth, so I recognized a master hand."[1] According to Tobin, "My 1955 piece, 'A Dynamic Aggregate Model,' may be my favorite; it was the most fun to write. It differed from the other growth literature by explicitly introducing monetary government debt as a store of value, a vehicle of saving alternative to real capital, and by generating a business cycle that interrupted the growth process" (Breit and Spencer 1990, 130–31). That said, Tobin's analysis has failed to claim a place as a classic in the literature. Although the model in his 1955 paper has "the key features of the one-sector neoclassical growth model (a neoclassical two-factor production function in capital and labour, smooth capital-labour substitution, competitive factor markets)," and although "it includes several other features (outside fiat money in the asset menu, money wage inflexibility and

We thank Donald Hester and participants at the 2008 *HOPE* conference, especially Pedro Duarte, for helpful comments. Durlauf acknowledges support of the National Science Foundation.

1. Tobin (1955, 103) thanked Solow for comments on the paper.

History of Political Economy 41 (annual suppl.) DOI 10.1215/00182702-2009-023

business cycle fluctuations)," Tobin's model "has not received the credit it deserves" (Buiter 2003, F596).

Tobin's (1965, 1968) subsequent work on long-run economic growth and capital formation in a monetary economy (see also Haliassos and Tobin 1990 and Tobin with Golub 1998) proved more influential, even though it was less ambitious. Tobin's Fisher Lecture to the Econometric Society, "Money and Economic Growth" (1965), attracted considerable attention (see Johnson 1967; Solow 1970, chap. 4; Foley and Sidrauski 1971; Stein 1971; and Patinkin 1972). According to Athanasios Orphanides and Solow (1990, 257),

> Tobin's 1965 paper succeeded in framing the question that has domi-
> nated the literature since: Does the rate of monetary growth have any
> long-run effect on the real rate of interest, capital-intensity, output and
> welfare? He also established the framework within which the question
> would be debated: portfolio choice, where fiat money is one of several
> competing assets. It has turned out to be difficult to assess the "practi-
> cal" relevance of the Tobin effect precisely because equally plausible
> models of portfolio balance can yield quite different answers. . . . Once
> again, we observe that seemingly small variations in a model change
> the conclusion regarding the effect of inflation on capital accumulation.

This facet of Tobin's work generated a literature, but it is not a major component of current growth economics.

In this article, we review Tobin's main contributions to growth economics and discuss some reasons why they have not, so far, proved of lasting influence. Tobin's efforts to integrate short-run and long-run macroeconomic phenomena, an objective echoed in a number of current approaches to macroeconomics, rely on very different assumptions than these newer approaches. Hence current growth theory does not reflect Tobin's overall vision. Yet this vision may still prove to be important.

A Dynamic Aggregative Model

The state of the art when Tobin (and Solow and Trevor Swan) turned to growth theory was represented by Roy Harrod (1939, 1948, 1952) and Evsey Domar (1946, 1957). The models of Harrod and Domar were widely interpreted as assuming fixed factor proportions and savings propensities, resulting in an unstable, "knife-edge" equilibrium. While Nicholas Kaldor (1956) proposed to eliminate this instability by making the propensity to save endogenous, depending on the distribution of income between wages and profits, Tobin (1960) found the implications of this device untenable. Harold Pilvin (1953), Tobin (1955), Solow (1956), and Swan (1956) eliminated the knife-edge property of the equilibrium path via a richer specification of the aggregate production function: substitution between capital and labor rendered steady-state growth a stable equilibrium (although Swan denied that Harrod's theory led to a knife-edge equilibrium and argued that he was only formalizing Harrod's adjustment mechanism).

Tobin (1955, 103) objected that

> contemporary theoretical models of the business cycle and of economic growth typically possess two related characteristics: (1) they assume production functions that allow for no substitution between factors, and (2) the variables are all real magnitudes; monetary and price phenomena have no significance. Because of these characteristics, these models present a rigid and angular picture of the economic process: straight and narrow paths from which the slightest deviation spells disaster, abrupt and sharp reversals, intractable ceilings and floors. The models are highly suggestive, but their representation of the economy arouses the suspicion that they have left out some essential mechanisms of adjustment. The purpose of this paper is to suggest a simple aggregative model that allows for substitution possibilities and for monetary effects.

Tobin (1955) had factor substitution possibilities in common with Solow (1956) and Swan (1956), but the introduction of money in growth models was distinctively Tobin's contribution, in keeping with the central role of money in his life's work in economics. While the models of Solow and Swan yielded only steady-state paths of capacity growth in a fully employed economy, Tobin's 1955 model had three possibilities: steady growth, cycles, or "continuing underemployment—'stagnation' during which positive investment increases the capital stock and possibly the level of real income. This outcome, like the cycle, depends on some kind of price or monetary inflexibility" (103).

Tobin assumed that the aggregate production function exhibited constant returns in capital and labor, so that the marginal products of the factor inputs depend only on the proportion in which inputs are used. Tobin's model was thus in line with Solow's and Swan's. Tobin moved beyond their single-asset world by introducing money. There are only two stores of value:

physical capital (K) and currency (M). M has an exogenous own-rate of interest (assumed to be zero), and the quantity of M is also exogenous, with changes in the money supply level generated by government budget surpluses or deficits. Letting p denote prices, real wealth (W) is equal to $K + M/p$, and portfolio balance (owners of wealth are content with the division of their wealth between capital and money) is determined by the standard money market equilibrium condition $M/p = L(K, r, Y)$. The partial derivatives of L (the liquidity preference function) with respect to its three arguments are nonnegative, strictly negative, and strictly positive, respectively. "Requirements for transactions balances of currency are assumed, as is customary, to depend on income. . . . Given their real wealth, W, owners of wealth will wish to hold a larger amount of capital, and a smaller amount of currency, the higher the rent on capital, r. Given the rent on capital, owners of wealth will desire to put some part of any increment of their wealth into capital and some part into currency" (Tobin 1955, 105). Wealth owners are assumed to be risk averse: "The principle of 'not putting all your eggs in one basket' explains why a risk-avoiding investor may well hold a diversified portfolio even when the expected returns of all the assets in it are not identical. For the present purpose it explains why an owner of wealth will hold currency in excess of transactions requirements, even when its expected return is zero and the expected return on capital is positive" (106–7).

Tobin identified portfolio balance as "the one of the four building blocks of the model that introduces possibly unconventional and unfamiliar material into the structure" (105). Several of his section headings look unconventional from the vantage point of what has become the neoclassical growth model: "Technical Progress and Price Deflation," "Monetary Expansion as an Alternative to Price Deflation," "Wage Inflexibility as an Obstacle to Growth," "Wage Inflexibility and Cyclical Fluctuations," and "Wage Inflexibility and Stagnation." In their 1956 articles on the neoclassical growth model, both Solow and Swan assumed that full employment was maintained by appropriate Keynesian policies operating offstage. Tobin (1955) incorporated both cyclical fluctuations and long-run capacity growth in one model. Because his article covered so much ground, the role of capital-labor substitution in a one-sector growth model stood out more clearly in Solow 1956 and Swan 1956, where it was the central theme, than in Tobin 1955, which aimed to "provide a link, generally absent in other models, between the world of real magnitudes and the world of money and prices" (113). The portfolio balance framework (along with assuming that the supply of labor depends on the real wage, rather than being exogenous) led Tobin, unlike Solow or Swan, to a model in which "growth is possible at a great variety of rates and is not necessarily precluded when the labor supply grows slowly or remains constant" (113) because an appropriate inflation rate can induce capital deepening.

Tobin reached further conclusions beyond the scope of the neoclassical growth model: "In the absence of monetary expansion and technological progress . . . growth with stable or increasing employment cannot continue if the money-wage rate is inflexible downward. Given wage inflexibility, the system may alternate between high and low levels of employment and, concurrently, between periods of price inflation and deflation. . . . Alternatively, the system may 'stagnate' at less than full employment, quite conceivably with capital growth and reduction of employment occurring at the same time" (113).

Although Tobin 1955 was reprinted in such widely read collections as Stiglitz and Uzawa 1969 and Sen 1970, it proved to play little role in growth economics. This lack of impact is reflected in the single textual reference to the paper in Frank Hahn and Robin Matthews's (1964) classic survey of growth theory.

Why did Tobin's 1955 paper, despite its scholarly brilliance, fail to influence growth economics? One reason is that the range of topics covered and the multiplicity of possible outcomes lessened its impact, as compared with Solow 1956 or Tobin 1965, each of which had a clear, unmistakable central message. Buiter (2003, F596) shares this view: "It is probably the vast ambition of the paper and its failure to deliver on all of its objectives that account for the too limited recognition it has received."

A second reason may involve the model's utility in terms of empirical analysis. Solow's model has proved extraordinarily useful for interpreting empirical patterns, of which Kaldor's famous stylized facts are the best-known example. It is important to recognize that the link between the Solow model and empirical growth patterns emerged after the publication of the paper; Solow 1970 provides links between theory and empirics that are absent in Solow 1956. Perhaps equally important, Solow's theoretical analysis was quickly followed by "Technical Change and the Aggregate Production Function" (1957), which played a key role in empirical growth work in the 1960s through early 1980s (see, e.g., Denison 1967, 1985) and indeed continues to be relevant. In contrast, the theoretical success of Tobin's "Dynamic Aggregative Model" concerned issues whose empirical salience was unclear. The capacity of a model to produce stagnation, for example, was of empirical interest from the perspective of the Great Depression, but not for the postwar economic experience. More generally, "A Dynamic Aggregative Model" did not provide new insights on the growth/fluctuations relationship beyond an approach in which long-run phenomena are modeled via the Solow model and short-run phenomena are modeled via IS-LM analysis.

Tobin's major influence on growth economics came later in "Money and Economic Growth" (1965).

Money and Economic Growth

Tobin (1965) returned to analyzing the effect of monetary factors on the capital intensity of a growing economy. The message of this paper is clearly summarized in its concluding paragraph:

> In classical theory, the interest rate and the capital intensity of the economy are determined by "productivity and thrift," that is, by the interaction of technology and savings propensities. This is true both in the short run, when capital is being accumulated at a rate different from the growth of the labor force, and in the long-run stationary or "moving stationary" equilibrium, when capital intensity is constant. Keynes gave reasons why in the short run monetary factors and portfolio decisions modify, and in some circumstances dominate, the determination of the interest rate and the process of capital accumulation. . . . a similar proposition is true for the long run. The equilibrium interest rate and degree of capital intensity are in general affected by monetary supplies and portfolio behavior, as well as by technology and thrift. (684)

Although Tobin was concerned with finding a long-run analogue to John Maynard Keynes's short-run integration of real and monetary factors, this analysis, unlike his paper of a decade earlier, excluded "the familiar possibility . . . that downward stickiness of money wages prevents or limits deflation and substitutes underproduction and underemployment" (684). In "A Dynamic Aggregative Model," much had depended, or appeared to depend, on money wage rigidity, diverting attention from the importance of having two assets rather than one in a growth model, which stood out unmistakably in "Money and Economic Growth." Eliminating price rigidities from the analysis, Tobin directly addressed the distinction between neutrality and superneutrality of money, and argued that superneutrality fails because of portfolio substitution effects. As Don Patinkin (1987) noted, by doing this Tobin challenged Irving Fisher's (1896, 1907) classic arguments, which concluded that superneutrality, via the Fisher effect on interest rates, will be violated only if economic actors suffer from expectational errors (as Fisher believed they did); interestingly, Tobin did not highlight this disagreement in his Irving Fisher Lecture or in a biographical sketch of Fisher (Tobin 1987).

Tobin (1965, 676) noted that "in a closed economy clearly the important alternative stores of value are monetary assets. It is their yields which set limits on the acceptable rates of return on real capital and on the acceptable degree of capital intensity." He treated money and capital as substitutes from the viewpoint of the wealth holder, that is, they are alternative stores of value.[2] A higher rate of monetary expansion and hence of inflation raises the opportunity cost of holding real money balances (reduces the real rate of return on holding money) and so leads to portfolio balance with a lower real rate of return on capital and a greater capital intensity. A somewhat similar analysis, for an increase in the inflation rate in a short-run IS-LM model rather than a long-run growth model (and hence dealing with the flow of investment rather than the stock of capital), had been made by Robert Mundell (1963), who pointed out that investment depends on real interest but money demand on nominal interest, so that a change in the expected rate of inflation changes the level of output and real interest at which the IS curve intersects the LM curve.

Tobin's 1965 conclusion challenged economists used to thinking of the nonneutrality of money as a short-run phenomenon, attributable to rigid money wages: in the long run, inflation had real costs, but somehow did not affect real behavior or real variables (see Stein 1971 and Foley and Sidrauski 1971 on responses to Tobin 1965). As Solow (1970, 69–70) put the matter, "It appears, then, that money is not neutral in a growing economy, at least not in this very long-run sense: the real characteristics of the steady state depend on the rate of monetary growth. . . . The study of the non-steady-state behaviour of a monetary economy raises questions more difficult than any we have seen so far. They have only begun to be studied in the literature and there is still a lot to be found out" (see also Orphanides and Solow 1990, 233–34).

2. Tobin (1968) remarked, "An economic historian would be puzzled by the implication of section 1 that the development of monetary and financial institutions is in some sense bad for real investment. Without the safe assets made available by these institutions, how would the thrift of the cautious saver have been mobilized? The conflict is largely superficial. Financing of capital accumulation is the story of inside money, not of outside money."

The key to Tobin's result that a higher money supply growth rate leads to greater capital intensity was his treatment of capital and money holdings as substitutes in wealth portfolios (perfect substitutes in Tobin 1968),[3] together with the assumption that real private saving is a given fraction of real disposable income. With those two assumptions, an inflation-induced reduction in the holding of money increases capital. This general finding has not proved robust across economic environments. Different results were obtained by Stanley Fischer (1974, 1979) who instead considered the demand for money by business firms, which are assumed to hold cash balances as a way to reduce transactions costs rather than as a store of wealth. For firms, money functions as a factor of production,[4] and Fischer suggested that money and capital, considered as factor inputs, would be complements, rather than substitutes. In that case, smaller real money balances (because of inflation) would mean a lower marginal product of capital at any level of the capital stock, and so a lower real rate of return that would cause savers to hold a lower level of real wealth. Further, it has proved that what might appear to be innocuous changes in model specification can reverse the long-run effects of changes in money growth on output. For example, an overlapping generations model with agents who live for two periods can provide explicit optimizing foundations for the Tobin effect (Drazen 1981), with higher inflation increasing the capital stock, provided that the seigniorage from money creation is given to the young, but the reverse is true if the seigniorage is given to the old—but in another overlapping generations model, the Tobin effect dominates even if all the seigniorage is given to the old (Orphanides and Solow 1990, 245–46; Haliassos and Tobin 1990, 300–301).[5]

On the Costs and Benefits of Alternative Money Growth Rules

Tobin (1986b, 10) stated that in 1965, "I did not introduce explicitly the real costs of keeping money scarce but simply emphasized the gains from

3. Tobin (1968) also demonstrated that, if technology is changing, a steady state with a transactions requirement for money will exist only if technical progress is Harrod-neutral and occurs at the same steady rate for both transactions technology and production of goods.

4. Levhari and Patinkin (reprinted in Patinkin 1972) included money in the production function in 1968.

5. Tobin (1980) expressed strong reservations about how overlapping generations models incorporate fiat money, so he might not have welcomed such support (although, as Buiter [2003, F590–593] notes, Tobin found the overlapping generations framework useful for analyzing social security systems).

capital accumulation. One purpose of this paper is to remedy the imbalance of the old paper." After reviewing criticisms of his earlier paper by authors such as Miguel Sidrauski and Fischer, Tobin (1986b, 10–11) observed, "Clearly the infinite horizons attributed to savers are a crucial element in models which deny that money and capital are substitutes in wealth holdings. Savers with shorter horizons, for example, mortal life-cycle savers, will have finite capacities for accumulating wealth. They will not be willing to hold whatever amounts of every asset provide returns that meet some constant threshold of time preference. . . . In my paper here, wealth demand is modeled as life-cycle savings theory." Tobin 1986b also differed from his 1965 article by having a government budget constraint (which returned to the modeling assumption of "A Dynamic Aggregative Model"), with budget deficits financed by creation of fiat money, so that he could model "the long-run tradeoff between 'taxation' of money balances by inflation and explicit taxation of the earnings of capital and labor" (1986b, 14).

Friedman (1969, 1–50) had earlier examined the social loss from scarcity of real money balances when fiat money (unlike gold) is socially costless to produce, taking capital intensity as unaffected by monetary policy, and so found that it would be optimal to satiate the economy with real balances by having deflation equal to the real rate of return on capital, so that the private opportunity cost of holding real cash balances (nominal interest) is equal to zero, the social cost of creating real balances. Edmund Phelps (1979, vol. 1, chaps. 6–8) argued that, in the absence of nondistorting lump-sum taxes, it would not be optimal to set the inflation tax to zero when other distorting taxes were imposed to pay for public goods.[6] The "golden rule" literature found that the level of capital intensity that maximizes steady-state consumption occurs when the real rate of return on capital equals the growth rate of the economy (Allais 1947; Phelps 1979). Tobin (1986b) brought these two literatures together, analyzing the tradeoff between deviations from real balance satiation and deviations from golden rule capital intensity, and concluded that in some cases it would be optimal to have positive inflation, increasing capital intensity at the cost of reducing real balances.

Tobin's analysis of the joint effects of money growth on real balance levels and capital accumulation had relevance to policy debates at the time.

---

6. However, for models that view money as an intermediate good (rather than, e.g., putting money in the utility function as Sidrauski did), there is a public finance argument against taxing intermediate goods.

Martin Feldstein (1979) had argued that, as long as the growth rate of the economy is at least as large as the discount rate, any finite temporary loss in output is worth paying to achieve a permanent reduction in inflation, but Tobin's trade-off sidestepped Feldstein's result, because the gain in output from increased capital intensity is just as permanent as the reduction in shoe-leather costs from increased real cash balances. Tobin (1986b, 23) concluded, "The main point is that the position of the economy may be . . . one characterized simultaneously by: positive inflation, after-tax real interest rate less than the growth rate, and steady-state consumption less than it would be with a lower tax rate and higher inflation. . . . It cannot be excluded *a priori* as Feldstein has done." While Tobin won this particular theoretical argument, debates over trade-offs of this type have become relatively unimportant in the modern macroeconomic literature, which typically assumes away the possibility of Tobin's type of long-run nonneutrality when deciding on monetary policy. But it does accommodate the view that reducing business cycle volatility can be justified even if it requires long-run inflation.

Economic Growth as an Objective of Government Policy

Tobin's subsequent growth writings are very much policy driven. Tobin (1964, 1) told the American Economic Association, "Growth has become a good word. And the better a word becomes, the more it is invoked to bless a variety of causes and the more it loses specific meaning. At least in professional economic discussion, we need to give a definite and distinctive meaning to growth as a policy objective. Let it be neither a synonym for good things in general nor a fashionable way to describe other economic objectives. Let growth be something it is possible to oppose as well as to favor, depending on judgments of social priorities and opportunities." In keeping with his articles on how expansionary monetary policy could increase the capital intensity of steady-state growth, Tobin (1964, 10–11) argued "(1) that the government might legitimately have a growth policy, and indeed could scarcely avoid having one, even if private markets were perfect; (2) that capital markets are far from perfect and that private saving decisions are therefore based on an overconservative estimate of the social return to saving; and (3) that the terms on which even so advanced an economy as our own can trade present for future consumption seem to be very attractive." Tobin began his concluding paragraph by remarking cautiously that "the evidence is uncertain and there is a clear need for more refined and reliable estimates of the parameters on which the issue turns." But he promptly moved on to a much more definite statement: "I believe the evidence suggests that policy to accelerate growth, to move the economy to a higher path, would pay. That is, the return to a higher saving and investment ratio would be positive, if evaluated by a reasonable set of social time preference interest rates. This seems to me the strongest reason for advocating growth policy."

Tobin (1964) underlines his belief that real variables were not independent, even in long-run growth, of monetary variables, which monetary and fiscal policy could alter. He felt that imperfect capital markets and overly cautious savers would, in the absence of government policy to promote capital accumulation, keep capital intensity below the golden rule level that would maximize consumption per capita. Positive externalities of investment (not just investment in research and development, but any form of Arrow's "learning by doing" in which B can learn from A's doing) make the social return on capital accumulation greater than the private return. Tobin argues that government can and should improve social welfare by raising steady-state per capita consumption by using monetary policy and (since the two are linked through money creation to finance budget deficits) fiscal policy to increase capital intensity. This theme in Tobin's work carried over to long-run growth theory the concerns of two works that deeply influenced Tobin from the start of his career: the first economics book he ever read, Keynes's *General Theory* (1936) on the role for government to improve the welfare of a monetary economy by offsetting shortfalls in investment, and John R. Hicks's "Suggestion for Simplifying the Theory of Money" (1935) on applying economic analysis to understand why people hold money even though other assets pay higher returns (see Dimand 2004 on these influences).

While Tobin's writings on growth became increasingly policy oriented, he did not stray far from his earlier theoretical contribution. Among his later writings, Tobin (1986a, 1986b) and Haliassos and Tobin (1990) formalized the welfare trade-off between capital intensity and scarcity of real money balances. In these papers, Tobin posed the question of the effect of financial factors on long-run economic growth, the interrelatedness of real and monetary variables, that was central to his work in monetary economics. He did so in a style consistent with his other work, using asset demand functions with restrictions on partial derivatives and linking markets through the adding-up constraint on wealth rather than through the budget constraint of an assumed representative agent (see Solow 2004 and Dimand 2004 on Tobin's methodology). But the answers to the questions Tobin posed on the growth effects of monetary policy proved very sensitive to seemingly minor modifications in how models are specified, so that Orphanides and Solow (1990, 257) found that "we end where Stein ended 20 years ago."

Tobin as a Growth Theorist from the Vantage Point of Modern Macroeconomics

Tobin's efforts to integrate short-run and long-run macroeconomic outcomes, as developed in "A Dynamic Aggregative Model" and "Money and Economic Growth," are remarkably prescient in terms of subsequent general methodological developments in macroeconomics, while the specific ways he proposed to achieve this synthesis have not generally been adopted. The real business cycle approach of Finn Kydland and Edward Prescott explicitly attempts to achieve this integration, but does so in a way that is the converse of Tobin's. While Tobin's objective was to integrate what are conventionally regarded as short-run factors such as wage and price rigidity and portfolio balance requirements into the long-run determination of output, the Kydland-Prescott program attempts to interpret short-run fluctuations via traditional long-run factors such as shocks to the aggregate production function. This strategy is reflected in the key role that the Brock-Mirman (1972) stochastic growth model and associated generalizations play in the real business cycle literature. Tobin never found the methodology of real business cycles persuasive,[7] nor did he accept that it had consistent microeconomic foundations in any meaningful way. He was critical of representative agent models that avoid Keynesian coordination problems only by assuming that the economy behaves as if there were only one agent, of overlapping generations models that provide rigorous foundations for a positive value of fiat money only by assuming that no other assets exist, and of modelers who claim consistent microeconomic foundations while neglecting stock/flow consistency (Tobin 1980; Colander [1999] 2007; Solow 2004; Dimand 2004).

In contrast, the primary legatee of Tobin's views on short-run fluctuations, the new Keynesian macroeconomics school, generally avoids

---

7. When Colander ([1999] 2007, 400) asked him about real business cycle theorists, Tobin replied, "Well, that's just the enemy."

addressing growth issues. This literature very much focuses on explaining short-run data patterns and evaluating alternative policy rules, with a primary focus on monetary policy. This school of thought explicitly distinguishes between cyclical and trend components to data, whether the trend is based on a deterministic function of time, unit roots, or some distinction between more and less smooth data components such as the cycles produced by the Hodrick-Prescott filter. Michael Woodford's monumental *Interest and Prices* (2003) does not contain any discussion of growth issues (or any reference to any of Tobin's work). The evaluation of monetary policy is conducted entirely on the basis of cyclical behavior.

Relative to the time period in which Tobin worked, economic growth plays a much more prominent role in contemporary macroeconomics. The new growth literature, as initiated by Robert Lucas and Paul Romer, does contain facets that are reminiscent of Tobin's ideas, though these are often indirect. To focus our discussion of the contemporary literature, we consider the papers published in a 1996 issue of the *Federal Reserve Bank of St. Louis Review*, which contains the proceedings of one of the bank's annual economic policy conferences, this one titled "Price Stability and Economic Growth." This issue well summarizes macroeconomic thinking about the inflation-growth nexus at the end of the first decade of the new growth economics via two theoretical papers (Chari, Jones, and Manuelli 1996; Choi, Smith, and Boyd 1996) and two empirical studies (Barro 1996; Bruno and Easterly 1996). V. V. Chari, Larry E. Jones, and Rodolfo E. Manuelli (1996, 56) conclude that

> inflation rates per se have negligible effects on growth rates, but financial regulations and the interaction of inflation with such regulations have substantial effects on growth. This analysis suggests that researchers interested in studying the effects of monetary policy should shift their focus away from printing money and towards the study of banking and financial regulation.

In isolation, this sounds very much similar to the style of macroeconomics pioneered by Tobin. However, the formal analysis both in Chari, Jones, and Manuelli 1996 and in Choi, Smith, and Boyd 1996 uses very different microeconomic foundations from Tobin's. Chari, Jones, and Manuelli employ cash-in-advance and shopping time models (in which there is a trade-off between time spent shopping and the use of money) to understand money demand; Tobin-style portfolio considerations do not arise. Sangmok Choi, Bruce D. Smith, and John H. Boyd employ a framework closer in spirit to Tobin, but focus on how inflation can exacerbate adverse selection problems in financial markets. When these considerations are absent, their model produces results similar to Tobin's. However, in a market where default on the part of borrowers is a problem, greater inflation leads to selection toward riskier types. For our purposes, what is important is that both of the papers emphasize how inflation can lower growth, in direct opposition to Tobin's focus on how inflation, by making capital a more attractive asset, can enhance growth.

This emphasis on how inflation can reduce growth reflects the consensus in the empirical growth literature that this is in fact the case. Both the Barro and the Bruno and Easterly contributions to the 1996 conference find a negative relationship between inflation and growth, although this effect appears to be nonlinear: the evidence is stronger when one isolates the effects of very high inflation rates, rates outside the experience of the OECD economies. This evidence appears to be relatively robust in the sense that evidence of a negative relationship between inflation and growth survives in the presence of a range of competing explanations (see Durlauf, Kourtellos, and Tan 2008 for a recent study of this type). While interpreting the cross-country growth regressions underpinning this conclusion is problematic (see Brock and Durlauf 2001 and Durlauf, Johnson, and Temple 2005 for a delineation of the issues), the consensus that inflation is not growth enhancing has been associated with theoretical approaches very different from that employed by Tobin. On the other hand, Tobin's emphasis on financial intermediation as fundamental to understanding the monetary transmission mechanism is reflected in the modern money-growth literature.

Finally, there is an important sense in which Tobin's views on growth reflect a different orientation than that of the contemporaneous growth literature. Tobin's writings did not make broad claims about the growth differences between economies but rather focused on growth in contexts such as the United States; this orientation is also found in Solow's classic growth papers. Further, Tobin's focus was typically not on the determinants of steady-state growth; his analysis of a positive relationship between money and growth has to do with equilibrium levels of capital intensity, which influence the steady-state level of output (suitably normalized by population and the state of technology) but not the steady-state growth rate of per capita output per se. For steady-state behavior, Tobin (1998, 149) wrote,

> A list of sensible policies, one might say conservative policies, includes basic science, research and development, education and training, public

---

infrastructure, and carefully designed incentives for both private and public sectors to consume less and invest more. If everyone is patient with gains measured in tenths of a percentage point over the coming decades, these policies can pay off. With luck, new technologies may bring dramatic *improvements* in the growth rate. The computer and communications revolutions may well bear fruit in the next century.

The analysis of knowledge and technical progress as endogenous outcomes had to wait for another generation of macroeconomists, exemplified by Philippe Aghion and Peter Howitt (1999), in addition to Romer and Lucas.

Conclusion

The questions Tobin raised about money and long-run economic growth are still important, but definitive answers to them remain elusive even in light of the new growth economics. Tobin's vision of the integration of short-run and long-run macroeconomic phenomena is, ironically, primarily accepted by the real business cycle view of macroeconomics, one that is antithetical to Tobin's perspective on economic fluctuations. We conjecture that this may not prove the case in the next decades of growth analysis, as efforts to integrate the shorter and longer run move toward a more balanced view of supply and demand factors.

References

Aghion, Philippe, and Peter Howitt. 1999. *Endogenous Growth Theory.* Cambridge: MIT Press.

Allais, Maurice. 1947. *Économie et intérêt.* Paris: Imprimerie Nationale.

Barro, Robert. 1996. Inflation and Growth. *Federal Reserve Bank of St. Louis Review* 78.3:153–69.

Breit, William, and Roger W. Spencer, eds. 1990. *Lives of the Laureates: Thirteen Nobel Economists.* 3rd ed. Cambridge: MIT Press.

Brock, William A., and Steven N. Durlauf. 2001. Growth Empirics and Reality. *World Bank Economic Review* 15:229–72.

Brock, William A., and Leonard J. Mirman. 1972. Optimal Economic Growth and Uncertainty: The Discounted Case. *Journal of Economic Theory* 4:479–513.

Bruno, Michael, and William Easterly. 1996. Inflation and Growth: In Search of a Stable Relationship. *Federal Reserve Bank of St. Louis Review* 78:139–46.

Buiter, Willem. 2003. James Tobin: An Appreciation of His Contributions to Economics. *Economic Journal* 113:F585–F631.

Chari, V. V., Larry E. Jones, and Rodolfo E. Manuelli. 1996. Inflation, Growth, and Financial Intermediation. *Federal Reserve Bank of St. Louis Review* 78:41–58.

Choi, Sangmok, Bruce D. Smith, and John H. Boyd. 1996. Inflation, Financial Markets, and Capital Formation. *Federal Reserve Bank of St. Louis Review* 78:9–35.

Colander, David. [1999] 2007. Conversations with James Tobin and Robert J. Shiller on the "Yale Tradition." In *Inside the Economist's Mind: Conversations with Eminent Economists*, edited by Paul A. Samuelson and William A. Barnett. Malden, Mass: Blackwell.

Denison, Edward. 1967. *Why Growth Rates Differ.* Washington, D.C.: Brookings Institution Press.

———. 1985. *Trends in American Economic Growth, 1929–1982.* Washington, D.C.: Brookings Institution Press.

Dimand, Robert W. 2004. James Tobin and the Transformation of the IS-LM Model. In *The IS-LM Model: Its Rise, Fall, and Strange Persistence*, edited by Michel De Vroey and Kevin D. Hoover. *HOPE* 36 (supplement): 165–89.

Domar, Evsey D. 1946. Capital Expansion, Rate of Growth, and Employment. *Econometrica* 14:137–47.

———. 1957. *Essays in the Theory of Economic Growth.* New York: Oxford University Press.

Drazen, Allan. 1981. Inflation and Capital Accumulation under a Finite Horizon. *Journal of Monetary Economics* 8:247–60.

Durlauf, Steven N., Jonathan Temple, and Paul A. Johnson. 2005. Growth Econometrics. In *Handbook of Economic Growth*, edited by P. Aghion and S. Durlauf. Amsterdam: North-Holland.

Durlauf, Steven N., Andros Kourtellos, and Chih Ming Tan. 2008. Are Any Growth Theories Robust? *Economic Journal* 118:329–46.

Feldstein, Martin S. 1979. The Welfare Cost of Permanent Inflation and Optimal Short-Run Economic Policy. *Journal of Political Economy* 87:749–68.

Fischer, Stanley. 1974. Money and the Production Function. *Economic Inquiry* 124:517–33.

———. 1979. Capital Accumulation on the Transition Path in a Monetary Optimizing Model. *Econometrica* 47:1433–39.

Fisher, Irving. 1896. *Appreciation and Interest.* New York: Macmillan for the American Economic Association. Reprinted in Fisher 1997, vol. 1.

———. 1907. *The Rate of Interest.* New York: Macmillan. Reprinted in Fisher 1997, vol. 3.

———. 1997. *The Works of Irving Fisher.* 14 vols. Edited by William J. Barber, assisted by Robert W. Dimand and Kevin Foster, consulting editor James Tobin. London: Pickering and Chatto.

Foley, Duncan K., and Miguel Sidrauski. 1971. *Monetary and Fiscal Policy in a Growing Economy.* New York: Macmillan.

Friedman, Milton. 1969. *The Optimum Quantity of Money and Other Essays.* Chicago: Aldine.

Hahn, Frank H., and Robin C. O. Matthews. 1964. The Theory of Economic Growth: A Survey. *Economic Journal* 74:774–902.

Haliassos, Michael, and James Tobin. 1990. The Macroeconomics of Government Finance. In vol. 2 of *Handbook of Monetary Economics*, edited by Benjamin Friedman and Frank H. Hahn. Amsterdam: North-Holland. Reprinted in Tobin 1996.

Harrod, Roy F. 1939. An Essay in Dynamic Theory. *Economic Journal* 49:14–33.

———. 1948. *Towards a Dynamic Economics*. London: Macmillan.

———. 1952. *Economic Essays*. London: Macmillan.

Hicks, John R. 1935. A Suggestion for Simplifying the Theory of Money. *Economica*, n.s., 2.1:1–19.

Johnson, Harry G. 1967. *Essays in Monetary Economics*. Cambridge: Harvard University Press.

Kaldor, Nicholas. 1956. Alternative Theories of Distribution. *Review of Economic Studies* 23:83–100.

Keynes, John Maynard. 1936. *The General Theory of Employment, Interest, and Money*. London: Macmillan.

Levhari, David, and Don Patinkin. 1968. The Role of Money in a Simple Growth Model. *American Economic Review* 58:713–53.

Mundell, Robert A. 1963. Inflation and Real Interest. *Journal of Political Economy* 71:280–83.

Orphanides, Athanasios, and Robert M. Solow. 1990. Money, Inflation, and Growth. In vol. 1 of *Handbook of Monetary Economics*, edited by Benjamin M. Friedman and Frank H. Hahn. Amsterdam: North-Holland.

Patinkin, Don. 1972. *Studies in Monetary Economics*. New York: Harper and Row.

———. 1987. Neutrality of Money. In *New Palgrave Dictionary of Economics*, edited by John Eatwell, Murray Milgate, and Peter Newman. London: Palgrave Macmillan.

Phelps, Edmund S. 1979. *Studies in Macroeconomic Theory*. 2 vols. New York: Academic.

Pilvin, Harold. 1953. Full Capacity versus Full Employment Growth. *Quarterly Journal of Economics* 67:545–52.

Sen, Amartya K., ed. 1970. *Growth Economics*. Harmondsworth, U.K.: Penguin.

Solow, Robert M. 1956. A Contribution to the Theory of Economic Growth. *Quarterly Journal of Economics* 70:65–94.

———. 1957. Technical Change and the Aggregate Production Function. *Review of Economics and Statistics* 39:312–20.

———. 1970. *Growth Theory: An Exposition*. Oxford: Clarendon.

———. 2004. The Tobin Approach to Monetary Economics. *Journal of Money, Credit, and Banking* 36:657–63.

Stein, Jerome L. 1971. *Money and Capacity Growth*. New York: Columbia University Press.

Stiglitz, Joseph E., and Hirofumi Uzawa, eds. 1969. *Readings in the Modern Theory of Economic Growth*. Cambridge: MIT Press.

Swan, Trevor. 1956. Economic Growth and Capital Accumulation. *Economic Record* 32:334–61.

Tobin, James. 1955. A Dynamic Aggregative Model. *Journal of Political Economy* 63:103–15.

———. 1960. Toward a General Kaldorian Theory of Distribution: A Note. *Review of Economic Studies* 27:119–20.

———. 1964. Economic Growth as an Objective of Government Policy. *American Economic Review: Papers and Proceedings* 54:1–20.

———. 1965. Money and Economic Growth. *Econometrica* 33:671–84.

———. 1968. Notes on Optimal Monetary Growth. *Journal of Political Economy* 76:833–59.

———. 1980. The Overlapping Generations Model of Fiat Money: Discussion. In *Models of Monetary Economies*, edited by John H. Kareken and Neil Wallace. Minneapolis: Federal Reserve Bank of Minneapolis.

———. 1986a. The Monetary and Fiscal Policy Fix: Long Run Implications. *American Economic Review: Papers and Proceedings* 76:213–18.

———. 1986b. On the Welfare Macroeconomics of Government Financial Policy. *Scandinavian Journal of Economics* 88:9–24.

———. 1987. Irving Fisher. In *New Palgrave Dictionary of Economics*, edited by John Eatwell, Murray Milgate, and Peter Newman. London: Palgrave Macmillan.

———. 1996. *Essays in Economics*. Vol. 4. Cambridge: MIT Press.

———. 1998. Can We Grow Faster? In *The Rising Tide: The Leading Minds of Business and Economics Chart a Course toward Higher Growth and Prosperity*, edited by J. Jasinowski. New York: John Wiley. Reprinted in Tobin 2003.

———. 2003. *World Finance and Economic Stability: Selected Essays of James Tobin*. Cheltenham, U.K.: Edward Elgar.

Tobin, James, with the collaboration of Stephen S. Golub. 1998. *Money, Credit, and Capital*. Boston: McGraw-Hill.

Woodford, Michael. 2003. *Interest and Prices*. Princeton, N.J.: Princeton University Press.

Solow and Growth Accounting: A Perspective from Quantitative Economic History

Nicholas Crafts

Robert Solow's 1957 paper was a landmark in the development of growth accounting. As is well known, it was not the first paper to make an explicit decomposition of the sources of growth into contributions from factor inputs and from output per unit of total input. This had been done several times since the pioneering paper by Jan Tinbergen (1942). Nor was it original to claim that virtually all recent labor productivity growth in the United States had come from the residual contribution of total factor productivity (TFP); research at the NBER summarized by Solomon Fabricant (1954) and, with more detail, by Moses Abramovitz (1956) had already come to pretty much the same conclusion. The culmination of the NBER work was the magisterial volume by John Kendrick (1961), which found that 80.0 and 88.5 percent of the growth of labor productivity between 1869 and 1953 and between 1909 and 1948, respectively, was due to TFP.

But it was Solow 1957 that put the growth economics into growth accounting, making clear its interpretation in terms of the distinction between shifts of and moves along the aggregate production function. If a Cobb-Douglas production function with constant returns to scale is assumed,

$$Y = AK^{\alpha}L^{1-\alpha}, \tag{1}$$

I am grateful to Steven Durlauf, Mary Morgan, and two anonymous referees for helpful comments on an earlier version. Lennart Schon and Gianni Toniolo kindly provided data. I am responsible for all errors.

History of Political Economy 41 (annual suppl.) DOI 10.1215/00182702-2009-024

where Y is output, K is capital, L is labor, and A is TFP, while α and $(1 - \alpha)$ are the elasticities of output with respect to capital and labor, respectively, then the basic growth accounting formula is

$$\Delta\ln(Y/L) = \alpha\Delta\ln(K/L) + \Delta\ln A. \tag{2}$$

As Zvi Griliches (1996, 1328) said, "This clarified the meaning of what were heretofore relatively arcane index number calculations and brought the subject from the periphery of the field to the center."[1] Although it was clear that the residual would capture any kind of shift in the production function, the interpretation that Solow's paper (1957, 320) invited and that the concluding summary of his paper contained was that seven-eighths of the increase in American labor productivity between 1909 and 1949 was attributable to technical change.

The challenge was clearly to refine both understanding and measurement of the residual to go beyond "crude TFP" as in equation (2). Solow himself soon proposed an alternative version of growth accounting, which entailed calculating the effective stock of capital on the assumption that technical change was embodied in new vintages of capital. He suggested a formulation in which the embodied rate of technical change was 5 percent per year and the elasticity of output with respect to capital was 0.36, implying that technical change contributed 1.8 percent per year to U.S. economic growth between 1929 and 1957 or only about 70 percent of labor productivity growth (Solow 1963, 82).

However, the work of Edward Denison (1962) was a much more influential approach to accounting for the residual. This developed an explicit measurement of the contribution of labor quality, in particular through the effect of education on earnings, to recent American labor productivity growth, and reduced the contribution of the residual to a little under half using the production function

$$Y = AK^{\alpha}(LE)^{1-\alpha}, \tag{3}$$

where E is the average educational quality of the labor force. The growth accounting formula becomes

$$\Delta\ln(Y/L) = \alpha[\Delta\ln(K/L)] + (1 - \alpha)\Delta\ln E + \Delta\ln A. \tag{4}$$

---

1. Solow was aware of the earlier contributions by Abramovitz and Fabricant, which are cited. He clearly saw himself as clarifying the economic interpretation of their results and underlining the strong assumptions needed to interpret the residual as technical change (Solow 1957, 317).

Denison also suggested that economies of scale were responsible for about half of the remaining residual, though he had no way to justify what was no more than an assumption. Shortly thereafter, Denison (1967) applied his methodology to early postwar European economic growth and offered a fuller but still-unsubstantiated account of the sources of the residual distinguishing between economies of scale and improvements in resource allocation.[2] The trajectory of this work was to downsize rather sharply the contribution of technical change to labor productivity growth.

Another major development in the practice of growth accounting was the publication of Dale Jorgenson and Griliches (1967). These authors made revisions to the crude measure of TFP that reduced it from 1.6 to 0.1 percent per year for the United States during 1945–65. They focused on measuring capital services and produced a much more sophisticated (and data-demanding) index of capital input growth while also correcting labor quality for changes in education in a conceptually similar way to Denison. Jorgenson and Griliches concluded that the residual accounted for only a small fraction of productivity growth and stressed that looking at (conventionally measured) TFP growth as "manna from heaven" was seriously misleading.

Up to this point, mainstream economic history had not really been touched by these developments, and historical national income accounting was only beginning to produce estimates of long-run growth in various countries. Simon Kuznets was at the center of efforts to improve this quantification and together with Abramovitz edited a series of commissioned monographs that aimed to develop long-run growth accounts for industrialized countries. Several of these volumes eventually came to fruition, including J.-J. Carre et al. (1975) on France, Kazushi Ohkawa and Henry Rosovsky (1972) on Japan, and Robin Matthews et al. (1982) for the United Kingdom together with a succession of papers from the study of the United States, culminating in Abramovitz and Paul David (2001).[3] Denison-style research was undertaken at the Organisation for Economic Co-operation and Development (OECD) and produced explicitly comparable growth accounts for six countries from 1913 of which the best-known version was in Maddison 1987, later updated in Maddison 1996. As further usable historical national-income accounts have become available, the

---

2. As Abramovitz (1962, 763), by no means an unsympathetic reviewer, said of Denison's earlier work, "Crucial questions regarding the sources of growth are settled . . . by the author's ex cathedra pronouncements."

3. Carre et al. was originally published in French in 1972.

country coverage of long-run historical growth accounting has expanded, and papers in this tradition continue to be published. In recent years, these have included Max Schulze (2007) on Austria-Hungary, Pedro Lains (2003) on Portugal, and Leandro Prados de la Escosura and Joan Roses (2007) on Spain.

Clearly, growth accounting has played a considerable role in research on economic growth by economic historians. The present article seeks to assess the importance that variants of the technique have had and addresses the following questions.

- How has growth accounting been used by economic historians?
- What generalizations about the long-run sources of modern economic growth in the advanced countries emerged from this growth accounting?
- Where did the innovation of growth accounting most importantly change the lessons of history?

The Use of Growth Accounting in Economic History

This section considers how economic historians set about using the tools of growth accounting at the macroeconomic level. In the late 1950s and early 1960s there were good reasons for a renewed emphasis on the central task of economic history as quantifying and explaining long-run growth, given the burgeoning interest in economic development and the considerable funding opportunities to which this gave rise (de Rouvray 2005). This was indeed the Kuznetsian agenda.

Kuznets himself was not an exponent of growth accounting, but he did offer an informal analysis of the sources of long-run growth in advanced economies since the onset of modern economic growth in which he concluded that the growth of capital per worker could not have accounted for more than about one-quarter of the growth of per capita income (Kuznets 1971). Nevertheless, several growth accounting studies appeared between 1972 and 1982 in the series that he edited with Abramovitz.

More than anything else, the early (pre–new growth economics) studies followed Denison's agenda of downsizing the residual and adopted (variants of) at least some of his adjustments to reduce the extent of unexplained TFP growth. The most comprehensive attempt was made by Angus Maddison (1987). As shown in table 1, these analyses all followed Denison in taking account of labor quality in particular in terms of adopting his approach to estimating the contribution of education. Although

Table 1   Downsizing the Residual: Early Studies

	Education	Work Intensity	Capital Quality	Embodied Technical Change	Increasing Returns to Scale	Structural Change
Carre et al. 1975	x		(x)			x
Ohkawa and Rosovsky 1972	x		(x)			
Abramovitz and David 1973	x		x			
Matthews et al. 1982	x	x				
Bergson 1983	x				x	x
Maddison 1987	x		(x)	x	x	x

Notes: "Capital Quality" is full use of the Jorgenson methodology, and (x) in that column denotes adjustment simply for age of capital stock; "Education" denotes use of Denison 1962-type adjustments to labor inputs for years of schooling.

there were well-recognized doubts about this methodology, it had a stronger empirical foundation than his other major adjustments, which were widely seen as ad hoc; it did not appear to require econometric wizardry, and data were often reasonably easy to obtain.[4]

Solow's own suggestion that the way to address the issue of the embarrassing residual was to treat technical change as embodied in successive vintages of capital clearly had some appeal but seems to have been regarded as too difficult to implement, in particular in terms of the econometrics of pinning down the rate of improvement of capital quality (Nadiri 1970). Only Maddison (1987, 663) attempted this refinement, and he described his choice of an embodiment factor of 1.5 percent per year as "illustrative." The infrequency of attempts to implement the full Jorgenson-type methodology is perhaps attributable to its data demands.[5]

4. Recent reviews of the evidence that do consider some of the econometric issues suggest that Denison's methodology is probably acceptable; see Krueger and Lindahl 2001.

5. The Jorgenson approach is to construct a quantity index of capital services in which the growth rate of each capital asset is weighted by its user cost (rental price) adjusted for tax and assumed to be equal to its marginal product. This requires information on the rate of return, rate of depreciation, and rate of price inflation for each asset. This is much more difficult to implement than the more usual perpetual-inventory approach based on adding up past investment expenditure at constant prices and assuming a lifetime for capital.

Table 2   Downsizing the Residual: Recent Studies

	Education	Human Capital	Capital Quality	Embodied Technical Change	Research and Development	Capacity Utilization
Rossi and Toniolo 1992						x
van Ark and de Jong 1996	x				x	
Abramovitz and David 2001	x		x	x	x	
Lains 2003		x				
Schulze 2007		x				
Prados and Roses 2007	x			x		

Notes: "Capacity Utilization" indicates estimates based on the methodology in Morrison 1988 to allow for fixed factors, adjustment costs, and economies of scale; "Capital Quality" is full use of the Jorgenson methodology; "Education" denotes use of Denison 1962-type adjustments to labor inputs for years of schooling; "Human Capital" indicates use of an augmented Solow approach with human capital as a separate factor of production as in Mankiw et al. 1992.

The more recent studies listed in table 2 have appeared in the era of the new growth economics. In principle, this might have had significant effects on the formulas used for growth accounting because the specification of the production function would change (Barro 1999). In practice, the methods used by economic historians have not been greatly affected. In particular, it has remained general practice to regard the share of profits in national income as an acceptable proxy for the elasticity of output with respect to capital, the key parameter, and to believe that this will normally be in the range 0.3 to 0.4. This is in accordance with assessments of the evidence both by growth accounting practitioners (Collins and Bosworth 1996) and by econometricians (Aiyar and Dalgaard 2005).

In two cases research and development has been treated as a factor of production, and in two other cases the Denison approach to adjusting labor inputs for educational quality has been superseded by the augmented Solow approach of treating human capital as a separate factor in the production function

$$Y = AK^{\gamma}H^{\mu}L^{\theta}, \tag{5}$$

where γ, μ, and θ are the elasticities of output with respect to capital, human capital, and labor, respectively, which sum to 1, and H is the stock of human capital.

The growth accounting formula becomes

$$\Delta\ln(Y/L) = \gamma\Delta\ln K + \mu\Delta\ln H - (1 - \theta)\Delta\ln L + \Delta\ln A. \qquad (6)$$

Finally, Nicolo Rossi and Gianni Toniolo (1992) were unusual in not imposing conventional assumptions; rather, they employed a data-demanding econometric methodology to estimate the true contribution of technical change to TFP growth by correcting for fixed factors of production, adjustment costs, and scale economies.

The modal stance has been to benchmark growth performance on the basis of conventional assumptions that facilitate comparisons. In this tradition, the general belief of these authors is that TFP growth is only partly a reflection of technical change, but detailed quantification of the sources of TFP growth has remained elusive. Maddison (1987), rather like Denison, concluded that much of the Solow residual was typically attributable to some combination of labor quality, improved allocation of resources, changes in the utilization of factors of production, reductions in technology gaps, and economies of scale, leaving only a modest share "unexplained"—and perhaps reflecting disembodied technical change (see table 3).

Maddison's list of the components of rapid TFP growth in the European golden age is broadly in line with conventional economic histories, but precise quantification is, of course, very difficult, and there is no consensus on the details.[6] Maddison himself acknowledged that his exercise was rather speculative, and papers in the empirical-growth literature cast doubt on its reliability without, however, amounting to an alternative decomposition. For example, Stephen Broadberry (1998) proposes a different calculation for the effect of structural change that would increase its magnitude considerably, Harald Badinger (2005) offers an econometric estimation of the productivity implications of economic integration that suggests foreign trade was more important than Maddison suggests, while the analysis of convergence provided by Robert Barro and Xavier Sala-i-Martin (1995) indicates that Maddison may have given too much weight to catch-up in addition to structural change.

---

6. The results of a data envelopment analysis also give strong support to the claim that TFP growth during the European golden age was boosted considerably by improvements over time in the efficiency of factor use (Jerzmanowski 2007).

Table 3   Accounting for Growth in Maddison's (1987) Six-Country Study (% per year)

	France	Germany	Japan	The Netherlands	U.K.	U.S.A.
1913–50						
Y/HW Growth	2.01	1.05	1.72	1.58	1.57	2.42
K/HW	0.59	0.19	0.62	0.43	0.42	0.43
TFP	1.42	0.96	1.10	1.15	1.15	1.99
Capital quality	0.45	0.45	0.45	0.45	0.45	0.45
Labor quality	0.36	0.22	0.61	0.27	0.32	0.35
Capacity use	0.00	−0.13	−0.24	0.00	0.00	0.00
Labor hoarding	0.00	−0.20	−0.56	0.00	0.00	0.00
Catch-up	0.00	0.00	0.00	0.00	0.00	0.00
Structural	0.09	0.20	0.62	0.00	−0.04	0.29
Foreign trade	0.01	−0.04	0.02	0.05	0.00	0.01
Scale	0.03	0.04	0.07	0.07	0.04	0.08
Other	0.00	0.00	0.00	0.00	0.00	0.00
Unexplained	0.48	0.32	0.13	0.41	0.38	0.81
1950–73						
Y/HW Growth	5.12	5.96	7.82	4.44	3.18	2.50
K/HW	1.10	1.64	2.02	1.09	1.04	0.65
TFP	4.02	4.32	5.80	3.35	2.14	1.85
Capital quality	0.56	0.53	0.58	0.57	0.52	0.51
Labor quality	0.35	0.18	0.52	0.40	0.09	0.29
Capacity use	0.00	0.25	0.39	0.00	0.00	0.00
Labor hoarding	0.00	0.32	0.90	0.00	0.00	0.00
Catch-up	0.52	0.68	1.02	0.38	0.14	0.00
Structural	0.46	0.36	1.22	−0.07	0.10	0.12
Foreign trade	0.19	0.21	0.26	0.65	0.16	0.05
Scale	0.15	0.18	0.28	0.14	0.09	0.11
Other	−0.02	−0.02	−0.02	0.22	−0.02	−0.04
Unexplained	1.81	1.63	0.64	1.06	1.06	0.81

Two cases where the authors thought hard about the applicability in a particular historical context of the standard assumptions of a Cobb-Douglas production function with neutral technical change deserve to be highlighted. First, Abramovitz and David (1973, 2001) developed a view of the nineteenth-century U.S. economy that focuses on the capital-using bias of technical change and a low elasticity of substitution (σ) between factors of production in that era such that conventionally measured TFP growth *underestimates* the rate of technical change.[7] Second, Robert Allen (2003) confronted the suggestion that the Soviet growth experience is better represented by a production function with a very low elasticity of substitution, which would imply that the conventional methodology overestimates capital's contribution to growth (because it fails to register the extent of diminishing returns to capital) and that TFP growth was quite respectable. He provides a convincing rebuttal of this argument, noting inter alia that technological possibilities were similar to those in the West and that there is clear evidence of massive waste of capital that connotes negative TFP growth in the later years.

A further possible use of growth accounting is to evaluate the contribution of general purpose technologies to economic growth. This requires appropriate aggregation of sectoral TFP growth rates, which was set out by Evsey Domar (1961), who demonstrated that the correct weights were sectoral gross outputs divided by GDP. The formula adopted later on by economists investigating the implications of ICT was

$$\Delta \ln(Y/L) = \alpha_{KO} \Delta \ln(KO/L) + \alpha_{KICT} \Delta \ln(KICT/L) \qquad (7)$$
$$+ \phi \Delta \ln A_{ICT} + \eta \Delta \ln A_O,$$

where ϕ and η are Domar weights, as above, $KICT$ is capital used in ICT production, KO is the rest of the capital stock, A_{ICT} is TFP in ICT production, and A_O is TFP in the rest of the economy. Given that ϕ and α_{KICT} are very small initially, it is easy to see why a new general purpose technology adds very little to overall labor productivity growth.[8]

In the 1960s the equivalent investigation concerned railroads and nineteenth-century American growth, and, indeed, the defining moment for cliometrics in the 1960s was the railroads controversy (de Rouvray 2005). This famous debate revolved around the use of the social savings measure (roughly an upper-bound approximation of the consumer surplus gain) by Robert Fogel (1964) to evaluate the counterfactual value of national income without the railroad. Obviously, an alternative way to measure the contribution of this new technology to economic growth would have been to use growth accounting with Domar weights. Indeed, the social

---

7. In this context a factor-saving bias means that technological change acts as if it augments one factor of production by more than the other with implications for relative factor prices and also, if $\sigma \neq 1$, for factor shares. This means that the standard growth accounting formula has to be corrected to obtain an estimate of the "true" rate of technological change.

8. For the period 1973–95, the weights reported by Oliner and Sichel (2000) were $\phi = 1.4$ percent and $\alpha_{KICT} = 3.3$ percent.

savings approximates to the own TFP growth contribution of the new sector ($\phi \Delta \ln A_{rail}$) (Crafts 2004).

Fogel's choice of methodology was understandable in terms of its links to cost-benefit analysis and of his desire to isolate the "unique contribution" of railroads in his assault on the claim that railroads were indispensable to American economic growth in the nineteenth century.[9] Nevertheless, it slowed down the diffusion of growth accounting into economic history and was not really conducive to developing an understanding of why general purpose technologies have an effect on labor productivity growth that is very small at the outset but then rises through time and of why TFP growth might be quite modest in the throes of an industrial revolution.

Has Long-Run Labor Productivity Growth Been Dominated by TFP Growth?

Solow's finding that seven-eighths of U.S. labor productivity growth during 1909–49 was accounted for by TFP growth (where no separate allowance is made for educational quality of the labor force) is still pretty much what would be obtained applying his method to today's data. This does not, however, mean that this result has also been found by economic historians consistently for other periods and different countries, even though Kuznets (1971) suggested that it probably would be.

Table 4 reports that on the basis of conventional growth accounting for the United States over the long run, the picture is one of dominance of "Solow's TFP" (education + TFP in the table) from the late nineteenth century till the end of the post–World War II boom in the late 1960s. However, table 3 also shows that before 1890 and after 1966 the sum of the education and TFP components contributes at best only 50 percent of labor productivity growth.[10]

In fact, at face value, given that TFP growth is below 0.5 percent per year prior to 1890, the estimates in table 4 invite the conclusion that technical change was insignificant in the American economy for much of the nineteenth century and only came to prominence with the rise of the science-based industries and R&D in the so-called second industrial

9. Fogel did not include a capital deepening component because he argued that in the absence of railroads the capital would have been accumulated in some other activity where it also would have obtained normal returns.

10. Solow's estimates were for "crude" TFP growth, which equals the sum of education and TFP in table 4.

Table 4   Sources of U.S. Labor Productivity Growth over the Long Run (% per year)

	Labor Productivity	Capital Deepening	Education	TFP
1800–55	0.4	0.2	0.0	0.2
1855–90	1.1	0.7	0.0	0.4
1890–1905	1.9	0.5	0.1	1.3
1905–27	2.0	0.5	0.2	1.3
1929–48	2.0	0.1	0.4	1.5
1948–66	3.1	0.8	0.4	1.9
1966–89	1.2	0.6	0.3	0.3
1990–2003	1.8	0.9	0.1	0.8

Note: These estimates are obtained by the various authors on the basis of equations using the specification of equation (4). Sources: Abramovitz and David 2001 except for final period from Bosworth and Collins 2003 as updated on Web site.

revolution. This runs counter to standard historical discussions, however, and is certainly not the interpretation made by Abramovitz and David (1973, 2001). If, as they suggest, the nineteenth-century U.S. economy was characterized by a low elasticity of substitution between factors together with capital-using technical change, then TFP growth may have been considerably stronger than shown in table 4, which assumes that $\sigma = 1$. Whereas the crude TFP growth estimates give a rate of 0.24 percent per year for 1835 to 1890, if, instead, estimates are obtained using the assumption of an aggregate production function with the properties that Abramovitz and David believe that the evidence supports, this would generate a revised estimate for TFP growth of 0.9 percent per year and thus restore it to a dominant role.[11]

For the late-twentieth-century slowdown, it is also likely that the impression given by table 4 is misleading. Here the main issue relates to measuring output growth. Michael Boskin et al. (1996) thought that, for a variety

11. This calculation is based on the formula given by Dani Rodrik (1997) that the correction to TFP growth = $0.5\alpha((1-\sigma)/\sigma)(1-\alpha)(\Delta K/K - \Delta L/L)(\Delta A_L/A_L - \Delta A_K/A_K)$ where the term in the last parenthetical captures the degree of factor-saving bias in technological progress measured as the difference between the rate of labor augmentation and the rate of capital augmentation. The formula is parameterized using values suggested in Abramovitz and David 2001, including $\sigma = 0.3$, and applying them to 1835–90, the period that is singled out by these authors.

of reasons, inflation had been overestimated (and thus real GDP growth and TFP growth had been underestimated by a similar amount) in the national accounts and that the correction required was of the order of 0.6 percent per year. Again, this would raise the contribution of crude TFP growth well above that of capital deepening without quite reaching the seven-eighths mark.[12]

The estimates reported earlier in the first three rows of table 3 would suggest that, if Solow's methodology had been employed, a predominant role would have been found for unexplained TFP growth in other OECD countries in the period where TFP dominated in the United States. Maddison (1987) himself argued that the Solow residual could largely be explained and derived an "unexplained" component reported in the last row of the table that is typically well below half that in row three. Maddison's preferred account of the European and Japanese golden age, 1950–73, highlights large gains from improvements in efficiency and the quality of factors of production rather than disembodied technical change.

In table 5 the picture of modern economic growth in Europe through the 1970s is filled out on the basis of a Solow-type growth accounting. The estimates reported there show only two cases (Great Britain in 1801–31 and Portugal in 1910–34) where the TFP contribution to labor productivity growth is as much as 80 percent. A distinctive aspect of table 5 is that as modern economic growth spread across nineteenth-century Europe, TFP growth was initially quite modest, and any tendency for TFP growth to dominate capital deepening is generally a post-1890 or post-take-off phenomenon.

As Paul Krugman (1994) highlighted, and as economic historians in the Gerschenkronian tradition might have predicted, rapid catch-up growth in the East Asian developmental states looks rather different from the earlier OECD experience.[13] In Korea, Singapore, and Taiwan the contribution of capital deepening has been formidable and exceeded that of TFP growth in the period 1960–90.[14] There is a strong contrast with

12. The Boskin bias in inflation measurement does not appear to generalize to other periods (cf. Costa 2001).

13. In a very influential contribution, Alexander Gerschenkron (1962) proposed that the growth of "backward" follower countries would differ from that of their predecessors. In particular, there would be a much greater emphasis on capital accumulation and a key role for what would later be called the "developmental state" in implementing this.

14. Rodrik (1997) argued that the East Asian growth accounting estimates were biased; applying a similar correction formula to that in footnote 3 might add around 0.8 percent per year to TFP growth, which would change the detail but not the substance of this point.

Table 5   Ingenuity and Abstention in the Shift to Modern
Economic Growth (% per year)

	Labor Productivity Growth	Capital Deepening Contribution	TFP Growth
Austria			
1870–90	0.90	0.64	0.26
1890–1910	1.69	0.66	1.03
Germany			
1871–91	1.10	0.39	0.71
1891–1911	1.76	0.58	1.18
Great Britain			
1700–60	0.40	0.14	0.26
1760–1801	0.20	0.07	0.13
1801–31	0.50	0.10	0.40
1831–73	1.25	0.35	0.90
1873–1913	0.90	0.38	0.52
Hungary, 1870–1910	1.65	1.18	0.47
Italy			
1920–38	0.88	0.38	0.50
1951–73	4.51	1.61	2.90
The Netherlands			
1850–70	1.02	0.50	0.52
1870–90	0.94	0.61	0.33
1890–1913	1.35	0.46	0.89
Portugal			
1910–34	1.17	0.09	1.08
1934–47	0.78	0.90	−0.12
1947–73	4.47	2.46	2.01
Spain			
1850–83	1.2	1.6	−0.4
1884–1920	1.0	0.8	0.2
1920–29	2.0	0.6	1.4
1930–52	0.0	0.3	−0.3
1951–74	5.5	1.7	3.8
Sweden			
1850–90	1.18	1.12	0.06
1890–1913	2.77	0.94	1.83
1913–50	2.01	0.87	1.14
1950–73	3.68	1.82	1.86
USSR			
1928–40	2.5	2.0	0.5
1940–50	1.5	−0.1	1.6
1950–70	4.0	2.6	1.4
1970–85	1.6	2.0	−0.4

Table 5   Ingenuity and Abstention in the Shift to Modern
Economic Growth (% per year) (*cont.*)

	Labor Productivity Growth	Capital Deepening Contribution	TFP Growth
Korea, 1960–90	5.06	2.84	2.22
Singapore, 1960–90	4.97	3.34	1.63
Taiwan, 1960–90	6.07	3.17	2.90
China, 1978–2004	7.3	3.2	4.1
India, 1978–2004	3.3	1.3	2.0

Notes: All estimates impose equation (2) and are recalibrated with $\alpha = 0.35$; Great Britain is U.K. after 1831. Sources: Derived from data presented in the following original growth accounting studies: Austria and Hungary: Schulze 2007; Germany: Broadberry 1998; Great Britain: Crafts 1995 and Matthews, Feinstein, and Odling-Smee 1982; Italy: Rossi, Sorgato, and Toniolo 1992; The Netherlands: Albers and Groote 1996; Portugal: Lains 2003; Spain: Prados de la Escosura and Roses 2007; Sweden: Krantz and Schon 2007 and Schon 2004; USSR: Ofer 1987; Korea, Singapore, and Taiwan: Bosworth and Collins 2003; China and India: Bosworth and Collins 2008.

the well-known cases of Italy, Japan, and Spain in the golden age.[15] But table 5 also shows that catch-up growth comes in different flavors in modern times, as is reflected in the growth accounting estimates for China and India.

Finally, as is well known, growth in the Soviet Union did not follow the Solovian TFP-dominated trajectory. Table 5 shows that the Soviet economy succeeded for quite a while in mobilizing capital accumulation but had a weak record in TFP growth—note the comparison with golden age Western Europe—reflecting both poor resource allocation and inability to incentivize innovation (Ofer 1987).

In sum, it appears that the U.S. growth record that Solow (1957) analyzed was far from typical of the experience of the industrialized economies in the two centuries since the Industrial Revolution. Generally speaking, even without the refinements suggested by subsequent authors that tend to downsize the role of TFP, the contribution of TFP growth to labor productivity growth is well below seven-eighths. Had Solow's first growth accounting estimate been made in the 1950s for Spain or Sweden, the results would have been far less sensational.

15. Portugal, however, is more similar to East Asia.

Growth Accounting and the Lessons of History

In the late 1950s the "capital-fundamentalist" view of economic development predominated. In terms of economic history this was encapsulated
in the idea of take-off based on a doubling of the investment rate proposed
by Walt Rostow (1960) and based on his understanding of the British
industrial revolution. This was contested terrain, however, and was clearly
not Kuznets's view of the transition to modern economic growth. Much of
the work at this time in assembling the facts of long-run growth was in the
end working to undermine Rostow's analysis, and this was already clear
at the major conference organized to review the evidence for the "stages
of economic growth" (Rostow 1963). Solow attended this meeting and
in his oral comments noted a much-reduced emphasis on capital accumulation as, prompted by the discovery of the residual, economic historians were turning to narratives that, in Donald McCloskey's (1981, 108)
striking phrase, stressed ingenuity rather than abstention.

Growth accounting estimates for the British industrial revolution were
produced by Charles Feinstein (1981) who interpreted the results as incon-
sistent with capital fundamentalism and highlighted the large proportion
of labor productivity growth accounted for by TFP growth. Subsequent
research produced much-revised estimates of the rate of economic growth
in the late eighteenth and early nineteenth centuries (Crafts and Harley
1992), which had implications for TFP growth prior to 1830, as shown in
table 6. While the conclusion that capital deepening contributed relatively
little to labor productivity growth was sustained, the TFP growth rate during the Industrial Revolution was markedly reduced, a result that seemed
paradoxical to those brought up on the idea that famous inventions were
the hallmark of this period.

Clearly, especially given the imperfections of the underlying economic
data, a persuasive narrative is required if these estimates are to gain widespread acceptance. To some extent, this can be provided on the basis of the
arithmetic of growth by pointing to the large weight of sectors such as
domestic service that are known to have been untouched by technology
and the small initial size of industries that were transformed, such as cot-
ton textiles (Mokyr 2004). And to some extent, the limits to TFP growth
during the Industrial Revolution can be understood through the lens of
endogenous growth theory, which would point to weaknesses in incentive
structures and in science, technology, and education (Crafts 1995).

Nevertheless, some of the strongest support comes from further explorations in growth accounting. Independent estimates based on the dual

Table 6   Growth Accounting and the British Industrial Revolution (% per year)

	Labor Productivity	Capital Deepening	Steam-Capital Deepening	TFP	Steam TFP
Feinstein 1981					
1761–1800	0.3	0.1		0.2	
1801–30	1.3	0.0		1.3	
1831–60	1.1	0.3		0.8	
Crafts 1995					
1760–1801	0.2	0.1		0.1	
1801–31	0.5	0.1		0.4	
Crafts 2004					
1760–1800			0.004		0.005
1800–30			0.02		0.001
1830–60			0.19		0.10

Note: Steam contributions include both stationary steam engines and railways.

approach using evidence on real rewards to factors of production broadly support the Crafts-Harley view (Antras and Voth 2003), which might be expected when it is remembered that the Industrial Revolution is notorious for the slow growth of real wages, but the growth accounting equivalences are often overlooked. Further insights come from examining the contribution of steam to labor productivity growth. Until about 1830 this was slight, as table 6 reports. The major effect of steam on economic growth awaited the era of high-pressure steam in the second half of the nineteenth century.[16]

In fact, the British industrial revolution offers an interesting twist on the so-called Solow productivity paradox. In a comment made in July of 1987, Solow referred to a paradox as he remarked about the purported revolution in productivity brought on by the computer: "You can see the computer age everywhere except in the productivity statistics" (Triplett 1999). Steam power was not in fact very cost effective initially, and only

16. This should not have been a surprise to anyone familiar with the early cliometrics literature, which highlighted how small were the initial social savings of the steam engine (von Tunzelmann 1978) and the railway (Hawke 1970), but the implications for interpreting productivity growth were clarified only when these estimates were converted into their growth accounting equivalent in Crafts 2004.

about 165,000 horsepower were in use even as late as 1830 (Kanefsky 1979) when the steam engine capital income share was 0.4 percent and the steam engines' Domar weight was 1.7 percent (Crafts 2004). So, in this earlier episode the paradox is that you could see steam hardly anywhere and certainly not in the productivity statistics. The point in both cases is that the arithmetic of growth accounting as in equation (7) immediately reveals why the initial effect of new general purpose technologies such as steam and ICT will be underwhelming. That said, it is worth noting that by the standards of the steam age the growth contribution of ICT in the late 1980s was already quite stunning.[17]

Growth accounting underpins two key messages about modern economic growth that are now widely understood but were not well appreciated in the 1950s. First, the idea of a take-off into sustained economic growth based on a great leap forward in capital accumulation is a serious misunderstanding of the experience of the Industrial Revolution. Second, even really major technological breakthroughs have quite muted effects on economic growth at the level of the aggregate economy.

Conclusions

Growth accounting has been attractive to quantitative economic historians because it has been seen as a transparent yet flexible framework for describing the proximate sources of growth. On the whole, the use of the technique has been growth theory "lite" and has probably owed more to Denison than to Solow. Generally speaking, economic historians have opted for relatively simple versions of the technique and have been wary of adopting variants based on anything other than those consistent with a Cobb-Douglas production function. This has been facilitated by a body of evidence that suggests that the share of profits in national income is a reasonable estimate of the elasticity of output with respect to capital. Issues relating to labor quality have been dealt with better than those relating to capital quality. Economic historians have not generally interpreted Solow's residual as a measure of technical change; indeed, they have argued that TFP growth can either over- or underestimate technical change. Attempts

17. The contribution of steam to British labor productivity peaked at about 0.4 percent per year in the third quarter of the nineteenth century about a century after James Watt's patent (Crafts 2004). By contrast, the estimates in Oliner, Sichel, and Stiroh 2007 show the contribution of ICT to American labor productivity growth as 0.74 percent per year during 1973–95.

to quantify components of Solow's residual, other than education, have not commanded widespread support.

Overall, research has confirmed that (crude) TFP growth is a more important source of labor productivity growth than physical-capital deepening. The Asian tigers appear to be the main exception to this generalization. Where it is possible to make long-run comparisons, the dominance of TFP growth over capital deepening seems to have peaked in the mid-twentieth century when TFP growth was much more rapid than one hundred years earlier. The extent to which the twentieth century was more technologically progressive than the nineteenth century is difficult to ascertain because the (uncertain) extent to which the conventional benchmarking assumptions of growth accounting result in measurement errors has probably varied a good deal over the long run. Awareness of this problem is greatly enhanced by an understanding of neoclassical growth theory and underlines that making this connection, as Solow did, was a major step forward, although its potential has been underappreciated by economic historians.

The use of growth accounting in economic history has underpinned two big messages that were certainly not understood when Solow (1957) appeared. First, famous and far-reaching technological changes such as the invention of the steam engine raise the rate of growth of labor productivity appreciably only with a considerable lag. Second, the idea of the take-off propagated by Rostow is seriously misleading as a description of the transition to modern economic growth in the old industrial economies.

References

Abramovitz, M. 1956. Resource and Output Trends in the United States since 1870. *American Economic Review Papers and Proceedings* 46:5–23.

———. 1962. Economic Growth in the United States: A Review Article. *American Economic Review* 52:762–82.

Abramovitz, M., and P. A. David. 1973. Reinterpreting Economic Growth: Parables and Realities. *American Economic Review Papers and Proceedings* 63:428–39.

———. 2001. Two Centuries of American Macroeconomic Growth: From Exploitation of Resource Abundance to Knowledge-Driven Development. Discussion Paper No. 01–05, Stanford Institute for Economic Policy Research.

Aiyar, S., and C.-J. Dalgaard. 2005. Total Factor Productivity Revisited: A Dual Approach to Development Accounting. *IMF Staff Papers* 52:82–102.

Albers, R., and P. Groote. 1996. The Empirics of Growth. *De Economist* 144:429–44.

Allen, R. C. 2003. *Farm to Factory*. Princeton, N.J.: Princeton University Press.

Antras, P., and H.-J. Voth. 2003. Factor Prices and Productivity Growth during the English Industrial Revolution. *Explorations in Economic History* 40:52–77.

Badinger, H. 2005. Growth Effects of Economic Integration: Evidence from the EU Member States. *Review of World Economics* 141:50–78.

Barro, R. J. 1999. Notes on Growth Accounting. *Journal of Economic Growth* 4:119–37.

Barro, R. J., and X. Sala-i-Martin. 1995. *Economic Growth*. New York: McGraw-Hill.

Bergson, A. 1983. Technological Progress. In *The Soviet Economy: Toward the Year 2000*, edited by A. Bergson and H. S. Levine. Boston: Allen and Unwin.

Boskin, M. J., E. R. Dulberger, R. J. Gordon, Z. Griliches, and D. W. Jorgenson. 1996. *Towards a More Accurate Measure of the Cost of Living*. Washington, D.C.: U.S. Government Printing Office.

Bosworth, B. P., and S. M. Collins. 2003. The Empirics of Growth: An Update. *Brookings Papers on Economic Activity* 2:113–206.

———. 2008. Accounting for Growth: Comparing China and India. *Journal of Economic Perspectives* 22.1:45–66.

Broadberry, S. N. 1998. How Did the United States and Germany Overtake Britain? A Sectoral Analysis of Comparative Productivity Levels. *Journal of Economic History* 58:375–407.

Carre, J.-J., P. Dubois, and E. Malinvaud. 1975. *French Economic Growth*. Stanford, Calif.: Stanford University Press.

Collins, S. M., and B. P. Bosworth. 1996. Economic Growth in East Asia: Accumulation versus Assimilation. *Brookings Papers on Economic Activity* 2:135–203.

Costa, D. 2001. Estimating Real Income in the United States from 1888 to 1994: Correcting CPI Bias Using Engel Curves. *Journal of Political Economy* 109:1288–310.

Crafts, N. 1995. Exogenous or Endogenous Growth? The Industrial Revolution Reconsidered. *Journal of Economic History* 55:745–72.

———. 2004. Productivity Growth in the Industrial Revolution: A New Growth Accounting Perspective. *Journal of Economic History* 64:521–35.

Crafts, N., and C. K. Harley. 1992. Output Growth and the Industrial Revolution: A Restatement of the Crafts-Harley View. *Economic History Review* 45:703–30.

Denison, E. F. 1962. *The Sources of Economic Growth in the United States and the Alternatives before Us*. New York: Committee for Economic Development.

———. 1967. *Why Growth Rates Differ*. Washington, D.C.: Brookings Institution.

de Rouvray, C. 2005. Economists Writing History. PhD diss., London School of Economics.

Domar, E. D. 1961. On the Measurement of Technological Change. *Economic Journal* 71:709–29.

Fabricant, S. 1954. Economic Progress and Economic Change. In *NBER 34th Annual Report*. New York.

Feinstein, C. H. 1981. Capital Accumulation and the Industrial Revolution. In vol. 1 of *The Economic History of Britain*, edited by R. Floud and D. McCloskey. Cambridge: Cambridge University Press.

Fogel, R. W. 1964. *Railroads and American Economic Growth: Essays in Econometric History.* Baltimore, Md.: Johns Hopkins University Press.

Gerschenkron, A. 1962. *Economic Backwardness in Historical Perspective.* Cambridge, Mass.: Belknap.

Griliches, Z. 1996. The Discovery of the Residual: A Historical Note. *Journal of Economic Literature* 34:1324–30.

Hawke, G. R. 1970. *Railways and Economic Growth in England and Wales, 1840–1870.* Oxford: Clarendon.

Jerzmanowski, M. 2007. Total Factor Productivity Differences: Appropriate Technology vs. Efficiency. *European Economic Review* 51:2080–110.

Jorgenson, D. W., and Z. Griliches. 1967. The Explanation of Productivity Change. *Review of Economic Studies* 34:249–83.

Kanefsky, J. F. 1979. The Diffusion of Power Technology in British Industry. PhD diss., University of Exeter.

Kendrick, J. W. 1961. *Productivity Trends in the United States.* Princeton, N.J.: Princeton University Press.

Krantz, O., and L. Schon. 2007. *Swedish Historical National Accounts, 1800–2000.* Lund: Almqvist and Wiksell International.

Krueger, A. B., and M. Lindahl. 2001. Education for Growth: Why and for Whom? *Journal of Economic Literature* 39:1101–36.

Krugman, P. 1994. The Myth of Asia's Miracle. *Foreign Affairs* 73.6:62–78.

Kuznets, S. S. 1971. *Economic Growth of Nations.* Cambridge, Mass.: Belknap.

Lains, P. 2003. Catching Up to the European Core: Portuguese Economic Growth, 1910–1990. *Explorations in Economic History* 40:369–86.

Maddison, A. 1987. Growth and Slowdown in Advanced Capitalist Economies: Techniques of Quantitative Assessment. *Journal of Economic Literature* 25:649–98.

———. 1996. Macroeconomic Accounts for European Countries. In *Quantitative Aspects of Post-war European Economic Growth*, edited by B. van Ark and N. Crafts. Cambridge: Cambridge University Press.

Mankiw, N. G., D. Romer, and D. N. Weil. 1992. A Contribution to the Empirics of Economic Growth. *Quarterly Journal of Economics* 107:407–37.

Matthews, R. C. O., C. H. Feinstein, and J. C. Odling-Smee. 1982. *British Economic Growth, 1856–1973.* Stanford, Calif.: Stanford University Press.

McCloskey, D. N. 1981. The Industrial Revolution, 1780–1860: A Survey. In vol. 1 of *The Economic History of Britain since 1700*, edited by R. Floud and D. McCloskey. Cambridge: Cambridge University Press.

Mokyr, J. 2004. Accounting for the Industrial Revolution. In vol. 1 of *The Cambridge Economic History of Modern Britain*, edited by R. Floud and P. Johnson. Cambridge: Cambridge University Press.

Morrison, C. J. 1988. Quasi-Fixed Inputs in US and Japanese Manufacturing: A Generalized Leontief Restricted Cost Function Approach. *Review of Economics and Statistics* 70:275–87.

Nadiri, M. I. 1970. Some Approaches to the Theory and Measurement of Total Factor Productivity: A Survey. *Journal of Economic Literature* 8:1137–77.

Ofer, G. 1987. Soviet Economic Growth, 1928–1985. *Journal of Economic Literature* 25:1767–833.

Ohkawa, K., and H. Rosovsky. 1972. *Japanese Economic Growth: Trend Acceleration in the Twentieth Century.* Stanford, Calif.: Stanford University Press.

Oliner, S. D., and D. E. Sichel. 2000. The Resurgence of Growth in the Late 1990s: Is Information Technology the Story? *Journal of Economic Perspectives* 14.4:3–22.

Oliner, S. D., D. E. Sichel, and K. J. Stiroh. 2007. Explaining a Productive Decade. *Brookings Papers on Economic Activity* 1:81–152.

Prados de la Escosura, L., and J. Roses. 2007. The Sources of Long-Run Growth in Spain, 1850–2000. Centre for Economic Policy Research Discussion Paper No. 6189, London.

Rodrik, D. 1997. TFPG Controversies, Institutions, and Economic Performance in East Asia. Centre for Economic Policy Research Discussion Paper No. 1587, London.

Rossi, N., and G. Toniolo. 1992. Catching Up or Falling Behind? Italy's Economic Growth, 1895–1947. *Economic History Review* 45:537–63.

Rossi, N., A. Sorgato, and G. Toniolo. 1992. Italian Historical Statistics, 1890–1990. Working Paper No. 92–18, University of Venice, Dipartimento di Scienze Economiche.

Rostow, W. W. 1960. *The Stages of Economic Growth.* Cambridge: Cambridge University Press.

———, ed. 1963. *The Economics of Take-Off into Sustained Growth.* London: Macmillan.

Schon, L. 2004. Total Factor Productivity in Swedish Manufacturing in the Period 1870–2000. In *Exploring Economic Growth,* edited by S. Heikkinen and J.-L. van Zanden. Amsterdam: Aksant Academic Publishers.

Schulze, M.-S. 2007. Origins of Catch-Up Failure: Comparative Productivity Growth in the Habsburg Empire, 1879–1910. *European Review of Economic History* 11:189–218.

Solow, R. M. 1957. Technical Change and the Aggregate Production Function. *Review of Economics and Statistics* 39:312–20.

———. 1963. *Capital Theory and the Rate of Return.* Amsterdam: North-Holland.

Tinbergen, J. 1942. Zur Theorie der Langfirstigen Wirtschaftsentwicklung. *Weltwirtschaftliches Archiv* 55:511–49.

Triplett, Jack E. 1999. The Solow Productivity Paradox: What Do Computers Do to Productivity? *Canadian Journal of Economics* 32.2:309–34.

van Ark, B., and H. de Jong. 1996. Accounting for Economic Growth in the Netherlands since 1913. *Economic and Social History of the Netherlands* 7:199–242.

von Tunzelmann, G. N. 1978. *Steam Power and British Industrialisation to 1860.* Oxford: Clarendon.

Solow in the Tropics

John Toye

> "Growth Economics" is often taken to be particularly associated with
> the problem of "developing the underdeveloped." The appearance of a
> branch of theory called Growth Theory, at a time when the economics of
> underdevelopment has been a major preoccupation of economists, has
> made it look as if there must be a real connexion. I much doubt if there is.
> —John Hicks, *Capital and Growth* (1965)

Thus wrote Sir John Hicks, over forty years ago. According to him, growth
theory treats of economic growth in general, while development economics is a practical subject that draws on any theory relevant to it (including sociological theory). Hicks (1965, 3–4) added, "If there is any branch
of economic theory which is especially relevant to [development econom-
ics], it is the Theory of International Trade." The present article is about
why growth theory and development economics remained separate for a
generation after Robert Solow's (1956, 1957) pathbreaking contributions
to growth theory, and how and why the two are coming together now, as
neoclassical growth theory and statistical techniques based on it are being
applied to the formal analysis of economic development.

I am most grateful to Mauro Boianovsky, John Knight, and Adrian Wood for comments,
criticisms, and constructive suggestions on various drafts of this article; to Nick Crafts and
other participants in the *HOPE* 2008 conference at Duke University for their perceptive
observations; and to two anonymous referees for helpful guidance.

History of Political Economy 41 (annual suppl.) DOI 10.1215/00182702-2009-025

The sequence of discussion is as follows, by section: the question of whether the Solow model was intended to be applied to tropical countries; the model's prediction of convergence of countries' per capita income levels; links between growth models, trade models, and trade policy; the impact of the Solow model on the World Bank's activities; the use of growth accounting and growth regressions as diagnostics for developing countries; earlier insights into the growth process that the Solow model eclipsed; and some concluding remarks.

Does the Solow Model Apply to the Tropics?

The original Solow growth model had a beautiful simplicity, using the device of a variable capital-output ratio to return an economy to steady-state growth. It was quickly recognized as "a major step in the history of growth theory" (Sen 1970, 21). With respect to its analytical purchase, however, the choice of Roy Harrod's model for modification was unusual at the time. Harrod's was a theory of the requirements of steady-state growth at full employment, not a theory of the determinants of economic growth. When Amartya Sen asked whether the model should be read as a description of how capitalist economies actually work, or of the consequences of maintaining full employment, Solow's clarification was that "the idea is to trace full employment paths, no more" (Sen 1970, 23–24 n. 15).

Yet within what was still a requirements theory, Solow presumably would have held—as had Harrod (1951, 272 n. 1)—that his account of the forces that lead to and maintain equilibrium growth was "intended to be a study of causes." Solow has subsequently sounded slightly rueful that his model concentrated on the "price and interest rate dynamics that would support an equilibrium path" of growth. He has regretted having unleashed "a standing temptation to sound like Dr Pangloss" (Solow 1988, 309). The doctrine of Dr. Pangloss, however, was that *this is the best of all possible worlds.* By contrast, if its price and interest rate dynamics were indeed a study of causes, the Solow growth model tells us that, in the long term, there is another, better world—a world of full-employment growth, and that it is possible to reach it. Some even say that in the model steady-state growth "could hardly be avoided" (Ruttan 1998, 3–4). Far from imitating Pangloss's complacent conservatism, the vital characteristic of the initial Solow growth model was that it had a visionary quality. It was a theory in both senses: a programmatic idea of how things should be, and a scheme of explanation of how that program would come to be realized.

Development economics, by contrast, derived from a different portion of Keynes's legacy, the one that focused on identifying practical policy problems, on public advocacy, and on persuading policymakers to adopt intelligent solutions. The key problem of development economics had emerged during the Second World War in the less-developed regions of Europe, where disguised unemployment was believed to prevail.[1] The problem was how to raise incomes in these regions, *under specific constraining conditions*, namely, without waiting on further technical progress, without making any impact on existing international trade flows, and in the absence of much local entrepreneurship. The recommended policy was for the government to undertake large-scale capital investment in a range of complementary light industries, drawing labor out of disguised unemployment and into productive employment (Rosenstein-Rodan 1943). Development economics and policy began as an exercise in thinking *inside* the box—evaluating what to do for the best in a specific constrained situation.

The process of labor transfer in labor surplus countries was then given more formal shape in models of economic dualism, again with specific contextual assumptions, for example, in the paradigmatic model of Arthur Lewis (1954). When advising on economic policy, Lewis always referred back to strands of the complex sociological tangle that he had tried to unravel in his *Theory of Economic Growth* (1955). Yet it was his formal model whose features were attractive to many economists of development. Chronic underemployment was a key stylized fact about underdeveloped countries, so it was not a full-employment model. Moreover, while surplus labor remains, the accumulation of capital does not run into diminishing returns.[2]

Was the Solow model also intended to apply to developing countries? Bill Easterly (2002, 55–56) says that Solow "never mentioned tropical countries in any of his writings; in fact, he never applied his model to any other country besides the United States [so] Solow is not to blame for how his model was applied to the tropical countries." This is not quite right. Justifying the omission of land from the aggregate production function,

1. For details of the considerable influence of refugee German and Eastern European economists on the genesis of development economics, see Hagemann 2007, 340–48.

2. Some economists, such as T. W. Schultz (1964), denied the existence of labor whose marginal product was zero, but a zero marginal product of labor in the subsistence sector is neither a necessary nor a sufficient condition for Lewis-type labor transfer to occur (Sen 1966).

Solow (1956, 67 n. 2) stated that "one can imagine the theory applying as long as arable land can be hacked out of the wilderness at essentially constant cost," and he cited Ethiopia as an underdeveloped country that had no shortage of land.[3] The fact that he applied his model only to the United States does not entail that he believed that it did not apply elsewhere. On the contrary, he explains the motivation for his model in terms of intellectual discomfort with the models designed not just by Harrod and Domar but "also by Arthur Lewis in a slightly different context." "I believe I remember that writings on economic development often asserted that the key to a transition from slow growth to fast growth was a sustained rise in the savings rate. The recipe sounded implausible to me. I can no longer remember exactly why, but it did" (Solow 1988, 307–8). This tilt at the Lewis model does not really strike home, however, because that model does not address the issue of steady-state growth in a capitalist economy; rather, it asks how a transition occurs from an economy that is subsistence based to an economy that is fully capitalist (Lewis 1954, 155). Lewis's proposed answer was by means of a capitalist sector that continually reinvests its profits while drawing surplus labor from the subsistence sector at a constant real wage rate. Whatever the merits of this answer, the point is that it was addressed to a different question from Solow's. Further, it is debatable whether a model of the long-run steady state is the best way to think about economic development. As was still being urged fifty years later: "This process [of economic development] could be seen as inherently a transition, from one form of economy to something very different[, and] the stylized apparatus of balanced growth paths might have little to say about many events that are central to this transition" (Temple 2005, 436).

Nevertheless, Solow's remark implies that the geographic scope of his model was intended to include underdeveloped countries, at least those with unlimited supplies of cultivable land. Nor would such an intention be unreasonable, since the object of his model is to trace equilibrium growth paths. The important question to ask, however, with respect to developed and developing economies alike, is how such models can be applied appropriately. Their approach to growth theory is obviously different from that which would be used if the aim were to provide the best possible explanation of the variety of historical growth experience. While concentration

3. Solow assumed unlimited supplies of land, rather than (with Lewis) unlimited supplies of labor.

on the steady-state solution and its properties is entirely defensible, it sets limits on the extent to which the theory is applicable to reality. Solow gave his own understanding of these limits in 2001:

> In my view growth theory was conceived as a model of the growth of an industrial economy. . . . I have never applied such a model to a developing economy, because I thought the underlying machinery would apply mainly to a planned economy or a well developed market economy. *This is not a matter of principle, just wariness.* (283; emphasis added)

The Convergence Debate

The main conclusion of Solow's 1957 paper on growth accounting was that U.S. growth was the result not of capital accumulation but (seven-eighths of it) of the famous "residual." At the same time, the Solow-Swan model with its assumptions of a single universally available technology, diminishing returns to capital, and constant returns to scale provided the basis of a theoretical argument for the faster growth of poor countries than rich ones, and thus the worldwide convergence in levels of per capita income.[4] In response to different initial stocks of capital, and thus different rates of return to investment, domestic savings should temporarily increase or decrease. This implies that, before reaching the steady-state growth path, poor countries will grow faster than rich countries. However, since the steady-state growth rate is determined only by the rate of technical progress, and since technical progress is assumed to be available to all countries as a free good, ultimately all countries, whatever their initial incomes per head, will converge on the same steady-state rate of growth (Ray 1998, 74–82).

Although it is easy to see that this does not happen in the real world, a naive rebuttal of the prediction of unconditional convergence does not do justice to the Solow model. One can argue that the convergence prediction should be conditional on differences in saving and population growth rates, implying different steady-state growth paths and the absence of an inverse relation between initial income level and the rate of income growth. When capital accumulation is augmented to include both physical

---

4. As Jeffrey A. Frankel (2003, 190) has remarked: "I assume that the *aficionados* all recognize that the Solow residual 'school of thought' is the opposite of the Solow growth model school of thought, but I am guessing that this confuses many of our students."

and human varieties, about 80 percent of the observed differences in per capita incomes were estimated to be attributable to differences in these two variables (Mankiw, Romer, and Weil 1992). Yet this rehabilitation of the Solow model in an augmented version has not proved wholly convincing either. Theoretically, conditional convergence might be the result of the transfer of resources from a low productivity sector (agriculture) to a high productivity sector (industry), that is, the process that Lewis modeled, rather than a decline in the marginal product of capital (Thirlwall 2002, 33–34).[5]

Econometrically, the Mankiw, Romer, and Weil result has attracted a volley of objections, along the lines that the estimates are systematically biased (see, e.g., Temple 1999, 134–35; Bosworth and Collins 2003, 124–25; Helpman 2004, 27–28; McCombie 2006, 151–56; Bliss 2007, 73–85). Although the issue is still contested, attention has now switched elsewhere. It may be that, to the limited extent that national per capita incomes have converged, the augmented Solow model provides the explanation for it, but many commentators think that that result should be regarded as fragile. Moreover, estimates of the pace of conditional convergence suggest that it is very slow.

Growing doubts about convergence by the mid-1980s prompted Paul Romer and Robert Lucas to devise growth models in which technical progress is endogenous, essentially as a result of the externalities of knowledge production or education.[6] While retaining the framework of competition and diminishing returns to capital, these models exhibit increasing returns in the aggregate. They explain why capital does not necessarily accumulate faster in poor countries or, when capital is mobile, flow from high to low per capita income countries. Thus they neither imply even conditional convergence nor rule out any catching up. Endogenous growth models added some limited degrees of realism to the Solow model and, in not making any definite prediction about convergence, are compatible with key facts many development economists were beginning to observe—examples of failure to converge (sub-Saharan Africa) coexisting with a few remarkable examples of catching up (East Asia).

5. Once structural change is added to the augmented Solow model, it can do a better job of mimicking the actual growth rates of developing countries, even China's. In the doubly augmented model, the assumption that technical progress is exogenous, and is the same for all countries, is retained, however.

6. The basic idea for neoclassical endogenous models comes from Arrow's (1962) classic paper on the economic implications of learning by doing.

Growth Models, Trade Models, and Trade Policy

The original Solow model, like the Lewis model, was a closed economy model. Thus the context of the convergence debate was a set of isolated Solow-type economies, each of which was responding to its initial position relative to its own steady-state growth path. This setup contrasted with the concerns of the pioneer development economists, like Hans Singer and Raùl Prebisch, who focused on the consequences for growth and global inequality of the actual linkages through investment and trade of developed and undeveloped economies (Toye and Toye 2004, 110–36). The modeling of Ronald Findlay (1979, 1980) captured one of these global linkages. He successfully yoked a Solow model to a Lewis model in a global North-South model of dependent development, via deteriorating Southern terms of trade.

In a world where Solow-type economies are linked up by perfectly integrated capital markets, a uniform rate of profit will be established, and with access to identical technology, will move capital per worker to a common level. Despite differences in population growth and savings, economies will converge in terms of output per worker. Even without capital mobility, Solow-type economies that engage in trade will, using the special assumptions of Heckscher-Ohlin, tend to equalize factor prices, which implies a considerable move toward income equalization, though factor quantities in each economy would still differ (Ros 2000, 184–87).[7]

Many development economists failed to detect the working of such equalizing impulses in the international economy of the 1960s, so the question for them was "why were they not more powerful?" One answer often given was that the models' numerous restrictive assumptions were violated in reality, so it was idle to search for equalizing impulses. Those who felt comfortable with the models' assumptions, however, took a different tack, pointing to the obstacles to free trade that policymakers in developing countries had erected. A key tool for estimating the obstructive impact of these obstacles to trade was Max Corden's (1966, 1971) measure of the effective rate of protection, which calculated the degree of protection in relation not to the price of the final good but to the domestic value-added of the good. This measure was employed in several multicountry studies of

---

7. In the opinion of Bliss (2007, 238), "There is a makeshift feel to these [trade and growth] models, [which] is unsurprising if one considers that both growth, and trade, have been modelled independently, according to their particular requirements."

developing countries' trade regimes in the 1970s. Those done under the auspices of the Organisation for Economic Co-operation and Development (OEDC) are summarized in Little, Scitovsky, and Scott 1970. Bela Balassa et al. (1971) presented the results of World Bank–sponsored research. The U.S. National Bureau of Economic Research (NBER) series on foreign trade regimes and economic development (1974–78) concluded with summary volumes by Jagdish Bhagwati (1978) and Anne Krueger (1978).[8] All of these series of studies revealed very high levels of effective protection in many developing countries, including some that created negative value-added, that is, where the value of domestic production at world prices was lower than the value of its imported inputs at world prices!

The substantial intellectual effort sunk into these studies had important and varied consequences for development economics and policy. It showed what could be done by the sustained application of formal economic analysis and encouraged the appearance of new academic journals that featured formal analysis of trade and payments problems, such as the *Journal of International Economics*, which Bhagwati edited between 1971 and 1986. It also opened up important political economy questions about why trade was so distorted by government policies, thereby undermining the idea of governments as promoters of the public interest. Finally, it could be cited in support of trade liberalization as a growth-promoting reform in developing countries, although growth theorists are likely to agree with Solow that "sheer efficiency gains from trade cannot [raise the steady-state growth rate] except temporarily" (Snowdon and Vane 1999, 280). The case for trade raising the long-run growth rate has to suppose the existence of a technology gap that trade can subsequently close.

Impact of the Solow Model on the World Bank

When the World Bank expanded its lending to developing countries in the 1960s, it turned hardly at all to growth models for guidance. In 1973, its first historians could declare: "One will look in vain in the Bank files, both current and old, for any evidence of accepted theories of development or models of the development process" (Mason and Asher 1973, 458). The World Bank was (and indeed remains) an organization that takes a pragmatic view of economic doctrines. Its activities revolve around the

8. Other economists who were closely involved in this group of studies and who later became influential in the World Bank were Michael Michaely and Michael Bruno.

central functions of borrowing and lending, and its views of the development process have been closely related to achieving success in these practical activities.

Initially, its objective was lending for public overhead capital, and its vehicle was the project. Through the 1960s, however, the Bank broadened its horizons. In this, it was probably influenced by the post-1957 research spurt in growth accounting based on OECD country data. Edward Denison (1962) emphasized human capital's contribution to growth, and education's contribution to producing human capital, and this was the first area of the Bank's research interest. This led the Bank to examine other unconventional inputs into growth, such as technological innovations and improvements in the functioning of factor and product markets. Then, "estimates were attempted of the relative contribution [to growth] of conventional inputs—land, labour and capital—against the totality of unconventional inputs" (Mason and Asher 1973, 482). It seems that the Bank was willing to learn from the technique of growth accounting while fighting shy of any overt association with its new theoretical basis, the Solow model.

The arrival at the Bank of Robert McNamara (president, 1970–81) and Hollis Chenery (as his economic adviser) initiated big changes at the Bank—both a rapid expansion of lending and a zeal for the managing of lending by quantitative methods. Countries' capital needs were now estimated from Chenery and Strout's (1966) two-gap model, which became embodied in the Bank's minimum standard model—and subsequently its revised minimum standard model (RMSM). Although the two-gap model soon fell from academic favor, it lived on in the Bank's operational practice, and the RMSM's investment-growth relation is indeed of pure Harrod-Domar lineage (Easterly 2002, 34–35). Like the even longer-lived Polak model at the IMF, RMSM has survived because it is serviceable. It facilitates, standardizes, and makes routine the tasks of the agency, whatever it may lack in intellectual sophistication, as Chenery (1983, 22) explained: "A man who has actually done an analysis for the Minister of Finance or Head of Planning in a country is permanently affected by that process. He will not go back to the less useful parts of economics in the future." In contrast, the neoclassical growth model has never provided the Bank with an operational tool.

During the McNamara-Chenery era, the Bank's newly increased research activities examined the internal income distribution of developing countries, that is, the problem of poverty, as well as of international income inequality. This more radical approach (inspired by Dudley Seers) took the Bank into new territory (Chenery 1983, 5–6). Choice of technique was now viewed through the prism of income distribution, trying to answer the question, "Would a simpler technology for highway building or sewerage projects do more to raise the incomes of the rural poor?" Henry Bruton (1955, 327–28) had already suggested that developing countries had a problem—that importing an improved technology would move the capital-labor ratio in the opposite direction from that required to achieve greater employment of their abundant factor, labor. By contrast, Solow's conception of technology as a universal library of blueprints freely available ruled out the existence of a technology gap that required some countries to import improved technology from others endowed with different factor proportions, because they had no alternative source. In the Solow model, the problem of inappropriate technology simply could not arise: there was no technology gap for trade to close. Yet E. F. Schumacher's (1973) slogan "small is beautiful" proclaimed the need for a new intermediate technology, neither the capital-intensive technology imported from the West nor the labor-intensive but low-productivity technology found in the subsistence and informal sectors of the underdeveloped economy. So in an effort to change project design choices to make them more pro-poor, the Bank's project evaluation criteria were modified to give greater weight to the incomes of the poor. There were, however, many influential people in whose eyes this modification was too radical, validating excessive government intervention in the marketplace. Their moment came when McNamara retired before appointing Chenery's successor, thereby giving the new president, Tom Clausen, a former commercial banker, a free hand.

Clausen's choice was Anne Krueger. She had demonstrated her ability in growth accounting on standard neoclassical assumptions, attributing more than half of the difference in per capita income levels between developed and developing countries to the difference in their human capital endowments. She had interpreted this result as invalidating Hicks's claim of no connection between growth theory and development economics (Krueger 1968, 656–57). She enhanced her reputation further in the 1970s, through her contributions to the U.S. NBER foreign trade regimes studies (1974a, 1978). Krueger also showed how controls on foreign trade could produce corruption and unproductive activities associated with rent-seeking (1974b). This work was significant because, as Hicks had argued, trade was the branch of theory most relevant to development economics and thus an appropriate entry point for those seeking to enlarge the role of formal theory in development economics.

Krueger now made herself the main conduit by which neoclassical economics entered the Bank. Her transformation of the research staff there was more than just the normal sweep of a new broom. Only eight of the thirty-seven staff in the Development Research Department remained three years after her arrival, the rest discarded as technically incompetent advocates of state intervention. The new policy message was to be the pro-market one that price signals work, that the effects of market liberalization favor the poor, and thus that special antipoverty strategies are redundant. Research that threw doubt on these messages was actively discouraged (Kapur, Lewis, and Webb 1997, 1193–95 nn. 47, 48). In short, it was Krueger's tenure at the Bank (1982–87) that established the neoliberal policy agenda that fed into the Washington Consensus on desirable economic reform in developing countries.

Part of this agenda was to pour cold water on the claim that developing countries faced a technological gap. Ian Little, who was closely associated with the World Bank research department at this time, argued that empirically there was a wide range of capital-labor ratios for producing the great majority of products. Even when equipment was imported, there were different ways to use it to make its operation more labor intensive (Little 1984, 176–81). Little also rejected the idea that the proprietary knowledge of multinational corporations contributed to the technological dependency of developing countries. In his view, since there are always ways to get around such problems, excessive capital intensity in production in developing countries must be attributed to ignorance, plus the prejudices of local politicians, engineers, and managers in its favor (249). By arguments such as these, the idea of a universal library of blueprints freely available to all was put back on its feet briefly, only to be challenged again by the newer growth models that made technical change endogenous.

Development Accounting
and the Complex Sociological Tangle

In the wake of the convergence debate, development accounting (the cross-country analogue of growth accounting) has been used to derive conclusions about economic performance in developed and developing countries. Solow's wariness about this enterprise has not dampened the enthusiasm of newcomers to this field. Robert E. Hall and Charles Jones (1999), for example, have produced output-to-input decompositions showing that the differences in output levels between rich and poor countries result less from differences in capital inputs (both physical and human) than from differences in TFP. Is this a useful exercise? There are well-known measurement problems involved in making estimates of TFP levels. These include the crudeness of the underlying data on inputs and the fact that the method assumes that the share of the inputs in income is the same in all countries. This creates a major problem for interpreting the TFP estimate because, as a residual, it includes both specification error and measurement error.[9] It includes all unmeasured differences in the quality of inputs—technological differences; differences in organizational efficiency in the use of inputs; differences in government regulations and policies. It has been noted that more refined methods of measuring inputs normally lead to reductions in the TFP estimate.

One might be inclined to attribute the large estimated differences in productivity levels between developing and developed countries to (1) the concentration of most of the world's R&D expenditure in the latter countries—a fact highlighted in Singer 1975—and (2) the existence of a threshold level of income or skill that has to be passed before technology transfer to developing countries can take place (Baumol, Nelson, and Wolff 1994). Differences in TFP levels between countries indicate only that some countries (the now-industrialized countries) started accumulating capital earlier than others and have continued longer and more persistently than others.

When one turns to decompositions of output growth rates, it becomes clear that there are major contrasts between groups of countries in different parts of the developing world. Where, over the last fifty years, the growth of capital inputs per worker has been low (say, less than 2 percent a year), for example, in sub-Saharan Africa, Latin America, and the Middle East, the rate of growth of measured TFP has been slight or even negative. Where the growth of capital inputs per worker has been high, for example, in East and South Asia, the growth of TFP has also been high (Bosworth and Collins 2003, 122–23).[10] This suggests that the policy advice to developing countries often derived from levels accounting results, namely, "de-emphasize savings and investment, and emphasize

9. Commenting on Solow 1957, Hicks (1960, 129), for example, suggested the very small share of output growth explained by capital accumulation might be "an illusion which has only arisen because the particular production function chosen does not allow sufficient scope for the effect of capital accumulation on productivity."

10. Between 1960 and 2000, China had higher measured TFP growth (2.6 percent a year) than did the industrial countries (1 percent). Presumably, some of the Chinese figure reflects a poor agricultural economy in transition to a capitalist economy with Chinese characteristics.

technical change and technology adoption," does not make a great deal of sense. As Solow suggested with his vintages model (1959), improvements in technology and upgraded labor skills are embodied in each new vintage of physical and human capital. Policies that emphasize technology at the expense of capital formation, or vice versa, are unlikely to succeed, because of their many sources of interdependence.

Perhaps for that reason, these development and growth accounting exercises often provoke a desire to push one stage farther back. Accounting for the proximate causes of growth (capital inputs, productivity) tempts the researcher back into the complex sociological tangle to find more fundamental causes of productivity disparities than induced technical change and technology adoption. Hall and Jones, for example, hypothesized that the fundamental determinant of a country's economic performance was its social infrastructure (a combination of institutions and policies), which determines the economic environment within which human and physical capital is accumulated. This conjecture was tested by growth regressions employing various proxy indices for social infrastructure. While their hypothesis is plausible, their tests of it—using an ad hoc methodology and employing less than convincing institutional proxies—were not adequately challenging.

Eclipses: Creative Destruction and Polarized Societies

As with all innovations, Solow's growth model brought both benefits and costs. The benefits were obvious: the extension of the scope of formal analysis and a new model that was fully articulated, amenable to clear demonstration, and therefore also excellent student examination material. Today, the original and augmented Solow models, along with several varieties of endogenous growth model, are essential elements in the development economics curriculum and indeed hold the pride of place in most development economics textbooks and courses. At the same time, the well-chosen simplification that a good model requires imposes a cost, eclipsing ideas that contribute to understanding but cannot yet be rendered in formal mathematical terms.[11] These ideas, however important, are exiled to the catchall of "the complex sociological tangle."

11. Economic theorists, as Amartya Sen once pointed out, follow the precept of the Victorian corset maker: "If madam is entirely comfortable in it, she requires a smaller size."

The brilliance of the neoclassical vision inevitably put into the shade some competing conceptions of capitalist growth and development. Following Friedrich Engels, Karl Marx, and Joseph Schumpeter, some pioneer development economists had emphasized the double-edged consequences of growth—in Schumpeter's phrase, its creative destruction. Albert Hirschman (1958, 56), for example, was mindful that

> in general[,] economic development means transformation rather than creation *ex novo*: it brings disruption of traditional ways of living, of producing, of doing things, in the course of which there have always been many losses; old skills become obsolete, old trades are ruined, city slums mushroom, crime and suicide multiply, etc., etc. And to these social costs many others must be added, from air pollution to unemployment.

The destructive side of transformative growth meant that it normally created pecuniary external *diseconomies*. Past capitalist development had proceeded by allowing firms to merge freely to internalize external economies, creating ever-larger firms. However, these firms tended to be protected from having to internalize all the external *diseconomies* that they generated.

By contrast, central planning of investments by the state would internalize external economies and diseconomies alike. In this situation, central planners would have an incentive to avoid investments in new products or new processes that would cause existing capacity to become obsolete prematurely (59–60).[12] Instead, each new investment should be allowed to induce additional investments that become profitable, as a result either of backward or of forward linkages. To the extent that public investment or public regulation was felt to be required, it should be induced by the local-level exercise of political "voice" in a decentralized representative system (Hirschman 1970).

Also eclipsed was Simon Kuznets's notion of economic development as a unified and unique historical phenomenon. He argued that the British industrial revolution had been preceded by a period of sustained preparation lasting several centuries, but, once industrial capitalism had taken hold in Britain, it gradually diffused to other parts of the world. Hicks (1960, 132) endorsed this view: "The long run growth of the economy is

---

12. An apparent result of this mechanism at work was the weakness of TFP growth in the former Soviet Union.

not a thing that repeats itself; it does not repeat itself in different nations; their growth is all part of a single world story. One cannot argue from what did happen in the United States in a certain period so as to establish laws of economic development." Further, the single-world story comprised much more than the spread and acceleration of economic growth, and a rising tempo of technical innovation, capital formation, and productivity increase. Faster growth would have been impossible without a set of inter-related transitions—agrarian transition, industrialization, urbanization, and major alterations in demographic behavior. A one-sector growth theory, based on assumptions of homothetic preferences, neutral total-factor productivity growth, and instantaneous market adjustment, necessarily has difficulty in explaining such transitions.

Yet quickening growth and its accompanying transitions have a powerful impact on the labor force. They induce internal migration, movements out of occupations in one economic sector and into new ones in different sectors. Change on this scale causes social and political conflict, as established groups, experiencing or foreseeing the contraction of their economic base, struggle to resist or slow down the process. For Kuznets (1980, 420), the important point was "the inevitable presence, in a society within which social groups [rapidly] shift from one set of conditions of work and life to another, of a mixture of gains and losses for which the market does not provide an agreed-on social valuation." Consequently, the cost (or benefit) of rapid transitions within the economy cannot be found by inspecting changes over time in the national accounts totals.

Social conflicts induced by structural changes have to be resolved so as to preserve a sufficient consensus for growth and change—and yet not at a cost that would retard it unduly. His agreement with Hirschman on this point is clear. The state must be so constituted that it can act as an authoritative referee, able to facilitate consensus decision making to mitigate the negative effects of economic change, in order to reduce social resistance to the continuation of growth. Kuznets thus pointed us toward a better understanding of the critical role that institutions play in facilitating economic growth.

Conclusion

Was there a real connection between development economics and growth theory? The answer is yes and no. Yes, in that, as Solow tells us, his desire to work on growth theory was stimulated by the fact that he, like everyone in the 1950s, was interested in economic development. "I was passively interested in economic development, but I have never been actively interested—in a research way—in what happens in underdeveloped countries. . . . I knew I was not going to work on development issues, but it did get me interested in the area of economic growth" (Snowdon and Vane 1999, 273). No, in that, as he also tells us, "growth theory, *par excellence*, yielded to model building," while "on the whole the personality types in the profession who became interested in economic development were not model builders. . . . So even Arthur Lewis thought of his 1954 paper as a minor sideline to his book *The Theory of Economic Growth*" (275).

Thus for a generation after the original Solow model, growth theory and development economics connected only sporadically, since the latter was occupied principally with the question of transition between different types of economy, while the former was not.[13] The prediction extracted from the original Solow model of convergence of per capita income levels in the long run provided the main link between growth and development economics. Although the claim that an augmented Solow model performs well in respect of this prediction has been disputed, it has stimulated new models, using a double augmentation, that is, incorporating both human capital and inter-sector labor transfer as a source of average productivity increase (Temple and Woessmann 2006). Thus today the original Lewis theme has not disappeared, nor is it merely coupled up with a Solow model (à la Findlay), but it has been nested inside the augmented Solow framework, as part of a more comprehensive approach to formal growth modeling.

The endogenous growth models of the 1980s introduced into formal growth models some features that development economists had previously identified as significant for development, but which the original Solow model did not accommodate. These include induced innovation, investments with aggregate increasing returns, and the transfer of technology from developed to developing countries. Their incorporation into endogenous growth models has reawakened research interest in the security of property rights, patent and intellectual property laws, competition policy, and international business regulation.

---

13. Findlay (1979, 1980) successfully yoked Solow and Lewis together in a global North-South model of dependent development, but the link via terms of trade was oversimple, and an undifferentiated South ignored the great variety of development experiences in the South that was already evident.

Growth (and development) accounting, which the original Solow model rationalized, has since the 1980s been applied to developing countries, and estimates of differences in TFP levels and growth rates have been interrogated for their meaning and their contribution to policy formulation. They have provided a springboard for a revival of interest in the fundamental causes of growth, including historical differences in institutional trajectories (Acemoglu, Johnson, and Robinson 2001, 2002). Other than that, their findings have been used to castigate development economists at large as "capital fundamentalists" (believers that capital accumulation, but not technical progress, drives growth), who (Easterly claims) malignly influenced the development policies of the World Bank.[14] Yet Arrow (1962, 155) was surely right when he said that "no economist would have denied the role of technological change in economic growth"; what is at issue is the true size of the residual. Unfortunately, this empirical question remains hard to settle decisively and is, in any case, moot in its policy implications.

I have suggested that the increasing formalization of development economics during the last fifty years derives less from various growth theories, or—as in Easterly's narrative—from what growth accounting tells us about the components of growth, than from advances made in trade theory, which (as Hicks noted) is especially relevant to development economics. Further, within trade theory, the conduit of change was less the pure theory of international trade than the close analysis of particular trade policies and their undesirable consequences. In this subject area, the combination of formal treatment, standard assumptions, and, above all, the ability to speak directly to policy issues has proved a winner. By that I do not mean that more formal analysis inevitably produces a superior understanding of the dilemmas of economic development—only that since the 1980s it has succeeded in changing the whole tenor of the economic development debate.

References

Acemoglu, D., S. Johnson, and J. A. Robinson. 2001. The Colonial Origins of Comparative Development: An Empirical Investigation. *American Economic Review* 91.5:1369–401.
———. 2002. Reversal of Fortune: Geography and Institutions in the Making of the Modern World Income Distribution. *Quarterly Journal of Economics* 117.4:1231–94.

14. Easterly presents capital fundamentalism as the first of a series of failed panaceas advocated by development economists, others being education, population restraint, and debt relief.

Arestis, P., J. McCombie, and R. Vickerman, eds. 2006. *Growth and Economic Development: Essays in Honour of A. P. Thirlwall.* Cheltenham, U.K.: Elgar.

Arrow, K. J. 1962. The Economic Implications of Learning by Doing. *Review of Economic Studies* 29.3:155–73.

Arrow, K. J., S. Karlin, and P. Suppes, eds. 1959. *Mathematical Models in the Social Sciences.* Stanford, Calif.: Stanford University Press.

Balassa, B., et al. 1971. *The Structure of Protection in Developing Countries.* Baltimore, Md.: Johns Hopkins University Press.

Baumol, W., R. R. Nelson, and E. N. Wolff. 1994. *Convergence of Productivity.* New York: Oxford University Press.

Bhagwati, J. N. 1978. *Anatomy and Consequences of Exchange Control Regimes.* Cambridge, Mass.: Ballinger.

Bliss, C. 2007. *Trade, Growth, and Inequality.* Oxford: Oxford University Press.

Bosworth, B. P., and S. M. Collins. 2003. The Empirics of Growth: An Update. *Brookings Papers on Economic Activity* 2:113–206.

Bruton, H. J. 1955. Growth Models and Underdeveloped Economies. *Journal of Political Economy* 63:322–36.

Cairncross, A., and M. Puri, eds. 1975. *The Strategy of International Development: Essays in the Economics of Backwardness.* London: Macmillan.

Chenery, H. B. 1983. Interview. World Bank Oral History Archive, Washington, D.C.

Chenery, H. B., and A. M. Strout. 1966. Foreign Assistance and Economic Development. *American Economic Review* 56.4, pt. 1:679–733.

Corden, W. M. 1966. The Structure of a Tariff System and the Effective Protective Rate. *Journal of Political Economy* 74:221–37.

———. 1971. *The Theory of Protection.* Oxford: Oxford University Press.

Denison, E. F. 1962. *The Sources of Economic Growth in the United States and the Alternatives before Us.* New York: Committee for Economic Development.

Easterly, W. 2002. *The Elusive Quest for Economic Growth: Economists' Adventures and Misadventures in the Tropics.* Cambridge: MIT Press.

Findlay, R. 1979. Economic Development and the Theory of International Trade. *American Economic Review* 69.2:186–90.

———. 1980. The Terms of Trade and Equilibrium Growth in the World Economy. *American Economic Review* 70.3:291–99.

Frankel, J. A. 2003. Comment on Bosworth and Collins 2003. *Brookings Papers on Economic Activity* 2:189–99.

Hagemann, H. 2007. German-Speaking Economists in British Exile, 1933–45. *Banca Nazionale del Lavoro Quarterly Review* 60.242:323–63.

Hall, R. E., and C. I. Jones. 1999. Why Do Some Countries Produce So Much More Output per Worker Than Others? *Quarterly Journal of Economics* 114.1:83–116.

Harrod, R. F. 1951. Notes on Trade Cycle Theory. *Economic Journal* 61.242:261–75.

Helpman, E. 2004. *The Mystery of Economic Growth.* Cambridge, Mass.: Belknap Press.

Hicks, J. 1960. Thoughts on the Theory of Capital—the Corfu Conference. *Oxford Economic Papers*, n.s., 12.2:123–32.

———. 1965. *Capital and Growth.* Oxford: Clarendon.

Hirschman, A. O. 1958. *The Strategy of Economic Development*. New Haven, Conn.: Yale University Press.

——. 1970. *Exit, Voice, and Loyalty*. New Haven, Conn.: Yale University Press.

Kapur, D., J. P. Lewis, and R. Webb. 1997. *The World Bank: Its First Half Century*. Vol. 1. Washington, D.C.: Brookings Institution Press.

Krueger, A. O. 1968. Factor Endowments and *Per Capita* Income Differences among Countries. *Economic Journal* 78.311:641–59.

——. 1974a. *Foreign Trade Regimes and Economic Development: Turkey*. Cambridge, Mass.: Ballinger.

——. 1974b. The Political Economy of Rent-Seeking. *American Economic Review* 64.3:291–303.

——. 1978. *Foreign Trade Regimes and Economic Development: Liberalization Attempts and Consequences*. Cambridge, Mass.: Ballinger.

Kuznets, S. 1980. Driving Forces of Economic Growth: What Can We Learn from History. *Weltwirtliches Archiv* 116:409–31.

Lewis, W. A. 1954. Economic Development with Unlimited Supplies of Labour. *Manchester School* 22.2:139–91.

——. 1955. *The Theory of Economic Growth*. London: Allen and Unwin.

Little, I. M. D. 1984. *Economic Development: Theory, Policy, and International Relations*. New York: Basic Books.

Little, I. M. D., T. Scitovsky, and M. F. G. Scott. 1970. *Industry and Trade in Some Developing Countries*. Oxford: Oxford University Press.

Mankiw, N. G., D. Romer, and D. N. Weil. 1992. A Contribution to the Empirics of Economic Growth. *Quarterly Journal of Economics* 107:407–38.

Mason, E. S., and R. E. Asher. 1973. *The World Bank since Bretton Woods*. Washington, D.C.: Brookings Institution.

McCombie, J. 2006. The Nature of Economic Growth and the Neoclassical Approach: More Questions Than Answers? In Arestis, McCombie, and Vickerman 2006.

Ray, D. 1998. *Development Economics*. Princeton, N.J.: Princeton University Press.

Ros, J. 2000. *Development Theory and the Economics of Growth*. Ann Arbor: University of Michigan Press.

Rosenstein-Rodan, P. 1943. Problems of Industrialization in Eastern and Southeastern Europe. *Economic Journal* 53.210–11:202–11.

Ruttan, V. W. 1998. The New Growth Theory and Development Economics: A Survey. *Journal of Development Studies* 35.2:1–26.

Schultz, T. W. 1964. *Transforming Traditional Agriculture*. New Haven, Conn.: Yale University Press.

Schumacher, E. F. 1973. *Small Is Beautiful: Economics as If People Mattered*. London: Blond and Briggs.

Sen, A. 1966. Peasants with and without Dualism. *Journal of Political Economy* 74:425–50.

——, ed. 1970. *Growth Economics*. Harmondsworth, U.K.: Penguin Books.

Singer, H. W. 1975. The Distribution of Gains Revisited. In Cairncross and Puri 1975.

Snowdon, B., and H. R. Vane. 1999. *Conversations with Leading Economists: Interpreting Modern Macroeconomics*. Cheltenham, U.K.: Elgar.

Solow, R. M. 1956. A Contribution to the Theory of Economic Growth. *Quarterly Journal of Economics* 70:65–94.

———. 1957. Technical Change and the Aggregate Production Function. *Review of Economics and Statistics* 39:312–20.

———. 1959. Investment and Technical Progress. In Arrow, Karlin, and Suppes 1959.

———. 1988. Growth Theory and After. *American Economic Review* 78 (March–June): 307–17.

———. 2001 Applying Growth Theory across Countries. *World Bank Economic Review* 15.2:283–88.

Temple, J. 1999. The New Growth Evidence. *Journal of Economic Literature* 37 (March): 112–56.

———. 2005. Dual Economy Models: A Primer for Growth Economists. *Manchester School* 73.4:435–78.

Temple, J., and L. Woessmann. 2006. Dualism and Cross-Country Growth Regressions. *Journal of Economic Growth* 11:187–228.

Thirlwall, A. P. 2002. *The Nature of Economic Growth*. Cheltenham, U.K.: Elgar.

Toye, J., and R. Toye. 2004. *The UN and Global Political Economy*. Bloomington: Indiana University Press.

The Solow Model, Poverty Traps, and the Foreign Aid Debate

Brian Snowdon

> The neoclassical model is still the most useful theory of growth
> we have. It will continue to be the first growth model taught
> to students and the first growth model used by policy analysts.
> —Gregory Mankiw, "The Growth of Nations" (1995)

The 1940s and 1950s were an exciting and remarkably productive period in the fields of economic development and economic growth. A rich and prolific literature featured some of the most influential and well-known contributions in the history of economics. Discussions of economic development were dominated by "Big Ideas" relating to balanced growth, low-level traps, vicious circles, cumulative causation, dualism, savings ratios, big push, leading sectors, elasticity pessimism, import substitution, economic planning, take-offs into self-sustained growth, and foreign aid requirements (see Meier 2005).

Against this background, by far the most influential and durable contribution to the analysis of economic growth was Robert Solow's 1956 paper, "A Contribution to the Theory of Economic Growth," which established the benchmark neoclassical growth model. Solow's landmark paper remains "one of those rare pieces which quite literally changed the face of

The author is grateful for the helpful comments from two anonymous referees, as well as those from participants at the *HOPE* conference, "Robert Solow and the Development of Growth Economics," held at Duke University, 25–27 April 2008.

History of Political Economy 41 (annual suppl.) DOI 10.1215/00182702-2009-026

economics and launched a thousand theoretical ships" (Blinder 1989). One important theoretical ship that has recently set sail again is the idea that some very poor countries appear to be caught in a poverty trap requiring a "big push" from foreign aid in order to escape. A case in point is a 2004 article by Jeffrey Sachs and colleagues; as discussed later in this article, Sachs et al. make extensive use of a modified Solow model to provide theoretical support for increasing the flow of foreign aid to sub-Saharan Africa (SSA). There is a strong similarity between Sachs et al. 2004 and Richard Nelson's influential paper from 1956, the same year in which Solow's contribution appeared. Nelson's model of a "low level equilibrium trap" persuaded many economists that developing countries would need substantial inflows of external assistance if they were to escape extreme poverty and begin the process of sustained growth.

The burgeoning contemporary research into the causes of economic growth, poverty traps, and convergence clubs, as well as the need to identify the deeper determinants of substantial cross-country differentials in income per capita, has brought the Solow model, and modifications thereof, into the heart of the contemporary development debate after decades of neglect in this field. This article reviews and provides a critical commentary on the literature relating to the Solow model, economic development, poverty traps, and the case for foreign aid as a solution to the SSA growth tragedy.

The Solow Model and the Economics of Development

The importance of economic growth as a necessary condition for sustained improvements in human material welfare and poverty reduction is confirmed by numerous empirical studies (Dollar and Kraay 2002). When it comes to investigating the proximate causes of growth, the dynamics of transition to steady states, and the potential for catch-up and convergence between low- and high-income per capita countries, Solow's model, together with subsequent extensions and refinements, has proved an invaluable and adaptable framework of analysis. The model is parsimonious, rigorous, and flexible, and provides many useful insights into the causes of economic growth (Mankiw 1995). And yet, although the neoclassical growth model was central to the 1960s growth accounting debates relating to the high-income developed nations, strangely, and in sharp contrast to the highly visible Harrod-Domar (H-D) model, compared with today, the

Solow growth model is largely inconspicuous in the mainstream development literature during the period 1956–85. For example, in the classic and widely used collections of readings edited by Amar Agarwala and Sampat Singh (1971, first published in 1958), and Ian Livingstone (1971), there is *no* discussion of the Solow model. Further evidence that the Solow model played little part in the early development literature comes from Diana Hunt, who in her 1989 survey notes that "neoclassical growth theory is not surveyed here, partly because it did not form part of the intellectual heritage of development economists in the 1940s and early 1950s, *but also because it has had no appreciable influence on development economics*" (34; emphasis added).

Why did development economics and growth theory evolve along separate paths for almost three decades in the post-1956 period? Building on Paul Krugman's (1992) insightful analysis, Solow (1999, 275) offers the following explanation:

> On the whole the personality types in the profession who became interested in economic development were not model builders. They were collectors of data and generalizers from rough empirical data, like Simon Kuznets; or they were like Ted Schultz, really deeply into underdeveloped agriculture, or they were people interested in history and backwardness for its own sake. That sort of temperament is not suited to model building. Growth theory *par excellence*, yielded to model building. So even Arthur Lewis thought of his 1954 paper as a minor sideline to his book *The Theory of Economic Growth* (1955). The people who got interested in the theory of economic growth were interested in model building.

Today the situation is very different. Since the mid-1980s, interest in the Solow model, and model building in general, among development economists has revived. Although the H-D model still finds a place in most development textbooks, it rarely warrants much more than a passing comment in modern macro or growth textbooks (e.g., compare the brief discussion in Barro and Sala-i-Martin 2004 with the extensive treatment in Jones 1975). Unlike the years of "high development theory" (Krugman 1992), the Solow model now receives extensive treatment in most textbooks on economic development (e.g., compare Higgins 1959 with Perkins, Radelet, and Lindauer 2006). In large part this can be attributed to the versatility of Solow's model and the insights it provides on the convergence-divergence debate (Islam 2003). Although dominated by the Solow and

Romer models, another notable change is the welcome and growing tendency in macro and growth textbooks to give increasing attention to the "deeper" political economy determinants of growth and development (see, e.g., Acemoglu 2008).

What were the main influences that led Solow (2007, 4) into the research that culminated in his 1956 "contribution to the theory of economic growth"? According to Solow (1999), he became interested in growth for three main reasons. First, in the early 1950s many economists were becoming increasingly absorbed in the daunting economic problems facing the developing countries. However, in terms of his own research, Solow became "passively" rather than "actively" interested in economic development ("I got to thinking about development issues and I had read Arthur Lewis"). Second, Solow's linear programming research with Robert Dorman and Paul Samuelson (1958) stimulated his thinking about intertemporal optimization and economic growth. Third, Solow (1999, 273–74) was "suspicious of the Harrod-Domar model. . . . I thought there must be a way of modelling growth that does not have the knife edge property of the Harrod-Domar model."

While Solow never intended his model to address the specific problems facing developing countries, it does provide a coherent framework for thinking about the connection between growth, capital accumulation, and economic development. Capital accumulation was already central in the 1950s development models of Harrod-Domar, Walt Rostow, Ragnar Nurkse, and Arthur Lewis (Meier 2005). However, when there are diminishing returns to the accumulation of capital, a policy emphasis on increasing investment-GDP ratios will not lead to sustained economic growth; rather, long-run growth is driven by (exogenous) technological progress. Therefore it is hardly surprising that Solow's one-sector neoclassical growth model failed to have a substantial impact on the development literature, given this was an era of development thinking heavily influenced by dual-sector models, surplus labor, structuralism, and "capital fundamentalism" (King and Levine 1994).[1]

In his thought-provoking tale of "economists' misadventures in the tropics," Bill Easterly (2001) provides a stinging critique of "capital fundamentalism." Because of diminishing returns, Solow's growth model contains

1. Mauro Boianovsky (2010) defines capital fundamentalism as "the notion that physical capital accumulation, instead of technical change or investment in human capital, determines the rate of growth of income per capita."

the "surprising" result that investment is not the key to long-run growth, even if it plays a role in the transition to the steady-state growth path. However, this "shocker" failed to influence the thinking of the development "experts" in the major international financial institutions who mistakenly continue to view the "accumulation of productive assets" as the "foundation of economic growth."

Augmenting the Solow Model:
From Solow to Romer, Barro, and Mankiw

The revival of interest in growth theory and empirics since the mid-1980s has had a significant influence on the economic development literature as well as reigniting interest in the Solow model as a versatile framework for investigating the issue of convergence. While part of this revival of interest in growth analysis reflected the return of macroeconomic stabilization in the developed economies during the 1980s, it also reflects the intellectual stimulus provided by the new endogenous growth theories. Even though these models were more about developed than developing countries, in his seminal paper Paul Romer (1986) highlights the growing body of evidence supporting the lack of convergence in per capita incomes between developed and developing countries. This was a significant contributing factor influencing Romer's quest to construct a growth model based on increasing returns. Indeed, the existence of convergence and divergence clubs is one of the key stylized facts of international economic development that has allowed the Solow model to become a central component in the debate on the evolution of world inequality.

In response to Romer's challenge to the conventional neoclassical theory of growth, Greg Mankiw, David Romer, and David Weil (1992) developed their "modified" Solow model that can explain international differences in growth rates as the result of convergence to different steady states and is consistent with the idea that "the accumulation of capital broadly defined is the key to international differences in economic growth rates" (Mankiw 1995, 308). However, the biggest push toward integrating the modern analysis of growth and development was given by Robert Barro's (1991) highly influential cross-country regression paper. Barro's cross-country empirical work was firmly embedded in the extended Solow neoclassical model; a major finding from his research is that the "neoclassical model's central idea of conditional convergence receives strong support from the data." As Barro (1997, x) observes, "It is surely an irony that one of the lasting contributions of endogenous growth theory is that it stimulated empirical work that demonstrated the explanatory power of the neoclassical growth model." While Solow (1999) remains "very suspicious" of cross-country regression results, the new empirical literature focusing on the convergence issue undoubtedly created a synergy between the growth and development literature and was a major influence in placing the Solow model at the heart of modern discussions of economic development, including the SSA "growth tragedy" (Mankiw 1995; Snowdon and Vane 2005).

The Sub-Saharan Growth Tragedy

The lack of significant progress in SSA is *the* outstanding development failure of the last quarter of the twentieth century relative to the expectations and aspirations present at the time of decolonization. This problem remains the greatest development challenge facing the world in the twenty-first century (Easterly and Levine 1997; Artadi and Sala-i-Martin 2003; Sala-i-Martin 2006). As Angus Maddison's (2004) data reveal, although during the relatively stable period, 1950–73, GDP per capita growth in Africa was a respectable 2 percent, this fell to a dismal 0.19 percent for the period 1972–2001. This is in sharp contrast to the well-documented "miracle" growth experienced by the East Asian economies.

The reasons for the poor economic performance of most of SSA since the decolonization period remain highly controversial. Paul Collier and Jan Gunning (1999) consider several plausible explanations:

1. *adverse external influences and conditions* including the legacy of colonialism, slavery (Nunn 2008), "Cold War" politics, and the restrictive trade policies of high income countries;
2. *terms of trade volatility* and heavy dependence on a small number of primary exports;
3. *damaging economic policies*, including protectionism, excessive regulations, fiscal profligacy, incentives to "rent seeking" and "directly unproductive" behavior, hostility toward FDI, and excessive public ownership and statism;
4. *unfavorable demographic factors*, especially rapid population growth;
5. *geographical constraints*, relating to climate, soils, topography and disease ecology, the "natural resource curse," and the problems faced by countries landlocked by hostile neighbors;

6. *internal political instability*, authoritarianism, corruption, bureaucratic inefficiency, poor governance and lack of accountable democratic institutions;
7. *ethnic diversity*, absence of trust and lack of social capital;
8. *lack of adequate physical and social infrastructure*, failure to provide secure property rights and contract enforcement.

While growth theory and the experience of East Asia suggest that SSA countries have enormous potential for catch-up and convergence, this potential is unlikely to materialize in countries with inadequate growth-supporting political and economic institutions. However, Jeffrey Sachs (2005, 2008) has recently become *the* leading advocate of the argument that SSA is caught in a "poverty trap" that requires a "big push" to escape via a substantial increase in foreign aid flows. Moreover, by using modifications to the Solow model to make their case, Sachs et al. (2004) illustrate just how versatile the neoclassical theoretical framework can be when discussing a major issue in development theory and policy.

The Foreign Aid Controversy:
From Harrod-Domar to the Solow Model

One long-running controversy in development economics, where the Solow model has now become central to the debate, relates to the role that foreign aid can play in helping low-income countries escape from extreme poverty. While economists agree that a *necessary* condition for the elimination of extreme poverty is sustained economic growth, the idea that a substantial increase in the flow of foreign aid, to regions such as SSA, is necessary to promote such growth remains highly controversial. Indeed the debate relating to the effectiveness of foreign aid in promoting growth and development remains plagued with problems relating to causality, measurement, and ideology (Friedman 1958; Bauer 1971; Easterly 2006b; Riddell 2007).

During the first two "development decades" (1950–70) the case for increasing foreign aid to stimulate economic growth and escape from a low-level equilibrium initially centered on the H-D model rather than the Solow model. The "capital fundamentalism" of the H-D model became a key ingredient within the framework of development planning and the estimation of aid requirements. The implications of this simple growth model were dramatic and somewhat reassuring. The problem of generating an increase in economic growth could be achieved by simply increasing the resources devoted to capital accumulation.

The familiar H-D growth equation, $G = s/v$, simply states that the growth rate (G) of GDP is jointly determined by the savings ratio (s) and the incremental capital-output ratio (ICOR $= v$). The higher the savings (investment) ratio and the lower the ICOR, the faster will an economy grow. For example, if a developing country desired to achieve a target growth rate of per capita income, $\Delta(Y/P)$, of 2 percent per annum (i.e., a growth target that will ensure that living standards double every thirty-five years), and population (P) is estimated to be growing at $n = 2$ percent per annum, then economic planners could calculate the savings rate required to achieve a target rate of aggregate GDP growth (G^*) equal to 4 percent according to equation (1).

$$G^* = [\Delta(Y/P) + n] = s^*/v. \tag{1}$$

If $v = 4$, this implies that G^* will be realized only with a desired savings ratio (s^*) of 0.16, or 16 percent of GDP (i.e., $G^*v = s^*$). If $s^* > s$, there is a "savings (foreign exchange) gap," and planners would need to devise policies to plug this gap (Chenery and Strout 1966). If domestic sources of finance proved inadequate to achieve G^*, then foreign aid could fill the savings gap. As (2) illustrates, aid requirements (Ar) could simply be calculated as $s^* - s = Ar$.

$$G^* = [s + Ar]/v_1 = s^*/v. \tag{2}$$

It is assumed in such formulations that the boost given to growth by an injection of aid resources will eventually cause a jump in the domestic savings rate such that self-sustaining growth is achieved, thereby ending the need for further aid inflows.

However, a major weakness of the H-D approach is the assumption of a stable ICOR. Aid inflows are likely to raise the ICOR (lower the productivity of capital) as a result of channeling aid into easy-to-monitor, large, prestigious projects that will stand as monuments to the generosity of the politically motivated donors (Griffin 1970). Economists soon became aware of a second major flaw in the "aid requirements" or "financing gap" model. The model assumes that aid inflows are channeled into investment, one-to-one. But it quickly became apparent that foreign aid, with the objective of closing the savings gap, did not necessarily boost total savings and in many cases reduced domestic savings (Easterly 2006b). This is equivalent to a proportion (α_c) of the aid inflow being consumed, that is, aid is highly *fungible* (see Griffin 1970; Boone 1996). As equation (3) illustrates, if aid has a negative impact on the ICOR, and a significant proportion of the aid is consumed, the impact of aid on growth is substantially reduced and could even be negative.

$$G = [s + (1 - \alpha_c)Ar]/v_2, \tag{3}$$

where α_c is large, and $v_2 > v_1$. In this "pessimistic" scenario, G^* is unlikely to be achieved via attempts to boost domestic savings with inflows of foreign aid (Snowdon 2007).

Ignoring these early doubts, the case for increasing foreign aid has reemerged as a major international policy issue and is linked, via modifications to the standard Solow model, to the idea that some developing countries are trapped in a permanent condition of poverty.

Poverty Traps, Foreign Aid, and the Sachs-Solow Model

In a recent influential paper, Jeffrey Sachs et al. (2004) argue that most SSA countries are caught in a "poverty trap" that is heavily influenced by geographically rooted low agricultural productivity, heavy disease burdens, and relative physical isolation. In such circumstances, the optimistic neoclassical vision that market forces combined with improved governance can remedy the development problem in many very poor countries, irrespective of their initial poverty, is rejected. A practical solution requires targeted investments, large in scale and financed by foreign aid, in infrastructure, disease control, and selective measures to promote a "green revolution" in agriculture.

That poor countries can be caught in a poverty trap is of course an old idea in economics, dating back at least to 1798 and the work of Thomas Malthus. During the 1950s this idea was revived by Ragnar Nurkse (1953) as the "vicious circle of poverty" model, and also in the influential paper by Richard Nelson (1956), whose theory of a "low level equilibrium trap" was used to explain persistent poverty. Nelson suggests that "foreign assistance, together with internal change, can play an important role in boosting an economy from the hold of the trap" (904).

Poverty traps (multiple equilibria) represent self-reinforcing inefficient steady-state equilibria at low levels of per capita income and can arise from a variety of sources, including both market and institutional failure (Azariadis and Stachurski 2005; Azariadis 2006). Paul Collier (2007) identifies four significant "traps" that ensnare the "bottom billion" of the world's population, namely, "internal conflict traps," "natural resource traps," "landlocked by bad neighbour traps," and "bad governance traps." One of the simplest and best-known poverty-trap mechanisms runs from extreme poverty to low rates of domestic saving and capital accumulation, to low or negative rates of growth of productivity (Ben-David 1998). In an open economy setting, with no restrictions on capital mobility, we should expect to see, ceteris paribus, capital flowing from rich to poor countries, attracted by higher potential returns, thereby accelerating capital accumulation. However, in reality, poor infrastructure, high rates of corruption, and political instability, by lowering the risk-adjusted rate of return to capital, discourage such FDI flows, thereby explaining the "Lucas paradox" (Lucas 1990).

Another potential poverty-trap mechanism arises from the inefficient operation of shallow financial markets in poor countries. Because credit and insurance markets are plagued by informational imperfections, risk-averse lenders require collateral before they are willing to make loans. Unfortunately, the poor obviously lack assets that they can use as collateral and remain credit constrained. Costas Azariadis and Allan Drazen (1990) argue that credit rationing, because of a lack of "financial depth," reduces investment in human capital with important adverse consequences for economic growth (De Soto 2000).

Sachs et al. (2004) argue that the solution to SSA's poverty trap lies in the initiation of a temporary "big push" on the investment front leading to a "step" increase in underlying productivity and a take-off into sustained growth. Given the nature and dynamics of the poverty trap, this big push requires substantial external assistance in the form of a Marshall Plan for SSA. To support their case Sachs et al. use modified versions of the Solow neoclassical growth model that include *critical thresholds . . . that must be reached before the forces of standard competitive theory take hold*" (Bowles, Durlauf, and Hoff 2006).

The standard Solow growth model is built around the familiar neoclassical aggregate production function (4) and focuses on the *proximate* causes of growth:

$$Y = A_t F(K, L), \tag{4}$$

where Y is real output, K is capital, L is the labour input, and A_t is a measure of exogenously determined "technology." The aggregate production function is assumed to be "well-behaved," that is, it satisfies the following three "Inada" conditions (Barro and Sala-i-Martin 2005). First, for all values of $K > 0$ and $L > 0$, $F(\bullet)$ exhibits positive but diminishing marginal returns with respect to both capital and labor, that is, $\partial F/\partial K > 0$, $\partial^2 F/\partial K^2 < 0$, $\partial F/\partial L > 0$, and $\partial^2 F/\partial L^2 < 0$. Second, the production function exhibits constant returns to scale such that $F(\lambda K, \lambda L) = \lambda Y$, that is, raising inputs by λ will also increase aggregate output by λ. Letting $\lambda = 1/L$ yields $Y/L = A_t F(K_t/L,1/L)$. This assumption allows (4) to be written down in intensive form as (5) where y = output per worker (Y/L) and k = capital per worker (K/L):

$$y = A_t f(k), \text{ where } f'(k) > 0, \text{ and } f''(k) < 0 \text{ for all } k. \qquad (5)$$

Equation (5) states that, for a given technology (A_t), output per worker is a positive function of the capital-labor ratio and exhibits diminishing returns. Third, as the capital-labor ratio approaches infinity ($k \rightarrow \infty$) the marginal product of capital (MPK) approaches zero; as the capital-labor ratio approaches zero, the marginal product of capital tends toward infinity ($MPK \rightarrow \infty$). The standard diagrammatic representation of the Solow model embraces the intensive form of the neoclassical aggregate production function that satisfies the above conditions. In a recent comment on these conditions, Sachs recalls that it took him twenty years to fully appreciate the implications of these mathematical properties of the neoclassical production function (Snowdon 2007).

How does capital accumulate? Where s = the domestic savings rate, n = the rate of population growth, and δ = the rate of depreciation, and dk/dt = *capital deepening*, then the well-known fundamental differential equation of the Solow model is given by (6):

$$dk/dt = sAf(k) - (n + \delta)k. \qquad (6)$$

The *capital widening* term $(n + \delta)k$ indicates the investment (saving) per worker necessary to hold the capital-labor ratio constant. In the Solow model, as long as $sAf(k) > (n + \delta)k$, output per worker will grow. When $sAf(k) = (n + \delta)k$, an economy has reached a steady-state equilibrium.

Sachs et al. (2004) argue that the textbook neoclassical growth model is a "special case" and the actual behavior of an economy at very low levels of output per worker is very different from the one portrayed in the standard neoclassical model in three important ways:

1. While in the conventional Solow model the *MPK* is nearly infinite at very low levels k, in reality, because production processes require a "minimum threshold of capital" (k^T), *MPK* is also low in poor

countries. Therefore, without the presence of basic infrastructure (roads, human capital, etc.) the productivity of small increments of k will be negligible. In figure 1, dk/dt only becomes positive above point k^T, and at low levels of k there are increasing returns to capital accumulation due to a *nonconvexity* in the production function.

2. As shown in figure 2, when k is very low, the savings rate is likely to be low, or even negative, because very poor people need to consume all of their income just to survive. However, saving increases with higher levels on output (income) per worker (capita), forming an "S" shaped function. With $sAf(k)$ less steep than $(n + \delta)k$ at low levels of k, then dk/dt is again negative below point k^T (Solow, 1956, also discusses alternative configurations of the savings function).

3. A third factor likely to prevent capital accumulation at low levels of k is rapid population growth. There is a strong correlation between low income per capita and fertility rates, and poor people, for perfectly rational reasons, aim to have large numbers of children. Figure 3 illustrates a Solow model with a demographic trap. Note how the $(n + \delta)k$ function is very steep at low levels of k. Therefore dk/dt is again negative below k^T.

While Sachs et al. argue that in very poor countries the "capital thresholds, savings traps, and demographic traps" are all likely to interact to produce a powerful "poverty trap," throughout their discussion they refer only to the "standard neoclassical model," never mentioning or citing Solow's 1956 paper. In doing so they miss the opportunity to note that Solow also considered nonstandard outcomes.[2] Indeed, as early as 1958, John Buttrick's *Quarterly Journal of Economics* paper demonstrated the relevance to development economics of the possibility of multiple equilibria in the Solow model.[3]

While the influential arguments of Sachs have provided a rallying point for the pro-aid lobby, many economists remain unconvinced that foreign

---

2. Solow (1956, 71) notes that "the steady adjustment of capital and output to a state of balanced growth comes about because of the way I have drawn the productivity curve." He also considers the impact of a "variable saving rate" (87–89) and "variable population growth" (90–91).

3. I am grateful to an anonymous referee who drew my attention to Buttrick's paper.

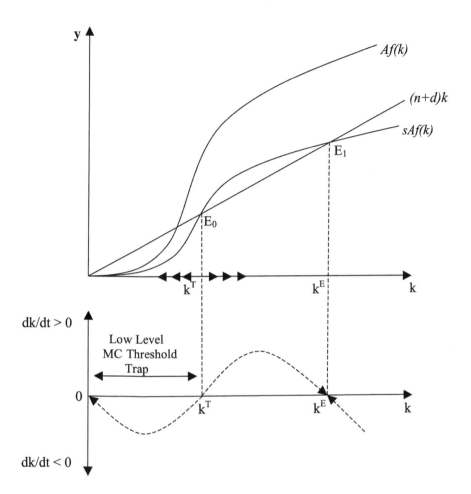

Figure 1 The Solow model with a minimum capital stock threshold.
Adapted and extended from Sachs et al. 2004.

aid is either necessary or sufficient for successful growth and development. Aart Kraay and Claudio Raddatz (2007) find little evidence supporting the existence of poverty traps, in their extensive survey of the literature. Azariadis and Jan Stachurski (2005) note that there are a large number of self-reinforcing mechanisms that can interact and potentially cause a poverty trap. In such cases, policy shocks will have "large and permanent

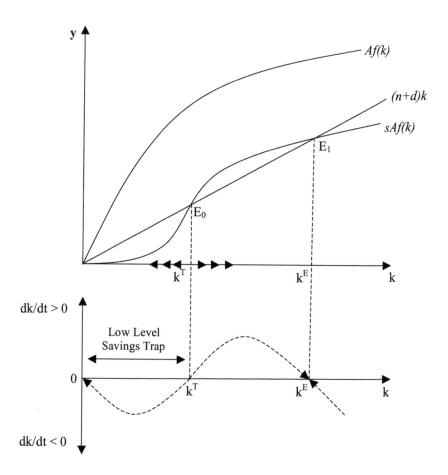

Figure 2 The Solow model with a savings trap. Adapted and extended from Sachs et al. 2004.

effects if one-off interventions can cause the formation of new and better equilibria." However, they also recognize that engineering such an outcome to achieve a more efficient equilibria in practice is very problematic, given the perverse influence of the prevailing structure of incentives in many developing countries, together with problems of corruption and the lack of information facing policymakers.

There is considerable variation in the motivation and behavior of aid donors, and the research of Alberto Alesina and David Dollar (2000) confirms that the criteria for bilateral aid allocations are dominated as much

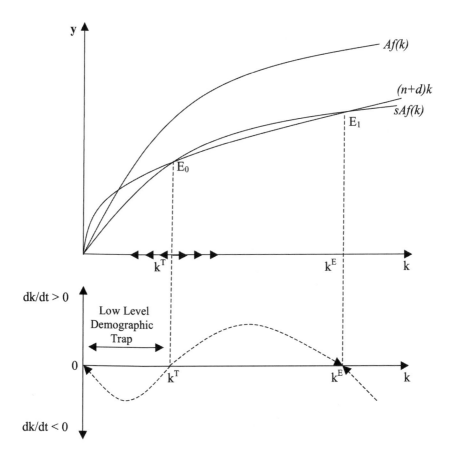

Figure 3 The Solow model with a demographic trap. Adapted and extended from Sachs et al. 2004.

by political and strategic considerations as they are by considerations of economic development. Alesina and Beatrice Weder (2002) demonstrate that there is no evidence that less corrupt governments receive more foreign aid than highly corrupt governments, and Jacob Svennson (2000) also provides evidence that inflows of foreign aid are associated with increased corruption and rent-seeking behavior, especially in countries where there are competing social groups.

According to the critics of aid, "capital fundamentalism" and the "aid-financed investment fetish" have led policymakers up the wrong path in their "elusive quest for growth." Indeed, Easterly (2006a, 2006b) argues that although the H-D model died long ago in academia, it is still influential among economists working in the major international financial institutions who continue to employ the H-D–Chenery-Strout methodology to calculate the investment and aid requirements needed for specific countries to achieve their growth targets. However, Easterly argues that the evidence that aid flows into investment on a one-for-one basis, and that there is a fixed linear relationship between growth and investment in the short run, is "soundly rejected" (see also Burnside and Dollar 2000; Easterly, Levine, and Roodman 2000; Rajan and Subramanian 2005).

To date, the "top down," "mega reform," planned administrative approach to solving the problem of world poverty involving large increases in the flow of foreign aid has not been a success (Easterly 2006a). What is the alternative? Easterly advocates a piecemeal gradualist "bottom up" approach in the spirit of Edmund Burke and Karl Popper. However, Easterly does concede that aid *could* be useful in achieving more modest objectives than Rostovian "take-offs" into "self sustaining growth," *if* incentive structures at ground level were improved and *if* the existing bureaucratic flaws within the international aid agencies could be corrected.

From Solow to the Fundamental Determinants of Growth

In the most recent wave of growth theory and empirics, modern political economy models have been used to investigate the *deeper* or *fundamental* determinants of growth, something the Solow model does not and was not designed to address. A major problem with formal growth models that focus on the *proximate* determinants of growth is that they necessarily ignore factors such as the influence of history, path dependency, ethnolinguistic fractionalization, and the numerous political and economic barriers to reform. Fortunately, recent political economy models of growth focus on factors such as the quality of governance, the origins of the legal system, ethnic diversity, social cohesion, democracy, trust, corruption, path dependency, political barriers, and institutions in general (Helpman 2004; Acemoglu 2008). Consequently, some of the most exciting developments in recent years have been those emerging as a result of the remarkable coming together of the fields of economic growth, economic development, and economic history. This has led to several insightful political economy contributions to our understanding of the deeper (fundamental) determinants of long-run economic growth and development. Key insights have emerged from the research of such scholars as Douglass North (2005), Dani Rodrik (2007), and Daron Acemoglu and James Robinson (2006).

Although there is obviously a great deal of interaction among the numerous factors influencing growth, perhaps the most promising framework for analyzing SSA's growth tragedy is one that emphasizes the role of institutions and political constraints. Rodrik (2007) has emphasized the importance of embedding a market economy within a set of non-market institutions and identifies five key institutions, namely, "property rights; regulatory institutions; institutions for macroeconomic stabilisation; institutions for social insurance; and institutions for conflict management." However, it is important to emphasize that these institutions "are not uniquely determined," and Rodrik rejects the discredited "neo-liberal social-economic model" associated with the more extreme versions of the Washington Consensus.

While the World Bank (2002) is giving increasing emphasis to the growth-retarding impact of weak institutions, and many economists are now persuaded that the incentive structure created by the institutional environment must be a key ingredient that determines the success or failure of countries in their "elusive quest for growth," there remains little consensus on the precise channels of causation running from institutions to economic growth. As Elhanan Helpman (2004) observes, "The study of institutions and their relation to economic growth is an enormous task on which only limited progress has been made so far."

To understand the political roots of economic success remains a crucial research area for economists, and the recent work of Acemoglu and North, and their coresearchers, is making a substantial contribution in this area (Acemoglu and Robinson 2006; North et al. 2007). A major problem facing almost all developing countries is how to make the formidably difficult transition from their current politico-economic status as *"limited access orders"* to becoming *"open access orders"* (North et al. 2007). Limited access orders are those where "social, economic, and political systems are based on limited entry and rent creation," while open access orders are characterized by the rule of law and open competition in both the political and economic spheres. While there may be leeway for aid to perform a role in the more "mature" limited-access societies, in fragile limited-access orders aid inflows could very well be highly destabilizing.

Conclusion

Fifty years on, the idea that many low-income countries in SSA are caught in a poverty trap is once more popular among economists who advocate some form of global Marshall Plan to defeat poverty. Sachs et al. (2004) reject the orthodox Solow model as a useful framework of analysis for poor countries because its key assumptions rule out the possibility of a poverty trap. While the three poverty-trap mechanisms built into the Solow model and highlighted by Sachs have intellectual appeal and are theoretically plausible, the lack of any systematic empirical evidence supporting them suggests that a very cautious response is appropriate to appeals for substantial increases in aid as a viable solution to SSA's poverty. There are numerous examples of countries (including the United Kingdom and United States) that have escaped from poverty via sustained growth where foreign aid has played little or no part. Furthermore, large inflows of aid, of the volume envisaged by Sachs, are not a dominant feature of the thirteen countries that have sustained rapid growth during the last forty years discussed in the 2008 *Commission on Growth and Development Report* (a commission, by the way, of which Bob Solow was a member).

The most significant barriers to economic progress in much of SSA have their origin in the destructive dynamics of internal political conflict combined with dysfunctional institutions and misguided economic policies, rather than minimum capital threshold, saving, and demographic poverty traps. Inefficient institutions, created and perpetuated by elites, are a major barrier to progress in many developing countries. As economists we should not be surprised when aid flowing into an environment dominated by mismanaged or corrupt institutions and inadequate governance fails to deliver a virtuous circle of enlightened reforms and the Holy Grail of sustained economic growth. In reality, the economic history of the world has repeatedly demonstrated how political barriers prevent economic progress. Nowhere is this problem more acute than in SSA.

References

Acemoglu, Daron. 2008. *Introduction to Modern Economic Growth*. Princeton, N.J.: Princeton University Press.

Acemoglu, Daron, and James Robinson. 2006. *Economic Origins of Dictatorship and Democracy*. Cambridge: Cambridge University Press.

Agarwala, Amar, and Sampat Singh, eds. 1971. *The Economics of Underdevelopment*. Oxford: Oxford University Press.

Alesina, Alberto, and David Dollar. 2000. Who Gives Foreign Aid to Whom and Why? *Journal of Economic Growth* 5.1:33–63.

Alesina, Alberto, and Beatrice Weder. 2002. Do Corrupt Governments Receive Less Foreign Aid? *American Economic Review* 92.4:1126–37.

Artadi, Elsa, and Xavier Sala-i-Martin. 2003. The Economic Tragedy of the Twentieth Century: Growth in Africa. NBER Working Paper 9865 (July): 1–33.

Azaridias, Costas. 2006. The Theory of Poverty Traps: What Have We Learned? In *Poverty Traps*, edited by Samuel Bowles, Steven N. Durlauf, and Karla Hoff. New York: Russell Sage Foundation.

Azariadis, Costas, and Allan Drazen. 1990. Threshold Externalities in Economic Development. *Quarterly Journal of Economics* 105.2:501–26.

Azariadis, Costas, and Jan Stachurski. 2005. Poverty Traps. In *Handbook of Economic Growth*, edited by Philippe Aghion and Steven N. Durlauf. Amsterdam: Elsevier.

Barro, Robert J. 1991. Economic Growth in a Cross Section of Countries. *Quarterly Journal of Economics* 106:404–43.

———. 1997. *Determinants of Economic Growth: A Cross Country Empirical Analysis*. Cambridge: MIT Press.

Barro, Robert J., and Xavier Sala-i-Martin. 2004. *Economic Growth*. 2nd ed. Cambridge: MIT Press.

Bauer, Peter. 1971. *Dissent on Development*. London: Weidenfeld and Nicholson.

Ben-David, Dan. 1998. Convergence Clubs in Subsistence Economies. *Journal of Development Economics* 55.1:153–59.

Blinder, Alan. 1989. In Honor of Robert W. Solow: Nobel Laureate in 1987. *Journal of Economic Perspectives* 3.3:99–105.

Boianovsky, Mauro. 2010. A View from the Tropics: Celso Furtado and the Theory of Economic Development. *HOPE*, forthcoming.

Boone, P. 1996. Politics and the Effectiveness of Foreign Aid. *European Economic Review* 40.2:289–328.

Bowles, Samuel, Steven N. Durlauf, and Karla Hoff, eds. 2006. *Poverty Traps*. New York: Russell Sage Foundation.

Burnside, Craig, and David Dollar. 2000. Aid, Policies, and Growth. *American Economic Review* 90.4:847–68.

Buttrick, John. 1958. A Note on Professor Solow's Growth Model. *Quarterly Journal of Economics* 72.4:633–36.

Chenery, Hollis B., and Alan M. Strout. 1966. Foreign Assistance and Economic Development. *American Economic Review* 56.4:679–733.

Collier, Paul. 2007. *The Bottom Billion: Why the Poorest Countries Are Failing and What Can Be Done about It*. Oxford: Oxford University Press.

Collier, Paul, and Jan Gunning. 1999. Explaining African Economic Performance. *Journal of Economic Literature* 37.1:64–111.

Commission on Growth and Development. 2008. *The Growth Report: Strategies for Sustained Growth and Inclusive Development*. www.growthcommission.org.

De Soto, Hernando. 2000. *The Mystery of Capital: Why Capitalism Succeeds in the West and Fails Everywhere Else*. New York: Basic Books.

Dollar, David, and Aart Kraay. 2002. Growth Is Good for the Poor. *Journal of Economic Growth* 7.3:95–125.

Dorfman, Robert, Paul A. Samuelson, and Robert M. Solow. 1958. *Linear Programming and Economic Analysis*. New York: McGraw Hill.

Easterly, William. 2001. *The Elusive Quest for Growth: Economists' Adventures in the Tropics*. Cambridge: MIT Press.

———. 2006a. The Big Push Déjà Vu: A Review of Jeffrey Sachs's *The End of Poverty: Economic Possibilities for Our Time. Journal of Economic Literature* 44.1:96–105.

———. 2006b. *The White Man's Burden: Why the West's Efforts to Aid the Rest Have Done So Much Ill and So Little Good*. New York: Penguin.

Easterly, William, and Ross Levine. 1997. Africa's Growth Tragedy: Policies and Ethnic Divisions. *Quarterly Journal of Economics* 112.4:1203–50.

Easterly, William, Ross Levine, and David Roodman. 2000. New Data, New Doubts: Comment On "Aid, Policies, and Growth by Burnside and Dollar." *American Economic Review* 94.3:774–80.

Friedman, Milton. 1958. Foreign Economic Aid: Means and Objectives. *Yale Review* 47:24–38.

Griffin, Keith. 1970. Foreign Capital, Domestic Savings, and Economic Development. *Bulletin of the Oxford University Institute of Economics and Statistics* 32.2:99–112.

Helpman, Elhanan. 2004. *The Mystery of Economic Growth*. Cambridge: Harvard University Press.

Higgins, Benjamin. 1959. *Economic Development: Problems, Principles, and Policies*. New York: Norton.

Hunt, Diana. 1989. *Economic Theories of Underdevelopment: An Analysis of Competing Paradigms*. London: Harvester Wheatsheaf.

Islam, Nazrul. 2003. What Have We Learned from the Convergence Debate? *Journal of Economic Surveys* 17.3:309–62.

Jones, Hywel. 1975. *An Introduction to Economic Growth*. Sunbury-on-Thames, U.K.: Thomas Nelson and Sons.

King, Robert G., and Ross Levine. 1994. Capital Fundamentalism, Economic Development, and Economic Growth. *Carnegie-Rochester Conference Series on Public Policy* 40.1:252–92.

Kraay, Aart, and Claudio Raddatz. 2007. Poverty Traps, Aid, and Growth. *Journal of Development Economics* 82.1:15–47.

Krugman, Paul. 1992. Towards a Counter-Counterrevolution in Development Theory. In *Proceedings of the World Bank Annual Conference on Development Economics 1992*. Washington, D.C.: World Bank.

Lewis, Arthur. 1954. Economic Development with Unlimited Supplies of Labour. *Manchester School* 22:139–91.

———. 1955. *The Theory of Economic Growth*. Homewood, Ill.: Irwin.

Livingstone, Ian, ed. 1971. *Economic Policy for Development*. Harmondsworth, U.K.: Penguin.

Lucas, R. E., Jr. 1990. Why Doesn't Capital Flow from Rich to Poor Countries. *American Economic Review* 80.2:92–96.

Maddison, Angus. 2004. Contours of the World Economy and the Art of Macromeasurement, 1500–2001. Ruggles Lecture. www.ggdc.net/maddison.

Mankiw, N. Gregory. 1995. The Growth of Nations. *Brookings Papers on Economic Activity* 1:275–326.

Mankiw, N. Gregory, David Romer, and David N. Weil. 1992. A Contribution to the Empirics of Economic Growth. *Quarterly Journal of Economics* 107.2:407–37.

Meier, Gerald M. 2005. *Biography of a Subject: An Evolution of Development Economics*. Oxford: Oxford University Press.

Nelson, Richard R. 1956. A Theory of the Low Level Equilibrium Trap. *American Economic Review* 46.5:894–908.

North, Douglass C. 2005. *Understanding the Process of Economic Change*. Princeton, N.J.: Princeton University Press.

North, Douglass C., John J. Wallis, Steven B. Webb, and Barry R. Weingast. 2007. Limited Access Orders in the Developing World: A New Approach to the Problems of Development. World Bank Research Policy Paper WPS4359 (September): 1–48.

Nunn, Nathan. 2008. The Long-Term Effects of Africa's Slave Trades. *Quarterly Journal of Economics* 123.1:139–76.

Nurkse, Ragnar. 1953. *Problems of Capital Formation in Underdeveloped Countries*. New York: Oxford University Press.

Perkins, D. W., S. Radelet, and D. L. Lindauer. 2006. *Economics of Development*. 6th ed. New York: Norton.

Rajan, Raghuram G., and Arvind Subramanian. 2005. Aid and Growth: What Does the Cross-Country Evidence Really Show? International Monetary Fund Working Paper 05/127.

Riddell, Roger. 2007. *Does Foreign Aid Really Work?* Oxford: Oxford University Press.

Rodrik, Dani. 2007. *One Economics Many Recipes: Globalisation, Institutions, and Economic Growth*. Princeton, N.J.: Princeton University Press.

Romer, Paul M. 1986. Increasing Returns and Long-Run Growth. *Journal of Political Economy* 94.5:1002–37.

Sachs, Jeffrey D. 2005. *The End of Poverty: Economic Possibilities for Our Time*. New York: Penguin.

———. 2008. *Common Wealth: Economics for a Crowded Planet*. London: Penguin.

Sachs, Jeffrey D., John W. McArthur, Guido Schmidt-Traub, Margaret Kruk, Chandrika Bahadur, Michael Faye, and Gordon McCord. 2004. Ending Africa's Poverty Trap. *Brookings Papers on Economic Activity* 1:117–216.

Sala-i-Martin, Xavier. 2006. The World Distribution of Income: Falling Poverty and . . . Convergence, Period. *Quarterly Journal of Economics* 121.2:351–97.

Snowdon, Brian. 2007. *Globalisation, Transition, and Development: Conversations with Eminent Economists*. Cheltenham, U.K.: Elgar.

Snowdon, Brian, and Howard R. Vane. 2005. *Modern Macroeconomics: Its Origins, Development, and Current State*. Cheltenham, U.K.: Elgar.

Solow, Robert M. 1956. A Contribution to the Theory of Economic Growth. *Quarterly Journal of Economics* 70.1:65–94.

———. 1999. Interview with Robert Solow. In *Conversations with Leading Economists: Interpreting Modern Macroeconomics*, edited by B. Snowdon and H. R. Vane. Cheltenham, U.K.: Elgar.

———. 2007. The Last 50 Years of Growth Theory and the Next 10. *Oxford Review of Economic Policy* 23.1:3–14.

Svensson, Jacob. 2000. Foreign Aid and Rent Seeking. *Journal of International Economics* 51.2:437–61.

World Bank. 2002. *Building Institutions for Markets*. New York: Oxford University Press.

Hotelling, Rawls, Solow: How Exhaustible Resources Came to Be Integrated into the Neoclassical Growth Model

Guido Erreygers

> My idea of heaven is an occasion when a piece of pretty economic
> theory turns out to suggest a program of empirical research
> and to have implications for the formulation of public policy.
> —Robert Solow, "An Almost Practical Step toward Sustainability"
> ([1992] 1994)

Textbooks or surveys of economic growth theory nowadays routinely include a chapter on natural resources or the environment (see, e.g., Jones 2002, chap. 9; Brock and Taylor 2005). In his exposition of neoclassical growth theory in the *Handbook of Macroeconomics* Robert Solow (1999, 655–57) also devoted a section to natural resources. But when neoclassical growth theory was developed in the 1950s, natural resources were not very prominent. It cannot be said that they were completely left out of consideration. W. Arthur Lewis (1955) discussed various ways in which resources bear on economic growth. Both Solow and Trevor Swan drew attention to the fact that the inclusion of a natural resource in constant supply would make their models more like those of the classical economists. Solow (1956, 67) merely hinted at this when he introduced

I am grateful to two anonymous referees, the participants of the *HOPE* 2008 conference, and the editors of this annual supplement for their comments on previous drafts. Special thanks to Mauro Boianovsky for unearthing correspondence between John Rawls and Robert Solow from the Solow Papers at the Rare Book, Manuscript, and Special Collections Library of Duke University.

History of Political Economy 41 (annual suppl.) DOI 10.1215/00182702-2009-027

the assumption "that there is no scarce nonaugmentable resource like land. . . . The scarce-land case would lead to decreasing returns to scale in capital and labor and the model would become more Ricardian." Swan (1956, 340–42), on the other hand, pondered this "Ricardian" or "classical" case more explicitly. Assuming constant returns to scale in capital, labor, and (fixed supply) land, he examined what would happen if the rate of population growth were always equal to the rate of output growth, so that output per capita remained constant. He showed that without technical progress the economy would inevitably lose "the unequal struggle against niggardly nature" (340): the rate of population (and output) growth would continuously fall and the economy would move in the direction of the worst possible stationary state, characterized by a capital-output ratio equal to zero. With technical progress occurring at a steady rate, however, the diminishing returns on the land could be offset and the economy would move in the direction of a stable equilibrium with a positive output per capita.

Not all natural resources are of the fixed-supply type. The distinctive character of exhaustible resources is that their use diminishes the available quantity. If (some of) these resources happen to be essential for production, growth theory simply cannot ignore them. That means in particular that growth theorists must face the issue of depletion, and either envisage a backstop (possibly end-of-the-world) scenario in which the resources will be effectively depleted or indicate how the economy could steer a course that pushes depletion to infinity.

In this article I examine how exhaustible resources came to be integrated into the neoclassical growth model. I begin by exploring the reasons why this integration happened only at the beginning of the 1970s. Then I concentrate on Solow's contributions to the literature on exhaustible resources, and I also analyze the influence of these contributions, especially with regard to the way in which economists now think about sustainability. Since my focus is on Solow, I would like to stress that this is *not* a full survey of exhaustible resources and neoclassical growth theory (additional insights may be gained by consulting, for instance, Toman, Pezzey, and Krautkraemer 1995).

The Hotelling Legacy

The absence of exhaustible resources in the first stages of the development of the neoclassical growth model had nothing to do with a lack of theory about these resources.[1] The foundations had been laid in the first half of the twentieth century, or even earlier, if one includes the largely descriptive work of W. R. Sorley (1889). In two articles in the *Quarterly Journal of Economics*, Lewis Cecil Gray (1913, 1914) had explored the economic aspects of resource conservation and exhaustion, at the same time drawing attention to the difficult ethical issues that these involved, such as discounting and intergenerational justice. A much more formal treatment was given in a seminal article by Harold Hotelling (1931). Acknowledging that the "static-equilibrium type of economic theory which is now so well developed" (139) was "plainly inadequate" to deal with exhaustible resources, he introduced a dynamic approach using the calculus of variations. He examined both the behavior of perfectly competitive resource owners and that of a monopolist. In the first case, he immediately derived that in equilibrium, one expects the net price of the resource at time t, p_t, to obey the formula

$$p_t = p_0 e^{rt}, \tag{1}$$

where r is the (constant) rate of interest. (An alternative way of expressing this condition is $\dot{p}/p = r$, with $\dot{p} \equiv dp/dt$.) The level p_0 would be determined by the conditions of demand and supply; at the date of exhaustion T the price of the resource would reach the level at which demand would fall to zero. Expression (1) is the now-famous Hotelling rule. This was only a tiny part of Hotelling's 1931 contribution. Large parts of the article were in fact devoted to examining the optimum course of exploitation, where the total discounted social value of the resource would be maximal. This implied the discussion of saving rules and discount rates, giving Hotelling the opportunity to comment, as one of the first, on Frank Ramsey's (1928) article on optimal saving.[2]

For decades Hotelling's contribution lay dormant. For instance, when Paul Samuelson (1960) reviewed Hotelling's work, he included the 1931 article among Hotelling's six major papers in economics, but did not discuss any specific details besides its emphasis on the calculus of variations. During the 1950s and 1960s relatively few economists were working on exhaustible resources, notable exceptions being Orris C. Herfindahl (1967), Anthony C. Scott (1967), and William Vickrey (1967)—whose papers were originally presented at a 1964 conference organized by the Committee on Taxation, Resources, and Economic Development—as well as

---

1. For a survey of the early history of exhaustible resource economics, see Robinson 1989.
2. On the Ramsey-Hotelling connection, see also Duarte (this volume).

Richard L. Gordon (1967). The volcano erupted in the 1970s, when there was a sudden outpouring of theoretical economic papers on exhaustible resources. But before I deal with Solow's contribution to that literature, I have to draw attention to two other developments.

The Doomsday Scenarios

The nexus between economic growth and ecological constraints had come under closer scrutiny in the middle of the 1960s. For economists, a major landmark was the publication of *Scarcity and Growth* by Harold Barnett and Chandler Morse (1963) under the auspices of the independent research institute Resources for the Future. This book, described as a "mixture of historical thought, theoretical model building, empirical testing, and general philosophizing" (Milliman 1963, 181), questioned the classical wisdom that natural resources would become scarcer in the course of history and cause diminishing returns. Mainly based on information of U.S. prices, Barnett and Morse saw very little sign of increasing scarcity of natural resources. Their optimistic thesis was resoundingly challenged by a number of publications on the limits to growth. The tone had been set by controversial books like *Silent Spring* by Rachel Carson (1962) and *The Population Bomb* by Paul Ehrlich (1968).

Economists, too, began to voice concerns about a looming conflict between economic growth and the environmental system. Kenneth Boulding (1966), for instance, compared the open-system "cowboy economy" to the closed-system "spaceman economy," and Nicholas Georgescu-Roegen (1971) pled for an alternative economic approach based on recognizing the importance of the entropy law. The issue grabbed the headlines of newspapers and magazines when Donella Meadows et al. (1972), using the systems-dynamics approach developed by Jay Forrester at the Massachusetts Institute of Technology, published the first report for the Club of Rome, painting a bleak picture of humanity's future.[3] Their model predicted that in the very near future crucial natural resources would be exhausted, making economic growth problematic. The message was echoed in the *Ecologist*'s "A Blueprint for Survival" issue, written by Edward Goldsmith et al. (1972) in advance of the United Nations Conference on the Human Environment held in June 1972 in Stockholm. The second report for the Club of Rome, presented by Mihajlo Mesarović and Eduard Pestel (1974), was

---

3. The Club of Rome was founded in 1968 at the initiative of Aurelio Peccei and Alexander King.

based on a much more refined computer model and gave a slightly less pessimistic view of the future. It contained a plea for a shift from undifferentiated, or exponential, growth to differentiated, or organic, growth, and offered a blueprint that would allow humanity to make the right choice at the turning point.

At the beginning of the 1970s economists in general were not terribly impressed by the messages of the catastrophic consequences of economic growth sent by the contemporary Cassandras. For example, in their essay "Is Economic Growth Obsolete?" written for the "Economic Growth" colloquium organized in December 1970 in San Francisco as part of the Fiftieth Anniversary Colloquium Series of the National Bureau of Economic Research, William Nordhaus and James Tobin (1972, 15) found "little reason to worry about the exhaustion of resources" and claimed that economic growth rates would probably increase over the coming decades. It comes, therefore, as no surprise that the reaction of economists to the Club of Rome's *Limits to Growth* report was overwhelmingly negative. The fact that the full model was published only two years after the first report (Meadows et al. 1974) certainly fueled suspicion about the validity of its predictions. The main criticism was that the World3 computer model simply extrapolated certain exponential growth tendencies and did not, or did not well enough, take into account that changing prices, substitution, and technical progress could fundamentally alter the patterns of future resource utilization.[4] A team of the Science Policy Research Unit of the University of Sussex published a detailed and at some points highly critical examination of the model and its subsystems (Cole et al. 1973). Solow too joined the debate and delivered a devastating critique of the "Doomsday Models" at a conference held in October 1972, describing the models as "bad science and therefore bad guides to economic policy" (Solow 1974c, 47). On the other hand, the outbreak of the first oil crisis in 1973 seemed to confirm that most industrialized countries depended heavily on an exhaustible resource that, according to *Limits to Growth*, was in danger of being depleted in a few decades' time.

Rawls and Saving

The beginning of the 1970s also saw the publication of one of the most influential books on political philosophy of the twentieth century: *A Theory*

---

4. In this respect, there is a striking similarity between *The Limits to Growth* and *The Coal Question* by William Stanley Jevons (1865).

of Justice by John Rawls (1971). Rawls's conception of justice as fairness, his criticism of utilitarianism, and his egalitarianism were but a few of the issues of particular interest to economists. In the present context the most relevant part of the book is chapter 5, "Distributive Shares," which contains an extensive section on "the problem of justice between generations" (sec. 44) in which Rawls, among other things, tried to find a just savings principle. Rawls acknowledged that the question of intergenerational justice "subjects any ethical theory to severe if not impossible tests" (284). Rawls was in fact forced to admit that his second, or difference, principle of justice did not apply to the savings question. This was due to "the natural fact that generations are spread out in time and actual exchanges between them take place only in one direction. We can do something for posterity but it can do nothing for us. This situation is unalterable, and so the question of justice does not arise" (291). Rawls's solution was to postulate that the just savings principle "is defined from the standpoint of the least advantaged in each generation. It is the representative men from this group as it extends over time who by virtual adjustments are to specify the rate of accumulation" (292). He then reformulated his difference principle by including the just savings principle as a constraint.

Rawls's statements with regard to intergenerational justice are hesitant and on purpose not always very precise. For instance, it is not clear how the maximin criterion should be applied in that context. Kenneth Arrow (1973) was one of the first to comment on Rawls's just saving principle. He advanced a more precise interpretation of the maximin criterion and examined what its implications would be for saving. He began by comparing the utilitarian and the Rawlsian criteria for a just distribution at a given moment of time. Assuming the existence of interpersonally comparable cardinal utility functions $u_i(c_i)$, where c_i is the consumption of person i, the utilitarian criterion could be formulated as

$$\max \left[\sum_i u_i(c_i) \right], \tag{2}$$

subject to the constraints imposed by technology, and so forth. By contrast, the Rawlsian maximin criterion would be

$$\max \left[\min_i u_i(c_i) \right], \tag{3}$$

again subject to the relevant constraints. In an intertemporal framework, however, both criteria must be adapted. The crucial problem now becomes the distribution of consumption over generations, which can be thought of as individuals living at different moments of time t. Arrow suggested the following adaptation of the utilitarian criterion:

$$\max\left[\sum_t \beta^t u(c_t)\right],\tag{4}$$

where β is the subjective discount rate. By analogy, the intertemporal maximin criterion would be

$$\max\left[\min_t u(c_t)\right].\tag{5}$$

Arrow (1973, 325) stressed that criterion (5) "would lead to zero savings in every generation for there is no way to compensate the first generation for any saving they may do, and they would be worse off than any of their successors." At some point Rawls had hinted at the assumption that parents care about their direct descendants. Following this lead, Arrow introduced the assumption that the utility of generation t depends not only on its own consumption, c_t, but also on that of the next generation, c_{t+1}. The modified intertemporal maximin rule then becomes

$$\max\left[\min_t v(c_t, c_{t+1})\right],\tag{6}$$

with $v(c_t, c_{t+1}) = u(c_t) + \beta u(c_{t+1})$. Given certain assumptions on the production and utility functions, Arrow derived that the optimal consumption profile under the intertemporal maximin rule would be of the type $(c_0, c_1, c_0, c_1, \ldots)$, which prompted him to remark that it "is at least questionable that the saw-tooth pattern corresponds to any intuitive idea of justice" (331). In the last part of the article Arrow showed that a modified version of the $v(.)$ function representing preferences over an infinite horizon would make the Rawlsian optimum approximate the utilitarian optimum.

Solow on Exhaustible Resources

Solow decided to study the issue of exhaustible resources in the beginning of the 1970s. In the Richard T. Ely Lecture that he gave at the eighty-sixth annual meeting of the American Economic Association in New York at the end of December 1973, he mentioned explicitly what motivated him to do so:

About a year ago, having seen several of those respectable committee reports on the advancing scarcity of materials in the United States and the world, and having, like everyone else, been suckered into reading the *Limits to Growth*, I decided I ought to find out what economic theory has to say about the problems connected with exhaustible resources. I read some of the literature, including Hotelling's classic article—the theoretical literature on exhaustible resources is, fortunately, not very large—and began doing some work of my own on the problem of optimal social management of a stock of a nonrenewable but essential resource. (Solow 1974a, 1–2)

The work to which Solow referred here was published in the "Symposium on the Economics of Exhaustible Resources," a special issue of the *Review of Economic Studies*, which appeared in 1974. This interesting collection of papers gives a good idea of the fervor with which economists were working on exhaustible resources at that time. Several articles and notes focused on the question of growth; I mention especially the paper on optimal depletion by Partha Dasgupta and Geoffrey Heal (1974)—Heal was one of the managing editors of the *Review of Economic Studies*—and two papers by Joseph Stiglitz, one focusing on the efficiency and optimality of growth in the presence of an exhaustible resource (1974a) and the other on whether a competitive economy would use the resource in the optimal way (1974b). Although nowadays one sometimes speaks of the Dasgupta-Heal-Solow-Stiglitz model (a recent example is Hamilton and Withagen 2007), I focus here exclusively on Solow.

Solow's contribution to the symposium was directly related to the ongoing debate on intergenerational justice. Rawls's book provided new fuel to the debate, and economists were keen to discuss the implications of Rawls's principles for (optimal) economic policies. This was also the position taken by Solow (1974b, 30), who chose to follow it to the extreme: "In this article I am going to be *plus Rawlsien que le Rawls*: I shall explore the consequences of a straightforward application of the max-min principle to the intergenerational problem of optimal capital accumulation."[5] As in Arrow's case, the Rawlsian criterion was presented as an alternative to the classical utilitarian criterion.[6]

Instead of introducing a modified intertemporal maximin rule of the type (6), Solow concentrated on the "straightforward" version (5). He

5. In February 1973 Solow had sent a copy of (a first draft of) his paper to Rawls, which led to an exchange of letters in February and March. In his first letter (dated 15 February) Rawls objected to Solow's suggestion that Rawls had "propose[d] the maximin criterion as a principle of justice between generations." He stressed that between generations the just savings principle is lexically prior to the maximin criterion. In his reply (dated 26 February) Solow accepted the validity of Rawls's objection ("Thanks for setting me straight") and announced that he had corrected the tone of what he had written. This might explain Solow's caveat of being more Rawlsian than Rawls himself. In March 1973 Solow and Rawls exchanged views on optimal saving and the Ramsey approach.

6. Although Arrow's article was published in 1973 and Solow's in 1974, it seems that the Solow paper was written before the Arrow paper. In fact, Arrow 1973 referred to Solow 1974b, but not the reverse.

applied it to a simple one-sector growth model, similar to the one used by Arrow. With a single consumption good and identical agents in every generation, the maximin rule requires that consumption per capita remains constant over time. To derive more precise results, assumptions had to be made on the production side of the economy. Solow assumed (1) a constant population, (2) a given technology, and (3) the absence of natural resources. Moreover, he postulated the existence of a well-behaved constant returns to scale production function $Q = F(K, L)$, which relates the net output Q to the inputs of capital and labor, K and L; in the intensive form this can be written as $Q = Lf(k)$, with $k \equiv K/L$. It turns out that in this case the largest per capita consumption level that can be kept constant over time is equal to $c_0 = F(K_0, L)/L = f(k_0)$, where K_0 is the initial capital stock. No generation adds anything to the capital stock; every generation entirely consumes the net product. This was the result already hinted at by Arrow ("zero savings in every generation").

In contrast to Arrow, Solow explored a wider variety of possibilities. First he relaxed the assumption of a constant population. With a population growing at the fixed rate n, the optimal per capita consumption level would be $c_0 = f(k_0) - nk_0$. Since the population is growing, the capital stock must increase at the same rate as the population in order to keep the capital-labor ratio k constant at the level k_0. Hence every generation must save in order to let the capital stock K grow at the rate n. In Solow's (1974b, 32) words, each generation must follow the dictum "widen, but don't deepen." Next, Solow additionally relaxed the assumption of a given technology and introduced labor-augmenting technical progress at a fixed rate. In this case no simple formula can be given for the optimal per capita consumption level, but Solow showed that the optimal trajectory is such that society gradually consumes its entire capital stock, which becomes zero when t tends to infinity.

The most important part of the article concerned the introduction of natural resources, more precisely exhaustible resources. Solow assumed the existence of a production function $Q = F(K, R, L)$, with R representing the rate of flow of an exhaustible resource. Actually, Solow rapidly moved to a more specific Cobb-Douglas form, $Q = e^{mt}K^\alpha R^\beta L^{1-\alpha-\beta}$, where m is the constant rate of Hicks-neutral technical progress. This function was chosen because it implies that the resource is "essential" (i.e., if $R = 0$, then $Q = 0$), but also because the marginal productivity of the resource tends to infinity when very little of it is used. Even with this more simple form, it was difficult to find an explicit solution of the optimal per capita consumption level in the most general case, that is, involving both positive population growth and technical progress. Solow did show, however, that the solution requires that "the *rate of change* of the marginal productivity of the resource should always equal the *level* of the marginal productivity of reproducible capital" (35–36), which is of course an alternative formulation of the Hotelling rule. By returning to the case of zero population growth and zero technical progress, Solow managed to obtain a more precise result. Assuming that $\alpha > 0$, $\alpha + \beta < 1$, and $\alpha > \beta$, Solow showed that there exists a positive per capita consumption level that can be maintained over time;[7] its maximum value can be expressed as

$$c_0 = \left[\frac{S_0}{L_0}\right]^{\frac{\beta}{1-\beta}} \left[\frac{K_0}{L_0}\right]^{\frac{\alpha-\beta}{1-\beta}} (\alpha - \beta)^{\frac{\beta}{1-\beta}} (1 - \beta), \tag{7}$$

where S_0 is the stock of the resource available at time 0. To maintain this level, society gradually consumes its stock of the exhaustible resource and replaces it by a larger stock of produced capital. This process of substitution requires that the fraction β of net output must be invested.

In all of these cases the Rawlsian criterion leads to a choice of a per capita consumption level c_0 determined by the initial values of K, S, and L. According to Solow, this was one of the main weaknesses of the criterion: "It requires an initial capital stock big enough to support a decent standard of living, else it perpetuates poverty, but it can not tell us why the initial capital stock should ever have been accumulated" (41). Nevertheless, Solow's overall verdict on the maximin rule was that it "seems to be a reasonable criterion for intertemporal planning decisions" (41). The presence of exhaustible resources did not fundamentally alter the results, although Solow carefully noted that

> this conclusion depends on the presumption that the elasticity of substitution between natural resources and labour-and-capital-goods is no less than unity—which would certainly be the educated guess at the moment. The finite pool of resources (I have excluded full recycling) should be used up optimally according to the general rules that govern the optimal use of reproducible assets. In particular, earlier generations are entitled to draw down the pool (optimally, of course!) so long as they add (optimally, of course!) to the stock of reproducible capital. (41)

7. Under competitive pricing, α and β are equal to the shares of capital and natural resources in net output; since in reality the share of capital tends to be much higher than the share of natural resources, the crucial assumption $\alpha > \beta$ seems plausible.

As in his 1956 article on the neoclassical growth theory, the model in Solow's 1974 article on exhaustible resources was stripped down to its essentials. The core assumptions were no population growth, no technical progress, no capital depreciation, a single exhaustible resource, zero resource extraction costs, and a Cobb-Douglas production technology with appropriate coefficients. The effects of relaxing some of these assumptions were already briefly examined in the 1974 article. Solow and Wan (1976) gave a more thorough analysis of the case in which there are positive extraction costs.

The Hartwick Rule

The symposium papers represented only a part of the research on exhaustible resources. Both the survey by Frederick Peterson and Anthony Fisher (1977) and the advanced textbook by Dasgupta and Heal (1979) provide useful summaries of the state of the art of exhaustible resource economics at the end of the 1970s. But perhaps the most important outcome of that wave of research was overlooked in the book by Dasgupta and Heal, and only very briefly mentioned in a footnote of the survey by Peterson and Fisher (1977, 703n). In December 1977 John M. Hartwick (1977, 972) had published a short paper in the *American Economic Review* on a solution for "the ethical problem of the current generation shortchanging future generations by 'overconsuming' the current product, partly ascribable to current use of exhaustible resources." Although Hartwick indicated that the idea for the solution had occurred to him after attending a seminar by Anthony Scott on resource policy, the paper is intimately connected to Solow's contribution to the symposium. In fact, the Hartwick rule—the name seems to have been given by Avinash Dixit, Peter Hammond, and Michael Hoel (1980)—is sometimes also referred to as the Hartwick-Solow rule.[8] It turned out to be a very influential contribution.

Hartwick's 1977 model was very similar to the one used by Solow. His assumptions nearly coincided with Solow's core assumptions mentioned above, the only difference being the introduction of a positive but constant resource extraction cost. What Solow did was to look for a path that yields a constant positive per capita consumption level; once such a path is found, one can derive the savings rule that will generate it. Hartwick, by contrast,

---

8. Hartwick (1978b, 353n) indicated that Anthony Scott had pointed him to a quote in which Hayek had expressed a similar idea.

started by postulating a particular savings rule and then derived the path of consumption it will generate. Hartwick called his savings function the "investment of resource rents" (IRR), because saving is supposed to be exactly equal to the net return of the exhaustible resource. In formal terms, the savings function is as follows:

$$\dot{K} = (F_R - a)R, \tag{8}$$

where $F_R \equiv dF/dR$ represents the marginal productivity of the resource and a its per unit extraction cost, so that $F_R - a$ is the per unit resource rent or royalty. The idea is that the net worth of the depleted amount of the exhaustible resource is transformed into an equivalent amount of produced capital instead of being consumed by the current generation. Efficiency in exploiting the exhaustible resource requires the satisfaction of the Hotelling rule (1). Here this implies:

$$\frac{d \log (F_R - a)}{dt} = F_K. \tag{9}$$

Given the IRR and Hotelling rules, represented by the two differential equations (8) and (9), the model can be solved when the initial values of K and R are given (the constant supply of labor is put equal to 1). Hartwick showed that if these values are such that the stock of the resource is exhausted in infinite time, then the economy follows a constant consumption path. In other words, the IRR savings rule, or Hartwick rule as it is now known, implies intergenerational equity in the Solow-Rawls sense. As observed by Hartwick (1977, 974), this result was implicit in the 1974b paper by Solow.[9]

In one sense Solow's paper was stronger than Hartwick's, because it contained an existence result: for a Cobb-Douglas technology with $\alpha > \beta$ and zero extraction costs, there always exists an infinite horizon trajectory characterized by a constant positive per capita consumption level, which is maintained by adhering to the IRR rule. Hartwick, on the other hand, was able to show that when extraction costs are positive, adhering to the IRR rule would still result in a constant consumption path. He also reported that Solow had pointed out to him that this result was valid for a large group of production functions, not just for the Cobb-Douglas. But the result would not hold anymore if there were capital depreciation (Hartwick 1977, 974).

9. Solow's conclusion was that a fraction β of output must be invested, that is, $\dot{K} = \beta Q$. Since in his case $a = 0$ and $F_R = \beta Q/R$, this boils down to the IRR rule.

In other papers from the end of the 1970s, Hartwick (1978a, 1978b) extended the analysis to the case of several exhaustible resources and to the case of the coexistence of an exhaustible and a renewable natural resource. Dixit, Hammond, and Hoel (1980) generalized the result to economies with several produced goods, labor types, and natural resources (both exhaustible and renewable). In their framework, they showed that the Hartwick rule can be expressed as "keep the total value of net investment under competitive pricing equal to zero" (Dixit, Hammond, and Hoel 1980, 551), a prescription sufficient to generate a constant consumption path. After that, numerous authors extended and qualified the Hartwick rule (see Asheim, Buchholz, and Withagen 2003 for a bold discussion of what the authors call the "myths and facts" on the Hartwick rule). The standard procedure is to assume a constant population, a given technology, competitive prices, and a time-invariant utility function.

Solow too contributed to this literature. In a paper originally presented at a conference on growth and distribution held in 1984 in Uppsala, he showed that with population growing at the rate n and Hicks-neutral technical progress occurring at the rate m, the adoption of the Hartwick rule would lead to per capita consumption growing at the "natural" rate $(m - \alpha n)/(1 - \beta)$. To generate a constant per capita consumption profile in such an economy, one would have to observe a rather complicated investment policy (Solow 1986, 145–46). More important, in the footsteps of Dixit, Hammond, and Hoel (1980), Solow established that the Hartwick rule implied the constancy of an appropriately defined capital stock, including both produced and natural resources, and through a contribution by Martin Weitzman (1976) Solow (1986, 146–48) derived that consumption could be seen as the interest of this capital stock. Therefore, even if it could not be shown that the Hartwick rule always produced the "right" results, the rule nevertheless constituted "a better-than-average rule of thumb" (148) because of its connection to the adage of maintaining capital intact.[10] As noted by Geir Asheim (1994) and Hartwick (1994), this linked the constant consumption level to a Hicksian income notion (Hicks 1939, chap. 14). Hartwick (1996) also showed that, for an efficient economy following the zero net investment policy, the concept of consumption as interest-on-capital

10. And Solow promptly used it to accuse the British government of "wasting the windfall of North Sea oil" (149). He repeated the accusation a few years later: "If I meet Mrs. Thatcher in heaven, since that is where I intend to go, the biggest thing I will tax her with is that she blew North Sea oil" (Solow 1993, 184). He contrasted this with the Norwegian policy aimed at converting (a large part of) the royalties into investment.

could be adapted to the case where labor services were seen as flows from a stock of human capital.

Sustainability and Substitutability

In 1987 the World Commission on Environment and Development (WCED) published its report *Our Common Future* and catapulted the notion of sustainable development to the top of the international community's agenda. Sustainable development was defined as "development that meets the needs of the present without compromising the ability of future generations to meet their own needs" (WCED 1987, 43). Taking growth as a proxy for development and per capita consumption levels as indicators of need satisfaction, one could say that the debate on the Solow-Hartwick results was, in fact, a discussion about the possibility of sustainable development *avant la lettre*.[11] It did not take long before a connection was made between the two. Solow himself contributed to this process through two nontechnical papers (based on lectures in 1991 and 1992) on the interpretation of sustainable development. In these he argued that sustainability should be understood as the conservation, "for the very long run," of the "generalized capacity to produce economic well-being" (Solow [1992] 1994, 24). That capacity depended of course on the availability and maintenance of society's capital, in the largest possible sense. Hence the crucial importance of investment:

> A concern for sustainability implies a bias toward investment. That does not mean investment *über alles*; it means just enough investment to maintain the broad stock of capital intact. It does not mean maintaining intact the stock of every single thing; trade-offs and substitutions are not only permissible, they are essential. (27)

He also suggested "an innovation in social accounting practice" (29) that would translate this principle into a pragmatic proposal: an estimation of the "true" value of resource depletion, indicating the amount of investment in other forms required to compensate for that specific loss of capital. The calculation, which would be by no means easy, could be extended to other natural resources and environmental assets.

11. In the case of a constant population, the WCED definition seems to require a constant capital stock, which makes it closely related to the Hicksian income notion. When the population grows, however, the capital stock should increase to maintain per capita consumption levels.

Solow's suggestion has been put into practice. Since the middle of the 1990s many environmental and resource economists, especially at the World Bank, have been working on methods to estimate "genuine" (or nowadays "net adjusted") savings, by correcting the traditional savings concept for changes in capital because of depletion, environmental degradation, education, and so forth. Recently a team led by Kirk Hamilton (World Bank 2006) completed the Millennium Capital Assessment, an ambitious attempt to estimate both the stocks and flows of produced, natural, and intangible assets. In one chapter (World Bank 2006, 49–60) the actual data for 2000 were compared with those that would have resulted from a "Hartwick rule counterfactual," that is, supposing that since 1970 countries had invested all rents from exhaustible resources into produced capital.[12] It turns out that some resource-rich countries like Venezuela would have accumulated a much larger capital stock if they had followed the Hartwick rule. These types of exercises may help clarify issues like the existence of a resource curse.

The work inspired by Solow, Hartwick, and many others (it seems appropriate to refer here to the contribution by Talbot Page [1977]) has been a success, in the sense that the link between sustainability and capital maintenance is now well recognized. For instance, in recent years the World Bank (2002, 13–35) has stressed that sustainability implies managing a broad portfolio of assets (human, natural, human-made, knowledge, and social). This designation is sufficiently vague to allow a variety of opinions about the composition of society's capital base. As a matter of fact, since the early 1990s there has been an ongoing debate about the substitutability of the different forms of capital, especially of natural and produced capital, in which the polar paradigms are those of weak and strong sustainability (see, e.g., Pearce and Atkinson 1995). I cannot go into that discussion here. I do want to point out that the distinction was at the heart of a sharp exchange of views on the pages of *Ecological Economics*, in a special issue dedicated to Nicholas Georgescu-Roegen. Already in 1979 Georgescu-Roegen had sharply criticized the substitutability assumptions underlying the Cobb-Douglas production function used by Solow and Stiglitz. Reiterating this criticism of the neoclassical production function, Herman Daly (1997, 265) invited Solow and Stiglitz to finally put an end

---

12. Two variants have been examined: the standard case in which genuine investment is always equal to zero, and another one in which genuine investment is kept at a constant positive level.

to their "conjuring tricks." In their cool and brief replies, both Solow (1997) and Stiglitz (1997) tried to clarify what they thought they had been doing at the beginning of the 1970s, and neither of them showed any signs of being prepared to confess they had deliberately misled the economic profession.[13]

Conclusions

I have tried to show that the integration of exhaustible resources into the neoclassical growth model in the beginning of the 1970s must be seen in the light of three contributing factors: (1) the "economics of exhaustible resources" legacy centered on the Hotelling rule; (2) the contemporary public and scientific debate on the "limits to growth"; and (3) the discussion among economists about the interpretation of Rawls's theory of justice in an intergenerational setting. Solow's contributions to this literature have been pathbreaking. He provided the framework for the Hartwick rule and suggested that sustainable consumption should be interpreted as interest-on-capital. This has undoubtedly shaped how economists think about sustainability today.

References

Arrow, Kenneth J. 1973. Rawls's Principle of Just Saving. *Swedish Journal of Economics* 75.4:323–35.

Asheim, Geir B. 1994. Net National Product as an Indicator of Sustainability. *Scandinavian Journal of Economics* 96.2:257–65.

Asheim, Geir B., Wolfgang Buchholz, and Cees Withagen. 2003. The Hartwick Rule: Myths and Facts. *Environmental and Resource Economics* 25.2:129–50.

Barnett, Harold J., and Chandler Morse. 1963. *Scarcity and Growth: The Economics of Natural Resource Availability.* Baltimore, Md.: Johns Hopkins University Press for Resources for the Future.

Boulding, Kenneth E. 1966. The Economics of the Coming Spaceship Earth. In *Environmental Quality in a Growing Economy*, edited by Henry Jarrett. Baltimore, Md.: Johns Hopkins University Press for Resources for the Future.

Brock, William A., and M. Scott Taylor. 2005. Economic Growth and the Environment: A Review of Theory and Empirics. In vol. 1B of *Handbook of Economic Growth*, edited by Philippe Aghion and Steven N. Durlauf. Amsterdam: Elsevier North-Holland.

13. For completeness I mention that many others joined the debate and contributed to the "Georgescu-Roegen versus Solow/Stiglitz" forum in the same issue of *Ecological Economics.*

Carson, Rachel. 1962. *Silent Spring.* Boston: Houghton Mifflin.

Cole, H. S. D., Christopher Freeman, Marie Jahoda, and K. L. R. Pavitt, eds. 1973. *Thinking about the Future: A Critique of "The Limits to Growth."* London: Chatto and Windus for Sussex University Press.

Daly, Herman E. 1997. Forum: Georgescu-Roegen versus Solow/Stiglitz. *Ecological Economics* 22.3:261–66.

Dasgupta, Partha, and Geoffrey Heal. 1974. The Optimal Depletion of Exhaustible Resources. *Review of Economic Studies*, Symposium on the Economics of Exhaustible Resources, 41:3–28.

———. 1979. *Economic Theory and Exhaustible Resources.* Cambridge: Cambridge University Press.

Dixit, Avinash, Peter Hammond, and Michael Hoel. 1980. On Hartwick's Rule for Regular Maximin Paths of Capital Accumulation and Resource Depletion. *Review of Economic Studies* 47.3:551–56.

Ehrlich, Paul. 1968. *The Population Bomb.* New York: Ballantine.

Georgescu-Roegen, Nicholas. 1971. *The Entropy Law and the Economic Process.* Cambridge: Harvard University Press.

———. 1979. Comments on the papers by Daly and Stiglitz. In *Scarcity and Growth Reconsidered*, edited by V. Kerry Smith. Baltimore, Md.: Johns Hopkins University Press.

Goldsmith, Edward, Robert Allen, Michael Allaby, John Davoll, and Sam Lawrence. 1972. A Blueprint for Survival. *Ecologist* 2.1:1–43.

Gordon, Richard L. 1967. A Reinterpretation of the Pure Theory of Exhaustion. *Journal of Political Economy* 75.3:274–86.

Gray, Lewis C. 1913. The Economic Possibilities of Conservation. *Quarterly Journal of Economics* 27.3:497–519.

———. 1914. Rent under the Assumption of Exhaustibility. *Quarterly Journal of Economics* 28.3:466–89.

Hamilton, Kirk, and Cees Withagen. 2007. Savings Growth and the Path of Utility. *Canadian Journal of Economics* 40.2:703–13.

Hartwick, John. 1977. Intergenerational Equity and the Investing of Rents from Exhaustible Resources. *American Economic Review* 67.5:972–74.

———. 1978a. Investing Returns from Depleting Renewable Resource Stocks and Intergenerational Equity. *Economics Letters* 1.1:85–88.

———. 1978b. Substitution among Exhaustible Resources and Intergenerational Equity. *Review of Economic Studies* 45.2:347–52.

———. 1994. National Wealth and Net National Product. *Scandinavian Journal of Economics* 96.2:253–56.

———. 1996. Constant Consumption as Interest on Capital. *Scandinavian Journal of Economics* 98.3:439–43.

Herfindahl, Orris C. 1967. Depletion and Economic Theory. In *Extractive Resources and Taxation*, edited by Mason Gaffney. Madison: University of Wisconsin Press.

Hicks, John R. 1939. *Value and Capital: An Inquiry into Some Fundamental Principles of Economic Theory.* Oxford: Clarendon.

Hotelling, Harold. 1931. The Economics of Exhaustible Resources. *Journal of Political Economy* 39.2:137–75.

Jevons, William Stanley. 1865. *The Coal Question*. London: Macmillan.

Jones, Charles I. 2002. *Introduction to Economic Growth*. 2nd ed. New York: Norton.

Lewis, W. Arthur. 1955. *The Theory of Economic Growth*. London: Allen and Unwin.

Meadows, Dennis L., William W. Behrens III, Donella H. Meadows, Roger F. Naill, Jørgen Randers, and Erich K. O. Zahn. 1974. *Dynamics of Growth in a Finite World*. Cambridge: Wright-Allen.

Meadows, Donella, Dennis L. Meadows, Jørgen Randers, and William W. Behrens III. 1972. *The Limits to Growth: A Report for the Club of Rome's Project on the Predicament of Mankind*. New York: Universe.

Mesarović, Mihajlo, and Eduard Pestel. 1974. *Mankind at the Turning Point: The Second Report to the Club of Rome*. New York: Dutton.

Milliman, Jerome W. 1963. Book review of Barnett and Morse 1963. *Southern Economic Journal* 30.2:181–83.

Nordhaus, William, and James Tobin. 1972. Is Growth Obsolete? In *Economic Growth*. New York: National Bureau of Economic Research.

Page, Talbot. 1977. *Conservation and Economic Efficiency*. Baltimore, Md.: Johns Hopkins University Press.

Pearce, David W., and Giles D. Atkinson. 1995. Measuring Sustainable Development. In *Handbook of Environmental Economics*, edited by Daniel W. Bromley. Oxford: Blackwell.

Peterson, Frederick M., and Anthony C. Fisher. 1977. The Exploitation of Extractive Resources: A Survey. *Economic Journal* 87.348:681–721.

Ramsey, Frank. 1928. A Mathematical Theory of Saving. *Economic Journal* 38.152:543–59.

Rawls, John. 1971. *A Theory of Justice*. Cambridge, Mass.: Belknap.

Robinson, Tim J. C. 1989. *Economic Theories of Exhaustible Resources*. London: Routledge.

Samuelson, Paul. 1960. Harold Hotelling as a Mathematical Economist. *American Statistician* 14.3:21–25.

Scott, Anthony C. 1967. The Theory of the Mine under Conditions of Scarcity. In *Extractive Resources and Taxation*, edited by Mason Gaffney. Madison: University of Wisconsin Press.

Solow, Robert M. 1956. A Contribution to the Theory of Economic Growth. *Quarterly Journal of Economics* 70.1:65–94.

———. 1974a. The Economics of Resources or the Resources of Economics. *American Economic Review* 64.2:1–14.

———. 1974b. Intergenerational Equity and Exhaustible Resources. *Review of Economic Studies*, Symposium on the Economics of Exhaustible Resources, 41:29–45.

———. 1974c. Is the End of the World at Hand? In *The Economic Growth Controversy*, edited by Andrew Weintraub, Eli Schwartz, and J. Richard Aronson. London: Macmillan.

———. 1986. On the Intergenerational Allocation of Natural Resources. *Scandinavian Journal of Economics* 88.1:141–49.

———. 1993. Sustainability: An Economist's Perspective. In *Economics of the Environment: Selected Readings*, edited by Robert Dorfman and Nancy S. Dorfman. 3rd ed. New York: Norton.

———. [1992] 1994. An Almost Practical Step toward Sustainability. In *Assigning Economic Value to Natural Resources*. Washington, D.C.: National Academy Press.

———. 1997. Reply. Georgescu-Roegen versus Solow/Stiglitz. *Ecological Economics* 22.3:267–68.

———. 1999. Neoclassical Growth Theory. In vol. 1A of *Handbook of Macroeconomics*, edited by John B. Taylor and Michael Woodford. Amsterdam: Elsevier.

Solow, Robert M., and Frederic Y. Wan. 1976. Extraction Costs in the Theory of Exhaustible Resources. *Bell Journal of Economics* 7.2:359–70.

Sorley, W. R. 1889. Mining Royalties and Their Effect on the Iron and Coal Trades. *Journal of the Royal Statistical Society* 52.1:60–98.

Stiglitz, Joseph E. 1974a. Growth with Exhaustible Natural Resources: Efficient and Optimal Growth Paths. *Review of Economic Studies*, Symposium on the Economics of Exhaustible Resources, 41:123–37.

———. 1974b. Growth with Exhaustible Natural Resources: The Competitive Economy. *Review of Economic Studies*, Symposium on the Economics of Exhaustible Resources, 41:139–52.

———. 1997. Reply. Georgescu-Roegen versus Solow/Stiglitz. *Ecological Economics* 22.3:269–70.

Swan, Trevor W. 1956. Economic Growth and Capital Accumulation. *Economic Record* 32.63:334–61.

Toman, Michael A., John Pezzey, and Jeffrey Krautkraemer. 1995. Neoclassical Economic Growth Theory and "Sustainability." In *Handbook of Environmental Economics*, edited by Daniel W. Bromley. Oxford: Blackwell.

Vickrey, William. 1967. Economic Criteria for Optimum Rates of Depletion. In *Extractive Resources and Taxation*, edited by Mason Gaffney. Madison: University of Wisconsin Press.

Weitzman, Martin. 1976. On the Welfare Significance of National Product in a Dynamic Economy. *Quarterly Journal of Economics* 90.1:156–62.

World Bank. 2002. *World Development Report 2003: Sustainable Development in a Dynamic World*. Washington, D.C.: World Bank.

———. 2006. *Where Is the Wealth of Nations? Measuring Capital for the 21st Century*. Washington, D.C.: World Bank.

World Commission on Environment and Development (WCED). 1987. *Our Common Future*. Oxford: Oxford University Press.

Part 4
Endogenous Growth,
the New Growth Economics

Solovian and New Growth Theory from the Perspective of Allyn Young on Macroeconomic Increasing Returns

Roger J. Sandilands

> There is no problem where there has been more loose thinking
> than in this of increasing returns. . . . Large production,
> not large scale production, permits increasing returns.
> —Allyn Young, "Nicholas Kaldor's Notes on Allyn Young's
> LSE Lectures, 1927–29" (1990)

Robert Solow's two seminal papers, "A Contribution to the Theory of Economic Growth" (1956) and "Technical Change and the Aggregate Production Function" (1957), induced a burgeoning literature on "endogenous" growth theory. His theoretical and empirical work was based on a constant-returns-to-scale neoclassical aggregate production function that harked back to Charles Cobb and Paul Douglas (1928), who tested J. B. Clark's marginal productivity theory of distribution. Solow's model is expounded in companion papers in this volume, so here it is necessary only to recall that his work was a reaction against the "knife-edge" instability of the Harrod-Domar model by invoking a general linear homogeneous production function with flexible factor prices and factor proportions to maintain full employment. The theory predicted a tendency to a steady state of zero growth in per-worker terms unless the production function is augmented by technical progress. "Labor-augmenting" innovations could maintain the output-capital ratio and constant factor shares. In his empirical 1957 paper he found that the Cobb-Douglas functional form fitted aggregate U.S. data (on growth of output per worker regressed

History of Political Economy 41 (annual suppl.) DOI 10.1215/00182702-2009-028

against capital per worker) as well as or better than any of the other forms with which he experimented.

The Cobb-Douglas paper appeared in the same year as Allyn Young's (1928a) on increasing returns. Earlier, Young had also elaborated the marginal productivity theory of distribution in some detail as a coauthor of the second (1908) edition of Richard T. Ely's *Outlines of Economics*. However, he had always been careful to differentiate static equilibrium theory and the individual profit-maximizing entrepreneur from the dynamics of the aggregate growth process through which are set the product and factor prices to which the entrepreneur adjusts.[1] Marginal productivity theory helps explain income distribution but not the determinants of marginal utility and productivity. The latter depend on conditions that affect demand and supply elasticities of products—hence of the factors—as incomes increase through time.[2]

It is thus unlikely that Young would have embraced the Cobb-Douglas-Solow production function with its unidirectional dependence of aggregate output on factor inputs and technology. In Young's theory of the circular flow, his concept of "increasing returns" is macroeconomic, arising from growth itself and hence dependent as much on demand as on supply, though Young emphasized that in the overall sense demand is the reciprocal of supply. Combined with the varying elasticities of supply of land, labor, and capital goods, factor prices and market opportunities are determined and entrepreneurs adjust accordingly. In the process, the Marshallian "representative firm"—and industries too—tend constantly to lose their identity and become increasingly specialized, employing increasingly specialized methods, hence becoming increasingly productive. This interplay questions how far output growth can be explained in Solovian fashion by the measured growth of capital and labor inputs weighted by their income shares if incomes mainly reflect relative scarcities that in turn depend on growth of GDP.[3]

---

1. J. B. Clark (1899, vi) himself wrote that his theory "tries completely to isolate the static forces that act in distribution from the dynamic forces."

2. In 1908 Young discussed the relation between the "annual product" (inclusive of capital goods) and the "social dividend" (sale of final goods and services), showing "the importance of the greater productivity of indirect, time using methods of production for the theory of interest" (quoted in Mehrling and Sandilands 1999, 73). This was an early exposition of what Young's student Frank Knight would later call the "wheel of wealth," or the circular flow of income mediated through time by the rate of interest. Young stressed the relation between product and factor demand, showing that rewards "imputed" to factors are not the same as their contributions.

3. In Ely et al. 1908, 324–35, Young criticizes Clark for fudging this circularity problem in respect of capital.

It is clear from his chapters on value theory in the various editions of *Outlines*, in lectures at the London School of Economics (LSE) during 1927–29 as recorded by Nicholas Kaldor (Young 1990), and in correspondence with Frank Knight throughout the 1920s, that there were distinct limitations to the Marshallian concept of normal price for understanding secular growth. As detailed in Sandilands 2000, Young spoke of the "togetherness" of economic phenomena so that the conventional Marshallian apparatus of supply and demand and Clark's marginal productivity theory could not be integrated to give the social picture or explain why growth tends to be self-sustaining rather than self-exhausting (as in Solow's model).

Also showing the development of his thinking is Young's (1913) critique of A. C. Pigou on social cost. Pigou had insisted that if expansion of a competitive industry with "decreasing returns" (rising supply curve) drives up factor prices for other industries, then this "external diseconomy" raises the social above the private cost, thus justifying a tax. Vice versa for competitive "increasing returns" industries if lower factor prices associated with a larger industry are not offset by the rising expenses of each firm as it expands. Young criticized Pigou for confusing transfer payments as real costs, and for failing to distinguish the independent effects of a larger firm size from those connected with an enlarged industry. He concluded that he could scarcely imagine a case where increasing returns, *in Pigou's sense*, could coexist with competition. Furthermore, it would be practically impossible to identify increasing and decreasing returns industries and then to internalize these misconceived Pigouvian externalities with taxes or subsidies.

But Young did not deny the significance of *Marshallian* external economies, as is clear from his 1928 presidential address.[4] However, his untimely death (March 1929) prevented him from developing the growth theory expounded there, and with the onset of the Great Depression interest in long-run growth waned in favor of depression economics until Roy Harrod and Evsey Domar renewed interest, but along different lines from Young's. Meantime, the cost controversy associated with others' interpretations of Pigou and the Marshallian representative firm was oriented toward the nature of the firm itself rather than the way the representative firm might evolve in the overall growth process. Young (1928a, 527) himself warned

---

4. Peter Newman (1987) misinterpreted Young's criticism of Pigou, suggesting that he later regretted his claim that cases of increasing returns in competitive industries must be rare. But there is no inconsistency. Young rejected Pigou's notion of external economies, but (subject to caveats) not Marshall's.

that he did not propose to discuss those "alluring" but narrower questions, and that the supply and demand apparatus being developed for that purpose "may stand in the way of a clear view of the more general or elementary aspects of the phenomena of increasing returns." Soon the imperfect and monopolistic competition theories of the firm in equilibrium would also distract attention from Young's disequilibrium view of monopolistic competition.

Instead, Solow (1956, 1957) came to dominate growth theory and related empirical work, following his finding that nearly 90 percent of the growth of labor productivity could not be explained by growth of capital per worker. The "residual" was an unexplained measure of labor-augmenting technical progress. The two main strands to subsequent work were, first, redefinition and measurement of factors with a distinction between skilled and unskilled labor and inclusion of human with physical capital, and second, special attention to the nature of "knowledge" and research and development expenditures. Most of this research has retained the neoclassical growth framework, but with the new variables placed comfortably within it. Thus instead of growth of aggregate output being driven only by inputs of capital and labor, it is also driven more explicitly by *effective* labor, with human capital increased through the knowledge that comes from education, training, and learning by doing.

A Youngian Evaluation of Attempts to Endogenize Solow's "Residual"

The distinctive feature of knowledge in the wealth of nations (to echo the title of David Warsh's [2006] enthusiastic "story of economic discovery" of modern endogenous growth theory, with Paul Romer heading a star cast) is that it is "non-rivalrous" and only partially and temporarily excludable by learning costs and patent protection. In the medium and long run, pure and applied scientific advances are widely learned and copied. These features are modeled to allow resources devoted to R&D—now seen as an explicit explanatory driver of growth—to depend on expected internal net benefits, but also emphasizing the external benefits of new knowledge.[5] It

---

5. Philippe Aghion and Peter Howitt (1998, 79) call imitators' dissipation of innovators' profits a "Schumpeterian business-stealing effect" that discourages innovation and lends support for monopoly and protectionism. By contrast, Young stressed the positive role of competition to maximize the pecuniary external economies inherent in the free market mechanism (see Chandra and Sandilands 2005, 2006, and parallel ideas in Baumol 2002).

is believed this explains why capital deepening is not subject to diminishing returns, thus converting the production function into one exhibiting increasing returns consistent with Young's seminal but rather "mushy" (as characterized by Krugman 1993) nonmathematical treatment of the subject.[6]

But does this modern theory really coincide with Young's emphasis on the size of the overall market in his treatment of knowledge, induced innovation, externalities, and the factor rewards? A major difference is that neoclassical theories are based on a mainly input-driven, supply-side view of the growth process. New kinds of inputs may be introduced, but in their production functions causation runs unidirectionally from inputs to outputs. This is true even of Marvin Frankel's (1962) model, based on Solow but with a "development modifier" that makes enterprise production functions depend on the *aggregate* capital stock per worker. Philippe Aghion and Peter Howitt (1998, 26–27) see this as an early but neglected endogenous growth model in tune with Romer (1986) where social returns on capital (the vehicle for accumulation of knowledge, especially when including human capital) so exceed private returns as to yield an *AK* production function (see also Romer 1994, 7–8, and Sandilands 2000). But Frankel still retains a Solovian framework in which growth is driven by capital without explaining what drives capital.

This is less true of Kenneth Arrow's (1962) model where learning-by-doing depends on the cumulative production experience. However, Alberto Ades and Edward Glaeser (1999) test whether learning-by-doing is as important as Young's stress on growth of market size. They find that insofar as scope for learning-by-doing is greater in advanced products in which rich countries specialize, it is less important than growth of markets in explaining why poor countries have the most to gain from trade liberalization, for they, with their narrower range of products, are more specialized. But the significance of specialization for Young is less the potential

---

6. Warsh (2006, 91) also deprecates Young as a rather fuzzy "literary" economist who (unlike Frank Ramsey on savings and optimal growth) "eschewed mathematics altogether." Yet Irving Fisher acclaimed him "decidedly the best mathematician among living American economists" (see Earl Hamilton, quoted in Sandilands 1999, 469). Observe, too, the math in the appendix to Young 1928a, mentioned in Young's letter to Frank Knight, 11 August 1928, showing it was prepared in advance of his September presidential address. Commenting on Knight's theory of price, Young wrote, "Where I don't follow you, of course, is in respect of increasing returns. . . . The economies which show themselves in increasing returns are the economies of *large* production, not of large-scale production. I have just sent a mathematical note on this matter to the printer."

economies of scale from a small number of products than the economies from a larger number of specialized firms producing and using a larger number of specialized products. Actually the range of firms and products expanded most in poorer countries such as China and India that grew most rapidly after opening up trade. This is in line with Yongsheng Zhang and Xueyan Zhao (2004)—following the extensive work of Xiaokai Yang (2003) on Youngian economics—that showed a declining average size of firm as growth proceeded in countries such as Mexico and South Korea.[7]

Young saw the supply and effectiveness of inputs as driven by aggregate *derived* demand or the force of overall market demand for goods and services whose size is in turn affected by the degree of competition and mobility in product and factor markets. However, when Young emphasizes demand, it is in the special sense of real *aggregate reciprocal demand* (abstracting from fluctuations arising from monetary disturbances).[8] Thus

> the capacity to buy depends upon capacity to produce. In an inclusive view, considering the market not as an outlet for the products of a particular industry, and therefore external to that industry, but as the outlet for goods in general, the size of the market is determined and defined by the volume of production. (Young 1928a, 533)

Consequently the Marshallian apparatus of sectoral supply and demand curves cannot adequately illumine the growth process. Young acknowledged Alfred Marshall's "fruitful distinction between the internal productive economies which a particular firm is able to secure as the growth of the market permits it to enlarge the scale of its operations and the economies external to the individual firm which show themselves only in changes of the organization of the industry as a whole" (527), but he thought Marshall underplayed the qualitative changes in the external field. The internal

---

7. Marshall (1920, 318) believed an increase in the size of the industry will generally increase the size of the representative firm and wrote, "The *law of increasing returns* may be worded thus: An increase of labour and capital leads generally to improved organization which increases the efficiency of the work of labour and capital." Young might complain that this is a supply-side "law" that misses the crucial role of demand, and that increased specialization often means smaller firms.

8. Some necessary qualifications, allowing for monetary disturbances and malinvestments, are found in Young 1928a to indicate that despite a powerful underlying, self-reinforcing secular trend, there may be cyclical interruptions: "There is a sense in which supply and demand, seen in the aggregate, are merely different aspects of a single situation. It is for this reason that some of the older economists held that general overproduction is impossible—a theorem which, though not really erroneous, has proved to be misleading" (145). Young's cycle theory is similar to Ralph Hawtrey's monetary theory; see Laidler 1993.

economies of the representative firm "dissolve into the internal and external economies of the more highly specialized undertakings which are its successors, and are supplemented by new economies." Further,

> insofar as it is an adjustment to a new situation created by the growth of the market for the final products of industry the division of labour among industries is a vehicle of increasing returns. It is more than a change of form incidental to the full securing of the advantages of capitalistic methods of production—although it is largely that—for it has some advantages of its own which are independent of changes in productive technique. (538)

Young thereby extended Smith's famous aphorism that the division of labor is limited by the size of the market—in turn limited by the degree of competition. Today, "we mean by the division of labour something much broader in scope than that splitting up of occupations and development of specialized crafts which Adam Smith mostly had in mind" (Young 1928a, 529). Instead it shows up as increasingly specialized firms and industries, using more roundabout methods and producing increasingly differentiated consumer and capital goods. Emphasis is on economics of specialization rather than economies of scale. Thus

> the principal economies which manifest themselves in increasing returns . . . are largely identical with the economies of the division of labour in its most important modern forms. In fact, these economies lie under our eyes, but we may miss them if we try to make of *large-scale* production (in the sense of production by large firms or large industries), as contrasted with *large* production, any more than an incident in the general process by which increasing returns are secured. (531)

Here, importantly, "large production" means not only large real (reciprocal) demand or size of market for an industry in which the single firm operates, but also the size of the whole economy in which the single industry operates, and indeed of the size of the effective world economy to which a country has access. With a larger market in Young's inclusive sense of "an aggregate of productive activities, *tied together by trade*" (533; emphasis added), an "increasingly intricate nexus of specialized undertakings has inserted itself between the producer of raw materials and the consumer of the final product" (538). Both the scale and nature of firms and industries in a growing economy are determined not only, and not mainly, by their own sales but by sales of the industry or economy to which they are ancillary.

In a "Marshall-Young-Romer" model, Romer (1989) attempts to formalize the significance of this "increasingly intricate nexus of undertakings." He posits that the greater the number of intermediate inputs the greater the productivity of given resources. Here the constraint on specialization is the fixed cost (giving rise to a U-shaped average cost curve) of each addition to the list of intermediate inputs produced by specialist firms. If each specialist is a monopolist, each one faces downward-sloping demand and excess profits that entice additional specialist firms. This reduces demand for each of the specialists (all assumed to have similar costs) until equilibrium is established with excess profits eliminated and price equal to average cost above the minimum on the U-shaped curve. This, then, is a model incorporating Chamberlinian monopolistic competition, so Euler's theorem cannot apply: conventional factor inputs receive less than their marginal products, and the excess compensates producers for the fixed costs of specialist goods that generate increasing returns. The larger the resources devoted to specialization (constrained by the discounted present value of expected benefits), the greater these returns.

Monopolistic competition is a feature common to many endogenous growth models (and of new trade theory too: e.g., Krugman 1990), but according to Earl Hamilton (in Sandilands 1999, 469), "Every worthwhile idea in E. H. Chamberlin's subsequent work on imperfect competition had been clearly expounded by Allyn Young in class long before Chamberlin put pen to paper." However, Young's LSE lectures (Young 1990) indicate that the number of specialist firms (whether producing intermediate inputs or more varied consumer goods) is ultimately constrained by the growth of the market, which determines how many resources it is worth devoting to this. In elaborating his theory of increasing returns, he stressed that "all costs are prime [i.e., variable] costs if you take the right period of time" (Young 1990, 49), and "underproduction is a feature of a state of growth. Plant cannot grow by infinitesimals; the [ever-changing] representative firm generally has more power than is necessary for immediate needs. It shows progress rather than depression and is evidently, in the long run, productive and economical or it would not be done" (48). Thus "surplus productive capacity is a normal and necessary condition of economic progress" (54), and increasing returns are consistent with intense competition. Monopolistic competition is inherent in Young's view of competition as a process in growth, intrinsically tied to qualitative changes to the increasingly specialized representative firm.

For Romer (1994), the focus moves away from specialization as the source of growth and instead stresses the nonrivalrous nature of knowledge "goods." He asserts, "If there are no nonrival goods, there are no increasing returns" (15). In Young, however, what is important is not knowledge as such but knowledge in use. Here he again differs from Romer in his emphasis on the importance of market size—and its growth—in making it economic to adapt and use existing as well as new knowledge that hitherto was known but uneconomic. It is not ignorance that prevents less-developed countries from using tractors instead of oxen. But even developed countries forgo the latest technology until it pays. New inputs, both of the conventional and unconventional (ideas) kind, become as much the result as the cause of economic growth. Thus the powerful concluding lines of Young's (1928a) presidential address:

> The division of labour depends upon the extent of the market, but the extent of the market also depends upon the division of labour. In this circumstance lies the possibility of economic progress, *apart from the progress which comes as a result of the new knowledge which men are able to gain*, whether in the pursuit of their economic or of their non-economic interests. (539–40; emphasis added)

Although in explaining this cumulative process Young wrote that Marshallian curve analysis "may divert attention to incidental or partial aspects of a process that ought to be seen as a whole" (533), nevertheless one might learn something from it if one enquires

> into the operations of reciprocal demand when the commodities are produced competitively under conditions of increasing returns and when the demand for each product is elastic, in the special sense that a small increase in its supply will be attended by an increase in the amounts of other commodities which can be had in exchange for it. Under such conditions an increase in the supply of one commodity *is* an increase in the demand for other commodities, and it must be supposed that every increase in demand will evoke an increase in supply. The rate at which any one industry grows is conditioned by the rate at which other industries grow, but since the elasticities of demand and of supply will differ for different products, some industries will grow faster than others. Even with a stationary population and in the absence of new discoveries in pure or applied science there are no limits to the process of expansion except the limits beyond which demand is not elastic and returns do not increase.

However, even in the reciprocal relationship between an inelastic-demand sector such as agriculture and the rest of the economy, producers of such commodities "often share in the advantages of the increase of the general scale of production in related industries, and so far as they do productive resources are released for other uses" (535). Thus agricultural costs may fall partly through innovations (including, but not only, through "general purpose technologies" such as computers) in fields such as steel, engines, and petrochemicals that only partly relate to the size of agriculture (just as the cost of steel etc. is reduced, directly or indirectly, by a fall in agricultural costs). And so long as wants are insatiable, the overall income elasticity of demand for all goods is unity (again abstracting from exogenous interruptions to secular growth).

If Youngian "macroeconomic" (Currie 1997) or "generalized" (Buchanan and Yoon 1999; Buchanan 2008) increasing returns, associated with a growing "aggregate of productive activities tied together by trade," arise from this increasingly complex nexus of specialized undertakings, the benefits involve increased transactions costs. Yang and Jeff Borland (1991), and Yang 2003, emphasize that with Youngian fragmentation of production, a new role emerges for coordination services such as transport and communications as well as research and advertising. However, Young (1928a) himself wrote,

> One who likes to conceive of all economic processes in terms of tendencies towards an equilibrium might even maintain that increasing returns, so far as they depend upon the economies of indirect methods of production and the size of the market, are offset and negated by their costs. . . . This would amount to saying that no real economic progress could come through the operation of forces engendered *within* the economic system—a conclusion repugnant to common sense. . . . The appropriate conception is that of a *moving* equilibrium, and . . . the costs which (under increasing returns) grow less rapidly than the product are not the "costs" which figure in an "equilibrium of costs and advantages." (535)

These increasing returns are also reaped by service sectors as the market grows. For example, all sectors require transport, but how far each sector enjoys a reduction in these costs depends, paradoxically, on others' increased use of it. Thus are costs associated with the securing of increasing returns differentiated from those involved in a conventional "equilibrium of costs and advantages." With increasing returns there is no equilibrium except a moving equilibrium of technical and organizational change that is cumulative, self-sustaining, *and endogenous to the size of the overall real market*—a demand-driven rather than an input-driven theory of growth.[9]

However, the rate is subject to various obstacles, natural (such as inelastic demand for a major sector like agriculture) or human-made, and these may be relaxed or exacerbated by exogenous events or policies. The latter would include not only better monetary management but also attacks on institutional obstacles to competition and mobility (notably those inhibiting movement out of sectors such as agriculture that face low demand elasticity but substantial increases in labor productivity).[10]

Regarding Marshall's statement that an industry's long-run supply schedule may fall, "given time for the organisation of industry," Young (1990, 47–8) wrote,

> But that is exactly the problem: how much time? . . . The "period of time" is relative to costs, and the costs are relative to the period of time. . . . A long-period supply curve is meaningless apart from the particular length of time considered: the curve is relative to the rate at which increasing returns exist. On the other side you cannot postulate a

9. See Nicholas Kaldor (1972) and Young's (1990, 45) statement (cited by Kaldor) that "seeking for equilibrium under increasing returns is as good as looking for a mare's nest." Young had a profound influence on Kaldor (see Thirlwall 1987) and may have inspired Kaldor's "technical progress function" in which the growth of labor productivity is a positive function of the growth of capital per worker that embodies technical progress ($\dot{q} = a + b\dot{k}$). With $0 < b' < 1$, the two growth rates converge toward a *sustainable* equilibrium rate of productivity growth. In addition, the constant term may shift up over time because of exogenous technical change or learning-by-doing—as with Erik Lundberg's "Horndal effect" mentioned by Mauro Boianovsky (this volume). But Kaldor thought that increasing returns are confined to manufacturing and debated this with Currie (quoted in Sandilands 1990, 296–303). Youngian specialization also enhances productivity via "disembodied" organizational changes requiring little extra capital. Another Swedish connection to Young is told by Bertil Ohlin in Sandilands 1999, 473. Ohlin relates that Young "impressed me immensely [at Harvard in 1922–23]. . . . He knew and understood his subject better than anyone else I have met. I tested him by means of a question about the 'Wicksell effect,' i.e., the special aspects of the marginal productivity of capital which at that time was practically unknown in most countries outside of Scandinavia. He immediately gave a fine account in a five minute speech before the students."

10. Stressed by Currie (1981, 1997) in his "leading-sector" theory of development (cf. Chandra 2006). Institutional reform in urban housing finance and the exchange-rate regime could liberate latent demand (in Young's reciprocal sense) for sectors whose expansion had hitherto been artificially repressed (thus repressing the rest of the economy too).

constant demand curve for a good over a long period. It would shift as a result of the very forces which are shifting the supply curve. We need a theory of an equilibrium rate of progress. Probably the optimum rate of progress which will keep the supply curve close up to the demand curve.[11]

These reciprocal curves depend on their interrelated elasticities, which helps clarify an otherwise elusive statement in Young 1928a, 534n:

> If the circumstance that commodity *a* is produced under conditions of increasing returns is taken into account as a factor in the elasticity of demand for *b* in terms of *a*, elasticity of demand and elasticity of supply may be looked upon as different ways of expressing a single functional relation.

However, consider an inelastic-demand sector such as agriculture. For the long period, its downwardly shifting short-period cost schedules will appear as a downward-sloping supply schedule that nearly coincides with its demand schedule. Even if its cost reductions (increasing returns) are similar to those in other industries, its long-period demand and supply schedules will *both* be more steeply sloped (less elastic) than for products with elastic demand. For the supply schedules, this may seem paradoxical. But long-run industry supply is derived from a series of shifting cost schedules for the firms (farms) in a competitive industry, while demand conditions will dictate how many firms remain in the industry. With inelastic demand that number will fall—and will fall faster the greater the exodus of labor from agriculture into sectors with higher elasticity of demand.

Factor Shares and the Labor-Saving Bias of Technical Progress

Another outgrowth of Solovian growth theory concerned the factor bias to the technical progress that accompanies growth. Paul Samuelson (1965, 1966), highlighted by Joseph Stiglitz (2006, 237), addressed the issue of whether a rise in the wage rate (which occurs in both the Young and

11. At the conference Professor Solow asked if increasing returns exhibit diminishing returns in moving, for example, from aircraft to airframes to engines to rotor blades produced by increasingly specialized firms. The above paragraphs show it depends on the time frame, the secular direction of the structure of demand, and the degree of competition and mobility.

Solow theories as productivity advances) is likely to induce a labor-saving bias to innovation, following William Fellner (1961) and Charles Kennedy (1964).[12]

Samuelson and Stiglitz deny any a priori reason for such a bias, for a higher wage rate need not increase unit wage costs when capital deepening raises labor productivity, so there is no incentive to bias marginal R&D expenditures in the labor-saving direction. But if technical progress were Hicks-neutral (with neither a labor-saving nor a capital-saving bias), capital deepening would raise capital's share progressively. In view of the historically observed labor-saving bias, Samuelson suggests a natural tendency for innovative effort simply to follow the (successful) labor-saving trend. And the actual labor-saving bias explains the relative constancy of labor's share despite capital deepening and rising wage rates.

An alternative explanation could be asymmetry in the response to a rise in the economy's "going wage" by relatively labor-intensive industries compared with more capital-intensive ones. Labor-intensive sectors whose labor productivity is below average do face rising unit wage costs, and thus face the greatest pressure to make labor-saving adjustments. Nevertheless, they are still likely to suffer a decline in their domestic and international comparative advantages (a kind of Balassa-Samuelson effect on their relative costs). The squeeze on these sectors releases resources for expanding capital-intensive sectors where labor's productivity is higher. Thus the economy's measured average labor productivity will increase without there necessarily having been any *further* labor-saving innovations in the expanding sectors. All that has happened is that labor will have shifted to sectors with higher labor productivity.

This is consistent with Young's stress on the way an expanding market makes it pay to introduce the more roundabout or indirect uses of labor that most powerfully raise productivity and lower costs. If lower costs are passed on through competition in lower prices or higher money wages, market demand increases further. This provides, endogenously, the

---

12. Samuelson (1966) was a rejoinder to Kennedy on "induced Harrod-neutral technical change" that keeps relative factor shares constant. If the capital-labor ratio rises, labor-saving innovation prevents capital's share from falling, thus also maintaining a relatively constant return on capital—one of Kaldor's famous "stylized facts." Kaldor's LSE lecture notes reveal that Young (1990, 99), following Cassel, also stressed this. Solow (1994, 49) notes that the assumption of constant returns to capital makes *increasing returns to scale* "inevitable," along with the modeling of monopolistic competition. But Young's increasingly specialized monopolistically competitive firms that are the vehicle of his *"increasing returns"* are not necessarily exploiting "returns to scale" from being larger than their predecessors.

incentive and the resources to continue investing and innovating (whether in a predominantly labor-saving direction or not). So long as capital accumulation keeps the return on new investment more or less constant, it means that despite or because of growing labor scarcity (which implies growing labor productivity[13]) the purchasing power of wages can keep rising without depressing investment incentives. The wage rate (but not necessarily the wages share) will rise relative to the return on physical capital.

These ratios (and absolute returns) are, to repeat, ultimately simply a matter of (derived) supply and demand. As Young (1990, 25) put it, "The values of the factors merely reflect the value which consumers attach to final products of such factors." Constantly on guard against the fallacy of composition, he also wrote:

> Fundamentally, there is no difference between productivity and scarcity. Scarcity is meaningless except in relation to human desires; so is productivity. This does not mean that you can create a product by creating scarcity. . . . An objection has been raised that it is "value," not "product" that counts. But one does not produce value; the market values what one produces. . . . Wages are paid for the value of what the workman produces. There must be some balancing of the factors of production. One should not fix one's eye too narrowly on the way the individual entrepreneur apportions his expenses. One cannot apply an additive process and find a picture of the whole economy. The older economists thought on the grand scale. Take this notion of the universality of diminishing returns, of diminishing productivity. The individual entrepreneur is relatively disadvantaged if he oversupplies himself with one factor. Following Von Thünen, modern economists, assuming land and machinery are given, draw decreasing productivity curves to labour. But what significance does this have? To what extent is this diminishing productivity a matter of the individual firm? Would integration give a good social picture? (Young 1990, 73)

In other words, capital deepening and the shape and productivity of the isoquants associated with a move across an aggregate Cobb-Douglas production function are being driven by both the past growth of output and the expected increase and pattern of demand that increasing incomes induce. This favors labor-intensive or capital-intensive goods and ser-

---

13. In value terms, giving rise to increased output being *imputed* to labor in higher wages even though the cause of rising labor productivity/scarcity lies elsewhere; see below.

vices according to differing elasticities of demand and relative product prices—in turn determined by relative elasticities of factor supplies in response to the demands.[14]

But many inherently labor-intensive services have high income elasticity of demand. Partly this is because of the nature of services like education and health.[15] Partly it is because Youngian increasing returns involve a thickening of the trade and exchange nexus (as stressed by Yang 2003) that requires labor-intensive services such as transport and communications, as well as training and research. Significantly, although their costs per unit also fall with labor-saving innovation, as a share of GDP they tend to rise because of their income-elastic demand. Thus the derived demand for labor may increase on account of demand-side forces even if there is an induced labor-saving innovation bias. The growth of services has been greatest in the more-advanced countries where most of the world's inventive activity occurs. This provides another Youngian demand-side explanation for relatively constant factor shares and return to investment. Single-product or "corn" models of growth (including Solow's[16]) cannot explain this.

Incidentally, a growth model that explicitly separates the fixed supply of classical land (claiming classical Ricardian rents) from the elastic supply of capital (claiming interest) would argue for a bias toward land-saving innovations. Without these, the "free" gifts of nature command higher transfer payments to whoever can claim property rights over them. Similarly, separating skilled and unskilled labor, a growing relative demand for skills may induce a bias in favor of skill-saving innovation.

Ultimately, to repeat, factor incomes are not so much the result of the value of their *contributions* to the growth of GDP. Rather they are what

14. Young's (1928, 540–42) appendix explains the italicized *problem* of breaking free of a conventional equilibrium of costs and benefits to secure an equilibrium rate of *potential* increasing returns. He invokes a special isoquant and indifference map, with different (reciprocal) sectoral supply and demand elasticities. Then: "To diminish the amount of the one commodity which must be sacrificed for a given increment of the other, some of the labour hitherto devoted to its production must be used indirectly, so that the increase of the annual output of the one lags behind the curtailing of the output of the other."

15. But Japan has made great advances with robots (as well as computers) to replace humans in these fields. (On "machine slavery," Young [quoted in Mehrling and Sandilands 1999, 243]) wrote, "One way, perhaps the most important way, out of the admitted evils of the machine system is through the more thorough utilization of the possibilities of that system.")

16. However, cf. Solow 1958 on the constancy of relative shares. He considers sectoral differences in the elasticity of substitution as factor price ratios change, but not the bias of technical progress or sectoral differences in demand elasticities. See also his conference speech in this volume.

the market *attributes* or *imputes* to them through the forces of supply and demand. Thus, when searching for the sources of growth, Samuelson (1980, 502) surely misleads policy when he writes, on the basis of the Solow model, that "a 1% increase in labour increases output by 3 times as much as a 1% increase in capital, if the exponent on L is 0.75."

This could induce misplaced complacency toward population growth and rapid immigration. It is macroeconomic supply and demand as well as physical productivity that determines factor payments and shares. Factors must have scarcity as well as productivity if firms are to pay them well. The market distributes the fruits of economic progress accordingly, in the form of pecuniary external benefits, with factors paid not for what they contribute but on how far competition and mobility reduce prices and induce factors to move to where they are most valued. Pecuniary externalities are thus inherent in a successful market system, not a sign of its failure. Failure comes from monopoly[17] and protectionist elements, including excessively strong patents—which Young (1990, 52) opposed. For, to repeat, it is not knowledge per se that matters but the freedom to apply knowledge as and when it pays, which depends on the fastest possible growth of market size and specialization—not on the largest size of the firm or industry as stressed by neo-Schumpeterian and neoclassical endogenous growth theories.

Conclusion

Ultimately, then (as Lauchlin Currie [1997] insisted), the main sources of growth are competition, mobility, and growth itself. But perhaps the contrast with recent neoclassical theorizing may best be inferred from Young's (1929, 237) own conclusion to an essay titled "The Sources of Wealth":

> Science teaches how to harness nature, and to use her powers for our own needs. For a short time, the advance of scientific knowledge may be "capitalized" in the form of valuable technical secrets, or in patent rights, but, in the long run, scientific knowledge, of whatever sort, becomes diffused. We pay no rent, interest or royalty to science as such. We merely have to pay for the technical equipment, for the capital, which is required if we are to make effective use of our accumulated fund of scientific knowledge. Appraised by his real contributions to wealth and welfare, not in dollars and cents, the scientist may easily outrank the millionaire

---

17. As distinct from *monopolistic competition*, insofar as this is central to increasing specialization and differentiation inherent in the phenomenon of increasing returns.

or the captain of industry. His contributions to society's capital are, in general, free. For that reason, they do not fall under the ordinary laws of supply and demand. There is no limitation of supply; there is no question of a larger or a smaller number of increments of supply. The scientist's contribution is, or becomes, a free good. Just because it is diffused and free, its *apparent* utility to society may be less. Ordinary capital, in order to have value, must have both utility (productivity) and scarcity. The scientist's contribution has productivity without scarcity.

In short, *attributions* (payments) to factors under increasing returns have only tenuous links with *contributions* to growth. Young's (1928a, 529) vision was thus an extension of "one of the most illuminating and fruitful generalisations which can be found anywhere in the whole literature of economics," namely, Smith's dictum that the division of labor is limited by the size (and openness) of the market. While modern growth theory focuses on the microeconomic foundations of neoclassical growth theory by noting how entrepreneurs allocate resources to innovation according to a profit-maximizing balancing of private costs and benefits that may also yield external benefits, Young's more classical approach stresses the macro foundations of microeconomics. The dynamic creative function of markets induces productivity-enhancing specialization and roundabout methods that yield self-sustaining macroeconomic increasing returns to which entrepreneurs respond in ways that defeat the otherwise self-exhausting accumulation process. As Ramesh Chandra (2003) aptly noted, Young's approach converts the economics of scarcity and diminishing returns into the economics of opportunity and increasing returns.

References

Ades, Alberto F., and Edward L. Glaeser. 1999. Evidence on Growth, Increasing Returns, and the Extent of the Market. *Quarterly Journal of Economics* 114 (August): 1025–45.

Aghion, Philippe, and Peter Howitt. 1998. *Endogenous Growth Theory.* Cambridge: MIT Press.

Arrow, Kenneth J. 1962. The Economic Implications of Learning by Doing. *Review of Economic Studies* 29:155–73.

Baumol, William J. 2002. *The Free-Market Innovation Machine.* Princeton, N.J.: Princeton University Press.

Buchanan, J. M. 2008. Let Us Understand Adam Smith. *Journal of the History of Economic Thought* 30.1:21–28.

Buchanan, James M., and Yong J. Yoon. 1999. Generalized Increasing Returns, Euler's Theorem, and Competitive Equilibrium. *HOPE* 31.3:511–23.

Chandra, Ramesh. 2003. Allyn Young Revisited. *Journal of Economic Studies* 30.1:46–65.

———. 2006. Currie's "Leading Sector" Strategy of Growth: An Appraisal. *Journal of Development Studies* 42.3:490–508.

Chandra, Ramesh, and Roger J. Sandilands. 2005. Does Modern Endogenous Growth Theory Adequately Represent Allyn Young? *Cambridge Journal of Economics* 29.3:463–73.

———. 2006. The Role of Pecuniary External Economies and Economies of Scale in the Theory of Increasing Returns. *Review of Political Economy* 18.2:193–208.

Clark, J. B. 1899. *The Distribution of Wealth*. New York: Macmillan.

Cobb, Charles, and Paul Douglas. 1928. A Theory of Production. *American Economic Review* 18 (March supplement): 139–65.

Currie, Lauchlin. 1981. Allyn Young and the Development of Growth Theory. *Journal of Economic Studies* 8.1:52–60.

———. 1997. Implications of an Endogenous Theory of Growth in Allyn Young's Macroeconomic Concept of Increasing Returns. *HOPE* 29.3:414–43.

Ely, Richard T., Thomas S. Adams, Max O. Lorenz, and Allyn A. Young. 1908. *Outlines of Economics*. 2nd ed. New York: Macmillan.

Fellner, William J. 1961. Two Propositions in the Theory of Induced Innovations. *Economic Journal* 71:305–8.

Frankel, M. 1962. The Production Function in Allocation and Growth: A Synthesis. *American Economic Review* 52.5:955–1022.

Kaldor, Nicholas. 1972. The Irrelevance of Equilibrium Economics. *Economic Journal* 82:1237–55.

Kennedy, Charles. 1964. Induced Bias in Innovation and the Theory of Distribution. *Economic Journal* 71:514–47.

Krugman, Paul. 1990. *Rethinking International Trade*. Cambridge: MIT Press.

———. 1993. Toward a Counter-Counterrevolution in Development Theory. In *Annual Conference on Development Economics 1992*. Washington, D.C.: World Bank.

Laidler, David. 1993. Hawtrey, Harvard, and the Origins of the Chicago Tradition. *Journal of Political Economy* 101 (December): 1068–103.

Lewis, Arthur. 1954. Economic Development with Unlimited Supplies of Labour. *Manchester School* 22 (May): 139–91.

Marshall, Alfred. 1920. *Principles of Economics*. 8th ed. London: Macmillan.

Mehrling, Perry G., and Roger J. Sandilands, eds. 1999. *Money and Growth: Selected Papers of Allyn Abbott Young*. London: Routledge.

Newman, Peter. 1987. Allyn Abbott Young. In vol. 4 of *New Palgrave Dictionary of Economics*, edited by J. Eatwell, M. Milgate, and P. Newman. New York: Palgrave Macmillan.

Romer, Paul M. 1986. Increasing Returns and Long-Run Growth. *Journal of Political Economy* 94.5:1002–37.

———. 1989. Capital Accumulation in the Theory of Long-Run Growth. In *Modern Business Cycle Theory*, edited by Robert J. Barro. Cambridge: Harvard University Press.

——. 1994. The Origins of Endogenous Growth. *Journal of Economic Perspectives* 8.1:3–22.

Samuelson, Paul A. 1965. A Theory of Induced Innovation on Kennedy–von Weisäcker Lines. *Review of Economics and Statistics* 47.4:343–56.

——. 1966. Rejoinder. *Review of Economics and Statistics* 48.4:444–48.

——. 1980. *Economics*. 11th ed. New York: McGraw-Hill.

Sandilands, Roger J. 1990. *The Life and Political Economy of Lauchlin Currie: New Dealer, Presidential Adviser, and Development Economist*. Durham, N.C.: Duke University Press.

——. 1999. New Evidence on Allyn Young's Style and Influence as a Teacher. *Journal of Economic Studies* 26.6:453–79.

——. 2000. Perspectives on Allyn Young in Theories of Endogenous Growth. *Journal of the History of Economic Thought* 22.3:309–28.

Solow, Robert M. 1956. A Contribution to the Theory of Economic Growth. *Quarterly Journal of Economics* 70 (February): 65–94.

——. 1957. Technical Change and the Aggregate Production Function. *Review of Economics and Statistics* 39 (August): 312–20.

——. 1958. A Sceptical Note on the Constancy of Relative Shares. *American Economic Review* 48 (September): 618–31.

——. 1994. Perspectives on Growth Theory. *Journal of Economic Perspectives* 8.1:45–54.

Stiglitz, Joseph E. 2006. Samuelson and the Factor Bias of Technological Change. In *Samuelsonian Economics and the Twenty-first Century*, edited by Michael Szenberg et al. Oxford: Oxford University Press.

Thirlwall, Anthony P. 1987. *Nicholas Kaldor*. New York: New York University Press.

Warsh, David. 2006. *Knowledge and the Wealth of Nations: A Story of Economic Discovery*. New York: Norton.

Yang, Xiaokai. 2003. *Economic Development and the Division of Labour*. Oxford: Blackwell.

Yang, Xiaokai, and Jeff Borland. 1991. A Microeconomic Mechanism for Economic Growth. *Journal of Political Economy* 99.3:460–82.

Young, Allyn A. 1913. Pigou's Wealth and Welfare. *Quarterly Journal of Economics* 27.4:672–86.

——. 1928a. Increasing Returns and Economic Progress. *Economic Journal* 38 (December): 527–42.

——. 1928b. Supply and Demand. In Mehrling and Sandilands 1999.

——. 1929. The Sources of Wealth. From *The Book of Popular Science*, in Mehrling and Sandilands 1999.

——. 1990. Nicholas Kaldor's Notes on Allyn Young's LSE Lectures, 1927–29. *Journal of Economic Studies* 17.3–4:18–114.

Zhang, Yongsheng, and Xueyan Zhao. 2004. Testing the Scale Effect Predicted by the Fujita-Krugman Urbanization Model. *Journal of Economic Behaviour and Organization* 55.2:207–22.

Endogenous Growth: Valuable Advance, Substantive Misnomer

William J. Baumol

> My impression is that the process of innovation is still treated rather
> mechanically in the new generation of "endogenous" growth models.
> —Robert Solow, "On Macroeconomic Models of
> Free-Market Innovation and Growth" (2006)

Much of what follows will undoubtedly tempt the reader to interpret the comments as denigration. But that is far from my intention, as an enthusiastic admirer of the work of both the empirical and theoretical macroeconomists. Rather, my purpose is to suggest only something of what the endogenous growth literature has really accomplished, differentiating this from what it may appear to have achieved. My only direct quarrel is with the use of the term *endogenous*, and, even here, I admit that the grounds for my complaint are not solid and may amount to little more than a dispute over the use of words.

The problem on which I will focus here, however, is more substantive than a mere verbal dispute. It is about advertising that is misleading (though, surely, inadvertently so). When I am told that a model is designed to deal with the endogenous side of its subject, this strongly suggests revelation of the structure of the underlying mechanism and the way that it works. It suggests something analogous to the transformation of a reduced-

I am deeply grateful to the Ewing Marion Kauffman Foundation for its generous support of this work.

History of Political Economy 41 (annual suppl.) DOI 10.1215/00182702-2009-029

form model into the corresponding structural model, with all that this transformation can reveal. But by and large, from what I have seen of the endogenous growth literature, it undertakes to explain its black box by revealing that another black box (somewhat more limited in size) is to be found in its innards. All of this is made endogenous by the premise that each black box affects the workings of the other, so that the two together constitute a mechanism that drives the growth of the economy. Indeed, it can even be held that the outer box is to a substantial degree directed by the smaller box inside it and that, in turn, the movement of the small box is guided by that of the exterior container. Hence, it is indeed arguable that such a construct satisfies the formal interpretation of an endogenous process and that the model contains the (largely undisclosed) innards of a functioning growth process. The new black box is even assigned a general description in the literature; for example, it may contain a variable representing the accumulation and aggregation of acquired knowledge. But, surely, there is more expected of a story whose mechanism is labeled *endogenous*, because the term leads us to expect a fuller set of insights. We are led to anticipate more explicit material describing how the machinery is constructed and how its parts interact and drive one another. In addition, I will suggest, at least some of these insights cannot be encompassed in a description that is exclusively macroeconomic.

Robert Solow recognizes that there is a problem of substance and attributes it, to a substantial degree, to possibly misguided orientation of the investigators. "Part of the problem, I suspect, is the ubiquitous focus in growth theory—'endogenous' or not—on the steady state growth rate as a theoretical object" (2006, 16). He goes on to say, "I have nothing against steady states. The problem is that insisting on them has led to growth mechanisms for endogenous technological change that have no other merit than that they do the endogenous-growth-rate trick" (17).

My only complaint about Solow's critique is that it is a bit harsh. The output of the authors in question surely does have more merit than these remarks may suggest. However, it fails to produce the insights that I expect of endogenous theory. The source of this problem is not the steady-state orientation but the reliance of these writers on the wrong tool for that purpose.

Their inappropriate tool, in short, is the macroeconomic approach. Here, let me not be misunderstood. Although the field in which I labor is micro, not macro, I am as enthusiastic an admirer as anyone of the concept and accomplishments of macroeconomics. But good tools often have their specialized uses—a micrometer is not well suited to turning screws. And it is my view that for more promising instruments for the study of the endogenous structure of the growth process, one must turn to microeconomics, or at least not avoid its use altogether.

To clarify the points I hope to make, I must offer a few comments on work that pursues "enhancement of realism" in economic models: its virtues and vices. The remarks on this subject will lead directly to my views on the contribution of macroeconomic analysis: the source of the invaluable insights it has offered to our discipline, characterizing its role as a powerful but specialized analytic tool. Then, finally, I will turn to the analysis of growth and argue the indispensability of a role for microeconomics if we are to arrive at an endogenous theoretical structure whose endogeneity is in itself illuminating.

Realism in Theory as Cost-Benefit Trade-off

All economic models can be characterized as deliberate untruths. For, if judiciously selected, it is in these misrepresentations that their primary virtue lies. That is, if such a model is to be tractable analytically, it must entail oversimplification of reality, often drastic oversimplification. It must systematically abstract from minor influences and relationships, even though there is hardly a situation in reality where they are not present in profusion. Such pruning of the many minor complications is essential for the construction of models that serve their evident purpose, insight into the explanation of real phenomena and real relationships. For, each complication that is incorporated into a model constructed for analytic purposes has a trade-off in reduced analytic tractability of the construct.[1]

Of course one cannot legitimately denigrate material that is purely descriptive, characterizes some phenomenon as fully as it can, and proceeds with an attempt to point out its every complication and the multitude of influences, however minor, by which it is driven.

But neither the human mind nor any of the investigative tools it has created are generally capable of embracing such an extensive catalog and studying its workings in their entirety. Consequently, one of the critical

---

1. One reader suggests that the views expressed here have some kinship with Milton Friedman's well-known defense of questionable premises, whose justification lies in their valid implications. But my point is rather different. What I defend is *simplification* of *valid* premises for the sake of analytic tractability.

skills of the theorist is the ability to carry out a pruning process that does not slash and burn the entire forest. Any models that result, evidently, are deliberately unrealistic. Thus a deliberate move to enhance the realism of such a model may turn out to be more vice than virtue. At the very least, the creator of such an improvement bears the responsibility of showing that it has not undermined the capability of subjecting the model to systematic analysis.

More than that, the complicator of the model can be urged to take on the obligation to show that it makes a significant difference—that the behavior of the model or some of its implications are substantially modified by the addition of the complication introduced. Or, perhaps, it is enough to show that nothing of any substantial importance follows from such an amendment of the model, thereby licensing analysts to proceed using the simpler predecessor model exclusively, without apology or further ado. But these remarks should indicate the grounds on which it can be held that an increase in the realism of a model is not a costless exercise and that, ideally, we may well wish to aim for something like an optimal compromise between realism and analytic tractability.

The Genius of the Macroeconomic Approach

But the preceding conclusion is itself an unacceptable oversimplification. A review of the literature confirms that there is no one optimal degree of realism, even for any particular economic model. A justifiable degree of complexity differs not only from one analytic issue to another but also substantially among analysts. Among the great economists there are evidently those whose talents include the ability to contribute valuable simplifications, while there are others whose contribution consists in pointing out significant complications and ways in which they can be dealt with effectively. Surely, David Ricardo was one of the great simplifiers, for example, in contributing a growth model of the entire economy, whose realism and current relevance we justly question, but which is still a working mechanism whose functioning can still be admired for its aesthetic qualities. Even more can be said in admiration of contributions such as the theory of comparative advantage. Surely, Ricardo's work is a model of felicitous oversimplification—of the process by which one can remove from the model of some phenomenon all of its distracting complications, without destroying its usefulness and the valuable insights it offers.

At the other extreme there is the work of Léon Walras, the heart of whose addition to the literature is the interdependence of the different parts of the economy and its implications. A crucial part of the value of this addition to our understanding is the creation of a body of analytical materials, the equations of general equilibrium, that enables us to take hold of this interdependence and that permits us to begin to see systematically how it all works out.

These two noted examples show clearly that there is no one optimal choice of degree of realism in the trade-off between complication and simplification. On the contrary, we need them both, and all investigators must choose for themselves where their talents lie and where the issue with which they are dealing leads them.

On the Genius and Special Contribution
of Macroeconomics

Macroeconomics can be interpreted as the most effective simplifying breakthrough in the history of economic ideas. Whether or not one is a Keynesian, as I consider myself to be, it will surely be acknowledged that the construction of so simple a model as that of John Maynard Keynes—one whose workings are transparent and fully coordinated, and that generates clear policy implications—was a stroke of genius. Of course, this is not meant to imply that the model of the *General Theory* is beyond criticism. We know all too well from the many cogent reviews and the enormous literature that have followed it that it urgently required further examination, exploration of appropriate modifications and additions, and perhaps even some substantial alterations.

But the one thing the work evidently does *not* need is complication for its own sake or for the sake of enhanced realism. Thus, for example, I have little sympathy for efforts to provide extensive microeconomic foundations for macroeconomic analysis. Microeconomic analysis is sufficiently advanced and sufficiently defensible that it can well stand on its own feet, requiring no support from my fellow microtheorists. And, as I have already argued, all usable models are untruths, at least to a degree. A reduction in the degree of divergence between some model and the corresponding reality is not necessarily an improvement, and certainly is not if its cost in terms of reduced analytic tractability is too great. My concern here is that efforts to make the growth models endogenous court that danger. But that is not the main question that can be raised about them.

Improving the Solow Growth Model?

Models such as Solow's pathbreaking construct generally have one of two patent goals (or both). The first, evidently, is to provide insight into the workings of the phenomenon under study, and the second is to permit empirical exploration by adaptation to available data. The first of these tasks is clearly carried out by the Keynesian model itself. I need hardly add that the second is performed masterfully by Solow with the aid of his construct. What, then, is to be gained by the addition of elements of endogeneity to the model?

The answer is that there is much to be gained, on two grounds. First, there is good reason to assert that the growth process of the economy, at least as it has proceeded in the last two centuries, does have significant endogenous components. I return to this last assertion presently. Second, there is no such thing in any analytic discipline as a construct that is the final word—it was surely appropriate for Einstein to propose substantial modifications of the Newtonian system.

The contributions to the literature that constitute endogenous growth theory do have much to be said for them. In particular, those who provided this material demonstrated great skill in the additions they introduced because the additions are substantive, defensible as to relevance, and yet do not complicate the model structure to a degree that renders them intractable for such purposes as econometric exploration. I have seen nothing in the resulting modifications of the models to which one can object—either on the ground that the addition deals with an insignificant phenomenon or on the ground that it substantially distorts the facts beyond the degree that must be considered acceptable in a model-building process.

I have already cited Solow's criticism of the macroeconomists' fixation on the steady state. But that is not one of my reservations. Rather, I propose only two possible grounds for doubt. The first is identification of the payoff. The second is, obviously, my major focus here, the degree to which the work really illuminates the endogenous elements inherent in the growth process.

On the first of these, it may be my ignorance of the macroeconomic literature that is to blame. However, I am not aware of any striking additional insight on the details of the growth mechanism that the initial contributions to the endogenous growth literature provided, beyond what one could have gathered from Solow's work and from other earlier writings. Yet this portion of the literature does draw our attention to the importance of *accumulation* of knowledge and human capital. But I may be pardoned for saying that such an observation could have been made and, very likely, was made, before. I am not implying by this that the effort was a waste of time. To demonstrate how explicit recognition of such relationships can be incorporated into the preceding literature, to show the resulting implications, and to do so without undermining analytic tractability is no minor accomplishment. On the contrary, it would be very valuable if all that it accomplished was nothing more than empirical verification of a held belief, since so often what is claimed to be obviously true turns out to be unequivocally incorrect. But this new work has shown us much more than that.

Thus, my verdict, for what it may be worth, is that this earlier part of the literature represents worthwhile effort with a clear-cut payoff. If the payoff is slightly more modest than might be inferred from the attention that it has received, that is beside the point. It is a valuable contribution that has managed to avoid the heavy costs that improvement of working and workable models often incurs.

It must be recognized, moreover, that more recent contributions to the literature have gone well beyond this. They have clarified much more of what transpires in the growth process and shown us much about how formal mathematical tools can be used to expand the theory and its insights. The magnificent Aghion-Howitt volume (1998) clearly is evidence enough about what further work in the arena can accomplish. Yet even this powerful body of analysis does not obviate the need for a complementary microtheoretic contribution, as illustrated by the fact that the word *entrepreneur* does not appear even once in the Aghion-Howitt index, despite the evidence about the important role played by entrepreneurs in the growth process and their central place in the Schumpeterian vision that is so central to much of the Aghion-Howitt discussion. This is no criticism of their work, for the primary focus and accomplishments of the entrepreneurial activities are surely best discerned with the aid of the microscope, rather than that of the telescope, which these two authors handle so deftly.

That leaves me with the remaining issue: does the recent literature provide what we can hope for from a microeconomic investigation of the endogenous aspects of the growth process?

Endogenous Growth and the Need for Microtheory

This article began with the notion that the insertion of one black box into another, even if it makes the relationship endogenous in the literal sense, fails to provide the substance that might well be hoped for. When dealing with a growth model, we want to know how the pertinent actors affect the pace and pattern of development and how those, in turn, influence the behavior of the actors. That is to say, we surely want to know something about the mechanism that produces the observed growth and, better yet, can help us understand the features of the economy's internal workings that can account for such phenomena as the explosion of growth in the wake of the Industrial Revolution, by telling us what modifications occurred *inside the economy* that led it to grow at a pace and to a degree that apparently was never before even distantly approximated.

But here we must go into detail of the kind that macrotheory deliberately suppresses, and does so out of necessity, to provide the sort of understanding at which it is uniquely adept. In other words, to get at the type of illumination that one can hope to derive from an endogenous construct it seems to me that one is driven to turn to microtheory. Let me therefore end by describing, as examples of these matters, some of the elements that will have to be provided from that quarter and by indicating what it is about them that is inherently micro rather than macro.

On Inherently Microeconomic Components of Endogenous Growth

The growth process, by general agreement and as supported by Solow's research, has undoubtedly had, as one of its primary drivers, the flow of invention. But mere invention has repeatedly been found to be insufficient. From the rapidly forgotten inventions of Tang and Sung China (whose variety and ingenuity continue to astonish us) to the substantial creative output of Soviet scientists and engineers, with their superb educational training, history is replete with examples of inventions that have been left unused. A most striking example is what may have been the first working steam engine:

> As much as two thousand years ago the power of steam was not only observed, but an ingenious toy was actually made and put in motion by it, at Alexandria. . . . What appears strange is, that neither the inventor of the toy, nor anyone else, for so long a time afterwards, should perceive that steam would move *useful* machinery as well as a toy. (Lincoln 1858, 5)

There is also good reason to conclude that a good part of this reiterated failure is to be attributed to the role of entrepreneurs, who were not absent but were diverted to activities other than the promotion of productive inventions. Incentives matter, as William Easterly (2001) has emphasized, and the incentives were frequently such as to reallocate the entrepreneurial resources of society in other directions. Often they did promote inventions, but not for productive purposes. In Rome, it was the promising military innovation that was valued and that was unlikely to be ignored. But the payoff to another activity was also not negligible—competing religious institutions, which were looking for devices that could impress their flocks with the magical powers of their priests, offered handsome rewards. That seems to have been the primary source of income of Heron of Alexandria, who invented a profusion of "toys" that served this purpose, notably the steam engine described above, which opened and closed the door of a temple without the intervention of any visible power source.

It is certainly arguable that all of this changed with the evolution of institutions (as a result of endogenous developments that I shall not go into here) and when the structure of payoffs changed drastically as a result. As microeconomics teaches at its core, a change in the payoffs offered to the inputs of the economy can be relied on to change the tasks to which they are allocated, and in this the entrepreneurs are no exception. From the later Middle Ages to the Industrial Revolution the relative payoff in wealth and prestige changed to favor reallocating entrepreneurial activity into more innovative and productive activities, and this, surely, is not an unimportant part of the endogenous growth story.[2]

Here, I take the liberty of summarizing the distinctive features of my own work in the arena, my excuse being that it may help bring out more clearly the goals I have been espousing here for the theoretical parts of my subject. There are three directions this work has taken, the "historical," the "macrocapitalistic," and the "basic microtheoretic."

I consider the historical portion the most indispensable, even if it is condemned to offer no unequivocal answers, because it seems to me that any growth analysis must be unsatisfying if it provides no insights on what is arguably the most remarkable development ever encountered by any economy: the outburst of growth following the eighteenth-century Industrial Revolution and the apparent absence of anything comparable in

---

2. It was my intention here to minimize references to my own work, but I must confess my weakness in acquiescing instantly to the request of an (anonymous) reviewer that I amplify the discussion by indicating the alternative approaches I have taken to the pertinent issues, particularly in my book *The Free-Market Innovation Machine* (2002), especially chapters 8, 14, and 15 (the chapters kindly singled out by the reviewer).

all of previous human history. A body of growth literature that makes no attempt to offer explicit light on this issue is, indeed, a performance of *Julius Caesar* without the conqueror of Gaul. My allusions, above, to the strange fate of technological breakthroughs in ancient Rome and China are meant more to serve as challenge than as provision of even very tentative answers.

I turn next to the macrocapitalistic approach, which is illustrated in the two concluding chapters of my 2002 book, *The Free-Market Innovation Machine*. In the vast oversimplification adopted in my model (chapter 15), I try explicitly to incorporate three key variables: the magnitude of the effort devoted to innovation, the cost that the process entails, and the consequences for the trajectory of the economy's productivity. Aside from the obvious relationships (innovative activity enhances productivity growth, higher cost reduces the demand for innovative activity), I note that much of innovative activity (notably thinking) can be viewed as having a substantial handicraft component, which reduces opportunities for labor saving and leads the costs of the activity to rise more quickly than the average for all products of the economy. Readers can now readily imagine how all of this connects (or, better yet, they can read the book). The innovation process contributes to the productivity growth of the economy. But that introduces the much-discussed cost disease, which increases the relative lag of productivity in the innovation process behind the average for the economy, raising its "real" cost, that is, its cost increases relative to the general price level. That, in turn, slows investment in innovation and thereby subsequently holds back the entire growth process. Relative innovation costs then fall back, and an oscillatory intertemporal trajectory is generated.

I am well aware that such an oscillatory time path is all too easily obtained by use of a difference equation model. But I suspect that the construct nevertheless offers us some insights and, to a degree, reduces dependence on the black boxes, whose desirability I have questioned above. Moreover, the construct and the behavior of its variables offer some insights on the prospects that the mechanism will ultimately lead to stagnancy and enable us to examine possible countermeasures (as I do in chapter 16).

Finally, I come to my third strand, the microtheoretic approach, to which my next book will be devoted (advertisement: the manuscript has already gone to Princeton University Press). There, I hope to have shown how directly the Schumpeterian entrepreneurship model of innovation can be formalized and how the resulting construct can be used to describe (theoretically) the process of determining the magnitude of investment in innovation, the earnings the activity will bring, and the pricing of the final outputs that will be produced, using as inputs the innovations created. In short, I claim to be able to do for entrepreneurship what value theory offers for other inputs and outputs in the elementary textbooks.

Of course, there is much more to the matter. But what has just been recounted makes no attempt at full coverage of the issues, but is offered to argue only one point. Accepting, as I do, the conclusion that much of the economic growth process is endogenous, it follows that macroeconomics alone cannot be relied on to carry out the task of its analysis. Full partnership with microeconomists is indispensable and, happily, microeconomists are beginning to accept that role.

References

Aghion, Philippe, and Peter Howitt. 1998. *Endogenous Growth Theory.* Cambridge: MIT Press.

Baumol, William J. 2002. *The Free-Market Innovation Machine: Analyzing the Growth Miracle of Capitalism.* Princeton, N.J.: Princeton University Press.

Easterly, William. 2001. *The Elusive Quest for Growth: Adventures and Misadventures in the Tropics.* Cambridge: MIT Press.

Lincoln, Abraham. 1858. *Lecture on Discoveries and Inventions.* showcase.netins.net/web/creative/Lincoln/speeches/discoveries.htm.

Solow, Robert. 1956. A Contribution to the Theory of Economic Growth. *Quarterly Journal of Economics* 70 (February): 65–94.

———. 2006. On Macroeconomic Models of Free-Market Innovation and Growth. In *Entrepreneurship, Innovation, and the Growth Mechanism of the Free-Enterprise Economies*, edited by Eytan Sheshinski, R. J. Strom, and W. J. Baumol. Princeton, N.J.: Princeton University Press.

The Rise and Fall of Cross-Country Growth Regressions

Steven N. Durlauf

In this article I describe the evolution of the use of cross-country growth regressions in economics over the last two decades. The rise of cross-country growth regressions was an important component of the sea change in economic research associated with the new growth economics. By their fall, I do not mean to suggest that such regressions are no longer used; the opposite is very much the case. Rather, the word *fall* concerns how these regressions have been interpreted in the context of growth theories. Certain forms of these regressions enjoyed a period in which they were taken as the statistical analogs of the law of motion implied by the neoclassical growth model in general and the Solow growth model in particular.[1] Since Robert Solow's original model is most commonly used to justify both the linear structure of cross-country regressions and the forms in which certain core variables appear, it will be my primary focus; Mankiw, Romer, and Weil 1992 continues to be the standard derivation of cross-country

I thank the NSF and the University of Wisconsin Graduate School for financial support and William Brock and Paul Johnson, who have deeply influenced my thinking on growth empirics. I thank Marcel Boumans and participants at the 2008 *HOPE* conference, "Robert Solow and the Development of Growth Economics," as well as two referees for comments on a previous draft.

1. References to the Solow growth model are not meant to slight Trevor Swan's (1956) contribution but to reflect the terminology conventionally used in the empirical growth literature.

History of Political Economy 41 (annual suppl.) DOI 10.1215/00182702-2009-030

growth regressions from Solow dynamics. Remarkably, this specification was commonly used even when the neoclassical model was augmented with growth determinants that Solow's original growth model took as either exogenous (e.g., technical change) or as fixed background variables (e.g., legal institutions). New growth theories have to a large extent been evaluated by adding empirical proxies to a linear regression justified by the dynamics of the Solow model. While the practice of comparing candidate growth determinants via their statistical significance in growth regressions continues, the stronger claims as to the interpretation of these exercises have greatly diminished. I argue that growth regressions are now used to generate a modern form of stylized facts, which provides a parallel to earlier ways in which growth theory and empirics were linked. However, I also argue that the particular stylized facts that have been developed are not ideal in terms of creating a synergy between theory and empirics.

The evolution of the interpretation of cross-country growth regressions is a good example of how theory, econometrics, and empirical practice evolve together. New growth theories stimulated the use of cross-country growth regressions to identify their empirical salience. Growth econometrics evolved as a way to bring theory and empirics closer together, but had the effect of uncovering limits to the theory-empirics relationship; in this sense the ubiquitous identification problem emerged in a growth context. Empirical practice has partially adjusted to the econometric criticisms, but primarily by relaxing the strong claims that were made earlier in the development of growth empirics. My view is that it would be very difficult to argue that this coevolution has been nearly as successful as parallel developments in the study of business cycles, let alone when compared with advances in microeconomics. After discussing the case of growth regressions, I draw some comparisons with business cycle theory and empirics.

Rise

The relationship between the Solow growth model and cross-country regressions was initially quite casual. In a generally neglected paper, Roger Kormendi and Philip Meguire (1985) conduct cross-country regression exercises that are conceptually identical to those that are now conventional; it is difficult to identify any methodological difference between their work and that subsequently found in Barro 1991 as discussed below.[2] (Barro's subsequent writings, e.g., Barro and Sala-i-Martin 1992, are more explicit in linking neoclassical dynamics to a linear regression.) Kormendi and Meguire motivate the inclusion of particular variables in their regression, specifically initial income and population growth, by appealing to "standard neoclassical growth theory" (143) and evidently regard this as sufficiently well known that they do not cite either Solow, Trevor Swan, or optimal growth variations because of David Cass or Tjalling Koopmans. One likely reason why their paper has received so little attention is that its focus is on the growth effects of macroeconomic variables such as the inflation rate. While variables of the type they studied have reemerged in the empirical growth literature (see Durlauf, Johnson, and Temple 2005 for a survey), Kormendi and Meguire were not interested in the neoclassical model per se. For them, the model suggests variables whose omission could have resulted in spurious correlations with respect to those growth determinants in which they were interested.

The seriousness with which the neoclassical growth model was taken as the basis for econometric work profoundly changed with the emergence of endogenous growth theory. Within the new growth economics, the neoclassical model naturally represented a comparison point against which to evaluate theories such as Romer 1986 and Lucas 1988, in which increasing returns to scale imply the possibility of perpetual growth without exogenous technical change. Barro 1991, which arguably launched the industry of identifying variables that explain cross-country growth differences, gave explicit motivation of Barro's exercise to evaluating the convergence property of Solow (and other) growth models. His analysis opens with "in neoclassical growth models such as Solow (1956) . . . a country's per capita income growth rate tends to be inversely related to its starting level of income per person" (Barro 1991, 407). So, while Barro 1991 is no more formal than Kormendi and Meguire 1985 in Barro's derivation of a statistical model corresponding to the neoclassical theory, his analysis

2. Kormendi and Meguire is not cited in either Barro 1991 or Mankiw, Romer, and Weil 1992. My own large-scale surveys on empirical growth research (Durlauf and Quah 1999 and Durlauf, Johnson, and Temple 2005) do cite the paper, but otherwise pay very little attention to it. My conjecture for this neglect is that Kormendi and Meguire's focus was on the role of macroeconomic policies on growth, policies that are generally associated with the business cycle, as opposed to lower-frequency dynamics. Policy variables of this type did subsequently emerge as candidates for growth explanation.

gives primary focus to the empirical implications of the neoclassical model. Barro and subsequent authors have interpreted the finding that the regression coefficient on initial income in these regressions is typically negative as evidence against the Romer and Lucas view.[3] If, ceteris paribus, lower initial income is associated with higher subsequent growth, this relationship implies that contemporaneous income differences are narrowing, a property that is in turn predicted by an aggregate production function in which the marginal product of capital is decreasing. The idea that the marginal product of capital (human or physical) was increasing in its level represents the key conceptual difference between the neoclassical and first-generation endogenous growth theories, as an increasing marginal product can produce growth in initial income differences and thereby capture the increasing international inequality observed since World War II.

The empirical relevance of the Solow model, and the interpretation of cross-country growth regressions as a complete econometric version of the growth dynamics implied by the model, is given its fullest development by N. Gregory Mankiw, David Romer, and David Weil (1992), who open their paper by describing their analysis as the direct legatee of Solow: "This paper takes Robert Solow seriously. . . . This paper argues that the predictions of the Solow model are, to a first approximation, consistent with the evidence" (407). "Our results indicate that the Solow model is consistent with the international evidence if one acknowledges the importance of human as well as physical capital" (423). Their analysis concludes that the Solow model can explain approximately 70 percent of cross-country growth variability from 1950 to 1985 for a large cross-section of countries.

The research program initiated by Barro and Mankiw, Romer, and Weil continues to deeply influence empirical growth research. Steven Durlauf, Paul Johnson, and Jonathan Temple (2005) find that growth regressions have been used to assess over forty distinct growth theories, with over 140 different variable choices to explore these theories. Further, the theoretical implications of the Solow growth model condition how these regressions are constructed. To the extent that an analyst wishes to move beyond the determinants of the Solow model,[4] additional explanatory

---

3. In the growth literature, this negative coefficient property is known as β-convergence. See Durlauf, Johnson, and Temple 2005, 2008 for an overview from statistical and economic perspectives.

regressors are added to those suggested by Solow; the statistical significance of these additional variables is interpreted as affecting the level of technology as occurs in Solow's original framework. Growth regressions of course do not exhaust modern growth empirics; while growth accounting exercises (themselves the product of a fundamental contribution, this time Solow 1957) play an important empirical role in current growth debates, cross-country regression analysis still maintains pride of place in empirical work.

A good example of the extent to which cross-country growth regressions, at their heyday, have been used to make substantive economic claims is the relationship between democracy and growth. Based on the statistical significance (or lack thereof) in a series of cross-country regressions, Barro (1996, 24) has made such general claims as the following:

> The analysis has implications for the desirability of exporting democratic institutions from the advanced developing economies to developing nations. The first lesson is that more democracy is not the key to more economic growth, although it may have a weak positive effect for countries that start with few political rights. The second message is that political freedoms tend to erode over time if they get out of line with a country's standard of living. . . . The more general conclusion is that the advanced western economies would contribute more to the welfare of poor nations by exporting their economic systems, notably property rights and free markets, rather than their political systems, which typically developed after reasonable standards of living had been attained. . . . in the long run, the propagation of Western-style economic systems would also be the effective way to expand democracy in the world.

Barro has made such country-specific claims as the following:

> Thus growth would likely be reduced by further democratization beyond the levels attained in 1994 in countries such as Malaysia and Mexico. Moreover, political liberalization has probably gone beyond the point

---

4. The Solow model implies that cross-country growth differences may be explained via initial income, the population growth rate, the human capital savings rate, and the physical capital savings rate. These are sometimes referred to as the Solow variables. Mankiw, Romer, and Weil (1992) provide specific forms of the variables, when the aggregate production function is Cobb-Douglas. These particular forms have not always been employed in subsequent work.

of growth maximization in places such as Chile, South Korea, and Taiwan. (Barro 1997, 59)

Controversy

In discussing the emergence of criticisms of cross-country growth regressions, I use Solow's view of his model as an organizing framework. Solow ranks among the visible critics of how cross-country growth regressions have been used to make broad substantive claims. As early as 1994, only three years after the publication of the Barro paper and two years after Mankiw, Romer, and Weil, he wrote that

> a particular style of empirical work seems to have sprung from the conjunction of growth theory with the immensely valuable body of comparative national-accounts data compiled by Summers and Heston (1991). It rests on international cross-section regressions with the average growth rates of different countries as the dependent variable and various politico-economic factors on the right-hand side that might easily affect the growth rate if the growth rate were easily affected. I had better admit that I do not find this a confidence-inspiring project. It seems altogether too vulnerable to bias from omitted variables, to reverse causation, and above all to the recurrent suspicion that the experiences of very different national economies are not to be explained as if they represent different "points" on some well-defined surface. . . . The temptation of wishful thinking hovers over the interpretation of these cross-section studies. It should be countered by cheerful skepticism. The wide range of explanatory variables has the advantage of offering partial shelter from the bias due to omitted variables. But this protection is paid for. As the range of explanation broadens, it becomes harder and harder to believe in an underlying structural, reversible relation that amounts to more than a sly way of saying that Japan grew rapidly and the United Kingdom grew more slowly over this or that period. (Solow 1994, 51)

He later remarked,

> I have been skeptical from the beginning about the interpretation of cross-country growth regressions. . . . In my view growth theory was conceived as a model of the growth of an industrial economy. Its parameters certainly could not be regarded as fixed forever, but maybe they would need to be reconsidered only over intervals of 30–50 years. . . .

So far as I remember, I have never applied such a model to a developing economy, because I thought the underlying machinery would apply mainly to a planned economy or a well-developed market economy. This is not a matter of principle, just wariness. (Solow 2001, 283)

Solow's criticisms correspond to three components of the criticisms of cross-country growth regressions:

1. *endogeneity*: the variables in both the neoclassical model and new growth alternatives are themselves endogenous, so that causal claims about determinants are invalid.
2. *model uncertainty*: there is no *a priori* basis for identifying the appropriate set of variables that represent explanations outside of those suggested by the neoclassical model, hence claims about any particular set of growth determinants are based on an ad hoc choice of model.
3. *exchangeability*: different countries do not represent draws from a common growth model, in particular a linear one; heterogeneity in the objects of analysis cannot be reduced to differences in the values of control variables and differences in the realizations of shocks to the growth process.

Each of these criticisms has been developed in detail as the empirical growth literature evolved and has in turn produced a range of responses. Endogeneity has, from the perspective of the literature, received the most attention. Early work, for example, Barro and Lee 1994, treated endogeneity from the perspective of classical simultaneous equations analysis and used lagged dependent variables in panel analogs to the original cross-section data sets; the justification for these types of instruments follows from assumptions about the lag structure of the growth process, which do not possess any economic basis; as such they were naturally susceptible to Christopher Sims's (1980) critique of the arbitrary use of exclusion restrictions to identify business cycle models. This style of analysis was, unsurprisingly in light of the history of simultaneous equations modeling in business cycle macroeconomics, supplanted by efforts to find instrumental variables whose legitimacy may be argued on substantive grounds. This search parallels the popularity of identification of natural experiments in microeconomics, which as shown by James Heckman (1996) is a form of instrumental variables estimation. One famous example is Daron Acemoglu, Simon Johnson, and James Robinson's (2001) use of settler mortality rates as an instrument for the effects of colonial institutions on growth; the idea underlying their empirical analysis is that higher mortality stemmed from exogenous geographic factors, leading to a lower migration from the colonial power to the colony, which in turn reduced the extent to which the colonizers' institutions were transplanted. Another example, from Frankel and Romer 1999, is the use of geographic variables to proxy for economic openness. Here the idea is that differences in geography have exogenously induced variation in the ability of countries to integrate themselves with the rest of the world. Jeffrey Frankel and David Romer claim that these instruments may be used to construct consistent parameter estimates that capture the causal effect of trade on growth.

The issue of model uncertainty, unlike endogeneity, generally has been addressed using relatively powerful econometric methods. Uncertainty about the appropriate set of growth determinants initially led to efforts to identify "robust" growth determinants. An early example comes from Ross Levine and David Renelt (1992), who applied extreme bounds analysis to a wide set of growth variables and concluded that the only robust growth variables were initial income and the share of investment in GDP, with coefficient signs as predicted by the neoclassical model. Modifications of extreme bounds analysis have also appeared, for example, in Sala-i-Martin 1997, which asks whether, across 95 percent of model specifications, a coefficient has the same sign. Neither extreme bounds analysis nor modified approaches have proved that influential in the growth literature. One reason is that the interpretation of the robustness criterion is problematic; the extreme bounds approach corresponds to a minimax decision problem, which is difficult to reconcile with the objectives of a growth exercise; alternatives such as Sala-i-Martin's do not have any decision-theoretic interpretation (Brock and Durlauf 2001). A more popular approach has involved the use of model averaging methods (Fernandez, Ley, and Steel 2001; Sala-i-Martin, Doppelhofer, and Miller 2004; Durlauf, Kourtellos, and Tan 2008). In this approach, the primary alternative involves model selection algorithms (Hoover and Perez 2004; Hendry and Krolzig 2004). Heterogeneity in cross-country experiences has been modeled via nonlinearities (Durlauf and Johnson 1995; Bloom, Canning, and Sevilla 2003) and random coefficients interpreted as realizations from a hyperdistribution (Canova 2004).

Exchangeability has been addressed in a host of ways. The most popular approach has been to allow for fixed effects in a panel growth regression; different countries are allowed to have idiosyncratic growth components, but these are assumed to be invariant across time. An early influential example is Islam 1995. This approach is not particularly in the spirit of Solow's argument, as it essentially assumed that, modulo a constant of proportionality, each country is described by the same aggregate production function. Another approach in ensuring exchangeability involves an explicit allowance for country-specific coefficients. Kevin Lee, M. Hashem Pesaran, and Ron Smith (1997, 1998) do this in the context of a panel analysis that uses one-year time increments (very short by growth analysis standards); Fabio Canova (2004) employs Bayesian methods in a cross section. While these approaches are closer to the spirit of Solow, they raise a conceptual issue that is delineated in an exchange between Lee, Pesaran, and Smith (1998) and Nazrul Islam (1998): at what point does the parameter heterogeneity become the object of interest, rather than the model, per se?

Other work in growth has attempted to treat exchangeability violations through the introduction of nonlinearity into growth regressions. An early example is Durlauf and Johnson (1995), who argued that different regimes exist for the aggregate production function. These regimes are associated with differences in initial income and literacy. This approach is related to work by David Bloom, David Canning, and Jaypee Sevilla (2003), which attempts to uncover the coexistence of multiple growth regimes, one corresponding to a poverty trap, the other to sustained growth. Other authors have focused on linking parameter heterogeneity to nonlinearity by modeling parameters as functions rather than constants. Thanasis Stengos's work is the key example of this strategy and predates subsequent authors who have used similar methods; see Liu and Stengos 1999 and Mamuneas, Savvides, and Stengos 2004. Durlauf, Andros Kourtellos, and Artur Minkin (2001) extend Stengos's thinking to perhaps its logical limit and produce a "local" Solow growth model in which each level of initial income and initial literacy is associated with a distinct aggregate production; to be precise, each of these initial conditions produces a distinct set of Cobb-Douglas production function parameters. Cross-country differences in production functions are implicitly measured by differences in initial conditions.

How can one summarize the state of practice for cross-country growth regressions? With respect to endogeneity, the instrumental variables proposals that have been made are widely used. This is so even though the validity of the instruments suffers from a basic conceptual problem (Brock and Durlauf 2001), namely, there are no good reasons why the instruments are orthogonal to the model errors. This parallels the dispute in the microeconometrics literature about natural experiments; see the debate between Heckman (1997, 1999) and Joshua Angrist and Guido Imbens (1999). For model uncertainty, model averaging techniques have become increasingly popular. As for exchangeability, fixed-effects corrections are ubiquitous for panel data analyses. On the other hand, nonlinear methods have not been widely adopted by empirical growth researchers.

Fall

The various critiques of cross-country growth regressions have perhaps had an influence in that these regressions are in general no longer interpreted in the way done by Mankiw, Romer, and Weil, that is, as a structural econometric analog of the Solow growth model.[5] One sees relatively little contemporary research on β-convergence, especially as a source for resolving the relative merits of the neoclassical and endogenous growth approaches. In contrast, one sees relatively simple growth regressions employed to buttress various substantive economic claims.

A good example of this evolution is the debate between the relative role of institutions (Acemoglu, Johnson, and Robinson 2001; Rodrik, Subramanian, and Trebbi 2004) versus geography (McArthur and Sachs 2001; Sachs 2003) in explaining long-term differences. To focus on one very prominent example, Dani Rodrik, Arvind Subramanian, and Francesco Trebbi (2004) argue in favor of a primary role of institutions as opposed to other fundamental growth factors based on a three-variable regression in which an empirical proxy for institutions "competes" against an empirical proxy for geography and an empirical proxy for the degree of integration with the rest of the world. The Solow variables are in essence ignored, on the basis that they are proximate rather than ultimate causes of growth. While neither side in the debate has explicitly denied that there may be separate roles for geography, integration, and institutions, there is considerable attention given to monocausal explanations. Relative to the work of Barro and Mankiw, Romer, and Weil, the empirical study of "fundamen-

5. My belief that the econometric criticisms of growth regressions have helped deflate the stronger claims on their interpretability is to some extent a conjecture, as it represents my impressions of the growth literature and not a detailed examination of how these criticisms diffused in the literature and across researchers. Another factor in their reduced significance is the rise of microeconomic data sets for developing economies, which has allowed for different ways to evaluate growth factors such as randomized experiments. See Banerjee 2008 for a spirited argument that these types of data analyses trump growth regressions as a methodology.

tal" determinants of growth is a step backward both in terms of the diversity of growth determinants that are considered and in terms of explicit links between a statistical framework and any underlying theoretical model. And it also seems to be a step backward in terms of substantive thinking. More econometrically sophisticated studies such as Bleaney and Nishiyama 2002 find that larger sets of growth determinants outperform smaller subsets of the type used to advocate particular theories; model averaging efforts have not buttressed claims about the importance of the particular theories on which various horse races are based. This is not surprising, since there is no a priori reason to expect cross-country growth behavior differences to reduce to a single major determinant or a very small set of determinants, which is exactly the upshot of advances that have been made in the modern theory.

Back to the Future

Nevertheless, in my judgment, it would be a mistake to dismiss this new, limited use of growth regressions. Cross-country regressions have begun to evolve into a tool for pattern recognition and construction of stylized facts. In considering the debate on the respective importance of institutions and geography, one can conclude that, modulo measures of malaria, it is difficult to identify a marginal value for geographic variables in explaining cross-country growth heterogeneity, whereas one can do so for institutional measures. For the specific context of Acemoglu, Johnson, and Robinson's work, the finding that mortality rates are correlated with growth differences is itself a data pattern of interest and one that theory ought to address.[6] This is a very different approach to empirical work from one in which patterns are used to "prove" that institutions matter.

By moving away from strong claims and focusing on the identification of sturdy empirical growth regularities, cross-country regressions can eventually play the same constructive role that Kaldor's stylized facts did in the neoclassical literature. Solow's original analysis was motivated by the desire to understand major features of long-run growth as experienced by advanced industrial economies, an experience in which growth did not

---

6. Albouy (2008) has questioned the construction of the settler mortality variable and argued that correct construction fails to replicate the initial claims made about its predictive power. This dispute is far from resolved. The dispute illustrates the measurement problem I have emphasized as a limit to empirical progress in growth economics.

produce either permanent mass unemployment or permanent mass labor shortages, as occurred outside knife-edge cases in the Harrod-Domar model.[7] Further, the linkage of the neoclassical model to Kaldor's stylized facts, as done in Solow's 1970 book, provided a range of dimensions along which the model could reasonably be concluded to provide empirical insights.

But unlike Kaldor's stylized facts, current analyses involve questions of statistical significance of regression coefficients as opposed to the identification of interesting empirical regularities.[8] (And here I refer to regularities beyond the brute fact that there is much heterogeneity in international experiences.) While these types of exercises address the fact of heterogeneity in cross-country growth experiences, they do not organize their analyses in ways to understand salient facts such as the discrepancy between sub-Saharan Africa and the rest of the world. Hence, while cross-country growth regressions have moved away from the structural claims of Mankiw, Romer, and Weil, they have yet, I believe, proceeded to explicitly identify regularities of the type that were so important in the development of the neoclassical theory. We simply do not have the equivalent of the Kaldor stylized facts to evaluate alternative growth theories.

This need for stylized facts also applies to policy evaluation; cross-country growth regressions are still used to make policy recommendations. From the perspective of policy-relevant regression analysis, the main need is for stylized facts that link policy heterogeneity and growth heterogeneity, facts that are not contingent on strong prior beliefs about the "true" growth model.[9] This modest view of how empirical research should inform growth policy is consistent with Solow's view on the contribution that theory can make. Solow's views of the policy implications of his model are very modest; his classic 1970 book states,

> Any theory that says something about the real world is likely to have implications for policy. But it is only good sense to realize that an abstract

7. Even here, Solow is remarkably modest; his 1956 paper does not emphasize the empirical salience of his analysis relative to the Harrod-Domar approach.

8. While *interesting* has a subjective component, it is not simply a matter of taste, as arguments can be made based on the current body of economic knowledge as to whether a given fact is or is not interesting; a similar point applies in arguing that one ethical claim is correct versus another (Nagel 1997).

9. Brock, Durlauf, and West (2003) argue that contemporary empirical practice in growth economics, when applied to growth policy, is flawed because it does not respect the decision-theoretic nature of the exercise; some ways to constructively proceed are made.

theory, like the one I have been developing, can only say abstract things about economic policy. At the very beginning, I described the aggregative theory of growth as a parable. You expect a parable to have a moral, but hardly to contain concrete instructions for the conduct of life. So here, when I talk of policy implications, I have to stay roughly at the same level of abstraction as the theory on which they are based. (71)

My conjecture is that stylized facts about the portfolios of policies that are highly correlated with successful growth experiences will prove to be policy relevant. More specific policy conclusions require detailed analysis of the individual country in question.

Conclusions: Parallels with the Evolution of Business Cycle Research

The evolution of empirical growth research, as exemplified in cross-country growth regressions, has interesting parallels with the evolution of business cycle analysis from the 1960s to the rational expectations revolution to contemporary perspectives. One of Solow's (1994, 49) criticisms of modern growth economics is that it takes too extreme a view of theory, particularly when the growth process is interpreted through a representative agent paradigm:

I cannot say the same about the use made of the intertemporally optimizing representative agent. Maybe I reveal myself as old-fashioned, but I see no redeeming value in using this construction, which Ramsey intended as a representation of the decision-making of an idealized policymaker, as if it were a descriptive model of an industrial capitalist economy. It adds little or nothing to the story anyway, while encumbering it with unnecessary implausibilities and complexities.

This criticism by Solow has, to a large extent, been accepted on the empirical side of growth economics, as evidenced by the removal of the neoclassical model from the forefront of cross-country growth analyses. While I believe that there needs to be more work in developing growth regressions as a source of stylized facts and as a source of policy-relevant evidence, it is certainly the case that their links to theory have been attenuated.

Solow has made similar criticisms of the developments in business cycle macroeconomics, as the leading model paradigm of dynamic stochastic general equilibrium models (DSGE) emerged; see Solow 2002 for some of his general views and Hahn and Solow (1995) for a fully delineated alternative to some of what passed at the time for microfoundations. Aspects of this type of criticism have guided developments in macroeconomics over the last decade. At one level, fully rigorous modeling has proved consistent with the incorporation of many of the substantive objections that were raised to the early incarnations of the DSGE. The robustness research program initiated by Lars Hansen and Thomas Sargent (see their 2007 book for a brilliant synthesis) has challenged the rational expectations assumption; the now-standard new Keynesian model includes a range of market frictions that were unheard-of in the early rational expectations literature. Further, macroeconomics has found a useful role for models based on relatively "weak" microfoundations. Much of the modern work on monetary policy evaluation is based on models in which expectations and lagged terms appear, but which are not explicitly generated by individual decision problems. While it is certainly the case that there exist variants of these models with fully delineated microfoundations (exemplified in Woodford's [2003] magisterial development of the new Keynesian model), it is the case that models with weak microfoundations have a current respectability. Yet these efforts to enrich business cycle theory have been consistent with the preservation of much closer links between the theory and empirics than now occurs in growth economics.[10]

Why are there differences between the theory-empirics nexus for business cycle and growth research? Here, I see two distinct reasons. A first reason is theoretical and concerns the open-endedness of growth models that, following Brock and Durlauf 2001, means the mutual compatibility of different growth theories. The research program developed by Lars Hansen, Finn Kydland, Robert Lucas, Edward Prescott, and Sargent on the microfoundations of macroeconomics focused on precisely articulated economic environments. The limitations of these assumptions became the source of the recent developments to which I have referred. It is no exaggeration to say that macroeconomics has progressed in a dialectic fashion; the logic of intertemporal decision making is fully instantiated in the current generation of recent macroeconomic models, as the post-1970 approach insisted on, but the assumptions of complete markets, instanta-

10. Here I am excluding the calibration of growth models from what is meant by empirical work. In my view, calibration is better thought of as a quantitative form of theory. While I believe most calibration advocates would be comfortable with the latter description, many would dispute my claim that calibration analysis is not a form of empirical analysis.

neous price adjustment, and the degree of information available to individual agents as to the correct structure of the economy have all been challenged, as has the ability of a representative agent model to fully capture the sources of aggregate fluctuations. While there is no consensus in macroeconomics with respect to these substantive assumptions, it seems clear that there is less disagreement than there was, say, twenty-five years ago. And I believe that this represents very clear progress in macroeconomic understanding.

The new growth theories, with the important exception of the question of constant versus increasing returns, are based on ideas that are essentially compatible with the substantive economic assumptions of the neoclassical model and with each other. As a result, one does not have the same dialectic process as occurred in the business cycle context. The profusion of new growth theories has in turn produced neither the successful replacement of past theories nor a synthesis across theories. My belief is that the business cycle literature had the critical advantage that the basic issues of contention between schools of thought, be they Keynesian, new Keynesian, new classical, or real business cycle theory, have long been well delineated. The universe of implied assumptions is a relatively well-defined one. As a result, different sets of assumptions are amenable to relatively straightforward empirical assessment. Further, different assumptions are often capable of either synthesis or relaxation. Open-endedness, in contrast, means that growth economics suffers from an abundance of theoretical riches and a shortage of clash between the theories. In light of the desire of the new growth theory to integrate the most and least advanced economies under a common framework, it is unsurprising that so many different theoretical explanations have emerged. In particular, the effort to integrate such disparate societies naturally led to the emergence of growth theories that work on very different time scales; the distinction between fundamental and proximate explanations is perhaps a misnomer, as what distinguishes institutions and savings rates is not that one deserves priority over another but that they move at different frequencies. This expansion of the timescale of admissible explanations itself is a source of open-endedness.

The second reason is empirical: growth theories are not subject to the same degree of critical evaluation as business cycle theories. In the case of business cycle theories, there is general agreement on the objects to be measured as well as (frequently) starkly different implications of theories for data, a classic example of which is the stability of the Phillips curve. In contrast, growth economics faces first-order measurement problems with respect to the candidate theories that are studied. It is one thing to argue that corruption affects growth; it is quite another to identify an appropriate measure of corruption. While the growth literature is replete with clever measures of the broad theories under debate, as well as clever suggestions for instrumental variables to allow for identification of causal effects, one has no consensus on the appropriate objects of study. Further, in the presence of mutually compatible theories as implied by open-endedness, the empirical distinctions between theories are blurred by the multicollinearity of their empirical analogues and the similarity of their empirical implications.

Open-endedness and measurement limitations do not necessarily condemn growth economics to a lack of progress. This is where growth regressions can play a role. By identifying appropriate stylized facts with respect to the heterogeneity of growth experiences, they can provide a basis for theory comparison. The problem with current growth regressions approaches is that while they have appropriately moved away from strong structural claims, they continue to focus on efforts to run horse races between theories, rather than the use of regressions to identify salient and economically significant data patterns. In this instantiation, they have lost what would seem to be a more fundamental objective of empirical work: construction of a baseline set of empirical facts for which growth theories are supposed to provide *understanding*. This interplay occurred over the course of the development of the neoclassical literature. When Solow suggests that the embedding of a growth model in an intertemporally optimizing framework has little value, I believe this is best understood as meaning that there is little gained in terms of understanding cross-country growth differences; the role of increasing returns in generating increasing inequality is qualitatively similar when appended to Solow's model or embedded in a fully developed general equilibrium framework. But this is a statement about the stylized facts that are focused on; a richer set of stylized facts may lead to different conclusions.

Of course, to declare the need for the new growth economics to produce a new set of stylized facts is trivial compared with producing them. Some work, such as Danny Quah's (1996) development of the "twin peaks" description of the cross-country income distribution, has successfully engaged in this task. My hope is that the present article communicates its importance and indicates how cross-country regressions can play a constructive role in growth analysis.

References

Acemoglu, D., S. Johnson, and J. Robinson. 2001. The Colonial Origins of Comparative Development: An Empirical Investigation. *American Economic Review* 91:1369–401.

Albouy, D. 2008. The Colonial Origins of Comparative Development: An Investigation of the Settler Mortality Data. Mimeo, University of Michigan.

Angrist, J., and G. Imbens. 1999. Comment on James J. Heckman, "Instrumental Variables: A Study of the Implicit Behavioral Assumptions Used in Making Program Evaluations." *Journal of Human Resources* 34:823–27.

Banerjee, A. 2008. Big Answers for Big Questions: The Presumption of Macroeconomics. Unpublished manuscript, Brookings Institution.

Barro, R. 1991. Economic Growth in a Cross-Section of Countries. *Quarterly Journal of Economics* 106:407–43.

———. 1996. Democracy and Growth. *Journal of Economic Growth* 1:1–27.

———. 1997. *Determinants of Economic Growth*. Cambridge: MIT Press.

Barro, R., and J.-W. Lee. 1994. Sources of Economic Growth (with commentary). *Carnegie-Rochester Conference Series on Public Policy* 40:1–57.

Barro, R., and X. Sala-i-Martin. 1992. Convergence. *Journal of Political Economy* 100:223–51.

Bleaney, M., and A. Nishiyama. 2002. Explaining Growth: A Contest between Models. *Journal of Economic Growth* 40:43–56.

Bloom, D., D. Canning, and J. Sevilla. 2003. Geography and Poverty Traps. *Journal of Economic Growth* 8:355–78.

Brock, W., and S. Durlauf. 2001. Growth Empirics and Reality. *World Bank Economic Review* 15:229–72.

Brock, W., S. Durlauf, and K. West. 2003. Policy Analysis in Uncertain Economic Environments (with discussion). *Brookings Papers on Economic Activity* 1:235–322.

Canova, F. 2004. Testing for Convergence Clubs in Income Per Capita: A Predictive Density Approach. *International Economic Review* 45:49–77.

Durlauf, S., and P. Johnson. 1995. Multiple Regimes and Cross-Country Growth Behaviour. *Journal of Applied Econometrics* 10.4:365–84.

Durlauf, S., and D. Quah. 1999. The New Empirics of Economic Growth. In *Handbook of Macroeconomics*, edited by J. Taylor and M. Woodford. Amsterdam: North-Holland.

Durlauf, S., P. Johnson, and J. Temple. 2005. Growth Econometrics. In *Handbook of Economic Growth*, edited by P. Aghion and S. Durlauf. Amsterdam: North-Holland.

———. 2008. Convergence. Mimeo.

Durlauf, S., A. Kourtellos, and A. Minkin. 2001. The Local Solow Growth Model. *European Economic Review* 45:928–40.

Durlauf, S., A. Kourtellos, and C. M. Tan. 2008. Are Any Growth Theories Robust? *Economic Journal* 118.527:329–46.

Fernandez, C., E. Ley, and M. Steel. 2001. Model Uncertainty in Cross-Country Growth Regressions. *Journal of Applied Econometrics* 16.5:563–76.

Frankel, J., and D. Romer. 1999. Does Trade Cause Growth? *American Economic Review* 89:379–99.

Hahn, F., and R. Solow. 1995. *A Critical Essay on Modern Macroeconomic Theory.* Cambridge: MIT Press.

Hansen, L., and T. Sargent. 2007. *Robustness.* Princeton, N.J.: Princeton University Press.

Heckman, J. 1996. Randomization as an Instrumental Variable. *Review of Economics and Statistics* 78:336–41.

———. 1997. Instrumental Variables: A Study of the Implicit Behavioral Assumptions Used in Making Program Evaluations. *Journal of Human Resources* 32:441–62.

———. 1999. Instrumental Variables: Response to Angrist and Imbens. *Journal of Human Resources* 34:828–37.

Hendry, D., and H.-M. Krolzig. 2004. We Ran One Regression. *Oxford Bulletin of Economics and Statistics* 66:799–810.

Heston, A., and R. Summers. 1991. The Penn World Table (Mark 5): An Expanded Set of International Comparisons, 1950–1988. *Quarterly Journal of Economics* 106:327–68.

Hoover, K., and S. Perez. 2004. Truth and Robustness in Cross-Country Growth Regressions. *Oxford Bulletin of Economics and Statistics* 66:765–98.

Islam, N. 1995. Growth Empirics: A Panel Data Approach. *Quarterly Journal of Economics* 110:1127–70.

———. 1998. Growth Empirics: A Panel Data Approach—a Reply. *Quarterly Journal of Economics* 113:325–29.

Kormendi, R., and P. Meguire. 1985. Macroeconomic Determinants of Growth: Cross-Country Evidence. *Journal of Monetary Economics* 16:141–63.

Lee, K., M. Pesaran, and R. Smith. 1997. Growth and Convergence in Multi-Country Empirical Stochastic Solow Model. *Journal of Applied Econometrics* 12:357–92.

———. 1998. Growth Empirics: A Panel Data Approach: A Comment. *Quarterly Journal of Economics* 113:319–23.

Levine, R., and D. Renelt. 1992. A Sensitivity Analysis of Cross-Country Growth Regressions. *American Economic Review* 82.4:942–63.

Liu, Z., and T. Stengos. 1999. Non-Linearities in Cross-Country Growth Regressions: A Semiparametric Approach. *Journal of Applied Econometrics* 14:527–38.

Lucas, R. 1988. On the Mechanics of Economic Development. *Journal of Monetary Economics* 22:3–42.

Mamuneas, T., A. Savvides, and T. Stengos. 2004. Economic Development and Return to Human Capital: A Smooth Coefficient Semiparametric Approach. *Journal of Applied Econometrics* 21:111–32.

Mankiw, N. G., D. Romer, and D. Weil. 1992. A Contribution to the Theory of Economic Growth. *Quarterly Journal of Economics* 107:407–37.

McArthur, J., and J. Sachs. 2001. Institutions and Geography: Comment on Acemoglu, Johnson, and Robinson. NBER Working Paper no. 8114.

Nagel, T. 1997. *The Last Word*. Oxford: Oxford University Press.

Quah, D. 1996. Twin Peaks: Growth and Convergence in Models of Distribution Dynamics. *Economic Journal* 106:1045–55.

Rodrik, D., A. Subramanian, and F. Trebbi. 2004. Institutions Rule: The Primacy of Institutions over Geography, and Integration in Economic Development. *Journal of Economic Growth* 9:131–65.

Romer, P. 1986. Increasing Returns and Long-Run Growth. *Journal of Political Economy* 94:1002–37.

Sachs, J. 2003. Institutions Don't Rule: Direct Effects of Geography on Per Capita Income. NBER Working Paper no. 9490.

Sala-i-Martin, X. 1997. I Just Ran Two Million Regressions. *American Economic Review* 87:178–83.

Sala-i-Martin, X., G. Doppelhofer, and R. Miller. 2004. Determinants of Long-Term Growth: A Bayesian Averaging of Classical Estimates (BACE) Approach. *American Economic Review* 94:813–35.

Sims, C. 1980. Macroeconomics and Reality. *Econometrica* 48:1–48.

Solow, R. 1956. A Contribution to the Theory of Economic Growth. *Quarterly Journal of Economics* 70:65–84.

———. 1957. Technical Change and the Aggregate Production Function. *Review of Economics and Statistics* 39:312–20.

———. 1970. *Growth Theory: An Exposition*. Oxford: Oxford University Press.

———. 1994. Perspectives on Growth Theory. *Journal of Economic Perspectives* 8:45–54.

———. 2001. Applying Growth Theory across Countries. *World Bank Economic Review* 15:283–88.

———. 2002. Interview. *Federal Reserve Bank of Minneapolis Bulletin*, September, 24–34.

Swan, T. 1956. Economic Growth and Capital Accumulation. *Economic Record* 32:334–61.

Woodford, M. 2003. *Interest and Prices*. Princeton, N.J.: Princeton University Press.

The Solow Residual as a Black Box: Attempts at Integrating Business Cycle and Growth Theories

Tiago Mata and Francisco Louçã

The intersection between growth and business cycle theory remains a controversial subject in economics. The question posed by this article is, What role did Robert Solow's "Technical Change and the Aggregate Production Function" (1957) play in recent attempts to integrate business cycle and growth theory? We argue that the "Solow residual" was a resource given to multiple uses, at times rhetorical and symbolic, at times instrumental for theory development, at others a social artifact.

The Solow residual is herein conceived as an object. We examine the history of fluctuations in growth theory in a narrative of model building, of the addition and subtraction of elements to models. Our views are informed by the concept of the black box associated with the work of Bruno Latour and colleagues (Latour 1987; Latour and Woolgar 1979). Their notion is that theoretical and experimental artifacts can attain a status of consensual acceptance that exempts them from close examination. It is in this sense that they are said to be "closed."[1]

Our use of the term *black box* is felicitous for another reason. The term has an established lineage in controversies over the role of innova-

We are indebted to the participants at the 2008 *HOPE* conference for their insightful commentary on this article. Lionello Punzo, Marcel Boumans, Nicholas Crafts, Michel De Vroey, and David Warsh were generous in offering suggestions and corrections both during and after the meetings. We also thank two anonymous referees who gave a careful and thoughtful reading of this article. Tiago Mata has benefited for the writing of this article from a postdoctoral fellowship (SFRH/BPD/30403/2006) from the Fundação para a Ciência e Tecnologia, Portugal.

1. For a test of Latour's semiotics, see Yuval Yonay's (1994) study of institutional economics.

History of Political Economy 41 (annual suppl.) DOI 10.1215/00182702-2009-031

tion in economic growth. We agree with Nathan Rosenberg's (1982) judgment that "economists have long treated technological phenomena as events transpiring inside a black box. . . . [and] adhered rather strictly to a self-imposed ordinance not to inquire too seriously into what transpires inside that box." Our story, which begins in 1982, at the time of Rosenberg's book, suggests that the box, when opened, became a source of multiple puzzles. But before we consider the uses given to the object, we have to observe how neoclassical growth theory canonized the Solow residual.

Solow's Residual and Growth's Black Box

The influence of Solow's "Technical Change and the Aggregate Production Function" cannot be overemphasized. The piece followed closely the publication of Solow's (1956) celebrated growth model and was intended as a contribution to the literature on growth.[2] Its startling conclusion was that "gross output per man hour doubled over the interval [1909–49], with 87 $\frac{1}{2}$ per cent of the increase attributable to technical change and the remaining 12 $\frac{1}{2}$ per cent to increased use of capital." Solow humbly acknowledged that the result lacked great depth or insight. He noted soon after that

> in every-day speech, talk of technological change calls to mind primarily single discontinuous inventions, like the electric light or the automobile or the electronic computer. . . . But most of this flavor disappears in statistical aggregates.
>
> Economists, who give the impression of having invented the idea of technological progress in the past 6 or 7 years, have something much more pedestrian in mind, . . . "increase in output per unit of input." It is a statistical artifact. (Solow 1963, 37)

It was immediately understood that such a large proportion of growth left unaccounted for by the factors of production was a problematic result. Frank Hahn and R. C. Matthews (1964, 832), in their "monumental" 120-page survey of growth theory, noted that "those who used the 'residual' approach were well aware that the residual, as its name implies, is a catch-all and that in practice the task of research would be to break it up into its constituent components."

---

2. For a survey of what was in the 1950s and 1960s a vibrant field of econometric study, see Walters 1963.

The field of growth accounting blossomed in the 1960s, particularly following the lead of Edward Denison (1962, 1979, 1985; Denison and Brookings Institution 1967, 1974). As Nicholas Crafts (this volume) establishes in his survey, the residual resisted the multiple accounting models. As Christopher Freeman (1988, 2) graphically put it: "The various 'growth accounting' exercises, even after allowing for an entire Kamasutra of variables, generally remain with a big unexplained 'residual' and fail to deal with the complementarities and interactions of these variables." Denison (1967, 283) was aware of the difficult interpretation of the residuals, which include "contributions of advances in the lag of average practice behind the best known but also the net effect of errors in the growth rates themselves, of errors in estimates of the contributions made by other sources of growth, and of omission of all sources not specifically estimated."

Alongside the accounting exercises, in theory development, Solow's contribution brought into focus the need to formalize "innovations" (Burmeister and Dobell 1970). Solow's own views on the multiple formulations of the aggregate production function leaned toward labor-augmenting technological progress and capital "vintages" with differing productivities. Yet, despite the insight afforded by these developments, the dynamic rested in the technology component represented by the residual, "to change the rate of growth of real output per head you have to change the rate of technological progress." Significantly, such improvements stood largely outside the model's explanatory purview, as follows from the statement that policy measures "involve considerations quite outside the model we have been discussing" (Solow 1970, 77).

The residual's resilience led to comfort in the belief that "innovation" was an indistinct and impenetrable stream whose source was in the domain of other branches of economics. The Solow residual was a statistical artifact, yet it seemed to decide on the division of labor between growth and other theoretical quarters. This occurred despite Solow's (1985) misgivings about sharply drawn divisions of labor or dogmatic acceptance of neoclassical theory. Solow's work had gained a life of its own in the research of other authors and was autonomous of his intentions or interpretations.[3]

---

3. Coupled with the subject of innovation was uncertainty. It was a difficulty that growth theory could not face and should hence ignore (Solow 1963, 15). Solow's deterministic standpoint remained unchanged, when two decades on, Solow wrote to Frank Hahn: "Regarding . . . fluctuations, Schumpeterian innovations, and all that. I find myself driven to the uncomfortable view that probability is not the right way to handle such things as innovations or other real shocks. . . . Last thing in the world I want to spend time on is axiomatizing Knightian uncertainty. Maybe some ad-hoc device to get away from simple-minded mean-value thinking. Maybe better to dodge the whole thing" (Solow 1984).

Shocks and Business Cycle's Black Box

In separate quarters Robert Lucas and his coauthors were championing in the 1970s a new approach to macroeconomics.[4] It was a model-building approach, where

> a "theory" is not a collection of assertions about the behavior of the actual economy but rather an explicit set of instructions for building a parallel or analogue system—a mechanical, imitation economy. A "good" model, from this point of view, will not be exactly more "real" than a poor one, but will provide better imitations. (Lucas 1980, 697)

The early literature commenting on new classical macroeconomics has emphasized the rational expectations hypothesis (Kantor 1979; Laidler 1981; Tobin 1981; Begg 1982; Blaug 1980; Sheffrin 1983),[5] but to Lucas the discriminating feature of his models was a new notion of equilibrium. Models were "constructed so as to predict how agents with stable tastes and technology will *choose* to respond to a new situation" (Lucas 1977, 12; emphasis in original). Lucas and Sargent (1979, 7) attributed earlier notions of equilibrium to a distant legacy of John Maynard Keynes and his *General Theory*, stating that "the term equilibrium was thought to refer to a system at rest," but "the meaning of the term equilibrium has changed so dramatically that a theorist of the 1930s would not recognize it. An economy following a multivariate stochastic process is now routinely described as being in equilibrium, by which is meant nothing more than that at each point in time" that markets clear and agents act in their own self-interest.[6]

Influential papers by Lucas (1972, 1975) embodied this program. Lucas's models describe a stationary process around a deterministic time trend representing a "natural rate of growth," whereas serially correlated variations of the levels of the economy motivated by exogenous random shocks create the cycles. The solution for the whole economy indicates the properties of the cyclical component, as agents confound variations

---

4. This work had its predecessors, most notably Milton Friedman. The terms of this monetarist ancestry are controversial; see Hoover 1988 for a review of that debate and Kim 1988 for an account of Austrian threads.

5. For a critical examination of rational expectations complex history, see Sent 1998.

6. Lucas's caricature of Keynes is not historically accurate. For Keynes equilibrium arose from the matching of individual plans of saving, hoarding, and investment. It is a rather more dynamic story than Lucas portrays. On the history of equilibrium notions in economics, see Weintraub 1991. Lucas (2004) has recently suggested that his background had a great deal more Keynesianism than he avowed in print in the 1970s. For a critical assessment of Lucas's education, see Louçã 2004.

of relative and general price levels (Dore 1993, 68, 75). The economic intuition is that agents confound unanticipated monetary shocks, with no real effects, with shocks in relative prices, implying substitution effects. The exogenous shocks have no permanent influence on the behavior of the system.

The seminal and canonical paper on real business cycles is Finn Kydland and Edward C. Prescott's "Time to Build and Aggregate Fluctuations" (1982).[7] The authors' stated purpose was to "integrate growth and business cycle theory," conceiving real shocks as their distinction from Lucas's business cycle models. As they later stated, "Economic activity in industrial market economies is characterized by sustained growth. Lucas defines business cycles as deviations of real GNP from trend. . . . But Lucas does not define trend, so his definition of business cycle deviation is incomplete" (Kydland and Prescott 1990, 6). Kydland and Prescott's (1982) "time-to-build" production function was composed of a persistent and a transitory element, interpreted as a technological shock.[8] Production was explicitly modeled with agents not only optimizing the investment-consumption decision but also allocating time between employment and leisure.[9]

7. In a bibliometric study of the most-cited academic articles post-1970, Kydland and Prescott 1982 was ranked sixty-first, being cited 814 times (Kim, Morse, and Zingales 2006). In 1972, William Brock and Leonard Mirman published in the *Journal of Economic Theory* a paper presenting a basic model of growth of a single sector with stochastic impulses to the production function, and established the proof of ergodicity required for time series econometrics. Real business cycle theorists do not ignore this work. But references are sparse, centered on the peculiar contribution of the ergodicity proof and not recognizing the core idea that was present in the 1972 paper and that anticipated the strategy of real business cycle models (Prescott 1986b; Plosser 1989). It is only in a footnote that Rodolfo Manuelli (1986, 3) notices that the model was the first to use stochastic shocks in the production function. In private correspondence with one of the authors, Brock argued for a very open modeling strategy. According to his view, the way forward should be based on an experimental recipe starting with Frank Ramsey and adding stochastic shocks for uncertainty (as in Brock and Mirman 1972), disutility of labor in the production function, money, sticky price vectors, and eventually some market failures. This unorthodox outlook on orthodoxy may explain why Brock and Mirman were denied progeny of real business cycle modeling.

8. A 1980 paper had speculated on the introduction of preference shocks alongside productivity ones, but the new version collapsed the former (Kydland and Prescott 1980).

9. There were four potential sources of persistence in the Kydland-Prescott model: autocorrelation of the exogenous technological shocks, time-dependent individual preferences, inventories as factors of production, and the "time-to-build" production function. K. Geert Rouwenhorst (1991) has argued that the "time-to-build" production function is insufficient to produce the cyclical behavior; for this the autocorrelation of exogenous shocks is required.

John Long and Charles Plosser (1983) gave the new class of models the label of "Real Business cycles."[10] Following work by Charles Nelson and Plosser (1982), they proposed a Cobb-Douglas production function with a single stochastic component, undermining the notion of a deterministic trend and replacing it by a nonstationary stochastic process with no tendency to return to a deterministic path.[11] The Long and Plosser model relaxed the assumption of the autocorrelation of shocks. Defining an input-output structure they examined the propagation of a shock and an individual's smoothing of windfall capital gains. They later realized that serial correlation was critical to produce fluctuations (King, Plosser, and Rebelo 1988). It is significant that the Long and Plosser piece was never as influential as the Kydland and Prescott model. Although the authors simulated the time paths of their model economy to reveal cycle-like movements, this result did not seek to match the economic record. The model was illustrative but unpersuasive in the new classical sense of providing an "imitation" of the real economy.

The real business cycle models developed from Lucas's program.[12] They assumed calibration in the place of econometric estimation, Kydland and Prescott (1982) comparing the time paths of their simulations with quarterly data for the U.S. postwar economy.[13] Puzzle solving was focused on tweaking the models' specifications to replicate the autocorrelation and comovements in U.S. time-series data.[14] The sources of fluctuations were not misperceptions but objective changes in the aggregate productivity function. The dynamic stochastic behavior of the model-worlds

10. Long and Plosser cite the working-paper version of Kydland and Prescott 1982, but their paper did not originate as a refinement of that model. In a personal communication of January 2008 to the authors, Plosser recalled that their paper was well underway before they saw the Kydland-Prescott one, adding, "We were intentionally trying to build a real model of fluctuations using growth theory. I think KP backed into that conclusion. Thus it is fair to say the papers were developed independently at about the same time."

11. The stochastic trend approach was further developed by James Stock and Mark Watson (1988a, 1988b), who hypothesize that variations in trends are responsible for an important part of the fluctuation of output in U.S. series. So did Stephen Beveridge and Nelson (1981) and Nelson and Plosser (1982), stating that business cycles can be defined as adjustments to changes in the growth paths.

12. Besides the intellectual kinship there is also a social connect. Lucas and Prescott met at Carnegie Mellon in the late 1960s and continued to collaborate for over two decades, well into Prescott's real business cycle years (Lucas and Prescott 1971, 1974; Prescott and Lucas 1972; Stokey, Lucas, and Prescott 1989). Arjo Klamer's (1984, 32–33) interview with Lucas captures this bond of friendship.

13. The calibration approach is not the only one available to the new classicals; see Cooley 1997. For an opposing view on the promise of calibration, see Hoover 1995.

14. For sympathetic surveys, see King and Rebelo 1999 and Rebelo 2005.

emerged out of microeconomic principles of maximization and out of a situation in which all markets are permanently cleared.

Lucas (1987, 46–47) was supportive of the new generation, in 1987 calling Kydland and Prescott's work the "current frontier in business cycle research" and adding that they offer "a formulation that combines intelligible general equilibrium theory with an operational, empirical seriousness. . . . I would like to call this progress."[15] Lucas was critical to the extent that the "model focuses exclusively on real (as opposed to monetary) neoclassical considerations, which I think is a mistake."[16]

By locating the emergence of real business cycle models in the context of new classical macroeconomics, we aim to show its genetic distance from growth theory. Solow 1957 was not mentioned in the two seminal pieces of real business cycle models (Kydland and Prescott 1982; Long and Plosser 1983). Solow was on record as quite dismissive of the new classical enterprise. In his presidential lecture to the American Economic Association, he portrayed the equilibrium outlook as unreasonable, saying it is "legitimate to wonder why the unemployed do not feel themselves to be engaged in voluntary intertemporal substitution, and why they queue up in such numbers when legitimate jobs of their usual kind are offered during a recession" (Solow 1980, 7).

Solow was not engaged by the enterprise, but that did not mean that his work was not influential. Although real business cycle models emerged from the new classical program, its adoption of the neoclassical production function borrowed from Solow. The goal was to integrate business cycle and growth, a prospect that Solow (1982) shared. Solow and the new classicals concurred that the "technology" component of the production function was its dynamic and independent element.

The Black Box Challenged

The notion of shock entered the discourse on the growing economy in the 1980s. Later in the decade, real business cycle theory's attempts to straddle growth and fluctuations became an item of controversy.[17] Our aim in

---

15. Lucas's assessment is not surprising given the close kinship between his models and Kydland and Prescott's work. The propagation side of their models is very similar; it is in the impulse element that they differ. See Lucas 1977.

16. See also the updated but largely unchanged commentary in Lucas 2007.

17. Reviewing real business cycle theory, Victor Zarnowitz (1985) did not think much of Kydland and Prescott's work.

this section is to highlight how the interpretation of the Solow residual became a crucial item of that debate.

The opening salvo of the controversy was fired by Prescott at a Carnegie-Rochester Conference on Public Policy in 1985, with an essay titled "Theory Ahead of Business Cycle Measurement" (Prescott 1986b), in which he offered an updated version of his 1982 model with Kydland. While Kydland and Prescott (1982) had studied variance and correlation for the output of different sectors of the economy, the new empirical target was to simulate the dynamics for the American economy post–Korean War for such aggregate variables as investment, inventory stock, capital stock, consumption, hours of work, productivity, and real interest rate. Prescott judged a satisfactory match between his simulation and the record, but he found discrepancies in labor's sensitivity to changes in output, the recorded elasticity being well below the model's solution. Prescott considered the mismatch to be due to empirical measurement lagging behind theory development.[18]

Contemporaneously, at a National Bureau of Economic Research (NBER) conference in March 1986 in Cambridge, Massachusetts, Martin Eichenbaum and Kenneth Singleton (1986) offered an assessment of monetary shocks (changes to M1) to explain variance of aggregate output. They concluded that monetary shocks had an insignificant causal power, which led them by default to endorse an explanation through real shocks. Real business cycle models were supplanting Lucas's money models. At this triumphant stage, Solow's work receives mention. Prescott (1986b) credited Solow and Trevor Swan as the originators of growth theory from which he claimed business cycle theory partly derived. But more salient than ancestor worship was Prescott's use of Solow's (1957) method to

18. It should interest the historian that Prescott had in mind a parallel between contemporary debates and the famous "measurement without theory controversy" between the Cowles Commission and the NBER. In a 1990 paper, where Kydland and Prescott examined the ancestry of their program—Mitchell, Frisch, Slutsky, and Lucas—they endorsed Tjalling Koopmans's (1947) critique of Burns and Mitchell 1946: a theory is needed before variables are selected. Yet, following Lucas's critique, they disagreed with Koopmans's use of structural systems of equations, considering that imposing such a straitjacket was a "grave disservice" (Kydland and Prescott 1990, 4). Prescott may have been primed toward the "measurement without theory" debates by the April 1985 Carnegie-Rochester conference where Salih Neftci gave a paper on the NBER's method of fluctuation analysis. The series editors read it as "the first serious reconsideration of Tjalling Koopmans's judgment, advanced more than 30 years ago, that the National Bureau methodology indulges in 'measurement without theory'" (Brunner and Meltzer 1986, 2).

obtain a measurement of technology.[19] Prescott concluded that economic fluctuations were optimal responses to uncertainty. Policy should be devoted to the institutional study of technology and an increase of its rate of change, in effect a proposition that echoed Solow's 1970 lectures. The policy brief of 1980s business cycle theory was aligned with that of 1960s neoclassical growth theory.

It was Lawrence Summers, speaking to the NBER Economic Fluctuations Group, who engaged with Prescott's overview (Summers 1986). Summers's list of objections sought to turn Prescott's paper on its head: "Theory was ahead of measurement" because theory had been constructed with unobservables that forever eluded definitive study. Not all of Summers's objections are of interest to our argument. The second objection, "Where are the shocks?" zoomed in on Prescott's interpretation of changes in total factor productivity as technological shocks albeit with a small measurement error. Summers asked for historical examples to assert the validity of this hypothesis and offered an alternative interpretation where changes in the Solow residual reflected businesses hoarding labor in response to economic downturns.

Both Prescott's and Summers's articles were published as a debate in the *Quarterly Review* of the Federal Reserve Bank of Minneapolis, and Prescott (1986a) was given the chance to reply to Summers. To the charge that no technological shocks were discernable in the historical record, Prescott called on Eugen Slutsky's finding that "some stable low-order linear stochastic difference equations have been known to generate cycles. They do not have a few large shocks, they have small shocks, one every period." Stating that economists lacked a theory of technological change, Prescott called on Solow 1957 to argue that given the "finding that more than 75 percent of the changes in per capital output are accounted for by changes in the technology parameter, the evidence for variation in the rate of technological change is strong." Summers's argument of labor hoarding was classed as a measurement problem in the labor component of the production function, distinct from the measurement of technology. Solow's authoritative findings were at this point a rhetorical resource in defense of real business cycle models (Hartley 2006).

19. The following year, 1987, Solow was awarded the Nobel Prize for economics. Alongside a paper by R. C. O. Matthews reviewing the laureate's contributions, Prescott wrote in the *Scandinavian Journal of Economics*, restating his 1986 findings. He reasserted that he had "challenged the widely held view that variations in the Solow technological parameter are too small to account for a significant amount of business cycle fluctuations" (Prescott 1988, 10).

The debate remained unsettled, since in 1989 the same arguments were repeated with a new cast of protagonists in the pages of the *Journal of Economic Perspectives*. Plosser was cast as defender of real business cycle theory. Mentioning Solow twice in his argument, Plosser refers to Solow 1957 as a piece of empirical research revealing that "changes in productivity and technology are the major factors determining economic growth." Further, "a crude but straightforward method [of obtaining some measure of the productivity shocks] is to follow the example provided by Solow" (Plosser 1989, 58).

Reprising Summers's criticisms, Gregory Mankiw reestimated the Solow residual to highlight substantial yearly variation. He clarified that "if the Solow residual is a valid measure of the change in the available production technology, then recessions are periods of technological regress" (Mankiw 1989, 84). Mankiw thus argued that for the 1982 recession there had been no reduction in the residual, contradicting the real business cycle argument. To counter the implausible interpretation, he proposed that cyclical changes in the Solow residual reflected firms' decisions to hold on to unnecessary and underutilized labor.

The interpretation of the Solow residual was center stage.[20] What is striking is that the Solow residual remained stable to a degree, as an object. In figure 1 there are two representations of the Solow residual. The numerical values were the same for both authors and were not in dispute. It is their readings that differed. Plosser (panel A) framed the residuals alone and hence interpreted a fluctuating time series of irregular interval, suggestive of a random walk. Mankiw, on the other hand, provided a greater time range, a much more cluttered and erratic depiction. Critically, Mankiw plotted the residuals (panel B) against the income series to stake the claim that the residual was quite literally a leftover. It was not the residual that was controversial but what it meant, or, in Mankiw's terms, which was the "more appealing interpretation"?

The differing interpretations of the Solow residual were not alone in demarcating the two perspectives. Probably more significant was the New Keynesians' disbelief in the automatic full employment of the Walrasian real business cycle models. Further, the latter reserved a role for monetary

---

20. Our side-by-side report of this set of controversies highlights a striking, if habitual, divide in American economics. In effect, this was another installment of the "saltwater vs. freshwater" controversy. Mankiw (1986, 139) made it quite explicit: "Real business cycle theory is one of the currently 'hot' topics in macroeconomics, especially among those who live closer to lakes than to oceans."

A *Figure 1*
Annual Growth Rate of Technology

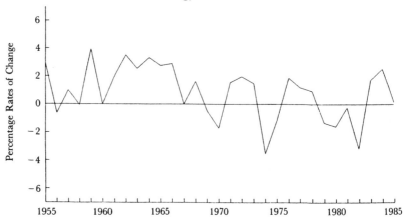

B *Figure 1*
Solow Residuals and Output Growth

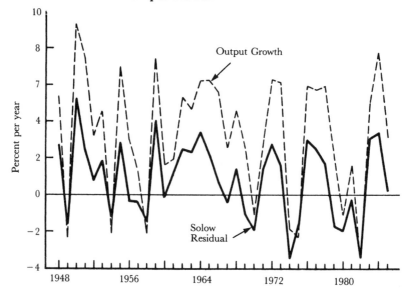

Figure 1 Plosser's (panel A) and Mankiw's (panel B) representations of the Solow residual. From Plosser 1989 and Mankiw 1989.

policy that was seemingly forbidden by the "real" emphasis of their opponents' models. Ironically, the Solow residual was not what set them apart, but what they shared. It was a convenient subject of their discussion because it was an object that stood at the boundary between the two communities.[21]

Opening the Box

As the Solow residual became a focus of debate, it moved from being a rhetorical and symbolic object to become a research puzzle. It is in relation to the opening of this black box that we can envisage the landscape of models.

Contemporaneously to the business cycle debates, the subject of neoclassical growth theory witnessed a resurgence of interest. This was largely due to the work of two Chicago men: Paul Romer and Lucas.[22] In the 1985 Marshall Lectures at Cambridge University, Lucas (1988) toyed with models of growth in which infinitely living families accumulated human capital. Further, human capital was formalized to have a spillover effect on the production function. Hence, while individual economic units faced constant returns to scale, the economy had increasing returns. Such work reinterpreted the Solow "technology" residual as disembodied human capital, a sediment of collective human capital. The more significant attack on growth theory was that of Romer (1986). He too sought to ban exogenous technological change from his competitive model. He specified a production function for technology production whose goods were in some measure nonexcludable, hence creating a positive externality. And although the production function of technology faced decreasing returns, output production had increasing returns.

The initial response of real business cycle theorists to the new classical versus New Keynesian controversy was tame. Real business cycle theorists met in June 1986 at the Portuguese Catholic University to discuss the state of their research program.[23] Kydland and Prescott (1988) reconfigured their model to allow capital utilization to vary, hence separating the service of capital from its stock measurement. The volatility of their model

21. The notion of "boundary object" connecting scientific communities is well established in the social study of science (Star and Griesemer 1989).

22. For a history of events, characters, and the economics of Paul Romer, see Warsh 2006.

23. The papers were only published in 1988 and substantially updated with the latest literature.

increased, although the nagging discrepancy between model and measured labor-output elasticity remained. Prescott (1988, 2006) never conceded to his critics that the real business cycle explanation required revision; he has consistently described the debate as settled to his advantage. In his Nobel lecture, Prescott dubbed his contribution part of a "revolution" that reunited macroeconomics with neoclassical economics. He took his 1986 findings that total factor productivity "shocks are the major contributor to fluctuations" to be "highly robust," lining up models akin to his as evidence (Prescott 2006, 11). Still, he was left to uncomfortably argue for the magic number of labor supply elasticity equals 3. Definitive proof hung on that proposition.[24]

Despite statements otherwise, Prescott has struggled with explaining the Great Depression (De Vroey and Pensieroso 2006). Following Cole and Ohanian (1999), Prescott separates the 1929–33 from the post-1933 period. While changes in total factor productivity may partly account for the 1929–33 downswing, they are unable to account for the American economy's failure to return to trend growth. Prescott (1999, 26) considered that, "given the considerable evidence against technology, monetary, or banking explanations, I am led . . . to the view that there must have been a fundamental [New Deal] change in labor market institutions and industrial policies that lowered steady-state, or normal, market hours." This result has been heralded as a "novel fact" given by theoretical investigation (Kehoe and Prescott 2002), but it hides an inability of the real business cycle models to provide plausible explanations of the economic historical record.

Prescott also developed a telling interest in the work initiated by Lucas and Romer. With a former graduate student, Stephen Parente, Prescott began by establishing the "development facts" models ought to emulate (Parente and Prescott 1993). They then designed a model of national technology adoption from an ever-increasing stock of world technology (Parente and Prescott 1994). Differences in relative income shares between nations were explained by an unobservable "technological capital" parameter that was deemed embodied in the firm but invisible to the aggregate data. The authors introduced a term of "cost of technology adoption" that did most of the explanatory work. Looking at the data for Japan, they concluded that "Japan was converging to some balanced growth path and in

---

24. Prescott's reliance on the high elasticity of labor has informed his examination of why Americans' working hours differ so widely from European ones (Prescott 2004). This has sparked an independent controversy that rages on; see Faggio and Nickell 2007.

1974 there was *regime change*, that is, a persistent and unanticipated change in the magnitude of the technology adoption barrier parameter" (Parente and Prescott 1994, 310). Hence the noisy flow of technology produced cycles, and it was the institutional interruption of its flow that set growth paths.

The Plosser branch of the real business cycle research program was more adventurous in rebuilding their models. To the 1986 conference, they restated their collapse of the trend-cycle distinction and with it the emergence of stochastic growth. They used the Lucas formulation to endogenize labor-augmenting technical progress. After Lucas's growth model had reinterpreted the "residual" as a social spillover from learning and human capital accumulation, one could hardly conceive of shocks originating out of this steady accumulation. Instead, the impulse was located in an equally mysterious and exogenous technology component in the production of human capital. It was a new black box within the old black box. Still, the move was not inconsequential. They found that "temporary disturbances to production possibilities . . . have permanent effects on the levels of economic activity, because they permit temporary changes in the amount of resources allocated to growth. Thus, endogenous growth models generate integrated time series, even when the underlying shocks are stationary" (King, Plosser, and Rebelo 1988b, 325).

An idiosyncratic strategy in real business cycle models is to embrace the ambiguity of the Solow residual. In a recent paper, Costas Azariadis and Leo Kaas (2007) propose, in the spirit of Prescott's Nobel lecture, that dynamic general equilibrium is a "theory of everything." In their grand scheme the Solow residual becomes an index that "conveys information not just about the aggregate technology frontier but also *how far inside* that frontier the economy operates." It is said to depend on "sectoral productivities; on financial variables like debt-equity ratios, interest rates, and the distribution of equity positions, and on institutional variables like property rights of lenders" and hence wealth distribution (Azariadis and Kaas 2007, 38).

Summers's and Mankiw's interpretation of the Solow residual as permeable to labor hoarding, and hence a poor measure of technological change, was substantively restated by Robert Hall (1986, 1990).[25] Hall argued that

---

25. The new classical response to Hall was given by Matthew Shapiro (1987), comparing output and factor price measures of productivity. He interpreted the null result of no differences between the two as proof that variation in output productivity (Solow residual) was not explained by changes to demand.

yearly movements in the Solow residual may potentially reflect market power, increasing returns, external technical complementarities, chronic excess capacity, unmeasured variations in work effort and hours, errors in measuring capital or output, and monopsony power in the labor market. He then added that the residual would not be sensitive to overhead labor or labor hoarding, wage smoothing, adjustment costs, or price rigidities.[26]

The New Keynesian models of the cycle have distinguished themselves for an emphasis on time and sector rigidities in the determination of wage contracts, prices, and investment plans (see Mankiw and Romer 1991). There is no class of New Keynesian growth models, but a strand in endogenous growth models bears some kinship.[27] Peter Howitt (1986) has interpreted the core of Keynes's message as revealing the prevalence of intertemporal coordination problems. Philippe Aghion and Howitt's research has sought to wire the New Keynesian adjustment processes with Schumpeterian insights for a study of long-run growth (Howitt 1994). This they accomplished in two papers in the early 1990s, one focusing explicitly on the concerns of the growth debate, the other on matters of unemployment (Aghion and Howitt 1992, 1994). Their highlight is that technology is disruptive: it renders old capital obsolete, leading to a destruction of jobs. Unemployment is "job search," as the adjustment process endemic to a changing economy. The connection between this proposal and the subject of the Solow residual and growth accounting was recently made explicit. Aghion and Howitt (2007) offer a hybrid neoclassical model with endogenous growth. The innovation dynamic is restated as an uncertain investment that is a function of the capital stock. The relationships between the factors and technology become more deeply entangled.

Conclusion

On the history of models that bring growth and fluctuation into a single frame, we have focused on the uses and meanings of a particularly prominent object: the Solow residual. The significance of Solow's 1957 work arose

26. James Hartley (2000) offers a microfoundations model that excludes the possibility of an aggregate production function. Under these conditions changes in technology will not register in the Solow residual.

27. This occurs despite the all-pervasive discredit of the trend-cum-cycle distinction. Following Nelson and Plosser 1982, Campbell and Mankiw (1987) have found that "innovations" were highly persistent in both U.S. quarterly postwar data and annual data from 1896 to 1984. Research by Shapiro and Mark Watson (1988) and King et al. (1991) have studied the contribution of changes in productivity to U.S. income data modeled as a stochastic trend: the first found its impact to be about one-third, the latter found it to be roughly two-fifths.

from having stabilized a method and result, the residual as reproducible object, a black box. This object was shown to traffic liberally across doctrinal divides in economics. Once on offer, the black box had a life of its own. Its relation to the original context and to the intentions and beliefs of its originator was severed. So while Denison used the residual in ways that were surely faithful to Solow, the new classicals employed it in ways that seemed counter to Solow's outlook. While the residual had always remained a problematic result in growth accounting, its borrowing by real business cycle theorists sought to establish it as a definitive representation of technology. Furthermore, in these models it was a short-run and stochastic technology, a novel and surprising interpretation.

As the claims of the new classicals came under scrutiny, so did the status and meaning of the object residual. The challenge by New Keynesians brought attention to it. The integration of growth and cycle has been shaped by the opening of this black box. Prescott has remained committed to his earlier interpretation of the Solow residual as stochastic technology. Others have sought to blanket a variety of supply shocks under the cover of the residual, abandoning attempts to decompose it. For the New Keynesians the "residual" was more evidence of market power and the need to integrate rigidities into the study of the cycle.

Solow (2007, 12) has consistently maintained the importance of the cycle in the modeling of growth, stating his worry "about the tendency of modern (American) macroeconomists to forget about the pathology of business cycles." But in a review of the recent growth literature he does not mention the models that market themselves as integrating growth and cycle (Solow 1994). His judgment on real business cycles has remained unappreciative. Writing for the prominent humanities journal *Daedalus*, Solow (1997, 52) casts real business cycle models with a minor role in the history of profession: "The bulk of the intellectual effort goes into the ways of showing that the data of observed fluctuations are compatible with the demands of the model. This is not easy because the key driving forces—irregular changes in tastes and technology—are not directly observable." However, his closing summary is intriguing, stating that "the more adventuresome advocates of Real Business Cycle Theory have found it necessary to modify many of the clean but extreme assumptions that give formal general equilibrium theory its artificial vanilla flavor. . . . it has come closer and closer to the more or less 'Keynesian' model it was supposed to discredit" (52–53). These more interesting developments are in our narrative the puzzling through the Solow residual and its continued privileged role in the construction of comprehensive models of economic dynamics.

References

Aghion, Philippe, and Peter Howitt. 1992. A Model of Growth through Creative Destruction. *Econometrica* 60.2:323–51.

———. 1994. Growth and Unemployment. *Review of Economic Studies* 61.3:477–94.

———. 2007. Capital, Innovation, and Growth Accounting. *Oxford Review of Economic Policy* 23.1:79–93.

Azariadis, Costas, and Leo Kaas. 2007. Is Dynamic General Equilibrium a Theory of Everything? *Economic Theory* 32.1:13–41.

Begg, David K. H. 1982. *The Rational Expectations Revolution in Macroeconomics: Theories and Evidence.* Baltimore, Md.: Johns Hopkins University Press.

Beveridge, Stephen, and Charles R. Nelson. 1981. A New Approach to Decomposition of Economic Time Series into Permanent and Transitory Components with Particular Attention to Measurement of the "Business Cycle." *Journal of Monetary Economics* 7.2:151–74.

Blaug, Mark. 1980. *The Methodology of Economics: or, How Economists Explain.* Cambridge: Cambridge University Press.

Brock, William A., and Leonard J. Mirman. 1972. Optimal Economic Growth and Uncertainty: The Discounted Case. *Journal of Economic Theory* 4:479–513.

Brunner, Karl, and Allan H. Meltzer. 1986. *The National Bureau Method: International Capital Mobility and Other Essays.* Amsterdam: North-Holland.

Burmeister, Edwin, and Rodney Dobell. 1970. *Mathematical Theories of Economic Growth.* [New York]: Macmillan.

Campbell, John Y., and N. Gregory Mankiw. 1987. Are Output Fluctuations Transitory? *Quarterly Journal of Economics* 102.4:857–80.

Cole, H. L., and L. E. Ohanian. 1999. The Great Depression in the United States from a Neoclassical Perspective. *Federal Reserve Bank of Minneapolis Quarterly Review* 23.1:2–24.

Cooley, T. F. 1997. Calibrated Models. *Oxford Review of Economic Policy* 13.3:55–69.

De Vroey, Michel, and Luca Pensieroso. 2006. Real Business Cycle Theory and the Great Depression: The Abandonment of the Abstentionist Viewpoint. *Contributions to Macroeconomics* 6.1. www.bepress.com/bejm/contributions/vol6/iss1/art13.

Denison, Edward Fulton. 1962. *The Sources of Economic Growth in the United States and the Alternatives before Us.* [New York]: Committee for Economic Development.

———. 1979. *Accounting for Slower Economic Growth: The United States in the 1970's.* Washington, D.C.: Brookings Institution.

———. 1985. *Trends in American Economic Growth, 1929–1982.* Washington, D.C.: Brookings Institution.

Denison, Edward Fulton, and Brookings Institution. 1967. *Why Growth Rates Differ: Postwar Experience in Nine Western Countries.* Washington, D.C.: Brookings Institution.

———. 1974. *Accounting for United States Economic Growth, 1929–1969.* Washington, D.C.: Brookings Institution.

Dore, Mohammed H. I. 1993. *The Macrodynamics of Business Cycles: A Comparative Evaluation.* Cambridge, Mass.: Blackwell.

Eichenbaum, Martin, and Kenneth J. Singleton. 1986. Do Equilibrium Real Business Cycle Theories Explain Postwar U.S. Business Cycles? *NBER Macroeconomics Annual* 1:91–135.

Faggio, Giulia, and Stephen Nickell. 2007. Patterns of Work across the OECD. *Economic Journal* 117.521:F416–F440.

Freeman, Christopher. 1988. Introduction. In *Technical Change and Economic Theory,* edited by G. Dosi, C. Freeman, R. Nelson, G. Silverberg, and L. Soete. London: Pinter Publishers.

Hahn, F. H., and R. C. O. Matthews. 1964. The Theory of Economic Growth: A Survey. *Economic Journal* 74.296:779–902.

Hall, Robert E. 1986. Market Structure and Macroeconomic Fluctuations. *Brookings Papers on Economic Activity* 2:265–338.

———. 1990. Invariance Properties of Solow's Productivity Residual. In *Growth/Productivity/Unemployment: Essays to Celebrate Bob Solow's Birthday,* edited by P. Diamond. Cambridge: MIT Press.

Hartley, James. 2006. Kydland and Prescott's Nobel Prize: The Methodology of Time Consistency and Real Business Cycle Models. *Review of Political Economy* 18:1–28.

Hartley, James E. 2000. Does the Solow Residual Actually Measure Changes in Technology? *Review of Political Economy* 12.1:27–44.

Hoover, Kevin D. 1988. *The New Classical Macroeconomics: A Sceptical Inquiry.* Oxford: Blackwell.

———. 1995. Facts and Artifacts: Calibration and the Empirical Assessment of Real Business Cycle Models. *Oxford Economic Papers* 47.1:24–44.

Howitt, Peter. 1986. The Keynesian Recovery. *Canadian Journal of Economics/Revue canadienne d'économique* 19.4:626–41.

———. 1994. Adjusting to Technological Change. *Canadian Journal of Economics/Revue canadienne d'économique* 27.4:763–75.

Kantor, Brian. 1979. Rational Expectations and Economic Thought. *Journal of Economic Literature* 17.4:1422–41.

Kehoe, Timothy J., and Edward C. Prescott. 2002. Great Depressions of the Twentieth Century. *Review of Economic Dynamics* 5:1–18.

Kim, E. Han, Adair Morse, and Luigi Zingales. 2006. What Has Mattered to Economics since 1970. *Journal of Economic Perspectives* 20:189–202.

Kim, Kyun. 1988. *Equilibrium Business Cycle Theory in Historical Perspective.* Cambridge: Cambridge University Press.

King, R. G., and Sergio Rebelo. 1999. Resuscitating Real Business Cycles. In *Handbook of Macroeconomics,* edited by J. B. Taylor and M. Woodford. Amsterdam: North-Holland.

King, Robert G., Charles I. Plosser, and Sergio T. Rebelo. 1988a. Production, Growth, and Business Cycles: I. The Basic Neoclassical Model. *Journal of Monetary Economics* 21.2–3:195–232.

———. 1988b. Production, Growth, and Business Cycles: II. New Directions. *Journal of Monetary Economics* 21.2–3:309–41.

King, Robert G., Charles I. Plosser, James H. Stock, and Mark W. Watson. 1991. Stochastic Trends and Economic Fluctuations. *American Economic Review* 81.4:819–40.

Klamer, Arjo. 1984. *Conversations with Economists: New Classical Economists and Opponents Speak Out on the Current Controversy in Macroeconomics.* Totowa, N.J.: Rowman and Allanheld.

Koopmans, Tjalling C. 1947. Measurement without Theory. *Review of Economic Statistics* 29.3:161–72.

Kydland, Finn E., and Edward C. Prescott. 1980. Dynamic Optimal Taxation, Rational Expectations, and Optimal Control. *Journal of Economic Dynamics and Control* 2:79–91.

———. 1982. Time to Build and Aggregate Fluctuations. *Econometrica* 50.6:1345–70.

———. 1988. The Workweek of Capital and Its Cyclical Implications. *Journal of Monetary Economics* 21.2–3:343–60.

———. 1990. Business Cycles: Real Facts and a Monetary Myth. *Federal Reserve Bank of Minneapolis Quarterly Review* 14.2:1–17.

Laidler, D. 1981. Monetarism: An Interpretation and an Assessment. *Economic Journal* 91.361:1–28.

Latour, Bruno. 1987. *Science in Action: How to Follow Scientists and Engineers through Society.* Cambridge: Harvard University Press.

Latour, Bruno, and Steve Woolgar. 1979. *Laboratory Life: The Social Construction of Scientific Facts.* Beverly Hills, Calif.: Sage.

Long, John B., Jr., and Charles I. Plosser. 1983. Real Business Cycles. *Journal of Political Economy* 91.1:39–69.

Louçã, Francisco. 2004. Swinging All the Way: The Education of Doctor Lucas and Foes. *HOPE* 36.4:689–734.

Lucas, Robert E., Jr. 1972. Expectations and the Neutrality of Money. *Journal of Economic Theory* 4.2:103–24.

———. 1975. An Equilibrium Model of the Business Cycle. *Journal of Political Economy* 83.6:1113–44.

———. 1977. Understanding Business Cycles. *Carnegie-Rochester Conference Series on Public Policy* 5:7–29.

———. 1980. Methods and Problems in Business Cycle Theory. *Journal of Money, Credit, and Banking* 12.4:696–715.

———. 1987. *Models of Business Cycles.* Oxford: Blackwell.

———. 1988. On the Mechanics of Economic Development. *Journal of Monetary Economics* 22.1:3–42.

———. 2004. Keynote Address to the 2003 *HOPE* Conference: My Keynesian Education. In *The IS-LM Model: Its Rise, Fall, and Strange Persistence*, edited by Michel De Vroey and Kevin D. Hoover. *HOPE* 36 (supplement): 12–24.

———. 2007. Remarks on the Influence of Edward Prescott. *Economic Theory* 32.1:7–11.

Lucas, Robert E., Jr., and Edward C. Prescott. 1971. Investment under Uncertainty. *Econometrica* 39.5:659–81.

———. 1974. Equilibrium Search and Unemployment. *Journal of Economic Theory* 7.2:188–209.

Lucas, Robert E., Jr., and Thomas Sargent. 1979. After Keynesian Macroeconomics. *Quarterly Review* 3.2:1–17.

Mankiw, N. Gregory. 1986. Comment. *Macroeconomics Annual* 1:139–46.

———. 1989. Real Business Cycles: A New Keynesian Perspective. *Journal of Economic Perspectives* 3.3:79–90.

Mankiw, N. Gregory, and David Romer. 1991. *New Keynesian Economics.* 2 vols. Cambridge: MIT Press.

Manuelli, Rodolfo E. 1986. Modern Business Cycle Analysis: A Guide to the Prescott-Summers Debate. *Federal Reserve Bank of Minneapolis Quarterly Review* 10.4:1–6.

Nelson, Charles R., and Charles R. Plosser. 1982. Trends and Random Walks in Macroeconomic Time Series: Some Evidence and Implications. *Journal of Monetary Economics* 10.2:139–62.

Ohanian, Harold L., and Lee E. Cole. 1999. The Great Depression in the United States from a Neoclassical Perspective. *Federal Reserve Bank of Minneapolis Quarterly Review* 23.1:2–24.

Parente, Stephen, and Edward C. Prescott. 1993. Changes in the Wealth of Nations. *Federal Reserve Bank of Minneapolis Quarterly Review* 17.2:3–16.

———. 1994. Barriers to Technology Adoption and Development. *Journal of Political Economy* 102.2:298–321.

Plosser, Charles I. 1989. Understanding Real Business Cycles. *Journal of Economic Perspectives* 3.3:51–77.

Prescott, Edward C. 1986a. Response to a Skeptic. *Federal Reserve Bank of Minneapolis Quarterly Review* 10.4:27–33.

———. 1986b. Theory Ahead of Business Cycle Measurement. *Federal Reserve Bank of Minneapolis Quarterly Review* 10.4:7–21.

———. 1988. Robert M. Solow's Neoclassical Growth Model: An Influential Contribution to Economics. *Scandinavian Journal of Economics* 90.1:7–12.

———. 1999. Observations on the Great Depression. *Federal Reserve Bank of Minneapolis Quarterly Review* 23.1:25–31.

———. 2004. Why Do Americans Work So Much More Than Europeans? *Federal Reserve Bank of Minneapolis Quarterly Review* 28.1:2–13.

———. 2006. The Transformation of Macroeconomic Policy and Research. *American Economist* 50.1:3–20.

Prescott, Edward C., and Robert E. Lucas Jr. 1972. A Note on Price Systems in Infinite Dimensional Space. *International Economic Review* 13.2:416–22.

Rebelo, Sergio. 2005. Real Business Cycle Models: Past, Present, and Future. *Scandinavian Journal of Economics* 107.2:217–38.

Romer, Paul M. 1986. Increasing Returns and Long-Run Growth. *Journal of Political Economy* 94.5:1002–37.

Rosenberg, Nathan. 1982. *Inside the Black Box: Technology and Economics.* Cambridge: Cambridge University Press.

Rouwenhorst, K. Geert. 1991. Time to Build and Aggregate Fluctuations: A Reconsideration. *Journal of Monetary Economics* 27.2:241–54.

Sent, Esther-Mirjam. 1998. *The Evolving Rationality of Rational Expectations: An Assessment of Thomas Sargent's Achievements.* Cambridge: Cambridge University Press.

Shapiro, Matthew D. 1987. Are Cyclical Fluctuations in Productivity Due More to Supply Shocks or Demand Shocks? *American Economic Review* 77.2:118–24.

Shapiro, Matthew D., and Mark W. Watson. 1988. Sources of Business Cycle Fluctuations. *NBER Macroeconomics Annual* 3:111–48.

Sheffrin, Steven M. 1983. *Rational Expectations.* Cambridge: Cambridge University Press.

Solow, Robert M. 1956. A Contribution to the Theory of Economic Growth. *Quarterly Journal of Economics* 70.1:65–94.

——. 1957. Technical Change and the Aggregate Production Function. *Review of Economics and Statistics* 39.3:312–20.

——. 1963. *Capital Theory and the Rate of Return.* Amsterdam: North-Holland.

——. 1970. *Growth Theory: An Exposition.* New York: Oxford University Press.

——. 1980. On Theories of Unemployment. *American Economic Review* 70.1:1–11.

——. 1982. Some Lessons from Growth Theory. In *Financial Economics: Essays in Honor of Paul Cootner,* edited by P. H. Cootner, W. F. Sharpe, and C. M. Cootner. Englewood Cliffs, N.J.: Prentice-Hall.

——. 1984. Letter to Frank Hahn, January 12. Robert Solow Papers, box 15. Rare Book, Manuscript, and Special Collections Library, Duke University.

——. 1985. Economic History and Economics. *American Economic Review* 75.2:328–31.

——. 1994. Perspectives on Growth Theory. *Journal of Economic Perspectives* 8.1:45–54.

——. 1997. How Did Economics Get That Way and What Way Did It Get? *Daedalus* 126.1:39–58.

——. 2007. The Last 50 Years in Growth Theory and the Next 10. *Oxford Review of Economic Policy* 23.1:3–14.

Star, Susan Leigh, and James R. Griesemer. 1989. Institutional Ecology, "Translations," and Boundary Objects: Amateurs and Professionals in Berkeley's Museum of Vertebrate Zoology, 1907–39. *Social Studies of Science* 19.3:387–420.

Stock, James H., and Mark W. Watson. 1988a. Testing for Common Trends. *Journal of the American Statistical Association* 83.404:1097–107.

——. 1988b. Variable Trends in Economic Times Series. *Journal of Economic Perspectives* 2.3:147–74.

Stokey, Nancy L., Robert Lucas, and Edward C. Prescott. 1989. *Recursive Methods in Economic Dynamics.* Cambridge: Harvard University Press.

Summers, Lawrence. 1986. Some Skeptical Observations on Real Business Cycle Theory. *Federal Reserve Bank of Minneapolis Quarterly Review* 10.4:22–26.

Tobin, James. 1981. The Monetarist Counter-Revolution Today—an Appraisal. *Economic Journal* 91.361:29–42.

Walters, A. A. 1963. Production and Cost Functions: An Econometric Survey. *Econometrica* 31.1–2:1–66.

Warsh, David. 2006. *Knowledge and the Wealth of Nations: A Story of Economic Discovery*. London: Norton.

Weintraub, E. Roy. 1991. *Stabilizing Dynamics: Constructing Economic Knowledge*. Cambridge: Cambridge University Press.

Yonay, Yuval P. 1994. When Black Boxes Clash: Competing Ideas of What Science Is in Economics, 1924–39. *Social Studies of Science* 24.1:39–80.

Zarnowitz, Victor. 1985. Recent Work on Business Cycles in Historical Perspective: A Review of Theories and Evidence. *Journal of Economic Literature* 23.2:523–80.

Contributors

William J. Baumol is professor of economics and academic director of the Berkley Center for Entrepreneurial Studies at New York University, and professor emeritus at Princeton University. He received his PhD from the University of London in 1949. After military service in Europe during World War II, he taught at the London School of Economics (1947–49), then served as a member of the faculty of Princeton University for forty-two years, and has since taught at New York University. He has written some forty professional books and five hundred articles and holds eleven honorary degrees and other honors in the United States and abroad.

Mauro Boianovsky is professor of economics at Universidade de Brasília, Brazil, where he teaches history of economic thought and theory of economic development. He has published a number of articles in professional journals and edited volumes, mostly on the history of macroeconomics. He is the editor of *Business Cycle Theory: Selected Texts, 1860–1939*, vols. 5–8 (Pickering and Chatto, 2005). He is currently vice president of the History of Economics Society (2009–10).

Marcel Boumans is associate professor of history and the methodology of economics at the University of Amsterdam and coeditor of the *Journal of the History of Economic Thought*. His research is marked by three Ms: modeling, measurement, and mathematics. His main research focus is on understanding empirical research practices from (combined) historical and philosophical perspectives. His current research project is on "science outside the laboratory." On these topics he has published a monograph, *How Economists Model the World into Numbers* (Routledge, 2005), and edited the volume *Measurement in Economics: A Handbook* (Elsevier, 2007).

Edwin Burmeister received his PhD from the Massachusetts Institute of Technology. Currently, he is Research Professor of Economics Emeritus at Duke University and Commonwealth Professor of Economics Emeritus at the University of Virginia. The former editor of the *International Economic Review*, he has been on the editorial boards of several other economics and finance journals. Mr. Burmeister has published numerous articles in mathematical economics and economic theory, particularly in the fields of financial economics, capital theory, economic growth, and macroeconomics. More recently he has studied the role that expectations play in determining interest rates and stock market prices. Mr. Burmeister is an elected Fellow of the Econometric Society and has been the recipient of seven National Science Foundation grants and an honorary Woodrow Wilson Fellowship. He was a John Simon Guggenheim Fellow and a visiting professor at the Australian National University during the 1974–75 academic year.

Nicholas Crafts is a professor of economic history and the director of the Centre for Competitive Advantage in the Global Economy at the University of Warwick. He has previously taught at several other universities including the London School of Economics, Oxford, Stanford, and UC Berkeley. His publications include *British Economic Growth during the Industrial Revolution* (Oxford University Press, 1985), *Economic Growth in Europe since 1945* (Cambridge University Press, 1996; edited with Gianni Toniolo), and "Steam as a General Purpose Technology: A Growth Accounting Perspective" (*Economic Journal*, 2004).

William Darity Jr. is a professor of economics at Duke University and the editor in chief of the *International Encyclopedia of the Social Sciences* (Macmillan Reference USA, 2008). He has published extensively on racial and ethnic economic inequality and on financial crises in developing countries.

Robert W. Dimand is a professor of economics at Brock University, St. Catharines, Ontario, and an adjunct professor of economics at McMaster University, Hamilton, Ontario. A graduate of McGill and Yale Universities, he is the author of *The Origins of the Keynesian Revolution* (Stanford University Press, 1988) and coauthor of volume 1 of *A History of Game Theory* (Routledge, 1996). He has edited or coedited a dozen books, and has published more than seventy-five journal articles, primarily on the history of macroeconomics, the early history of game theory, and the history of women in economics.

Pedro Garcia Duarte is an assistant professor of economics at the University of São Paulo (FEA-USP), Brazil. In May of 2007 he completed a doctoral degree in economics at Duke University with a thesis titled "Constructing Concepts of Optimal Monetary Policy in the Postwar Period." He is particularly interested in the history of postwar macroeconomics with an emphasis on how modeling strategies and techniques had their use stabilized over time. He has published articles in *HOPE* on this subject and he is now working on the uses of a time discount rate in growth models.

Steven N. Durlauf is Kenneth J. Arrow Professor of Economics at the University of Wisconsin and a research associate of the National Bureau of Economic Research. He is currently coeditor of the new journal *Quantitative Economics*. He has previously served as editor of the *Handbook of Economic Growth* and the *New Palgrave Dictionary of Economics* and coeditor of the *Journal of Applied Econometrics*. A Fellow of the Econometric Society, Durlauf received his BA in economics from Harvard and his PhD from Yale. His research covers macroeconomics, econometrics, social economics, and economic growth.

Guido Erreygers is a professor of economics at the University of Antwerp, Belgium. He obtained a PhD in economics from the University of Paris X-Nanterre. His research focuses on the history of economic thought, linear production theory, health inequality measurement, and intergenerational justice. He has published in a wide range of journals; he recently edited (with John Cunliffe) *The Origins of Universal Grants: An Anthology of Historical Writings on Basic Capital and Basic Income* (Palgrave Macmillan, 2004).

Harald Hagemann is a professor of economic theory at the University of Hohenheim, Stuttgart, Germany. He is a life member of Clare Hall, University of Cambridge, and is the chairman of the council of the European Society for the History of Economic Thought. His main areas of research are growth, structural change, new technologies and employment, and the history of economic analysis. Recent work also focuses on the history of modern business-cycle theory and the emigration of German-speaking economists after 1933.

Kevin D. Hoover is a professor of economics and philosophy at Duke University. He is the author of *The New Classical Macroeconomics, Causality in Macroeconomics* (Cambridge University Press, 2001), *The Methodology of Empirical Macroeconomics* (Cambridge University Press, 2001), and of numerous articles in macroeconomics, monetary economics, the history of economics, economic methodology, and the philosophy of science. He is past president of the History of Economics Society and past chairman of the International Network for Economic Methodology.

Francisco Louçã is a professor of economics at ISEG, Lisbon University. He is the author of *Turbulence in Economics* (Edward Elgar, 1997), *As Time Goes By* (Oxford University Press, 2002; with Chris Freeman), and *The Years of High Econometrics* (Routledge, 2007).

Tiago Mata is an assistant professor at the Amsterdam School of Economics, in the Netherlands. His research interests are on the sociology of economics and on the postwar history of economics with a particular concern for the role played by economic ideas in mass culture. He received the Joseph Dorfman Award for the Best Dissertation in the History of Economics in 2007, which will shortly be published as a book by Cambridge University Press.

Lionello F. Punzo is a full professor of economics at the University of Siena, a member of the Tourism Sustainability Group at the EC/DG Enterprise, and has taught in Europe, Japan, the United States, and Latin America. He has been a consultant for development projects of IDB, Europaid, and the Italian International Cooperation. His research in mathematical methodology and the history of economic analysis, growth, and development has been published in international journals. Among his books is *The Dynamics of a Capitalist Society* (Westview, 1987; with R. Goodwin); more recently he contributed to and edited *Growth, Cycle, and Structural Change: Mexico beyond NAFTA* (with M. P. Anyul) and *New Tools of Economic Dynamics* (Springer, 2005; with J. Leskow and M. Puchet).

Roger J. Sandilands is a professor of economics at the University of Strathclyde, Scotland. He is a graduate of Strathclyde and of Simon Fraser University, Canada. He taught for six years at the National University of Singapore and was a visiting professor at Sophia University, Tokyo, and Renmin University, Beijing. As a development economist he has worked extensively in Latin America, especially in Colombia at the National Planning Department with Lauchlin Currie (1902–1993), a student of Allyn Young at Harvard and a White House adviser to President Franklin Roosevelt. His biography of Currie was published by Duke University Press in 1990.

Brian Snowdon is currently a Senior Teaching Fellow at the University of Durham (U.K.), following his retirement in August 2008 as professor of economics and international business at Newcastle Business School, Northumbria University (U.K.). His main research interests are in the areas of macroeconomics and international growth and development. As well as numerous articles in academic journals, he has also authored or coauthored eleven books, including *Conversations on Growth, Stability, and Trade* (Edward Elgar, 2002); *An Encyclopaedia of Macroeconomics* (edited with H. R. Vane; Edward Elgar, 2002); and *Modern Macroeconomics: Its Origins, Development, and Current State* (with H. R. Vane; Edward Elgar, 2005). His most recent book, *Globalisation, Development, and Transition: Conversations with Eminent Economists,* was published by Edward Elgar in June 2007.

Robert M. Solow is an emeritus professor of economics at MIT. He was awarded the Nobel Prize in economics in 1987.

Barbara Spencer is the Asia Pacific Professor of Trade Policy in the Sauder School of Business at the University of British Columbia and a research associate at the National Bureau of Economic Research (NBER). She is a past president of the Canadian Economic Association and has served on a number of editorial boards, including the *Journal of International Economics* (1988–2000) and the *American Economic Review* (1988–91). She is best known for contributions (with James Brander) to strategic trade theory and is listed as a Highly Cited Researcher by the ISI Web of Science. She is the daughter of Trevor Swan.

John Toye is currently based at the Oxford Department of International Development, Oxford University. He has been successively a professor of development economics at the universities of Wales, Sussex, and Oxford in the United Kingdom. He was a director of the United Nations Conference on Trade and Development, from 1998 to 2000. He has written seven books, the first being *Public Expenditure and Development Policy in India* (Cambridge University Press, 1981) and the most recent being *The UN and Global Political Economy* (Indiana University Press, 2004), which he wrote with the historian Richard Toye.

Index